Michigan Sentencing Guidelines Manual

With Selected Statutes and Rules of Court

2007 EDITION

Mat#40511750

ISBN-13: 978-0-314-97042-8

PUBLISHER'S PREFACE

This pamphlet is designed to provide a comprehensive sentencing manual: it contains the text of the Michigan Sentencing Guidelines Manual, as revised in 2007, and related statutes and rules of court.

The Michigan Sentencing Guidelines Manual is a publication revised and produced annually by the Michigan Judicial Institute. Its content does not represent an authoritative statement by the Michigan Supreme Court.

The statutes are current through Public Act No. 7 of the 2007 Regular Session of the 94th Legislature. The court rules cover all amendments received through May 11, 2007. For subsequent amendments to statutes, see West's Michigan Legislative Service pamphlets, Interim Annotation Service pamphlets, or the MI-LEGIS and MI-ST-ANN databases on Westlaw. For subsequent amendments to court rules, see West's Michigan Legislative Service pamphlets or the MI-RULESUPDATES and MI-RULES databases on Westlaw.

This pamphlet replaces the 2006 Edition.

June, 2007

*

RELATED PRODUCTS FROM WEST

MICHIGAN COMPILED LAWS ANNOTATED

WEST'S MICHIGAN COMPILED LAWS–COMPACT EDITION

WEST'S MICHIGAN DIGEST, 2D

MICHIGAN REPORTER

MICHIGAN OFFICIAL REPORTS

MICHIGAN OFFICIAL APPEALS REPORTS

MICHIGAN COURT RULES PRACTICE

Text and Forms
Robert Dean, Elizabeth Norma Mckenna, Alan Saltzman,
Sheila Robertson Deming & Ronald S. Longhofer

Courtroom Handbook on Michigan Civil Procedure
Ronald S. Longhofer

Courtroom Handbook on Michigan Criminal Procedure
Alan Saltzman & Sheila Robertson Deming

Evidence, 2d
James K. Robinson, Ronald S. Longhofer & Norman C. Ankers

Courtroom Handbook on Michigan Evidence
James K. Robinson & Ronald S. Longhofer

TREATISES

Gillespie Michigan Criminal Law & Procedure with Forms, 2d

Hackett's Michigan and Federal Evidence
Wesley P. Hackett Jr.

Michigan Administrative Law
Don LeDuc

Michigan Civil Jurisprudence

Michigan Civil Practice Forms

Michigan Pleading & Practice, 2d

Michigan Probate: A Practice Systems Library Manual
Leonard Edelman & updates by John Payne

Michigan Nonstandard Jury Instructions: Civil and Criminal
Timothy Baughman, David C. Chardavoyne, Kenneth Mogill & Judge Cynthia
Stephens, Hon. William B. Murphy & John VandenHombergh

RELATED PRODUCTS

Michigan Lawyer's Manual
Roger A. Needham

Michigan Torts, 2d
Elmer E. White

Planning for Estates and Administration in Michigan
Frederick K. Hoops, Frederick H. Hoops III, & Daniel S. Hoops

Trial Handbook for Michigan Lawyers, 4th
Harry M. Philo

West's Jury Verdicts–Michigan Reports

MICHIGAN PRACTICE GUIDES

Civil Procedure Before Trial
Michigan Supreme Court Chief Justice Maura Corrigan, Judge William J. Giovan, Richard Bisio, Keefe A. Brooks & Larry J. Saylor

Civil Trials and Evidence
Judge Gerald E. Rosen, Judge Kurtis T. Wilder, Rodger D. Young & Thomas W. Cranmer

Civil Appeals
Michigan Supreme Court Justice Stephen J. Markman

Enforcing Judgments and Debts
U.S. Bankruptcy Court Judge James D. Gregg, Linda C. Scheuerman & Stephen S. LaPlante

Torts
Michigan Supreme Court Justice Clifford W. Taylor, George A. Googasian & Allen S. Falk

---

FORMS

Michigan Legal Forms

FinPlan Michigan Divorce Planner - (calculator)

Michigan SCAO Approved Forms

MCLA: Uniform Commercial Code Forms with Practice Comments, 3d
Cynthia Lee Starnes

Michigan Litigation Forms and Analysis
Theodore E. Hughes

HANDBOOKS & PAMPHLETS

Official Michigan Tax Guide

Michigan Civil Procedure Laws

Michigan Criminal and Motor Vehicle Law

Michigan Criminal Laws & Rules

Michigan Probate Laws & Rules

RELATED PRODUCTS

Michigan Family Laws & Rules

Michigan Rules of Court—State & Federal

Michigan Sentencing Guidelines

Michigan Child Support Formula Manual

Michigan Law Finder

Michigan Topical Digests for Employment, Family Law, Insurance, Personal Injury and Workers' Compensation

---

ONLINE RESEARCH

Westlaw®

KeyCite®

WestCheck.com™

CONTACT US

For more information about any of these Michigan research tools, please call your West Representative or **1–800–328–9352.**

NEED RESEARCH HELP?

You can get quality research results with free help—call the West Reference Attorneys when you have questions concerning Westlaw or West Publications at 1–800–733–2889.

INTERNET ACCESS

Contact the West Editorial Department directly with your questions and suggestions by e-mail at west.editor@thomson.com. Visit West's home page at west.thomson.com.

*

WESTLAW ELECTRONIC RESEARCH GUIDE

Westlaw—Expanding the Reach of Your Library

Westlaw is West's online legal research service. With Westlaw, you experience the same quality and integrity that you have come to expect from West books, plus quick, easy access to West's vast collection of statutes, case law materials, public records, and other legal resources, in addition to current news articles and business information. For the most current and comprehensive legal research, combine the strengths of West books and Westlaw.

When you research with westlaw.com you get the convenience of the Internet combined with comprehensive and accurate Westlaw content, including exclusive editorial enhancements, plus features found only in westlaw.com such as ResultsPlus™ or StatutesPlus.™

Accessing Databases Using the Westlaw Directory

The Westlaw Directory lists all databases on Westlaw and contains links to detailed information relating to the content of each database. Click **Directory** on the westlaw.com toolbar. There are several ways to access a database even when you don't know the database identifier. Browse a directory view. Scan the directory. Type all or part of a database name in the Search these Databases box. The Find a Database Wizard can help you select relevant databases for your search. You can access up to ten databases at one time for user-defined multibase searching.

Retrieving a Specific Document

To retrieve a specific document by citation or title on westlaw.com click **Find&Print** on the toolbar to display the Find a Document page. If you are unsure of the correct citation format, type the publication abbreviation, e.g., **xx st** (where xx is a state's two-letter postal abbreviation), in the Find this document by citation box and click **Go** to display a fill-in-the-blank template. To retrieve a specific case when you know one or more parties' names, click **Find a Case by Party Name**.

KeyCite®

KeyCite, the citation research service on Westlaw, makes it easy to trace the history of your case, statute, administrative decision or regulation to determine if there are recent updates, and to find other documents that cite your document. KeyCite will also find pending legislation relating to federal or state statutes. Access the powerful features of KeyCite from the westlaw.com toolbar, the **Links** tab, or KeyCite flags in a document display. KeyCite's red and yellow warning flags tell you at a glance whether your document has negative history. Depth-of-treatment stars help you focus on the most important citing references. KeyCite Alert allows you to monitor the status of your case, statute or rule, and automatically sends you updates at the frequency you specify.

ResultsPlus™

ResultsPlus is a Westlaw technology that automatically suggests additional information related to your search. The suggested materials are accessible by a set of links that appear to the right of your westlaw.com search results:

- Go directly to relevant ALR® articles and Am Jur® annotations.
- Find on-point resources by key number.
- See information from related treatises and law reviews.

StatutesPlus™

When you access a statutes database in westlaw.com you are brought to a powerful Search Center which collects, on one toolbar, the tools that are most useful for fast, efficient retrieval of statutes documents:

- Have a few key terms? Click **Statutes Index**.
- Know the common name? Click **Popular Name Table**.
- Familiar with the subject matter? Click **Table of Contents**.
- Have a citation or section number? Click **Find by Citation**.
- Interested in topical surveys providing citations across multiple state statutes? Click **50 State Surveys**.
- Or, simply search with **Natural Language** or **Terms and Connectors.**

When you access a statutes section, click on the **Links** tab for all relevant links for the current document that will also include a KeyCite section with a description of the KeyCite status flag. Depending on your document, links may also include administrative, bill text, and other sources that were previously only available by accessing and searching other databases.

Additional Information

Westlaw is available on the Web at www.westlaw.com.

For search assistance, call the West Reference Attorneys at
1–800–REF–ATTY (1–800–733–2889).

For technical assistance, call West Customer Technical Support at
1–800–WESTLAW (1–800–937–8529).

TABLE OF CONTENTS

Michigan Court Rules

Chapter

This sentencing guidelines manual has been prepared as an aid for those who use the guidelines enacted by the Michigan Legislature. The manual is intended to reflect with complete accuracy the substance of the law. However, in the event that the manual fails to comport exactly with the law, remember that the statute is the controlling authority.

General Information and Instructions for Using the Statutory Sentencing Guidelines

In general, the statutory sentencing guidelines apply only to felony offenses for which the penalty prescribed is an indeterminate sentence, and the sentencing court retains discretion in imposing an offender's sentence. That is, the guidelines are *not* applicable to offenses for which the applicable statute establishes a mandatory determinate penalty or a mandatory penalty of life imprisonment for conviction of the offense. MCL 769.34(5).

Specifically, the statutory sentencing guidelines apply to felony offenses listed in MCL 777.11 to 777.19 that were committed on or after January 1, 1999. MCL 769.34(2). The statutory sections listing the felony offenses to which the guidelines apply contain brief descriptions of the felonies listed there "for assistance only." MCL 777.6; MCL 777.11 to 777.19. The language contained in the statute defining the felony offense itself governs application of the sentencing guidelines. MCL 777.6. The statutory sentencing guidelines in effect on the date the offense was committed govern the calculation of an offender's minimum sentence. MCL 769.34(2).

When an offender is convicted of multiple offenses, a sentencing information report (SIR) should be completed for the sentencing offense that has the highest crime class. In instances where the sentences imposed will be served consecutively, an SIR should be completed for every crime that will be served consecutively.

STEP I. Score the Prior Record Variables

A. All seven prior record variables (PRVs) should be scored for all offenses. MCL 777.21(1)(b). PRVs 1 through 6 refer only to an offender's prior convictions. Concurrent and subsequent convictions should be scored in PRV 7, not in PRVs 1 through 6.

B. Each PRV consists of several statements to which a specific number of points are assigned. The statements appearing in each PRV quantify the specific sentencing characteristic addressed by that PRV. Determine which one or more of the statements addressed by the PRV apply to the offender and assign the point value indicated by the applicable statement with the highest number of points. Where no points are appropriate for a particular PRV, a score of zero (0) should be indicated. The total number of points assessed for all seven PRVs is the offender's "PRV level" and corresponds to the horizontal axis of the appropriate sentencing grid.

C. Whether a prior felony conviction or corresponding adjudication is of "high" or "low" severity is determined by reference to the crime class of the prior conviction or corresponding adjudication. An offense's crime class may be identified by consulting the offense lists contained in this manual. All guidelines offenses are listed in order of their MCL number (or alphabetically by offense description) and each offense's crime class is noted. Prior convictions classified in M2 (second-degree murder) or in classes A through D are "high severity" prior convictions; felonies in classes E through H are "low severity" prior convictions. In addition, prior convictions or adjudications punishable by a maximum term of imprisonment of 10 years or more and not listed in any crime class may qualify as prior high severity felony convictions; prior convictions or adjudications punishable by a maximum term of imprisonment of less than 10 years and not listed in any crime class may qualify as prior low severity felony convictions.

D. In scoring PRVs 1 to 5, do not use any conviction or juvenile adjudication that precedes a period of 10 or more years between the discharge date from a conviction or juvenile adjudication and the commission date of the next offense resulting in a conviction or juvenile adjudication. MCL 777.50. "Discharge date" means the date an individual is discharged from the jurisdiction of the court or the department of corrections.

Apply the "10-year gap rule" by determining the length of time between the discharge date of the offender's conviction or juvenile adjudication immediately preceding the commission date of the sentencing offense. If the time span is 10 years or more, that conviction or juvenile adjudication–and any convictions or adjudications that occurred earlier–must not be counted when scoring the offender's PRVs. If the time span between the commission date of the offender's sentencing offense and the discharge date of the offender's most recent conviction or adjudication is less than 10 years, that prior conviction or adjudication must be counted in scoring the offender's PRVs.

If the offender's most recent conviction or adjudication must be counted in scoring his or her PRVs, and if the offender has additional prior convictions or juvenile adjudications, determine the length of time between the commission date of the prior conviction or adjudication first scored and the discharge date of the next earlier conviction or adjudication. If the time span equals or exceeds 10 years, that conviction or adjudication may not be counted. If the time span is less than 10 years, that conviction or adjudication may be counted in scoring the offender's PRVs. Use the process described above until a time span equal to or greater than 10 years separates the discharge date of an earlier conviction or adjudication from the commission date of the next conviction or adjudication or until no previous convictions or adjudications remain.

If a discharge date is not available, determine the date by adding the amount of time the defendant was placed on probation or the length of the minimum term of incarceration to the date the defendant was convicted (not the date the defendant was sentenced) and use that date as the discharge date.

STEP II. Score the Offense Variables

A. The crime group of the sentencing offense determines which offense variables (OVs) must be scored. The offenses to which the guidelines apply are sorted into six crime groups (MCL 777.5(a)-(f)):

Crimes against a person ("Person")
Crimes against property ("Property")
Crimes involving a controlled substance ("CS")
Crimes against public order ("Pub ord")
Crimes against public safety ("Pub saf")
Crimes against public trust ("Pub trst")

The applicable crime group may be identified by consulting the offense lists contained in this manual. All guidelines offenses are listed in order of their MCL number and in alphabetical order based on offense descriptions. Along with the MCL numbers are the crime group and crime class designations for each offense and the statutory maximum penalty for conviction of the offense.

B. Each OV consists of several statements to which a specific number of points are assigned. The statements appearing in each OV quantify the specific sentencing characteristic addressed by that OV. Determine which one or more of the statements addressed by the OV apply to the offender and assign the point value indicated by the applicable statement with the highest number of points. Where no points are appropriate for a particular OV, a score of zero (0) should be indicated. The total number of points assessed for all OVs is the offender's "OV level" and corresponds to the vertical axis of the appropriate sentencing grid.

C. For all crimes against a person, score OVs 1, 2, 3, 4, 7, 8, 9, 10, 11,12,13,14,19, and 20. MCL 777.22(1). Score OVs 5 and 6 for homicide, attempted homicide, conspiracy or solicitation to commit a homicide, or assault with intent to commit murder. MCL 777.22(1). Score OV 16 for a violation or attempted violation of MCL 750.110a (home invasion). MCL 777.22(1). Score OVs 17 and 18 if the offense or attempted offense involves the operation of a vehicle, vessel, ORV, snowmobile, aircraft, or locomotive. MCL 777.22(1).

D. For all crimes against property, score OVs 1, 2, 3, 4, 9, 10, 12, 13, 14, 16, 19, and 20. MCL 777.22(2).

E. For all crimes involving a controlled substance, score OVs 1, 2, 3, 12, 13, 14, 15, 19, and 20. MCL 777.22(3).

F. For all crimes against public order, score OVs 1, 3, 4, 9, 10, 12, 13, 14, 16, 19, and 20. MCL 777.22(4).

G. For all crimes against public safety, score OVs 1, 3, 4, 9, 10, 12, 13, 14, 16, 19 and 20. MCL 777.22(5). Score OV 18 if the offense or attempted offense involves the operation of a vehicle, vessel, ORV, snowmobile, aircraft, or locomotive. MCL 777.22(5).

H. For all crimes against public trust, score OVs 1, 3, 4, 9, 10, 12, 13, 14, 16, 19, and 20. MCL 777.22(4).

I. Guidelines offenses in MCL 777.18 require the commission of an underlying offense. In those cases, score OVs for both the crime group of the underlying offense and for the crime group of the offense as it is listed under MCL 777.18. MCL 777.21(4)(a).

STEP III. Identify the Crime Class and Proper Sentencing Grid

A. Substantive Offenses

Within each crime group, all offenses to which the guidelines apply are further categorized by the seriousness of the offense. This gradation of offense seriousness is indicated by the offense's crime class. An offense's crime class is designated by the letters "A" through "H" and "M2" (second-degree murder). M2 and A represent the most serious felony offenses, while the letters B through H represent the remaining guidelines offenses in decreasing order of their seriousness. An offense's crime class roughly corresponds to a maximum term of imprisonment for all offenses in that same crime class:

M2 / Class A offenses	Imprisonment for life or any term of years
Class B offenses	Imprisonment for up to 20 years
Class C offenses	Imprisonment for up to 15 years
Class D offenses	Imprisonment for up to 10 years
Class E offenses	Imprisonment for up to 5 years
Class F offenses	Imprisonment for up to 4 years
Class G offenses	Imprisonment for up to 2 years
Class H offenses	Jail or other intermediate sanction

In most cases, using the statutory maximum to divide the guidelines offenses into discrete crime classes resulted in categories of offenses that shared the same statutory maximum penalty. There are offenses that do not adhere to the standard, however. There is no legislative authority for the division of felonies into crime classes, and therefore, there is no prohibition against assigning an offense to a crime class that is inconsistent with the statutory maximum penalty for that offense. Rather, the statutory maximum as it appears in the statutory language defining the offense governs the upper limit of punishment possible for conviction of that offense.

For example, MCL 409.122(3) is a crime against a person designated as a class D felony. MCL 777.14b. According to the chart above, class D felonies are crimes for which a maximum sentence of 10 years of imprisonment may be appropriate. However, the maximum term of imprisonment authorized for conviction of MCL 409.122(3) is 20 years. Although the crime class designation will in most cases correspond to the maximum sentences listed in the chart above, the offense just discussed exemplifies the directive of MCL 777.6: the express language of the statute defining the offense itself governs application of the sentencing guidelines.

B. Attempted Offenses

The sentencing guidelines apply to attempted crimes if the crime attempted is a felony offense. MCL 777.19(1). An attempt to commit an offense falls within the same crime group (person, property, CS, pub ord, pub saf, pub trst) as the offense attempted. MCL 777.19(2). The attempt's crime class is determined by the class of the offense attempted:

> **Attempted offenses in classes A, B, C, or D:** the attempt is a class E offense. MCL 777.19(3)(a).
>
> **Attempted offenses in classes E, F or G:** the attempt is a class H offense. MCL 777.19(3)(b).
>
> **Attempted offenses in class H:** the guidelines do not apply to an attempt to commit a class H offense. Attempted "H" offenses are to be sentenced to intermediate sanctions as defined in MCL 769.31(b).

C. Offenses Designated as "SPEC" with "Variable" Statutory Maximums

Special scoring instructions apply to offenses listed in MCL 777.18 (e.g., conspiracy, allowing a prisoner to escape, inducing a minor to commit a felony, etc.). Offenses in MCL 777.18 are guidelines offenses predicated on the offender's commission of an underlying offense. Each offense is given a crime group designation for purposes of MCL 777.18 and that crime group designation may differ from the crime group designation of the offense on which the MCL 777.18 conviction is based. In such cases, OVs for both crime group designations must be scored.

For example, MCL 777.18 includes an offense identified as MCL 750.157c. MCL 750.157c prohibits an individual from recruiting or inducing a minor to commit a felony and under MCL 777.18, MCL 750.157c is designated as a crime against a person. This crime group designation under MCL 777.18 – "person" – remains the same no matter what offense forms the basis for charging the offender with violating MCL 750.157c. Suppose an offender is convicted under MCL 750.157c of inducing a minor to commit arson of real property. Arson of real property, MCL 750.73, is a class D crime against property for which the statutory maximum penalty is 10 years of imprisonment. The crime designation of the underlying offense (arson) differs from the crime group of the offense under MCL 777.18

(inducing a minor, MCL 750.157c). MCL 750.157c is a crime against a person and MCL 750.73 is a crime against property. When the crime group under MCL 777.18 differs from the crime group of the underlying offense, score OVs appropriate to the crime group of the underlying offense ***and*** OVs appropriate to the crime group designation under MCL 777.18. In the example just discussed, score OVs for crimes against a person and crimes against property.

The crime class for a guidelines offense under MCL 777.18 is determined by the crime class of the underlying offense(s). MCL 777.18 offenses are identified on the crime lists included with this manual as having a crime class of "SPEC." When there is only one underlying felony offense for an offense under MCL 777.18, use that felony's crime class. When there is more than one underlying felony offense, use the crime class of the felony offense with the highest crime class designation. When none of the underlying offenses is a felony offense, use crime class G. Because the penalties authorized by statute for conviction of the underlying offenses vary from offense to offense, the statutory maximum penalty for "SPEC" offenses is indicated as "Variable."

D. Habitual Offender Sentencing

The nine sentencing grids in MCL 777.61 to 777.69 represent the proper sentence ranges for offenders not being sentenced as habitual offenders. No separate grids reflecting the recommended sentence ranges for habitual offenders exist in the statutory provisions governing felony sentencing. However, statutory authority exists for determining the upper limit of an habitual offender's recommended minimum sentence by adding a specific percentage of the range calculated for first-time offenders to the upper limit in the cells of the existing sentencing grids. MCL 777.21(3)(a)-(c). The sentencing grids published in this manual are comprehensive grids and include the minimum sentence ranges recommended under the guidelines for all offenders – both first-time and habitual.

The appropriate sentence ranges for habitual offenders are calculated as follows:

Second Habitual Offender (HO2) – increase the upper limit of the appropriate cell by 25%.

Third Habitual Offender (HO3) – increase the upper limit of the appropriate cell by 50%.

Fourth Habitual Offender (HO4) – increase the upper limit of the appropriate cell by 100%.

Step IV. Determine the Recommended Minimum Sentence Range

A. Using the Sentencing Grids

Sentencing grids for all offenses to which the guidelines apply are located in MCL 777.61 to 777.69. There are nine different grids, one each for crimes in classes A, B, C, D, E, F, G, and H, and one for second-degree murder (M2). Each sentencing grid is divided into "cells" corresponding to the number of offense variable (OV) levels and prior record variable (PRV) levels applicable to the crime class represented in the grid. An offender's recommended minimum sentence range is indicated by the numeric range in the cell located at the intersection of the offender's "OV level" (vertical axis) and "PRV level" (horizontal axis) on the appropriate sentencing grid. MCL 777.21(1)(c). The recommended minimum sentence in each cell is expressed by a range of numbers (in months) or life imprisonment ("L").

Specific cells in some sentencing grids are differentiated from other cells by their classification as "prison cells," "straddle cells," and "intermediate sanction cells." With the exception of cells indicating that an intermediate sanction is appropriate, the terms "straddle cell" and "prison cell" are not expressly used in statutes governing application of the sentencing guidelines.

1. **Prison cells** are those cells for which the minimum sentence recommended exceeds one year of imprisonment. Prison cells are those cells that are unmarked in the sentencing grids, i.e., not shaded (as are straddle cells) and not asterisked (as are intermediate sanction cells). When an offender's OV and PRV levels place him or her in a prison cell, a minimum sentence within the range indicated in the cell is an appropriate sentence.

2. **Straddle cells** are those cells in which the lower limit of the recommended range is one year or less and the upper limit of the recommended range is more than 18 months. MCL 769.34(4)(c). Straddle cells appear shaded in the sentencing grids. When an offender's OV and PRV levels place him or her in a straddle cell, a minimum sentence within the range indicated in the cell OR an intermediate sanction (which may include a jail term of not more than 12 months) is an appropriate sentence.

3. **Intermediate sanction cells** are those cells in which the upper limit recommended by the guidelines is 18 months or less. MCL 769.34(4)(a). These cells are marked with an asterisk in the sentencing grids. When an offender's OV and PRV levels place him or her in an intermediate sanction cell, the court must sentence the offender to an intermediate sanction (which may include a jail term of 0-12 months or the cell maximum, whichever is less).

B. Additional Sentencing Considerations

1. Where the guidelines range will violate a statutorily mandated minimum sentence, the sentencing judge must sentence the offender to the minimum sentence mandated by statute. This is not a departure. MCL 769.34(2)(a).

2. The minimum sentence may not in any case (including a departure) exceed two-thirds of the statutory maximum sentence. MCL 769.34(2)(b).

3. Where the recommended minimum sentence under the guidelines falls in an intermediate sanction cell, the sentencing judge may sentence the offender below the cell range. MCL 769.34(4)(a).

4. Where the recommended minimum sentence falls in a straddle cell, the judge may sentence the offender below the cell range. MCL 769.34(4)(c)(*ii*).

5. If a statute mandates a minimum sentence for an offense and the statute authorizes the sentencing judge to impose a sentence that is less than that minimum sentence, imposing a sentence that exceeds the recommended sentence range but is less than the mandatory minimum sentence is not a departure from the guidelines. MCL 769.34(2)(a).

STEP V. Requirements for Departing from the Minimum Range

A judge may depart from the guidelines sentence range only where there are “substantial and compelling” reasons to do so. MCL 769.34(3).

The judge shall not use an individual’s gender, race, ethnicity, alienage, national origin, legal occupation, lack of employment, representation by appointed legal counsel, representation by retained legal counsel, appearance in propria persona, or religion to depart from the appropriate sentence range. MCL 769.34(3)(a). Furthermore, a departure shall not be based on an offense or offender characteristic already taken into account in determining the appropriate sentence range, unless the court finds from the facts contained in the court record, including the presentence investigation report, that the characteristic has been given inadequate or disproportionate weight. MCL 769.34(3)(b).

If the judge imposes a minimum sentence that represents an upward or downward departure from the appropriate sentence range, the court must state on the record the reasons for departure. MCL 769.34(3).

If the judge imposes a minimum sentence that is longer or more severe than the appropriate sentence range, the court shall advise the defendant on the record and in writing that he or she may appeal the sentence as provided by law on grounds that it is longer or more severe than the appropriate sentence range. MCL 769.34(7).

Definitions

This list is not meant to be exhaustive. Some prior record variables and offense variables are subject to definitions and instructions unique to those variables.

Adjudication: An adjudication is a finding of responsibility in a juvenile matter. An adjudication includes an adjudication set aside under MCL 712.18e or one that has been expunged.

Aircraft: The term as defined in MCL 259.2. MCL 777.1(a).

Cell: The intersection of an offender's OV level and PRV level in a sentencing grid.

Conviction: A "conviction" is an adjudication of guilt in a criminal matter. A conviction includes assignment to MCL 762.11 (Holmes Youthful Trainee Act) and convictions set aside under MCL 780.621 - 780.624 (expunged).

> **Prior conviction:** A conviction that was entered on the offender's criminal record before the commission date of the sentencing offense.
>
> **Concurrent conviction:** A conviction arising from the same course of conduct as the sentencing offense.
>
> **Subsequent conviction:** A conviction that was entered on the offender's criminal record after the commission date of the sentencing offense and is unrelated to the conduct from which the sentencing offense arose.

Crime group: All offenses to which the guidelines apply are categorized as belonging to one of six particular crime groups. The crime groups are: crimes against a person (person); crimes against property (property); crimes involving a controlled substance (CS); crimes against public order (pub ord); crimes against public safety (pub saf); and crimes against public trust (pub trst). MCL 777.5(a)–(f).

Crime class: All offenses to which the guidelines apply are classified as belonging to one of nine crime classes depending on crime type and seriousness. The crime classes are second-degree murder (M2) and classes A, B, C, D, E, F, G, and H.

Departure: A departure is defined by statute as a sentence imposed that is not within the appropriate minimum sentence range established under the sentencing guidelines. MCL 777.1(b); MCL 769.31(a). The appropriate minimum sentence range will sometimes be outside the indicated cell range. There are four statutorily correct or appropriate sentences outside of specific cell ranges that are not departures. They are: 1) when a mandatory minimum sentence is required, 2) when the cell exceeds the two-thirds limitation, 3) when a jail sentence is below a cell range in an intermediate sanction cell, and 4) when a jail sentence is below a cell range in a straddle cell.

Felony: A "felony" means a violation of a penal law of this state for which the offender, upon conviction, may be punished by death or by imprisonment for more than one year, or an offense expressly designated by law to be a felony. Convictions under federal law or the law of states other than Michigan are to be considered felony convictions if the offense was punishable by more than one year of incarceration or, when the statutory penalty is not available, if the crime was designated as a felony in the convicting jurisdiction at the time of the prior conviction.

Grid: Each sentencing grid provides a recommended minimum sentence range for combinations of the OV and PRV levels for each crime classification.

Guidelines sentence range: The set of numbers (in months or LIFE) in each cell from which the judge is required to impose a minimum sentence, absent a departure or other statutorily required sentence.

Homicide: Any crime in which the death of a human being is an element of that crime. MCL 777.1(c).

Intermediate sanction: Any sanction, other than imprisonment in a state prison or state reformatory, which may lawfully be imposed. MCL 777.1(d); MCL 769.31(b). Intermediate sanctions include, but are not limited to, one or more of the following:

1) Inpatient or outpatient drug treatment or participation in a drug treatment court.
2) Probation with any probation conditions required or authorized by law.
3) Residential probation.
4) Probation with jail.
5) Probation with special alternative incarceration.
6) Mental health treatment.
7) Mental health or substance abuse counseling.
8) Jail.
9) Jail with work or school release.
10) Jail with or without authorization for day parole.
11) Participation in a community corrections program.
12) Community service.
13) Payment of a fine.
14) House arrest.
15) Electronic monitoring.

Juvenile: A person over whom the Juvenile Division of the Probate Court or the Family Division of the Circuit Court has or had jurisdiction at the time of adjudication.

Misdemeanor: A "misdemeanor" means a violation of a penal law of this state that is not a felony, or a violation of an order, rule, or regulation of a state agency that is punishable by imprisonment or by a fine that is not a civil fine. Convictions under federal law or the law of states other than Michigan are to be considered misdemeanor convictions if the offense was punishable by one year or less of incarceration or, when the statutory penalty is not available, if the crime was designated as a misdemeanor in the convicting jurisdiction at the time of the prior conviction.

Off the road vehicle (ORV): The term as defined in MCL 324.81101. MCL 777.1(e).

Offense variables (OVs): The factors that are used to evaluate the seriousness of the offense and to determine the offender's OV score.

Definitions

OV level: An offender's OV score determines the offender's OV level. Depending on the specific sentencing grid, the OV levels are designated by roman numerals from I to VI along the vertical axis of the grid. The OV level's numeric designation increases as the offender's OV point total increases. The severity of the corresponding penalty increases successively from OV levels I through VI.

OV score: The total number of points scored for all OVs applicable to the sentencing offense.

Prior high severity felony conviction: A prior high severity felony conviction is: (1) a conviction for a crime listed in class M2, A, B, C, or D or for a felony under federal law or the law of another state that corresponds to a crime listed in class M2, A, B, C, or D if the conviction was entered before the sentencing offense was committed; (2) a conviction (entered before the sentencing offense was committed) for a crime punishable by a maximum term of imprisonment of 10 years or more that is not listed in class M2, A, B, C, D, E, F, G, or H; or (3) a conviction (entered before the sentencing offense was committed) under federal law or the law of another state for a crime punishable by a maximum term of imprisonment of 10 years or more that does not correspond to a crime listed in class M2, A, B, C, D, E, F, G, or H. MCL 777.51(2).

Prior high severity juvenile adjudication: A prior high severity juvenile adjudication is: (1) a juvenile adjudication for conduct that would be a crime listed in class M2, A, B, C, or D if committed by an adult or for conduct that would be a felony under federal law or the law of another state that corresponds to a crime listed in class M2, A, B, C, or D if committed by an adult if the order of disposition was entered before the sentencing offense was committed; or (2) an adjudication (entered before the sentencing offense was committed) for conduct that if committed by an adult would be a crime punishable by a maximum term of imprisonment of 10 years or more that is not listed in class M2, A, B, C, D, E, F, G, or H; or (3) an adjudication (entered before the sentencing offense was committed) for conduct that if committed by an adult would be a crime under federal law or the law of another state punishable by a maximum term of imprisonment of 10 years or more that does not correspond to a crime listed in class M2, A, B, C, D, E, F, G, or H. MCL 777.53(2).

Prior low severity felony conviction: A prior low severity felony conviction is: (1) a conviction for a crime listed in class E, F, G, or H or for a felony under federal law or the law of another state that corresponds to a crime listed in class E, F, G, or H if the conviction was entered before the sentencing offense was committed; or (2) a conviction (entered before the sentencing offense was committed) for a crime punishable by a maximum term of imprisonment of less than 10 years that is not listed in class M2, A, B, C, D, E, F, G, or H; or (3) a conviction (entered before the sentencing offense was committed) under federal law or the law of another state for a crime punishable by a maximum term of imprisonment of less than 10 years that does not correspond to a crime listed in class M2, A, B, C, D, E, F, G, or H. MCL 777.52(2).

Prior low severity juvenile adjudication: A prior low severity juvenile adjudication is: (1) an adjudication for conduct that would be a crime listed in class E, F, G, or H if committed by an adult or for conduct that would be a felony under federal law or the law of another state that corresponds to a crime listed in class E, F, G, or H if committed by an adult if the order of disposition was entered before the sentencing offense was committed; (2) an adjudication (entered before the sentencing offense was committed) for conduct that if committed by an adult would be a crime punishable by a maximum term of imprisonment of less than 10 years that is not listed in class M2, A, B, C, D, E, F, G, or H; or (3) an adjudication (entered before the sentencing offense was committed) for conduct that if committed by an adult would be a crime under federal law or the law of another state punishable by a maximum term of imprisonment of less than 10 years that does not correspond to a crime listed in class M2, A, B, C, D, E, F, G, or H. MCL 777.54(2).

Prior misdemeanor conviction: A conviction for a misdemeanor under a law of this state, a political subdivision of this state, another state, a political subdivision of another state, or the United States if the conviction was entered before the sentencing offense was committed. MCL 777.55(3)(a).

Prior misdemeanor juvenile adjudication: A juvenile adjudication for conduct that if committed by an adult would be a misdemeanor under a law of this state, a political subdivision of this state, another state, a political subdivision another state, or the United States if the order of disposition was entered before the sentencing offense was committed. MCL 777.55(3)(b).

Prior record variables (PRVs): The factors used to evaluate the offender's criminal history and determine the offender's PRV score.

PRV level: An offender's PRV score determines the offender's PRV level. An offender's PRV level is represented on the horizontal axis of each sentencing grid and is designated by capital letters from A to F according to the offender's PRV point total. PRV level A represents the column with the least number of points and PRV level F represents the column with the highest number of points. As with the OV level values, the severity of penalty increases with an offender's transit from PRV level A up to PRV level F. The point values corresponding with PRV levels A through F are the same for all nine sentencing grids so that an offender's criminal history is equally weighted no matter what the severity of the sentencing offense.

PRV score: The total number of points scored for all seven PRVs.

Snowmobile: The term as defined in MCL 324.82101. MCL 777.1(f).

Truth in sentencing (TIS): A designation of those felony offenses that are subject to disciplinary time if committed on or after December 15, 1998. Persons convicted of TIS offenses committed on or after 12-15-98 do not earn disciplinary credits and must serve at least the complete minimum sentence imposed by the court in a secure facility before becoming eligible for parole, with the exception of a few offenses for which there is Special Alternative Incarceration eligibility. Prisoners subject to TIS will be assessed "disciplinary time" for institutional misconduct, which is not added directly to the minimum sentence but is submitted to the parole board for its consideration in granting or denying parole. TIS is extended to all felony offenses committed on or after December 15, 2000.

Vehicle: The term as defined in MCL 257.79. MCL 777.1(g).

Vessel: The term as defined in MCL 324.80104. MCL 777.1(h).

PRVs and OVs – Crimes Against a Person

PRV 1

Prior High Severity Felony Convictions

(All "prior convictions" must satisfy the 10-year gap requirements of MCL 777.50.)

Pts	The offender has:	Instructions
75	3 or more prior high severity convictions.	A **"prior high severity felony conviction"** is a conviction for any of the following crimes if the conviction was entered before the commission date of the sentencing offense: • a crime listed in class M2, A, B, C, or D (or a felony under federal law or the law of another state that corresponds to a crime listed in class M2, A, B, C, or D), or • (effective January 9, 2007)* a felony that is not listed in ***any*** crime class (or a felony under federal law or the law of another state that does not correspond to a crime listed in ***any*** class) that is punishable by a maximum term of imprisonment of 10 years or more. MCL 777.51(2). *2006 PA 655.
50	2 prior high severity convictions.	
25	1 prior high severity conviction.	
0	No prior high severity convictions.	

PRV 2

Prior Low Severity Felony Convictions

(All "prior convictions" must satisfy the 10-year gap requirements of MCL 777.50.)

Pts	The offender has:	Instructions
30	4 or more prior low severity convictions.	A **"prior low severity felony conviction"** is a conviction for any of the following crimes if the conviction was entered before the commission date of the sentencing offense: • a crime listed in class E, F, G, or H (or a felony under federal law or the law of another state that corresponds to a crime listed in class E, F, G, or H), or • (effective January 9, 2007)* a felony that is not listed in ***any*** crime class (or a felony under federal law or the law of another state that does not correspond to a crime listed in ***any*** class) that is punishable by a maximum term of imprisonment of less than 10 years. MCL 777.52(2). *2006 PA 655.
20	3 prior low severity convictions.	
10	2 prior low severity convictions.	
5	1 prior low severity conviction.	
0	No prior low severity convictions.	

PRV 3

Prior High Severity Juvenile Adjudications

(All "prior convictions" must satisfy the 10-year gap requirements of MCL 777.50.)

Pts	The offender has:	Instructions
50	3 or more prior high severity juvenile adjudications.	A **"prior high severity juvenile adjudication"** is an adjudication for conduct that would be any of the following if committed by an adult, if the order of disposition was entered before the commission date of the sentencing offense: • a crime listed in class M2, A, B, C, or D (or a felony under federal law or the law of another state that corresponds to a crime listed in class M2, A, B, C, or D), or • (effective January 9, 2007)* a felony that is not listed in ***any*** crime class (or a felony under federal law or the law of another state that does not correspond to a crime listed in ***any*** class) that is punishable by a maximum term of imprisonment of 10 years or more. MCL 777.53(2). *2006 PA 655.
25	2 prior high severity juvenile adjudications.	
10	1 prior high severity juvenile adjudication.	
0	No prior high severity juvenile adjudications.	

PRV 4

Prior Low Severity Juvenile Adjudications

(All "prior convictions" must satisfy the 10-year gap requirements of MCL 777.50.)

Pts	The offender has:	Instructions
20	6 or more prior low severity juvenile adjudications.	A **"prior low severity juvenile adjudication"** is an adjudication for conduct that would be any of the following if committed by an adult, if the order of disposition was entered before the commission date of the sentencing offense: • a crime listed in class E, F, G, or H (or a felony under federal law or the law of another state that corresponds to a crime listed in class E, F, G, or H), or • (effective January 9, 2007)* a felony that is not listed in ***any*** crime class (or a felony under federal law or the law of another state that does not correspond to a crime listed in ***any*** class) that is punishable by a maximum term of imprisonment of less than 10 years. MCL 777.54(2). *2006 PA 655.
15	5 prior low severity juvenile adjudications.	
10	3 or 4 prior low severity juvenile adjudications.	
5	2 prior low severity juvenile adjudications.	
2	1 prior low severity juvenile adjudication.	
0	No prior low severity juvenile adjudications.	

PRV 5

Prior Misdemeanor Convictions and Prior Misdemeanor Juvenile Adjudications

(All "prior convictions" must satisfy the 10-year gap requirements of MCL 777.50.)

Pts	The offender has:	Instructions
20	7 or more prior misdemeanor convictions or prior misdemeanor juvenile adjudications.	A **"prior misdemeanor conviction"** is a conviction: • for a misdemeanor offense under Michigan law or the law of a political subdivision of Michigan, or under the law of another state or a political subdivision of another state, or under the law of the United States, • if the conviction was entered before the commission date of the sentencing offense. MCL 777.55(3)(a). A **"prior misdemeanor juvenile adjudication"** is a juvenile adjudication: • for conduct that, if committed by an adult, would be a misdemeanor under Michigan law or the law of a political subdivision of Michigan, or under the law of another state or a political subdivision of another state, or under the law of the United States, • if the order of disposition for the juvenile adjudication was entered before the commission date of the sentencing offense. MCL 777.55(3)(b).
15	5 or 6 prior misdemeanor convictions or prior misdemeanor juvenile adjudications.	
10	3 or 4 prior misdemeanor convictions or prior misdemeanor juvenile adjudications.	
5	2 prior misdemeanor convictions or prior misdemeanor juvenile adjudications.	
2	1 prior misdemeanor conviction or prior misdemeanor juvenile adjudication.	
0	No prior misdemeanor convictions or prior misdemeanor juvenile adjudications.	

Special Instructions for PRV 5:

- A prior conviction used to enhance the sentencing offense to a felony may not be counted under PRV 5. MCL 777.55(2)(b).
- Only prior convictions and adjudications for offenses expressly listed in PRV 5 may be counted as "prior misdemeanor convictions" or "prior misdemeanor juvenile adjudications" for purposes of scoring PRV 5:
  - only those prior misdemeanor convictions or prior misdemeanor juvenile adjudications that are offenses against a person or property, weapons offenses, or offenses involving controlled substances, and
  - all prior misdemeanor convictions and juvenile adjudications for operating or attempting to operate a vehicle, vessel, ORV, snowmobile, aircraft, or locomotive while under the influence of or impaired by alcohol, a controlled substance, or a combination of alcohol and a controlled substance. MCL 777.55(2)(a)–(b).

PRV 6
Offender's Relationship to the Criminal Justice System

Pts		Instructions
20	Offender is a prisoner of the department of corrections or serving a sentence in jail (includes an offender who is an escapee from jail or prison). MCL 777.56(3)(b).	PRV 6 assesses points based on an offender's relationship to the criminal justice system at the time the sentencing offense was committed. MCL 777.56. The scope of PRV 6 includes consideration of an offender's relationship with a criminal justice system outside the state of Michigan. The point values indicated by applicable statements in PRV 6 should be assessed against an offender who is involved with the criminal justice system of another state or the federal criminal justice system. "Delayed sentence status" includes (but is not limited to) an offender assigned or deferred under MCL 333.7411 (deferral for certain controlled substance offenses), MCL 750.350a (deferral under limited circumstances for parental kidnapping), MCL 762.11 to 762.15 (assignment to youthful trainee status), MCL 769.4a (deferral under limited circumstances for domestic assault), MCL 600.1076 (deferral involving drug treatment courts), and MCL 750.430 (deferral for impaired healthcare professionals).
15	Offender is incarcerated in jail awaiting adjudication or sentencing on a conviction or probation violation.	
10	Offender is on parole, probation, or delayed sentence status or on bond awaiting adjudication or sentencing for a felony.	
5	Offender is on probation or delayed sentence status or on bond awaiting adjudication or sentencing for a misdemeanor.	
0	Offender has no relationship to the criminal justice system.	

PRV 7
Subsequent or Concurrent Felony Convictions

Pts	The offender has:	Instructions
20	2 or more subsequent or concurrent felony convictions.	• A conviction for felony-firearm may not be counted under PRV 7. MCL 777.57(2)(b). • A concurrent felony conviction that will result in a mandatory consecutive sentence may not be counted under PRV 7. MCL 777.57(2)(c). • A concurrent felony conviction that will result in a consecutive sentence under MCL 333.7401(3)* may not be counted under PRV 7. MCL 777.57(2)(c). *Effective March 1, 2003, 2002 PA 666. Does not apply to offenses committed before March 1, 2003.
10	1 subsequent or concurrent felony conviction.	
0	No subsequent or concurrent felony convictions.	

PRVs and OVs – Crimes Against a Person

OV 1
Aggravated Use of a Weapon

Pts		Instructions
25	A firearm was discharged at or toward a human being or a victim was cut or stabbed with a knife or other cutting or stabbing weapon. MCL 777.31(1)(a).	• Each person in danger of injury or loss of life is counted as a victim for purposes of scoring OV 1. MCL 777.31(2)(a). • In cases involving multiple offenders, if one offender is assigned points for the use or the presence of a weapon, all offenders must be assigned the same number of points. MCL 777.31(2)(b). • Do not score five points if the sentencing offense is a conviction of MCL 750.82 (felonious assault) or MCL 750.529 (armed robbery). MCL 777.31(2)(e). • Score five points if an offender used an object to suggest that he or she had a weapon. MCL 777.31(2)(c). • Score five points if an offender used a chemical irritant, a chemical irritant or smoke device, or an imitation harmful substance or device. MCL 777.31(2)(d). • "Harmful biological substance," "harmful biological device," "harmful chemical substance," "harmful chemical device," "harmful radioactive material," "harmful radioactive device," and "imitation harmful substance or device" are defined in MCL 750.200h. MCL 777.31(3)(a). • "Incendiary device" includes gasoline or any other flammable substance, a blowtorch, fire bomb, Molotov cocktail, or other similar device. MCL 777.31(3)(b).
20	The victim was subjected or exposed to a harmful biological substance, harmful biological device, harmful chemical substance, harmful chemical device, harmful radioactive material, harmful radioactive device, incendiary device, or explosive device. MCL 777.31(1)(b).	
15	A firearm was pointed at or toward a victim or the victim had a reasonable apprehension of an immediate battery when threatened with a knife or other cutting or stabbing weapon. MCL 777.31(1)(c).	
10	The victim was touched by any other type of weapon. MCL 777.31(1)(d).	
5	A weapon was displayed or implied. MCL 777.31(1)(e).	
0	No aggravated use of a weapon occurred. MCL 777.31(1)(f).	

OV 2

Lethal Potential of Weapon Possessed or Used

Pts		Instructions
15	The offender possessed or used a harmful biological substance, harmful biological device, harmful chemical substance, harmful chemical device, harmful radioactive material, or harmful radioactive device. MCL 777.32(1)(a).	• In cases involving multiple offenders, if one offender is assessed points for possessing a weapon, all offenders must be assessed the same number of points. MCL 777.32(2). • "Harmful biological substance," "harmful biological device," "harmful chemical substance," "harmful chemical device," "harmful radioactive material," and "harmful radioactive device" are defined in MCL 750.200h. MCL 777.32(3)(a). • A "fully automatic weapon" is a firearm that ejects an empty cartridge and loads a live cartridge from the magazine for the next shot without requiring renewed pressure on the trigger for each successive shot. MCL 777.32(3)(b). • A "pistol," "rifle," or "shotgun" includes a revolver, semi-automatic pistol, rifle, shotgun, combination rifle and shotgun, or other firearm made in or after 1898 that fires fixed ammunition. A "pistol," "rifle," or "shotgun" does not include a fully automatic weapon or short-barreled shotgun or short-barreled rifle. MCL 777.32(3)(c). • An "incendiary device" includes gasoline or any other flammable substance, a blowtorch, fire bomb, Molotov cocktail, or other similar device. MCL 777.32(3)(d).
15	The offender possessed or used an incendiary device, an explosive device, or a fully automatic weapon. MCL 777.32(1)(b).	
10	The offender possessed or used a short-barreled rifle or a short-barreled shotgun. MCL 777.32(1)(c).	
5	The offender possessed or used a pistol, rifle, shotgun, or knife or other cutting or stabbing weapon. MCL 777.32(1)(d).	
1	The offender possessed or used any other potentially lethal weapon. MCL 777.32(1)(e).	
0	The offender possessed or used no weapon. MCL 777.32(1)(f).	

PRVs and OVs – Crimes Against a Person

OV 3
Degree of Physical Injury to a Victim

Pts		Instructions
100	A victim was killed. MCL 777.33(1)(a).	• In cases involving multiple offenders, if one offender is assessed points for death or physical injury, all offenders must be assessed the same number of points. MCL 777.33(3)(a). • Score 100 points if death results from the commission of the offense and homicide is not the sentencing offense. MCL 777.33(2)(b). Any crime in which the death of a person is an element of the crime is a "homicide." MCL 777.1(c). • Score 50 points under this variable if death results from an offense or attempted offense that involves the operation of a vehicle, vessel, ORV, snowmobile, aircraft, or locomotive and any of the following apply: – the offender was under the influence of or visibly impaired by the use of alcohol, a controlled substance, or a combination of alcohol and a controlled substance, MCL 777.33(2)(c)(i); – the offender had an alcohol content of 0.08 grams* or more per 100 milliliters of blood, per 210 liters of breath, or per 67 milliliters of urine, MCL 777.33(2)(c)(ii); or – the offender's body contained any amount of a controlled substance listed in schedule 1 under MCL 333.7212 or a rule promulgated under that section, or a controlled substance described in MCL 333.7214(a)(iv), MCL 777.33(2)(c)(iii). • Do not score five points if "bodily injury" is an element of the sentencing offense. MCL 777.33(2)(d). • "Requiring medical treatment" refers to an injury's need for treatment not whether a victim was successful in obtaining treatment. MCL 777.33(3). **Effective October 1, 2013, the alcohol content level increases to 0.10 grams or more.*
50	A victim was killed. MCL 777.33(1)(b). *(35 points for offenses committed before September 30, 2003. 2003 PA 134.)*	
25	Life threatening or permanent incapacitating injury occurred to a victim. MCL 777.33(1)(c).	
10	Bodily injury requiring medical treatment occurred to a victim. MCL 777.33(1)(d).	
5	Bodily injury not requiring medical treatment occurred to a victim. MCL 777.33(1)(e).	
0	No physical injury occurred to a victim. MCL 777.33(1)(f).	

OV 4
Degree of Psychological Injury to a Victim

Pts		Instructions
10	Serious psychological injury requiring professional treatment occurred to a victim. MCL 777.34(1)(a).	Ten points may be scored if the victim's serious psychological injury may require professional treatment. Whether the victim has sought treatment for the injury is not conclusive. MCL 777.34(2).
0	No serious psychological injury requiring professional treatment occurred to a victim. MCL 777.34(1)(b).	

OV 5

Psychological Injury Sustained by a Member of a Victim's Family

*Score for crime in "Person" crime group **only** if the sentencing offense is homicide, attempted homicide, conspiracy or solicitation to commit a homicide, or assault with intent to commit murder.*

<table>
<tr><th>Pts</th><th></th><th>Instructions</th></tr>
<tr><td>15</td><td>Serious psychological injury requiring professional treatment occurred to a victim's family member. MCL 777.35(1)(a).</td><td rowspan="2">• Assess 15 points if the family member's serious psychological injury may require professional treatment. The fact that treatment has not been sought is not determinative. MCL 777.35(2).
• Any crime in which the death of a person is an element of the crime is a "homicide." MCL 777.1(c).</td></tr>
<tr><td>0</td><td>No serious psychological injury requiring professional treatment occurred to a victim's family member. MCL 777.35(1)(b).</td></tr>
</table>

OV 6

Intent to Kill or Injure Another Individual

*Score for crime in "Person" crime group **only** if the sentencing offense is homicide, attempted homicide, conspiracy or solicitation to commit a homicide, or assault with intent to commit murder.*

<table>
<tr><th>Pts</th><th></th><th>Instructions</th></tr>
<tr><td>50</td><td>The offender had premeditated intent to kill or the killing was committed while committing or attempting to commit arson, criminal sexual conduct in the first or third degree, child abuse in the first degree, a major controlled substance offense, robbery, breaking and entering of a dwelling, home invasion in the first or second degree, larceny of any kind, extortion, or kidnapping or the killing was the murder of a peace officer or a corrections officer. MCL 777.36(1)(a).</td><td rowspan="4">• Unless the sentencing court has information that was not presented to the jury, an offender's OV 6 score must be consistent with the jury's verdict. MCL 777.36(2)(a).
• Ten points must be scored if a killing is intentional within the definition of second-degree murder or voluntary manslaughter but the death took place in a combative situation or in response to the decedent's victimization of the offender. MCL 777.36(2)(b).
• Any crime in which a person's death in an element of the crime is a "homicide." MCL 777.1(c).</td></tr>
<tr><td>25</td><td>The offender had unpremeditated intent to kill, the intent to do great bodily harm, or created a very high risk of death or great bodily harm knowing that death or great bodily harm was the probable result. MCL 777.36(1)(b).</td></tr>
<tr><td>10</td><td>The offender had intent to injure or the killing was committed in an extreme emotional state caused by an adequate provocation and before a reasonable amount of time elapsed for the offender to calm or there was gross negligence amounting to an unreasonable disregard for life. MCL 777.36(1)(c).</td></tr>
<tr><td>0</td><td>The offender had no intent to kill or injure. MCL 777.36(1)(d).</td></tr>
</table>

OV 7
Aggravated Physical Abuse

Pts		Instructions
50	A victim was treated with sadism, torture, or excessive brutality or conduct designed to substantially increase the fear and anxiety a victim suffered during the offense. MCL 777.37(1)(a).	• Each person placed in danger of injury or loss of life is a victim for purposes of scoring OV 7. MCL 777.37(2). • "Sadism" is "conduct that subjects a victim to extreme or prolonged pain or humiliation and is inflicted to produce suffering or for the offender's gratification." MCL 777.37(3). • Effective April 22, 2002, 2002 PA 137 deleted "terrorism"* from OV 7's list of behaviors meriting points. Although "terrorism" was eliminated from consideration under OV 7, the conduct previously defined as "terrorism" remains in OV 7's statutory language as "conduct designed to substantially increase the fear and anxiety a victim suffered during the offense." MCL 777.37(1)(a). *"Terrorism" is now addressed by OV 20. MCL 777.49a.*
0	No victim was treated with sadism, torture, or excessive brutality or conduct designed to substantially increase the fear and anxiety a victim suffered during the offense. MCL 777.37(1)(b).	

OV 8
Victim Asportation or Captivity

Pts		Instructions
15	A victim was asported to another place of greater danger or to a situation of greater danger or was held captive beyond the time necessary to commit the offense. MCL 777.38(1)(a).	• Each person in danger of injury or loss of life is a victim for purposes of scoring OV 8. MCL 777.38(2)(a). • Zero points must be scored if the sentencing offense is kidnapping. MCL 777.38(2)(b).
0	No victim was asported or held captive. MCL 777.38(1)(b).	

OV 9
Number of Victims

Pts		Instructions
100	Multiple deaths occurred. MCL 777.39(1)(a).	• A "victim" for purposes of scoring OV 9 is each person placed in danger of injury or loss of life or (effective March 30, 2007)* loss of property. MCL 777.39(2)(a). • 100 points are scored only in homicide cases. MCL 777.39(2)(b). Any crime in which a person's death is an element of the crime is a "homicide." MCL 777.1(c). *2006 PA 548.
25	10 or more victims were placed in danger of physical injury or death. 20 or more victims were placed in danger of property loss (effective March 30, 2007). MCL 777.39(1)(b).	
10	2 to 9 victims were placed in danger of physical injury or death. 4 to 19 victims were placed in danger of property loss (effective March 30, 2007). MCL 777.39(1)(c).	
0	Fewer than 2 victims were placed in danger of physical injury or death. Fewer than 4 victims were placed in danger of property loss (effective March 30, 2007). MCL 777.39(1)(d).	

OV 10
Exploitation of a Victim's Vulnerability

Pts		Instructions
15	Predatory conduct was involved. MCL 777.40(1)(a).	• Do not automatically score points for victim vulnerability just because one or more of the factors addressed by OV 10 are present in the circumstances surrounding the sentencing offense. MCL 777.40(2). • "Predatory conduct" is an offender's preoffense conduct directed at a victim for the primary purpose of victimization. MCL 777.40(3)(a). • To "exploit" a victim is to manipulate a victim for the offender's selfish or unethical purposes. MCL 777.40(3)(b). • A victim's "vulnerability" is the victim's readily apparent susceptibility to injury, physical restraint, persuasion, or temptation. MCL 777.40(3)(c). • "Abuse of authority status" means the offender used a victim's fear of or deference to an authority figure to exploit the victim. Examples of an authority figure include, but are not limited to, a teacher, parent, or physician. MCL 777.40(3)(d).
10	The offender exploited a victim's physical disability, mental disability, youth or agedness, or a domestic relationship or the offender abused his or her authority status. MCL 777.40(1)(b).	
5	The offender exploited a victim by his or her difference in size or strength, or both, or exploited a victim who was intoxicated, under the influence of drugs, asleep, or unconscious. MCL 777.40(1)(c).	
0	The offender did not exploit a victim's vulnerability. MCL 777.40(1)(d).	

OV 11
Criminal Sexual Penetration

<table>
<tr><th>Pts</th><th></th><th>Instructions</th></tr>
<tr><td>50</td><td>Two or more criminal sexual penetrations occurred. MCL 777.41(1)(a).</td><td rowspan="3">• All sexual penetrations of the victim by the offender arising out of the sentencing offense must be counted in scoring OV 11. MCL 777.41(2)(a).
• Multiple sexual penetrations of the victim by the offender occurring beyond the sentencing offense may be scored in OVs 12 or 13.* MCL 777.41(2)(b). However, if any conduct is scored under this variable, that conduct must not be scored under OV 12 and may only be scored under OV 13 if the conduct is related to the offender's membership in an organized criminal group. MCL 777.42(2)(c); MCL 777.43(2)(c).
• The one penetration on which a first- or third-degree criminal sexual conduct offense is based must not be counted for purposes of scoring OV 11. MCL 777.41(2)(c).
**OV 12 addresses criminal acts that occur within 24 hours of the sentencing offense and will not result in a separate conviction. OV 13 accounts for an offender's pattern of criminal conduct over a period of five years regardless of outcome.*</td></tr>
<tr><td>25</td><td>One criminal sexual penetration occurred. MCL 777.41(1)(b).</td></tr>
<tr><td>0</td><td>No criminal sexual penetrations occurred. MCL 777.41(1)(c).</td></tr>
</table>

OV 12
Number of Contemporaneous Felonious Criminal Acts

<table>
<tr><th>Pts</th><th></th><th>Instructions</th></tr>
<tr><td>25</td><td>Three or more contemporaneous felonious criminal acts involving crimes against a person were committed. MCL 777.42(1)(a).</td><td rowspan="7">• A felonious criminal act is contemporaneous if both of the following circumstances exist:
– the criminal act occurred within 24 hours of the sentencing offense, MCL 777.42(2)(a)(i), and
– the criminal act has not and will not result in a separate conviction, MCL 777.42(2)(a)(ii).
• Conduct scored in OV 11 must not be scored under this variable. MCL 777.42(2)(c).
• Violations of MCL 750.227b (possession of a firearm during the commission of a felony) should not be counted when scoring this variable. MCL 777.42(2)(b).</td></tr>
<tr><td>10</td><td>Two contemporaneous felonious criminal acts involving crimes against a person were committed. MCL 777.42(1)(b).</td></tr>
<tr><td>10</td><td>Three or more contemporaneous felonious criminal acts involving other crimes were committed. MCL 777.42(1)(c).</td></tr>
<tr><td>5</td><td>One contemporaneous felonious criminal act involving a crime against a person was committed. MCL 777.42(1)(d).</td></tr>
<tr><td>5</td><td>Two contemporaneous felonious criminal acts involving other crimes were committed. MCL 777.42(1)(e).</td></tr>
<tr><td>1</td><td>One contemporaneous felonious criminal act involving any other crime was committed. MCL 777.42(1)(f).</td></tr>
<tr><td>0</td><td>No contemporaneous felonious criminal acts were committed. MCL 777.42(1)(g).</td></tr>
</table>

OV 13

Continuing Pattern of Criminal Behavior

Effective March 1, 2003, 2002 PA 666 amended the instructions for OV 13 to include references to specific controlled substance offenses. Language appearing in bold type in the chart below applies to offenses committed on or after March 1, 2003, pursuant to 2002 PA 666.

<table>
<tr><th>Pts</th><th></th><th>Instructions</th></tr>
<tr><td>50</td><td>The offense was part of a pattern of felonious criminal activity involving 3 or more sexual penetrations against a person or persons less than 13 years of age. MCL 777.43(1)(a).</td><td rowspan="7">• To score this variable, all crimes within a period of five years, including the sentencing offense, must be counted without regard to whether the offense resulted in a conviction. MCL 777.43(2)(a).
• The existence of an organized criminal group may be inferred from the facts surrounding the sentencing offense, and the group's existence is more important than the presence or absence of multiple offenders, the age of the offenders, or the degree of sophistication demonstrated by the criminal group. MCL 777.43(2)(b).
• Do not consider conduct scored in OVs 11 or 12 unless the offense was related to membership in an organized criminal group. MCL 777.43(2)(c).
• Score 50 points only if the sentencing offense is first-degree criminal sexual conduct. MCL 777.43(2)(d).
• Only one controlled substance offense arising from the criminal episode for which the offender is being sentenced may be counted when scoring this variable.* MCL 777.43(2)(e).
• Only one crime involving the same controlled substance may be counted under this variable.* For example, conspiracy and a substantive offense involving the same amount of controlled substances cannot both be counted under OV 13. Similarly, possession and delivery of the same amount of controlled substances may not be counted as two crimes under OV 13. MCL 777.43(2)(f).
**Effective March 1, 2003. 2002 PA 666.*</td></tr>
<tr><td>25</td><td>The offense was part of a pattern of felonious criminal activity involving 3 or more crimes against a person. MCL 777.43(1)(b).</td></tr>
<tr><td>10</td><td>The offense was part of a pattern of felonious criminal activity involving a combination of 3 or more crimes against a person or property or a violation of MCL 333.7401(2)(a)(i) to (iii) or 333.7403(2)(a)(i) to (iii). MCL 777.43(1)(c).</td></tr>
<tr><td>10</td><td>The offense was part of a pattern of felonious criminal activity directly related to membership in an organized criminal group. MCL 777.43(1)(d).</td></tr>
<tr><td>10</td><td>The offense was part of a pattern of felonious criminal activity involving a combination of 3 or more violations of MCL 333.7401(2)(a)(i) to (iii) or 333.7403(2)(a)(i) to (iii). MCL 777.43(1)(e).</td></tr>
<tr><td>5</td><td>The offense was part of a pattern of felonious criminal activity involving 3 or more crimes against property. MCL 777.43(1)(f).</td></tr>
<tr><td>0</td><td>No pattern of felonious criminal activity existed. MCL 777.43(1)(g).</td></tr>
</table>

OV 14

Offender's Role

<table>
<tr><th>Pts</th><th></th><th>Instructions</th></tr>
<tr><td>10</td><td>The offender was a leader in a multiple offender situation. MCL 777.44(1)(a).</td><td rowspan="2">• Consider the entire criminal transaction in which the sentencing offense occurred when determining the offender's role. MCL 777.44(2)(a).
• In cases involving three or more offenders, more than one offender may be considered a leader. MCL 777.44(2)(b).</td></tr>
<tr><td>0</td><td>The offender was not a leader in a multiple offender situation. MCL 777.44(1)(b).</td></tr>
</table>

PRVs and OVs – Crimes Against a Person

OV 16
Degree of Property Damage

*Score for crime in "Person" crime group **only** if the sentencing offense is a violation or attempted violation of MCL 750.110a (home invasion).*

Pts		Instructions
10	Wanton or malicious damage occurred beyond that necessary to commit the crime for which the offender is not charged and will not be charged. MCL 777.46(1)(a).	• In cases involving multiple offenders or multiple victims, the appropriate point total may be determined by aggregating the value of property involved in the offense, including property involved in uncharged offenses or property involved in charges dismissed under a plea agreement. MCL 777.46(2)(a). • Use the value of the property to score this variable in cases where the property was unlawfully obtained, lost to the lawful owner, or destroyed. If the property was damaged, use the amount of money necessary to restore the property to its pre-offense condition. MCL 777.46(2)(b). • Money or property involved in admitted but uncharged offenses or in charges dismissed under a plea agreement may be considered in scoring this variable. MCL 777.46(2)(c).
10	The property had a value of more than $20,000.00 or had significant historical, social, or sentimental value. MCL 777.46(1)(b).	
5	The property had a value of $1,000.00 or more but not more than $20,000.00. MCL 777.46(1)(c).	
1	The property had a value of $200.00 or more but not more than $1,000.00. MCL 777.46(1)(d).	
0	No property was obtained, damaged, lost, or destroyed or the property had a value of less than $200.00. MCL 777.46(1)(e).	

OV 17
Degree of Negligence Exhibited

*Score for crime in "Person" crime group **only** if the offense or attempted offense involves the operation of a vehicle, vessel, ORV, snowmobile, aircraft, or locomotive.*

Pts		Instructions
10	The offender showed a wanton or reckless disregard for the life or property of another person. MCL 777.47(1)(a).	• If points are assessed against the offender for OV 6, ten points may not be scored under this variable. MCL 777.47(2). • Definitions for "aircraft," "ORV," "snowmobile," "vehicle," and "vessel" are referenced in MCL 777.1.
5	The offender failed to show the degree of care that a person of ordinary prudence in a similar situation would have shown. MCL 777.47(1)(b).	
0	The offender was not negligent. MCL 777.47(1)(c).	

OV 18

Degree to Which Alcohol or Drugs Affected the Offender

Score for crime in "Person" crime group ***only*** *if the offense or attempted offense involves the operation of a vehicle, vessel, ORV, snowmobile, aircraft, or locomotive.*

Effective September 30, 2003, 2003 PA 134 amended the statute governing point allocations for OV 18. Language appearing in the shaded areas of the chart below represents the variable as it applies to offenses that occurred before September 30, 2003. Unshaded areas contain the instructions for scoring OV 18 for offenses occurring on or after September 30, 2003, the amendment's effective date.

Pts		Instructions
20	The offender operated a vehicle, vessel, ORV, snowmobile, aircraft, or locomotive when his or her bodily alcohol content was 0.20 grams or more per 100 milliliters of blood, per 210 liters of breath, or per 67 milliliters of urine. MCL 777.48(1)(a).	• For purposes of scoring OV 18, "any bodily alcohol content" is either of the following: – an alcohol content of 0.02 grams or more but less than 0.08 grams per 100 milliliters of blood, per 210 liters of breath, or per 67 milliliters of urine,* MCL 777.48(2)(a), or – any presence of alcohol within a person's body from the consumption of alcohol except for alcohol consumption as part of a generally recognized religious service or ceremony, MCL 777.48(2)(b). • Definitions for "aircraft," "ORV," "snowmobile," "vehicle," and "vessel" are referenced in MCL 777.1. **continued on next page**
20	The offender operated a vehicle, vessel, ORV, snowmobile, aircraft, or locomotive when his or her bodily alcohol content was 0.20 grams or more per 100 milliliters of blood, per 210 liters of breath, or per 67 milliliters of urine.	
15	The offender operated a vehicle, vessel, ORV, snowmobile, aircraft, or locomotive when his or her bodily alcohol content was 0.15 grams or more but less than 0.20 grams per 100 milliliters of blood, per 210 liters of breath, or per 67 milliliters of urine. MCL 777.48(1)(b).	
15	The offender operated a vehicle, vessel, ORV, snowmobile, aircraft, or locomotive when his or her bodily alcohol content was 0.15 grams or more but less than 0.20 grams per 100 milliliters of blood, per 210 liters of breath, or per 67 milliliters of urine.	
10	The offender operated a vehicle, vessel, ORV, snowmobile, aircraft, or locomotive while the offender was under the influence of alcoholic or intoxicating liquor, a controlled substance, or a combination of alcoholic or intoxicating liquor and a controlled substance; or while the offender's body contained any amount of a controlled substance listed in schedule 1 under MCL 333.7212, or a rule promulgated under that section, or a controlled substance described in MCL 333.7214(a)(iv); or while the offender had an alcohol content of 0.08 grams or more but less than 0.15 grams per 100 milliliters of blood, per 210 liters of breath, or per 67 milliliters of urine or, beginning October 1, 2013, the offender had an alcohol content of 0.10 grams or more but less than 0.15 grams per 100 milliliters of blood, per 210 liters of breath, or per 67 milliliters of urine. MCL 777.48(1)(c).	
10	The offender operated a vehicle, vessel, ORV, snowmobile, aircraft, or locomotive when his or her bodily alcohol content was 0.10 grams or more but less than 0.15 grams per 100 milliliters of blood, per 210 liters of breath, or per 67 milliliters of urine, or while he or she was under the influence of intoxicating liquor or a controlled substance, or a combination of intoxicating liquor and a controlled substance.	
5	The offender operated a vehicle, vessel, ORV, snowmobile, aircraft, or locomotive while he or she was visibly impaired by the use of alcoholic or intoxicating liquor or a controlled substance, or a combination of alcoholic or intoxicating liquor and a controlled substance, or was less than 21 years of age and had any bodily alcohol content. MCL 777.48(1)(d).	

PRVs and OVs – Crimes Against a Person

OV 18

Degree to Which Alcohol or Drugs Affected the Offender

*Score for crime in "Person" crime group **only** if the offense or attempted offense involves the operation of a vehicle, vessel, ORV, snowmobile, aircraft, or locomotive.*

Effective September 30, 2003, 2003 PA 134 amended the statute governing point allocations for OV 18. Language appearing in the shaded areas of the chart below represents the variable as it applies to offenses that occurred before September 30, 2003. Unshaded areas contain the instructions for scoring OV 18 for offenses occurring on or after September 30, 2003, the amendment's effective date.

Pts		Instructions
5	The offender operated a vehicle, vessel, ORV, snowmobile, aircraft, or locomotive when his or her bodily alcohol content was 0.07 grams or more but less than 0.10 grams per 100 milliliters of blood, per 210 liters of breath, or per 67 milliliters of urine, or while he or she was visibly impaired by the use of intoxicating liquor or a controlled substance, or a combination of intoxicating liquor and a controlled substance, or was less than 21 years of age and had any bodily alcohol content.	**Beginning October 1, 2013, an alcohol content of 0.02 grams or more but less than 0.10 grams per 100 milliliters of blood, per 210 liters of breath, or per 67 milliliters of urine.*
0	The offender's ability to operate a vehicle, vessel, ORV, snowmobile, aircraft, or locomotive was not affected by an alcoholic or intoxicating liquor or a controlled substance or a combination of alcoholic or intoxicating liquor and a controlled substance. MCL 777.48(1)(e).	
0	The offender's ability to operate a vehicle was not affected by an intoxicating liquor or a controlled substance or a combination of intoxicating liquor and a controlled substance.	

OV 19

Threat to Security or Interference With the Administration of Justice

Pts		Instructions
25	The offender by his or her conduct threatened the security of a penal institution or court. MCL 777.49(a).	
15	The offender used force or the threat of force against another person or the property of another person to interfere with, attempt to interfere with, or that results in the interference with the administration of justice or the rendering of emergency services. MCL 777.49(b).	
10	The offender otherwise interfered with or attempted to interfere with the administration of justice. MCL 777.49(c).	
0	The offender did not threaten the security of a penal institution or court or interfere with or attempt to interfere with the administration of justice or the rendering of emergency services by force or the threat of force. MCL 777.49(d).	

OV 20
Terrorism

Pts		Instructions
100	The offender committed an act of terrorism by using or threatening to use a harmful biological substance, harmful biological device, harmful chemical substance, harmful chemical device, harmful radioactive material, harmful radioactive device, incendiary device, or explosive device. MCL 777.49a(1)(a).	• For purposes of scoring this variable, the terms "act of terrorism" and "terrorist" are defined in MCL 750.543b. MCL 777.49a(2)(a). • "Harmful biological substance," "harmful biological device," "harmful chemical substance," "harmful chemical device," "harmful radioactive material," and "harmful radioactive device" are defined in MCL 750.200h. MCL 777.49a(2)(b). • "Incendiary device" includes gasoline or any other flammable substance, a blowtorch, fire bomb, Molotov cocktail, or other similar device. MCL 777.49a(2)(c). • For purposes of OV 20, "terrorist organization" is defined in MCL 750.543c. MCL 777.49a(2)(d).
50	The offender committed an act of terrorism without using or threatening to use a harmful biological substance, harmful biological device, harmful chemical substance, harmful chemical device, harmful radioactive material, harmful radioactive device, incendiary device, or explosive device. MCL 777.49a(1)(b).	
25	The offender supported an act of terrorism, a terrorist, or a terrorist organization. MCL 777.49a(1)(c).	
0	The offender did not commit an act of terrorism or support an act of terrorism, a terrorist, or a terrorist organization. MCL 777.49a(1)(d).	

PRVs and OVs – Crimes Against Property

PRV 1

Prior High Severity Felony Convictions

(All "prior convictions" must satisfy the 10-year gap requirements of MCL 777.50.)

Pts	The offender has:	Instructions
75	3 or more prior high severity convictions.	A **"prior high severity felony conviction"** is a conviction for any of the following crimes if the conviction was entered before the commission date of the sentencing offense: • a crime listed in class M2, A, B, C, or D (or a felony under federal law or the law of another state that corresponds to a crime listed in class M2, A, B, C, or D), or • (effective January 9, 2007)* a felony that is not listed in ***any*** crime class (or a felony under federal law or the law of another state that does not correspond to a crime listed in ***any*** class) that is punishable by a maximum term of imprisonment of 10 years or more. MCL 777.51(2). *2006 PA 655.
50	2 prior high severity convictions.	
25	1 prior high severity conviction.	
0	No prior high severity convictions.	

PRV 2

Prior Low Severity Felony Convictions

(All "prior convictions" must satisfy the 10-year gap requirements of MCL 777.50.)

Pts	The offender has:	Instructions
30	4 or more prior low severity convictions.	A **"prior low severity felony conviction"** is a conviction for any of the following crimes if the conviction was entered before the commission date of the sentencing offense: • a crime listed in class E, F, G, or H (or a felony under federal law or the law of another state that corresponds to a crime listed in class E, F, G, or H), or • (effective January 9, 2007)* a felony that is not listed in ***any*** crime class (or a felony under federal law or the law of another state that does not correspond to a crime listed in ***any*** class) that is punishable by a maximum term of imprisonment of less than 10 years. MCL 777.52(2). *2006 PA 655.
20	3 prior low severity convictions.	
10	2 prior low severity convictions.	
5	1 prior low severity conviction.	
0	No prior low severity convictions.	

PRV 3

Prior High Severity Juvenile Adjudications

(All "prior convictions" must satisfy the 10-year gap requirements of MCL 777.50.)

Pts	The offender has:	Instructions
50	3 or more prior high severity juvenile adjudications.	A **"prior high severity juvenile adjudication"** is an adjudication for conduct that would be any of the following if committed by an adult, if the order of disposition was entered before the commission date of the sentencing offense: • a crime listed in class M2, A, B, C, or D (or a felony under federal law or the law of another state that corresponds to a crime listed in class M2, A, B, C, or D), or • (effective January 9, 2007)* a felony that is not listed in ***any*** crime class (or a felony under federal law or the law of another state that does not correspond to a crime listed in ***any*** class) that is punishable by a maximum term of imprisonment of 10 years or more. MCL 777.53(2). *2006 PA 655.
25	2 prior high severity juvenile adjudications.	
10	1 prior high severity juvenile adjudication.	
0	No prior high severity juvenile adjudications.	

PRV 4

Prior Low Severity Juvenile Adjudications

(All "prior convictions" must satisfy the 10-year gap requirements of MCL 777.50.)

Pts	The offender has:	Instructions
20	6 or more prior low severity juvenile adjudications.	A **"prior low severity juvenile adjudication"** is an adjudication for conduct that would be any of the following if committed by an adult, if the order of disposition was entered before the commission date of the sentencing offense: • a crime listed in class E, F, G, or H (or a felony under federal law or the law of another state that corresponds to a crime listed in class E, F, G, or H), or • (effective January 9, 2007)* a felony that is not listed in ***any*** crime class (or a felony under federal law or the law of another state that does not correspond to a crime listed in ***any*** class) that is punishable by a maximum term of imprisonment of less than 10 years. MCL 777.54(2). *2006 PA 655.
15	5 prior low severity juvenile adjudications.	
10	3 or 4 prior low severity juvenile adjudications.	
5	2 prior low severity juvenile adjudications.	
2	1 prior low severity juvenile adjudication.	
0	No prior low severity juvenile adjudications.	

PRV 5

Prior Misdemeanor Convictions and Prior Misdemeanor Juvenile Adjudications

(All "prior convictions" must satisfy the 10-year gap requirements of MCL 777.50.)

Pts	The offender has:	Instructions
20	7 or more prior misdemeanor convictions or prior misdemeanor juvenile adjudications.	A **"prior misdemeanor conviction"** is a conviction: • for a misdemeanor offense under Michigan law or the law of a political subdivision of Michigan, or under the law of another state or a political subdivision of another state, or under the law of the United States, • if the conviction was entered before the commission date of the sentencing offense. MCL 777.55(3)(a).
15	5 or 6 prior misdemeanor convictions or prior misdemeanor juvenile adjudications.	
10	3 or 4 prior misdemeanor convictions or prior misdemeanor juvenile adjudications.	
5	2 prior misdemeanor convictions or prior misdemeanor juvenile adjudications.	A **"prior misdemeanor juvenile adjudication"** is a juvenile adjudication: • for conduct that, if committed by an adult, would be a misdemeanor under Michigan law or the law of a political subdivision of Michigan, or under the law of another state or a political subdivision of another state, or under the law of the United States, • if the order of disposition for the juvenile adjudication was entered before the commission date of the sentencing offense. MCL 777.55(3)(b).
2	1 prior misdemeanor conviction or prior misdemeanor juvenile adjudication.	
0	No prior misdemeanor convictions or prior misdemeanor juvenile adjudications.	

Special Instructions for PRV 5:

- A prior conviction used to enhance the sentencing offense to a felony may not be counted under PRV 5. MCL 777.55(2)(b).
- Only prior convictions and adjudications for offenses expressly listed in PRV 5 may be counted as "prior misdemeanor convictions" or "prior misdemeanor juvenile adjudications" for purposes of scoring PRV 5:
  - only those prior misdemeanor convictions or prior misdemeanor juvenile adjudications that are offenses against a person or property, weapons offenses, or offenses involving controlled substances, and
  - all prior misdemeanor convictions and juvenile adjudications for operating or attempting to operate a vehicle, vessel, ORV, snowmobile, aircraft, or locomotive while under the influence of or impaired by alcohol, a controlled substance, or a combination of alcohol and a controlled substance. MCL 777.55(2)(a)–(b).

PRV 6
Offender's Relationship to the Criminal Justice System

Pts		Instructions
20	Offender is a prisoner of the department of corrections or serving a sentence in jail (includes an offender who is an escapee from jail or prison). MCL 777.56(3)(b).	PRV 6 assesses points based on an offender's relationship to the criminal justice system at the time the sentencing offense was committed. MCL 777.56. The scope of PRV 6 includes consideration of an offender's relationship with a criminal justice system outside the state of Michigan. The point values indicated by applicable statements in PRV 6 should be assessed against an offender who is involved with the criminal justice system of another state or the federal criminal justice system. "Delayed sentence status" includes (but is not limited to) an offender assigned or deferred under MCL 333.7411 (deferral for certain controlled substance offenses), MCL 750.350a (deferral under limited circumstances for parental kidnapping), MCL 762.11 to 762.15 (assignment to youthful trainee status), MCL 769.4a (deferral under limited circumstances for domestic assault), MCL 600.1076 (deferral involving drug treatment courts), and MCL 750.430 (deferral for impaired healthcare professionals).
15	Offender is incarcerated in jail awaiting adjudication or sentencing on a conviction or probation violation.	
10	Offender is on parole, probation, or delayed sentence status or on bond awaiting adjudication or sentencing for a felony.	
5	Offender is on probation or delayed sentence status or on bond awaiting adjudication or sentencing for a misdemeanor.	
0	Offender has no relationship to the criminal justice system.	

PRV 7
Subsequent or Concurrent Felony Convictions

Pts	The offender has:	Instructions
20	2 or more subsequent or concurrent felony convictions.	• A conviction for felony-firearm may not be counted under PRV 7. MCL 777.57(2)(b). • A concurrent felony conviction that will result in a mandatory consecutive sentence may not be counted under PRV 7. MCL 777.57(2)(c). • A concurrent felony conviction that will result in a consecutive sentence under MCL 333.7401(3)* may not be counted under PRV 7. MCL 777.57(2)(c). *Effective March 1, 2003, 2002 PA 666. Does not apply to offenses committed before March 1, 2003.
10	1 subsequent or concurrent felony conviction.	
0	No subsequent or concurrent felony convictions.	

PRVs and OVs – Crimes Against Property

OV 1
Aggravated Use of a Weapon

Pts		Instructions
25	A firearm was discharged at or toward a human being or a victim was cut or stabbed with a knife or other cutting or stabbing weapon. MCL 777.31(1)(a).	• Each person in danger of injury or loss of life is counted as a victim for purposes of scoring OV 1. MCL 777.31(2)(a). • In cases involving multiple offenders, if one offender is assigned points for the use or the presence of a weapon, all offenders must be assigned the same number of points. MCL 777.31(2)(b). • Do not score five points if the sentencing offense is a conviction of MCL 750.82 (felonious assault) or MCL 750.529 (armed robbery). MCL 777.31(2)(e). • Score five points if an offender used an object to suggest that he or she had a weapon. MCL 777.31(2)(c). • Score five points if an offender used a chemical irritant, a chemical irritant or smoke device, or an imitation harmful substance or device. MCL 777.31(2)(d). • "Harmful biological substance," "harmful biological device," "harmful chemical substance," "harmful chemical device," "harmful radioactive material," "harmful radioactive device," and "imitation harmful substance or device" are defined in MCL 750.200h. MCL 777.31(3)(a). • "Incendiary device" includes gasoline or any other flammable substance, a blowtorch, fire bomb, Molotov cocktail, or other similar device. MCL 777.31(3)(b).
20	The victim was subjected or exposed to a harmful biological substance, harmful biological device, harmful chemical substance, harmful chemical device, harmful radioactive material, harmful radioactive device, incendiary device, or explosive device. MCL 777.31(1)(b).	
15	A firearm was pointed at or toward a victim or the victim had a reasonable apprehension of an immediate battery when threatened with a knife or other cutting or stabbing weapon. MCL 777.31(1)(c).	
10	The victim was touched by any other type of weapon. MCL 777.31(1)(d).	
5	A weapon was displayed or implied. MCL 777.31(1)(e).	
0	No aggravated use of a weapon occurred. MCL 777.31(1)(f).	

OV 2
Lethal Potential of Weapon Possessed or Used

<table>
<tr><th>Pts</th><th></th><th>Instructions</th></tr>
<tr><td>15</td><td>The offender possessed or used a harmful biological substance, harmful biological device, harmful chemical substance, harmful chemical device, harmful radioactive material, or harmful radioactive device. MCL 777.32(1)(a).</td><td rowspan="6">• In cases involving multiple offenders, if one offender is assessed points for possessing a weapon, all offenders must be assessed the same number of points. MCL 777.32(2).
• “Harmful biological substance,” “harmful biological device,” “harmful chemical substance,” “harmful chemical device,” “harmful radioactive material,” and “harmful radioactive device” are defined in MCL 750.200h. MCL 777.32(3)(a).
• A “fully automatic weapon” is a firearm that ejects an empty cartridge and loads a live cartridge from the magazine for the next shot without requiring renewed pressure on the trigger for each successive shot. MCL 777.32(3)(b).
• A “pistol,” “rifle,” or “shotgun” includes a revolver, semi-automatic pistol, rifle, shotgun, combination rifle and shotgun, or other firearm made in or after 1898 that fires fixed ammunition. A “pistol,” “rifle,” or “shotgun” does not include a fully automatic weapon or short-barreled shotgun or short-barreled rifle. MCL 777.32(3)(c).
• An “incendiary device” includes gasoline or any other flammable substance, a blowtorch, fire bomb, Molotov cocktail, or other similar device. MCL 777.32(3)(d).</td></tr>
<tr><td>15</td><td>The offender possessed or used an incendiary device, an explosive device, or a fully automatic weapon. MCL 777.32(1)(b).</td></tr>
<tr><td>10</td><td>The offender possessed or used a short-barreled rifle or a short-barreled shotgun. MCL 777.32(1)(c).</td></tr>
<tr><td>5</td><td>The offender possessed or used a pistol, rifle, shotgun, or knife or other cutting or stabbing weapon. MCL 777.32(1)(d).</td></tr>
<tr><td>1</td><td>The offender possessed or used any other potentially lethal weapon. MCL 777.32(1)(e).</td></tr>
<tr><td>0</td><td>The offender possessed or used no weapon. MCL 777.32(1)(f).</td></tr>
</table>

PRVs and OVs – Crimes Against Property

OV 3
Degree of Physical Injury to a Victim

Pts		Instructions
100	A victim was killed. MCL 777.33(1)(a).	• In cases involving multiple offenders, if one offender is assessed points for death or physical injury, all offenders must be assessed the same number of points. MCL 777.33(3)(a). • Score 100 points if death results from the commission of the offense and homicide is not the sentencing offense. MCL 777.33(2)(b). Any crime in which the death of a person is an element of the crime is a "homicide." MCL 777.1(c). • Score 50 points under this variable if death results from an offense or attempted offense that involves the operation of a vehicle, vessel, ORV, snowmobile, aircraft, or locomotive and any of the following apply: – the offender was under the influence of or visibly impaired by the use of alcohol, a controlled substance, or a combination of alcohol and a controlled substance, MCL 777.33(2)(c)(i); – the offender had an alcohol content of 0.08 grams* or more per 100 milliliters of blood, per 210 liters of breath, or per 67 milliliters of urine, MCL 777.33(2)(c)(ii); or – the offender's body contained any amount of a controlled substance listed in schedule 1 under MCL 333.7212 or a rule promulgated under that section, or a controlled substance described in MCL 333.7214(a)(iv), MCL 777.33(2)(c)(iii). • Do not score five points if "bodily injury" is an element of the sentencing offense. MCL 777.33(2)(d). • "Requiring medical treatment" refers to an injury's need for treatment not whether a victim was successful in obtaining treatment. MCL 777.33(3). **Effective October 1, 2013, the alcohol content level increases to 0.10 grams or more.*
50	A victim was killed. MCL 777.33(1)(b). (*35 points for offenses committed before September 30, 2003. 2003 PA 134.*)	
25	Life threatening or permanent incapacitating injury occurred to a victim. MCL 777.33(1)(c).	
10	Bodily injury requiring medical treatment occurred to a victim. MCL 777.33(1)(d).	
5	Bodily injury not requiring medical treatment occurred to a victim. MCL 777.33(1)(e).	
0	No physical injury occurred to a victim. MCL 777.33(1)(f).	

OV 4
Degree of Psychological Injury to a Victim

Pts		Instructions
10	Serious psychological injury requiring professional treatment occurred to a victim. MCL 777.34(1)(a).	Ten points may be scored if the victim's serious psychological injury may require professional treatment. Whether the victim has sought treatment for the injury is not conclusive. MCL 777.34(2).
0	No serious psychological injury requiring professional treatment occurred to a victim. MCL 777.34(1)(b).	

OV 9
Number of Victims

Pts		Instructions
100	Multiple deaths occurred. MCL 777.39(1)(a).	• A "victim" for purposes of scoring OV 9 is each person placed in danger of injury or loss of life or (effective March 30, 2007)* loss of property. MCL 777.39(2)(a). • 100 points are scored only in homicide cases. MCL 777.39(2)(b). Any crime in which a person's death is an element of the crime is a "homicide." MCL 777.1(c). *2006 PA 548.
25	10 or more victims were placed in danger of physical injury or death. 20 or more victims were placed in danger of property loss (effective March 30, 2007). MCL 777.39(1)(b).	
10	2 to 9 victims were placed in danger of physical injury or death. 4 to 19 victims were placed in danger of property loss (effective March 30, 2007). MCL 777.39(1)(c).	
0	Fewer than 2 victims were placed in danger of physical injury or death. Fewer than 4 victims were placed in danger of property loss (effective March 30, 2007). MCL 777.39(1)(d).	

OV 10
Exploitation of a Victim's Vulnerability

Pts		Instructions
15	Predatory conduct was involved. MCL 777.40(1)(a).	• Do not automatically score points for victim vulnerability just because one or more of the factors addressed by OV 10 are present in the circumstances surrounding the sentencing offense. MCL 777.40(2). • "Predatory conduct" is an offender's preoffense conduct directed at a victim for the primary purpose of victimization. MCL 777.40(3)(a). • To "exploit" a victim is to manipulate a victim for the offender's selfish or unethical purposes. MCL 777.40(3)(b). • A victim's "vulnerability" is the victim's readily apparent susceptibility to injury, physical restraint, persuasion, or temptation. MCL 777.40(3)(c). • "Abuse of authority status" means the offender used a victim's fear of or deference to an authority figure to exploit the victim. Examples of an authority figure include, but are not limited to, a teacher, parent, or physician. MCL 777.40(3)(d).
10	The offender exploited a victim's physical disability, mental disability, youth or agedness, or a domestic relationship or the offender abused his or her authority status. MCL 777.40(1)(b).	
5	The offender exploited a victim by his or her difference in size or strength, or both, or exploited a victim who was intoxicated, under the influence of drugs, asleep, or unconscious. MCL 777.40(1)(c).	
0	The offender did not exploit a victim's vulnerability. MCL 777.40(1)(d).	

PRVs and OVs – Crimes Against Property

OV 12
Number of Contemporaneous Felonious Criminal Acts

Pts		Instructions
25	Three or more contemporaneous felonious criminal acts involving crimes against a person were committed. MCL 777.42(1)(a).	• A felonious criminal act is contemporaneous if both of the following circumstances exist: – the criminal act occurred within 24 hours of the sentencing offense, MCL 777.42(2)(a)(i), and – the criminal act has not and will not result in a separate conviction, MCL 777.42(2)(a)(ii). • Conduct scored in OV 11 must not be scored under this variable. MCL 777.42(2)(c). • Violations of MCL 750.227b (possession of a firearm during the commission of a felony) should not be counted when scoring this variable. MCL 777.42(2)(b).
10	Two contemporaneous felonious criminal acts involving crimes against a person were committed. MCL 777.42(1)(b).	
10	Three or more contemporaneous felonious criminal acts involving other crimes were committed. MCL 777.42(1)(c).	
5	One contemporaneous felonious criminal act involving a crime against a person was committed. MCL 777.42(1)(d).	
5	Two contemporaneous felonious criminal acts involving other crimes were committed. MCL 777.42(1)(e).	
1	One contemporaneous felonious criminal act involving any other crime was committed. MCL 777.42(1)(f).	
0	No contemporaneous felonious criminal acts were committed. MCL 777.42(1)(g).	

OV 13
Continuing Pattern of Criminal Behavior

Effective March 1, 2003, 2002 PA 666 amended the instructions for OV 13 to include references to specific controlled substance offenses. Language appearing in bold type in the chart below applies to offenses committed on or after March 1, 2003, pursuant to 2002 PA 666.

Pts		Instructions
50	The offense was part of a pattern of felonious criminal activity involving 3 or more sexual penetrations against a person or persons less than 13 years of age. MCL 777.43(1)(a).	• To score this variable, all crimes within a period of five years, including the sentencing offense, must be counted without regard to whether the offense resulted in a conviction. MCL 777.43(2)(a). • The existence of an organized criminal group may be inferred from the facts surrounding the sentencing offense, and the group's existence is more important than the presence or absence of multiple offenders, the age of the offenders, or the degree of sophistication demonstrated by the criminal group. MCL 777.43(2)(b). • Do not consider conduct scored in OVs 11 or 12 unless the offense was related to membership in an organized criminal group. MCL 777.43(2)(c). • Score 50 points only if the sentencing offense is first-degree criminal sexual conduct. MCL 777.43(2)(d). • Only one controlled substance offense arising from the criminal episode for which the offender is being sentenced may be counted when scoring this variable.* MCL 777.43(2)(e). • Only one crime involving the same controlled substance may be counted under this variable.* For example, conspiracy and a substantive offense involving the same amount of controlled substances cannot both be counted under OV 13. Similarly, possession and delivery of the same amount of controlled substances may not be counted as two crimes under OV 13. MCL 777.43(2)(f). **Effective March 1, 2003. 2002 PA 666.*
25	The offense was part of a pattern of felonious criminal activity involving 3 or more crimes against a person. MCL 777.43(1)(b).	
10	The offense was part of a pattern of felonious criminal activity involving a combination of 3 or more crimes against a person or property **or a violation of MCL 333.7401(2)(a)(*i*) to (*iii*) or 333.7403(2)(a)(*i*) to (*iii*)**. MCL 777.43(1)(c).	
10	The offense was part of a pattern of felonious criminal activity directly related to membership in an organized criminal group. MCL 777.43(1)(d).	
10	**The offense was part of a pattern of felonious criminal activity involving a combination of 3 or more violations of MCL 333.7401(2)(a)(i) to (iii) or 333.7403(2)(a)(i) to (iii).** MCL 777.43(1)(e).	
5	The offense was part of a pattern of felonious criminal activity involving 3 or more crimes against property. MCL 777.43(1)(f).	
0	No pattern of felonious criminal activity existed. MCL 777.43(1)(g).	

OV 14
Offender's Role

Pts		Instructions
10	The offender was a leader in a multiple offender situation. MCL 777.44(1)(a).	• Consider the entire criminal transaction in which the sentencing offense occurred when determining the offender's role. MCL 777.44(2)(a). • In cases involving three or more offenders, more than one offender may be considered a leader. MCL 777.44(2)(b).
0	The offender was not a leader in a multiple offender situation. MCL 777.44(1)(b).	

PRVs and OVs – Crimes Against Property

OV 16
Degree of Property Damage

Pts		Instructions
10	Wanton or malicious damage occurred beyond that necessary to commit the crime for which the offender is not charged and will not be charged. MCL 777.46(1)(a).	• In cases involving multiple offenders or multiple victims, the appropriate point total may be determined by aggregating the value of property involved in the offense, including property involved in uncharged offenses or property involved in charges dismissed under a plea agreement. MCL 777.46(2)(a). • Use the value of the property to score this variable in cases where the property was unlawfully obtained, lost to the lawful owner, or destroyed. If the property was damaged, use the amount of money necessary to restore the property to its pre-offense condition. MCL 777.46(2)(b). • Money or property involved in admitted but uncharged offenses or in charges dismissed under a plea agreement may be considered in scoring this variable. MCL 777.46(2)(c).
10	The property had a value of more than $20,000.00 or had significant historical, social, or sentimental value. MCL 777.46(1)(b).	
5	The property had a value of $1,000.00 or more but not more than $20,000.00. MCL 777.46(1)(c).	
1	The property had a value of $200.00 or more but not more than $1,000.00. MCL 777.46(1)(d).	
0	No property was obtained, damaged, lost, or destroyed or the property had a value of less than $200.00. MCL 777.46(1)(e).	

OV 19
Threat to Security or Interference With the Administration of Justice

Pts		Instructions
25	The offender by his or her conduct threatened the security of a penal institution or court. MCL 777.49(a).	
15	The offender used force or the threat of force against another person or the property of another person to interfere with, attempt to interfere with, or that results in the interference with the administration of justice or the rendering of emergency services. MCL 777.49(b).	
10	The offender otherwise interfered with or attempted to interfere with the administration of justice. MCL 777.49(c).	
0	The offender did not threaten the security of a penal institution or court or interfere with or attempt to interfere with the administration of justice or the rendering of emergency services by force or the threat of force. MCL 777.49(d).	

OV 20
Terrorism

<table>
<tr><th>Pts</th><th></th><th>Instructions</th></tr>
<tr><td>100</td><td>The offender committed an act of terrorism by using or threatening to use a harmful biological substance, harmful biological device, harmful chemical substance, harmful chemical device, harmful radioactive material, harmful radioactive device, incendiary device, or explosive device. MCL 777.49a(1)(a).</td><td rowspan="4">• For purposes of scoring this variable, the terms “act of terrorism” and “terrorist” are defined in MCL 750.543b. MCL 777.49a(2)(a).

• “Harmful biological substance,” “harmful biological device,” “harmful chemical substance,” “harmful chemical device,” “harmful radioactive material,” and “harmful radioactive device” are defined in MCL 750.200h. MCL 777.49a(2)(b).

• “Incendiary device” includes gasoline or any other flammable substance, a blowtorch, fire bomb, Molotov cocktail, or other similar device. MCL 777.49a(2)(c).

• For purposes of OV 20, “terrorist organization” is defined in MCL 750.543c. MCL 777.49a(2)(d).</td></tr>
<tr><td>50</td><td>The offender committed an act of terrorism without using or threatening to use a harmful biological substance, harmful biological device, harmful chemical substance, harmful chemical device, harmful radioactive material, harmful radioactive device, incendiary device, or explosive device. MCL 777.49a(1)(b).</td></tr>
<tr><td>25</td><td>The offender supported an act of terrorism, a terrorist, or a terrorist organization. MCL 777.49a(1)(c).</td></tr>
<tr><td>0</td><td>The offender did not commit an act of terrorism or support an act of terrorism, a terrorist, or a terrorist organization. MCL 777.49a(1)(d).</td></tr>
</table>

PRVs and OVs – Crimes Involving a Controlled Substance

PRV 1

Prior High Severity Felony Convictions

(All "prior convictions" must satisfy the 10-year gap requirements of MCL 777.50.)

Pts	The offender has:	Instructions
75	3 or more prior high severity convictions.	A **"prior high severity felony conviction"** is a conviction for any of the following crimes if the conviction was entered before the commission date of the sentencing offense: • a crime listed in class M2, A, B, C, or D (or a felony under federal law or the law of another state that corresponds to a crime listed in class M2, A, B, C, or D), or • (effective January 9, 2007)* a felony that is not listed in ***any*** crime class (or a felony under federal law or the law of another state that does not correspond to a crime listed in ***any*** class) that is punishable by a maximum term of imprisonment of 10 years or more. MCL 777.51(2). *2006 PA 655.
50	2 prior high severity convictions.	
25	1 prior high severity conviction.	
0	No prior high severity convictions.	

PRV 2

Prior Low Severity Felony Convictions

(All "prior convictions" must satisfy the 10-year gap requirements of MCL 777.50.)

Pts	The offender has:	Instructions
30	4 or more prior low severity convictions.	A **"prior low severity felony conviction"** is a conviction for any of the following crimes if the conviction was entered before the commission date of the sentencing offense: • a crime listed in class E, F, G, or H (or a felony under federal law or the law of another state that corresponds to a crime listed in class E, F, G, or H), or • (effective January 9, 2007)* a felony that is not listed in ***any*** crime class (or a felony under federal law or the law of another state that does not correspond to a crime listed in ***any*** class) that is punishable by a maximum term of imprisonment of less than 10 years. MCL 777.52(2). *2006 PA 655.
20	3 prior low severity convictions.	
10	2 prior low severity convictions.	
5	1 prior low severity conviction.	
0	No prior low severity convictions.	

PRV 3

Prior High Severity Juvenile Adjudications

(All "prior convictions" must satisfy the 10-year gap requirements of MCL 777.50.)

<table>
<tr><th>Pts</th><th>The offender has:</th><th>Instructions</th></tr>
<tr><td>50</td><td>3 or more prior high severity juvenile adjudications.</td><td rowspan="4">A "prior high severity juvenile adjudication" is an adjudication for conduct that would be any of the following if committed by an adult, if the order of disposition was entered before the commission date of the sentencing offense:
• a crime listed in class M2, A, B, C, or D (or a felony under federal law or the law of another state that corresponds to a crime listed in class M2, A, B, C, or D), or
• (effective January 9, 2007)* a felony that is not listed in any crime class (or a felony under federal law or the law of another state that does not correspond to a crime listed in any class) that is punishable by a maximum term of imprisonment of 10 years or more. MCL 777.53(2).
*2006 PA 655.</td></tr>
<tr><td>25</td><td>2 prior high severity juvenile adjudications.</td></tr>
<tr><td>10</td><td>1 prior high severity juvenile adjudication.</td></tr>
<tr><td>0</td><td>No prior high severity juvenile adjudications.</td></tr>
</table>

PRV 4

Prior Low Severity Juvenile Adjudications

(All "prior convictions" must satisfy the 10-year gap requirements of MCL 777.50.)

<table>
<tr><th>Pts</th><th>The offender has:</th><th>Instructions</th></tr>
<tr><td>20</td><td>6 or more prior low severity juvenile adjudications.</td><td rowspan="6">A "prior low severity juvenile adjudication" is an adjudication for conduct that would be any of the following if committed by an adult, if the order of disposition was entered before the commission date of the sentencing offense:
• a crime listed in class E, F, G, or H (or a felony under federal law or the law of another state that corresponds to a crime listed in class E, F, G, or H), or
• (effective January 9, 2007)* a felony that is not listed in any crime class (or a felony under federal law or the law of another state that does not correspond to a crime listed in any class) that is punishable by a maximum term of imprisonment of less than 10 years. MCL 777.54(2).
*2006 PA 655.</td></tr>
<tr><td>15</td><td>5 prior low severity juvenile adjudications.</td></tr>
<tr><td>10</td><td>3 or 4 prior low severity juvenile adjudications.</td></tr>
<tr><td>5</td><td>2 prior low severity juvenile adjudications.</td></tr>
<tr><td>2</td><td>1 prior low severity juvenile adjudication.</td></tr>
<tr><td>0</td><td>No prior low severity juvenile adjudications.</td></tr>
</table>

PRVs and OVs – Crimes Involving a Controlled Substance

PRV 5

Prior Misdemeanor Convictions and Prior Misdemeanor Juvenile Adjudications

(All "prior convictions" must satisfy the 10-year gap requirements of MCL 777.50.)

Pts	The offender has:	Instructions
20	7 or more prior misdemeanor convictions or prior misdemeanor juvenile adjudications.	A **"prior misdemeanor conviction"** is a conviction: • for a misdemeanor offense under Michigan law or the law of a political subdivision of Michigan, or under the law of another state or a political subdivision of another state, or under the law of the United States, • if the conviction was entered before the commission date of the sentencing offense. MCL 777.55(3)(a). A **"prior misdemeanor juvenile adjudication"** is a juvenile adjudication: • for conduct that, if committed by an adult, would be a misdemeanor under Michigan law or the law of a political subdivision of Michigan, or under the law of another state or a political subdivision of another state, or under the law of the United States, • if the order of disposition for the juvenile adjudication was entered before the commission date of the sentencing offense. MCL 777.55(3)(b).
15	5 or 6 prior misdemeanor convictions or prior misdemeanor juvenile adjudications.	
10	3 or 4 prior misdemeanor convictions or prior misdemeanor juvenile adjudications.	
5	2 prior misdemeanor convictions or prior misdemeanor juvenile adjudications.	
2	1 prior misdemeanor conviction or prior misdemeanor juvenile adjudication.	
0	No prior misdemeanor convictions or prior misdemeanor juvenile adjudications.	

Special Instructions for PRV 5:

- A prior conviction used to enhance the sentencing offense to a felony may not be counted under PRV 5. MCL 777.55(2)(b).
- Only prior convictions and adjudications for offenses expressly listed in PRV 5 may be counted as "prior misdemeanor convictions" or "prior misdemeanor juvenile adjudications" for purposes of scoring PRV 5:
  - only those prior misdemeanor convictions or prior misdemeanor juvenile adjudications that are offenses against a person or property, weapons offenses, or offenses involving controlled substances, and
  - all prior misdemeanor convictions and juvenile adjudications for operating or attempting to operate a vehicle, vessel, ORV, snowmobile, aircraft, or locomotive while under the influence of or impaired by alcohol, a controlled substance, or a combination of alcohol and a controlled substance. MCL 777.55(2)(a)–(b).

PRV 6
Offender's Relationship to the Criminal Justice System

Pts		Instructions
20	Offender is a prisoner of the department of corrections or serving a sentence in jail (includes an offender who is an escapee from jail or prison). MCL 777.56(3)(b).	PRV 6 assesses points based on an offender's relationship to the criminal justice system at the time the sentencing offense was committed. MCL 777.56. The scope of PRV 6 includes consideration of an offender's relationship with a criminal justice system outside the state of Michigan. The point values indicated by applicable statements in PRV 6 should be assessed against an offender who is involved with the criminal justice system of another state or the federal criminal justice system. "Delayed sentence status" includes (but is not limited to) an offender assigned or deferred under MCL 333.7411 (deferral for certain controlled substance offenses), MCL 750.350a (deferral under limited circumstances for parental kidnapping), MCL 762.11 to 762.15 (assignment to youthful trainee status), MCL 769.4a (deferral under limited circumstances for domestic assault), MCL 600.1076 (deferral involving drug treatment courts), and MCL 750.430 (deferral for impaired healthcare professionals).
15	Offender is incarcerated in jail awaiting adjudication or sentencing on a conviction or probation violation.	
10	Offender is on parole, probation, or delayed sentence status or on bond awaiting adjudication or sentencing for a felony.	
5	Offender is on probation or delayed sentence status or on bond awaiting adjudication or sentencing for a misdemeanor.	
0	Offender has no relationship to the criminal justice system.	

PRV 7
Subsequent or Concurrent Felony Convictions

Pts	The offender has:	Instructions
20	2 or more subsequent or concurrent felony convictions.	• A conviction for felony-firearm may not be counted under PRV 7. MCL 777.57(2)(b). • A concurrent felony conviction that will result in a mandatory consecutive sentence may not be counted under PRV 7. MCL 777.57(2)(c). • A concurrent felony conviction that will result in a consecutive sentence under MCL 333.7401(3)* may not be counted under PRV 7. MCL 777.57(2)(c). *Effective March 1, 2003, 2002 PA 666. Does not apply to offenses committed before March 1, 2003.
10	1 subsequent or concurrent felony conviction.	
0	No subsequent or concurrent felony convictions.	

PRVs and OVs – Crimes Involving a Controlled Substance

<table>
<tr><th colspan="3">OV 1
Aggravated Use of a Weapon</th></tr>
<tr><th>Pts</th><th></th><th>Instructions</th></tr>
<tr><td>25</td><td>A firearm was discharged at or toward a human being or a victim was cut or stabbed with a knife or other cutting or stabbing weapon. MCL 777.31(1)(a).</td><td rowspan="6">• Each person in danger of injury or loss of life is counted as a victim for purposes of scoring OV 1. MCL 777.31(2)(a).
• In cases involving multiple offenders, if one offender is assigned points for the use or the presence of a weapon, all offenders must be assigned the same number of points. MCL 777.31(2)(b).
• Do not score five points if the sentencing offense is a conviction of MCL 750.82 (felonious assault) or MCL 750.529 (armed robbery). MCL 777.31(2)(e).
• Score five points if an offender used an object to suggest that he or she had a weapon. MCL 777.31(2)(c).
• Score five points if an offender used a chemical irritant, a chemical irritant or smoke device, or an imitation harmful substance or device. MCL 777.31(2)(d).
• "Harmful biological substance," "harmful biological device," "harmful chemical substance," "harmful chemical device," "harmful radioactive material," "harmful radioactive device," and "imitation harmful substance or device" are defined in MCL 750.200h. MCL 777.31(3)(a).
• "Incendiary device" includes gasoline or any other flammable substance, a blowtorch, fire bomb, Molotov cocktail, or other similar device. MCL 777.31(3)(b).</td></tr>
<tr><td>20</td><td>The victim was subjected or exposed to a harmful biological substance, harmful biological device, harmful chemical substance, harmful chemical device, harmful radioactive material, harmful radioactive device, incendiary device, or explosive device. MCL 777.31(1)(b).</td></tr>
<tr><td>15</td><td>A firearm was pointed at or toward a victim or the victim had a reasonable apprehension of an immediate battery when threatened with a knife or other cutting or stabbing weapon. MCL 777.31(1)(c).</td></tr>
<tr><td>10</td><td>The victim was touched by any other type of weapon. MCL 777.31(1)(d).</td></tr>
<tr><td>5</td><td>A weapon was displayed or implied. MCL 777.31(1)(e).</td></tr>
<tr><td>0</td><td>No aggravated use of a weapon occurred. MCL 777.31(1)(f).</td></tr>
</table>

OV 2

Lethal Potential of Weapon Possessed or Used

<table>
<tr><th>Pts</th><th></th><th>Instructions</th></tr>
<tr><td>15</td><td>The offender possessed or used a harmful biological substance, harmful biological device, harmful chemical substance, harmful chemical device, harmful radioactive material, or harmful radioactive device. MCL 777.32(1)(a).</td><td rowspan="6">• In cases involving multiple offenders, if one offender is assessed points for possessing a weapon, all offenders must be assessed the same number of points. MCL 777.32(2).
• “Harmful biological substance,” “harmful biological device,” “harmful chemical substance,” “harmful chemical device,” “harmful radioactive material,” and “harmful radioactive device” are defined in MCL 750.200h. MCL 777.32(3)(a).
• A “fully automatic weapon” is a firearm that ejects an empty cartridge and loads a live cartridge from the magazine for the next shot without requiring renewed pressure on the trigger for each successive shot. MCL 777.32(3)(b).
• A “pistol,” “rifle,” or “shotgun” includes a revolver, semi-automatic pistol, rifle, shotgun, combination rifle and shotgun, or other firearm made in or after 1898 that fires fixed ammunition. A “pistol,” “rifle,” or “shotgun” does not include a fully automatic weapon or short-barreled shotgun or short-barreled rifle. MCL 777.32(3)(c).
• An “incendiary device” includes gasoline or any other flammable substance, a blowtorch, fire bomb, Molotov cocktail, or other similar device. MCL 777.32(3)(d).</td></tr>
<tr><td>15</td><td>The offender possessed or used an incendiary device, an explosive device, or a fully automatic weapon. MCL 777.32(1)(b).</td></tr>
<tr><td>10</td><td>The offender possessed or used a short-barreled rifle or a short-barreled shotgun. MCL 777.32(1)(c).</td></tr>
<tr><td>5</td><td>The offender possessed or used a pistol, rifle, shotgun, or knife or other cutting or stabbing weapon. MCL 777.32(1)(d).</td></tr>
<tr><td>1</td><td>The offender possessed or used any other potentially lethal weapon. MCL 777.32(1)(e).</td></tr>
<tr><td>0</td><td>The offender possessed or used no weapon. MCL 777.32(1)(f).</td></tr>
</table>

OV 3
Degree of Physical Injury to a Victim

Pts		Instructions
100	A victim was killed. MCL 777.33(1)(a).	• In cases involving multiple offenders, if one offender is assessed points for death or physical injury, all offenders must be assessed the same number of points. MCL 777.33(3)(a). • Score 100 points if death results from the commission of the offense and homicide is not the sentencing offense. MCL 777.33(2)(b). Any crime in which the death of a person is an element of the crime is a "homicide." MCL 777.1(c). • Score 50 points under this variable if death results from an offense or attempted offense that involves the operation of a vehicle, vessel, ORV, snowmobile, aircraft, or locomotive and any of the following apply: – the offender was under the influence of or visibly impaired by the use of alcohol, a controlled substance, or a combination of alcohol and a controlled substance, MCL 777.33(2)(c)(i); – the offender had an alcohol content of 0.08 grams* or more per 100 milliliters of blood, per 210 liters of breath, or per 67 milliliters of urine, MCL 777.33(2)(c)(ii); or – the offender's body contained any amount of a controlled substance listed in schedule 1 under MCL 333.7212 or a rule promulgated under that section, or a controlled substance described in MCL 333.7214(a)(iv), MCL 777.33(2)(c)(iii). • Do not score five points if "bodily injury" is an element of the sentencing offense. MCL 777.33(2)(d). • "Requiring medical treatment" refers to an injury's need for treatment not whether a victim was successful in obtaining treatment. MCL 777.33(3). **Effective October 1, 2013, the alcohol content level increases to 0.10 grams or more.*
50	A victim was killed. MCL 777.33(1)(b). *(35 points for offenses committed before September 30, 2003. 2003 PA 134.)*	
25	Life threatening or permanent incapacitating injury occurred to a victim. MCL 777.33(1)(c).	
10	Bodily injury requiring medical treatment occurred to a victim. MCL 777.33(1)(d).	
5	Bodily injury not requiring medical treatment occurred to a victim. MCL 777.33(1)(e).	
0	No physical injury occurred to a victim. MCL 777.33(1)(f).	

OV 12
Number of Contemporaneous Felonious Criminal Acts

Pts		Instructions
25	Three or more contemporaneous felonious criminal acts involving crimes against a person were committed. MCL 777.42(1)(a).	• A felonious criminal act is contemporaneous if both of the following circumstances exist: – the criminal act occurred within 24 hours of the sentencing offense, MCL 777.42(2)(a)(i), and – the criminal act has not and will not result in a separate conviction, MCL 777.42(2)(a)(ii). • Conduct scored in OV 11 must not be scored under this variable. MCL 777.42(2)(c). • Violations of MCL 750.227b (possession of a firearm during the commission of a felony) should not be counted when scoring this variable. MCL 777.42(2)(b).
10	Two contemporaneous felonious criminal acts involving crimes against a person were committed. MCL 777.42(1)(b).	
10	Three or more contemporaneous felonious criminal acts involving other crimes were committed. MCL 777.42(1)(c).	
5	One contemporaneous felonious criminal act involving a crime against a person was committed. MCL 777.42(1)(d).	
5	Two contemporaneous felonious criminal acts involving other crimes were committed. MCL 777.42(1)(e).	
1	One contemporaneous felonious criminal act involving any other crime was committed. MCL 777.42(1)(f).	
0	No contemporaneous felonious criminal acts were committed. MCL 777.42(1)(g).	

OV 13

Continuing Pattern of Criminal Behavior

Effective March 1, 2003, 2002 PA 666 amended the instructions for OV 13 to include references to specific controlled substance offenses. Language appearing in bold type in the chart below applies to offenses committed on or after March 1, 2003, pursuant to 2002 PA 666.

Pts		Instructions
50	The offense was part of a pattern of felonious criminal activity involving 3 or more sexual penetrations against a person or persons less than 13 years of age. MCL 777.43(1)(a).	• To score this variable, all crimes within a period of five years, including the sentencing offense, must be counted without regard to whether the offense resulted in a conviction. MCL 777.43(2)(a). • The existence of an organized criminal group may be inferred from the facts surrounding the sentencing offense, and the group's existence is more important than the presence or absence of multiple offenders, the age of the offenders, or the degree of sophistication demonstrated by the criminal group. MCL 777.43(2)(b). • Do not consider conduct scored in OVs 11 or 12 unless the offense was related to membership in an organized criminal group. MCL 777.43(2)(c). • Score 50 points only if the sentencing offense is first-degree criminal sexual conduct. MCL 777.43(2)(d). • Only one controlled substance offense arising from the criminal episode for which the offender is being sentenced may be counted when scoring this variable.* MCL 777.43(2)(e). • Only one crime involving the same controlled substance may be counted under this variable.* For example, conspiracy and a substantive offense involving the same amount of controlled substances cannot both be counted under OV 13. Similarly, possession and delivery of the same amount of controlled substances may not be counted as two crimes under OV 13. MCL 777.43(2)(f). **Effective March 1, 2003. 2002 PA 666.*
25	The offense was part of a pattern of felonious criminal activity involving 3 or more crimes against a person. MCL 777.43(1)(b).	
10	The offense was part of a pattern of felonious criminal activity involving a combination of 3 or more crimes against a person or property **or a violation of MCL 333.7401(2)(a)(*i*) to (*iii*) or 333.7403(2)(a)(*i*) to (*iii*)**. MCL 777.43(1)(c).	
10	The offense was part of a pattern of felonious criminal activity directly related to membership in an organized criminal group. MCL 777.43(1)(d).	
10	**The offense was part of a pattern of felonious criminal activity involving a combination of 3 or more violations of MCL 333.7401(2)(a)(i) to (iii) or 333.7403(2)(a)(i) to (iii).** MCL 777.43(1)(e).	
5	The offense was part of a pattern of felonious criminal activity involving 3 or more crimes against property. MCL 777.43(1)(f).	
0	No pattern of felonious criminal activity existed. MCL 777.43(1)(g).	

OV 14

Offender's Role

Pts		Instructions
10	The offender was a leader in a multiple offender situation. MCL 777.44(1)(a).	• Consider the entire criminal transaction in which the sentencing offense occurred when determining the offender's role. MCL 777.44(2)(a). • In cases involving three or more offenders, more than one offender may be considered a leader. MCL 777.44(2)(b).
0	The offender was not a leader in a multiple offender situation. MCL 777.44(1)(b).	

OV 15

Aggravated Controlled Substance Offenses

Effective March 1, 2003, 2002 PA 666 amended the statute governing point allocations for OV 15. Language appearing in the shaded areas of the chart below represents the variable as it applies to offenses that occurred before March 1, 2003. Unshaded areas contain the instructions for scoring OV 15 for offenses occurring on or after March 1, 2003, the amendment's effective date.

Pts		Instructions
100	The offense involved the manufacture, creation, delivery, possession, or possession with intent to manufacture, create, or deliver of 1,000 or more grams of any mixture containing a controlled substance classified in schedule 1 or 2 that is a narcotic drug or a drug described in MCL 333.7214(a)(iv). MCL 777.45(1)(a).	• Deliver" is the actual or constructive transfer of a controlled substance from one person to another person without regard to remuneration. MCL 777.45(2)(a). • A "minor" is an individual 17 years of age or less. MCL 777.45(2)(b). • "Trafficking" is the sale or delivery of actual or counterfeit controlled substances on a continuing basis to another person or persons for further distribution. MCL 777.45(2)(c). **continued on next page**
75	The offense involved the manufacture, creation, delivery, possession, or possession with intent to manufacture, create, or deliver of 450 grams or more but less than 1,000 grams of any mixture containing a controlled substance classified in schedule 1 or 2 that is a narcotic drug or a drug described in MCL 333.7214(a)(iv). MCL 777.45(1)(b).	
50	The offense involved the manufacture, creation, delivery, possession, or possession with intent to manufacture, create, or deliver of 50 or more grams but less than 450 grams of any mixture containing a controlled substance classified in schedule 1 or 2 that is a narcotic drug or a drug described in MCL 333.7214(a)(iv). MCL 777.45(1)(c).	
25	The offense involved the sale or delivery of a controlled substance other than marijuana or a mixture containing a controlled substance other than marijuana by the offender who was 18 years of age or older to a minor who was 3 or more years younger than the offender. MCL 777.45(1)(d).	
25	The offense involved the sale or delivery of a controlled substance other than marijuana or a mixture containing a controlled substance other than marijuana by the offender who was 18 years of age or older to a minor who was 3 or more years younger than the offender.	
20	The offense involved the sale, delivery, or possession with intent to sell or deliver 225 grams or more of a controlled substance classified in schedule 1 or 2 or a mixture containing a controlled substance classified in schedule 1 or 2.	
15	The offense involved the sale, delivery, or possession with intent to sell or deliver 50 or more grams but less than 225 grams of a controlled substance classified in schedule 1 or 2 or a mixture containing a controlled substance classified in schedule 1 or 2.	
10	The offense involved the sale, delivery, or possession with intent to sell or deliver 45 kilograms or more of marijuana or 200 or more of marijuana plants. MCL 777.45(1)(e).	
10	The offense involved the sale, delivery, or possession with intent to sell or deliver 45 kilograms or more of marijuana or 200 or more of marijuana plants.	

PRVs and OVs – Crimes Involving a Controlled Substance

OV 15

Aggravated Controlled Substance Offenses

Effective March 1, 2003, 2002 PA 666 amended the statute governing point allocations for OV 15. Language appearing in the shaded areas of the chart below represents the variable as it applies to offenses that occurred before March 1, 2003. Unshaded areas contain the instructions for scoring OV 15 for offenses occurring on or after March 1, 2003, the amendment's effective date.

Pts		Instructions
10	The offense is a violation of MCL 333.7401(2)(a)(i) to (iii) pertaining to a controlled substance classified in schedule 1 or 2 that is a narcotic drug or a drug described in MCL 333.7414(a)(iv) and was committed in a minor's abode, settled home, or domicile, regardless of whether the minor was present. MCL 777.45(1)(f).	
5	The offense involved the delivery or possession with the intent to deliver marijuana or any other controlled substance or a counterfeit controlled substance or possession of controlled substances or counterfeit controlled substances having a value or under such circumstances as to indicate trafficking. MCL 777.45(1)(g).	
5	The offense involved the delivery or possession with the intent to deliver marijuana or any other controlled substance or counterfeit controlled substance or possession of controlled substances or counterfeit controlled substances having a value or under such circumstances as to indicate trafficking.	
0	The offense was not an offense described in the categories above. MCL 777.45(1)(h).	
0	The offense was not an offense described in the categories above.	

OV 19

Threat to Security or Interference With the Administration of Justice

Pts		Instructions
25	The offender by his or her conduct threatened the security of a penal institution or court. MCL 777.49(a).	
15	The offender used force or the threat of force against another person or the property of another person to interfere with, attempt to interfere with, or that results in the interference with the administration of justice or the rendering of emergency services. MCL 777.49(b).	
10	The offender otherwise interfered with or attempted to interfere with the administration of justice. MCL 777.49(c).	
0	The offender did not threaten the security of a penal institution or court or interfere with or attempt to interfere with the administration of justice or the rendering of emergency services by force or the threat of force. MCL 777.49(d).	

OV 20
Terrorism

<table>
<tr><th>Pts</th><th></th><th>Instructions</th></tr>
<tr><td>100</td><td>The offender committed an act of terrorism by using or threatening to use a harmful biological substance, harmful biological device, harmful chemical substance, harmful chemical device, harmful radioactive material, harmful radioactive device, incendiary device, or explosive device. MCL 777.49a(1)(a).</td><td rowspan="4"><ul><li>For purposes of scoring this variable, the terms “act of terrorism” and “terrorist” are defined in MCL 750.543b. MCL 777.49a(2)(a).</li><li>“Harmful biological substance,” “harmful biological device,” “harmful chemical substance,” “harmful chemical device,” “harmful radioactive material,” and “harmful radioactive device” are defined in MCL 750.200h. MCL 777.49a(2)(b).</li><li>“Incendiary device” includes gasoline or any other flammable substance, a blowtorch, fire bomb, Molotov cocktail, or other similar device. MCL 777.49a(2)(c).</li><li>For purposes of OV 20, “terrorist organization” is defined in MCL 750.543c. MCL 777.49a(2)(d).</li></ul></td></tr>
<tr><td>50</td><td>The offender committed an act of terrorism without using or threatening to use a harmful biological substance, harmful biological device, harmful chemical substance, harmful chemical device, harmful radioactive material, harmful radioactive device, incendiary device, or explosive device. MCL 777.49a(1)(b).</td></tr>
<tr><td>25</td><td>The offender supported an act of terrorism, a terrorist, or a terrorist organization. MCL 777.49a(1)(c).</td></tr>
<tr><td>0</td><td>The offender did not commit an act of terrorism or support an act of terrorism, a terrorist, or a terrorist organization. MCL 777.49a(1)(d).</td></tr>
</table>

PRVs and OVs – Crimes Against Public Order

PRV 1

Prior High Severity Felony Convictions

(All "prior convictions" must satisfy the 10-year gap requirements of MCL 777.50.)

Pts	The offender has:	Instructions
75	3 or more prior high severity convictions.	A **"prior high severity felony conviction"** is a conviction for any of the following crimes if the conviction was entered before the commission date of the sentencing offense: • a crime listed in class M2, A, B, C, or D (or a felony under federal law or the law of another state that corresponds to a crime listed in class M2, A, B, C, or D), or • (effective January 9, 2007)* a felony that is not listed in ***any*** crime class (or a felony under federal law or the law of another state that does not correspond to a crime listed in ***any*** class) that is punishable by a maximum term of imprisonment of 10 years or more. MCL 777.51(2). *2006 PA 655.
50	2 prior high severity convictions.	
25	1 prior high severity conviction.	
0	No prior high severity convictions.	

PRV 2

Prior Low Severity Felony Convictions

(All "prior convictions" must satisfy the 10-year gap requirements of MCL 777.50.)

Pts	The offender has:	Instructions
30	4 or more prior low severity convictions.	A **"prior low severity felony conviction"** is a conviction for any of the following crimes if the conviction was entered before the commission date of the sentencing offense: • a crime listed in class E, F, G, or H (or a felony under federal law or the law of another state that corresponds to a crime listed in class E, F, G, or H), or • (effective January 9, 2007)* a felony that is not listed in ***any*** crime class (or a felony under federal law or the law of another state that does not correspond to a crime listed in ***any*** class) that is punishable by a maximum term of imprisonment of less than 10 years. MCL 777.52(2). *2006 PA 655.
20	3 prior low severity convictions.	
10	2 prior low severity convictions.	
5	1 prior low severity conviction.	
0	No prior low severity convictions.	

PRV 3
Prior High Severity Juvenile Adjudications
(All "prior convictions" must satisfy the 10-year gap requirements of MCL 777.50.)

Pts	The offender has:	Instructions
50	3 or more prior high severity juvenile adjudications.	A **"prior high severity juvenile adjudication"** is an adjudication for conduct that would be any of the following if committed by an adult, if the order of disposition was entered before the commission date of the sentencing offense: • a crime listed in class M2, A, B, C, or D (or a felony under federal law or the law of another state that corresponds to a crime listed in class M2, A, B, C, or D), or • (effective January 9, 2007)* a felony that is not listed in ***any*** crime class (or a felony under federal law or the law of another state that does not correspond to a crime listed in ***any*** class) that is punishable by a maximum term of imprisonment of 10 years or more. MCL 777.53(2). *2006 PA 655.
25	2 prior high severity juvenile adjudications.	
10	1 prior high severity juvenile adjudication.	
0	No prior high severity juvenile adjudications.	

PRV 4
Prior Low Severity Juvenile Adjudications
(All "prior convictions" must satisfy the 10-year gap requirements of MCL 777.50.)

Pts	The offender has:	Instructions
20	6 or more prior low severity juvenile adjudications.	A **"prior low severity juvenile adjudication"** is an adjudication for conduct that would be any of the following if committed by an adult, if the order of disposition was entered before the commission date of the sentencing offense: • a crime listed in class E, F, G, or H (or a felony under federal law or the law of another state that corresponds to a crime listed in class E, F, G, or H), or • (effective January 9, 2007)* a felony that is not listed in ***any*** crime class (or a felony under federal law or the law of another state that does not correspond to a crime listed in ***any*** class) that is punishable by a maximum term of imprisonment of less than 10 years. MCL 777.54(2). *2006 PA 655.
15	5 prior low severity juvenile adjudications.	
10	3 or 4 prior low severity juvenile adjudications.	
5	2 prior low severity juvenile adjudications.	
2	1 prior low severity juvenile adjudication.	
0	No prior low severity juvenile adjudications.	

PRVs and OVs – Crimes Against Public Order

PRV 5

Prior Misdemeanor Convictions and Prior Misdemeanor Juvenile Adjudications

(All "prior convictions" must satisfy the 10-year gap requirements of MCL 777.50.)

Pts	The offender has:	Instructions
20	7 or more prior misdemeanor convictions or prior misdemeanor juvenile adjudications.	A **"prior misdemeanor conviction"** is a conviction: • for a misdemeanor offense under Michigan law or the law of a political subdivision of Michigan, or under the law of another state or a political subdivision of another state, or under the law of the United States, • if the conviction was entered before the commission date of the sentencing offense. MCL 777.55(3)(a). A **"prior misdemeanor juvenile adjudication"** is a juvenile adjudication: • for conduct that, if committed by an adult, would be a misdemeanor under Michigan law or the law of a political subdivision of Michigan, or under the law of another state or a political subdivision of another state, or under the law of the United States, • if the order of disposition for the juvenile adjudication was entered before the commission date of the sentencing offense. MCL 777.55(3)(b).
15	5 or 6 prior misdemeanor convictions or prior misdemeanor juvenile adjudications.	
10	3 or 4 prior misdemeanor convictions or prior misdemeanor juvenile adjudications.	
5	2 prior misdemeanor convictions or prior misdemeanor juvenile adjudications.	
2	1 prior misdemeanor conviction or prior misdemeanor juvenile adjudication.	
0	No prior misdemeanor convictions or prior misdemeanor juvenile adjudications.	

Special Instructions for PRV 5:

- A prior conviction used to enhance the sentencing offense to a felony may not be counted under PRV 5. MCL 777.55(2)(b).
- Only prior convictions and adjudications for offenses expressly listed in PRV 5 may be counted as "prior misdemeanor convictions" or "prior misdemeanor juvenile adjudications" for purposes of scoring PRV 5:
  - only those prior misdemeanor convictions or prior misdemeanor juvenile adjudications that are offenses against a person or property, weapons offenses, or offenses involving controlled substances, and
  - all prior misdemeanor convictions and juvenile adjudications for operating or attempting to operate a vehicle, vessel, ORV, snowmobile, aircraft, or locomotive while under the influence of or impaired by alcohol, a controlled substance, or a combination of alcohol and a controlled substance. MCL 777.55(2)(a)–(b).

PRV 6

Offender's Relationship to the Criminal Justice System

Pts		Instructions
20	Offender is a prisoner of the department of corrections or serving a sentence in jail (includes an offender who is an escapee from jail or prison). MCL 777.56(3)(b).	PRV 6 assesses points based on an offender's relationship to the criminal justice system at the time the sentencing offense was committed. MCL 777.56. The scope of PRV 6 includes consideration of an offender's relationship with a criminal justice system outside the state of Michigan. The point values indicated by applicable statements in PRV 6 should be assessed against an offender who is involved with the criminal justice system of another state or the federal criminal justice system. "Delayed sentence status" includes (but is not limited to) an offender assigned or deferred under MCL 333.7411 (deferral for certain controlled substance offenses), MCL 750.350a (deferral under limited circumstances for parental kidnapping), MCL 762.11 to 762.15 (assignment to youthful trainee status), MCL 769.4a (deferral under limited circumstances for domestic assault), MCL 600.1076 (deferral involving drug treatment courts), and MCL 750.430 (deferral for impaired healthcare professionals).
15	Offender is incarcerated in jail awaiting adjudication or sentencing on a conviction or probation violation.	
10	Offender is on parole, probation, or delayed sentence status or on bond awaiting adjudication or sentencing for a felony.	
5	Offender is on probation or delayed sentence status or on bond awaiting adjudication or sentencing for a misdemeanor.	
0	Offender has no relationship to the criminal justice system.	

PRV 7

Subsequent or Concurrent Felony Convictions

Pts	The offender has:	Instructions
20	2 or more subsequent or concurrent felony convictions.	• A conviction for felony-firearm may not be counted under PRV 7. MCL 777.57(2)(b). • A concurrent felony conviction that will result in a mandatory consecutive sentence may not be counted under PRV 7. MCL 777.57(2)(c). • A concurrent felony conviction that will result in a consecutive sentence under MCL 333.7401(3)* may not be counted under PRV 7. MCL 777.57(2)(c). *Effective March 1, 2003, 2002 PA 666. Does not apply to offenses committed before March 1, 2003.
10	1 subsequent or concurrent felony conviction.	
0	No subsequent or concurrent felony convictions.	

PRVs and OVs – Crimes Against Public Order

OV 1
Aggravated Use of a Weapon

Pts	
25	A firearm was discharged at or toward a human being or a victim was cut or stabbed with a knife or other cutting or stabbing weapon. MCL 777.31(1)(a).
20	The victim was subjected or exposed to a harmful biological substance, harmful biological device, harmful chemical substance, harmful chemical device, harmful radioactive material, harmful radioactive device, incendiary device, or explosive device. MCL 777.31(1)(b).
15	A firearm was pointed at or toward a victim or the victim had a reasonable apprehension of an immediate battery when threatened with a knife or other cutting or stabbing weapon. MCL 777.31(1)(c).
10	The victim was touched by any other type of weapon. MCL 777.31(1)(d).
5	A weapon was displayed or implied. MCL 777.31(1)(e).
0	No aggravated use of a weapon occurred. MCL 777.31(1)(f).

Instructions

- Each person in danger of injury or loss of life is counted as a victim for purposes of scoring OV 1. MCL 777.31(2)(a).
- In cases involving multiple offenders, if one offender is assigned points for the use or the presence of a weapon, all offenders must be assigned the same number of points. MCL 777.31(2)(b).
- Do not score five points if the sentencing offense is a conviction of MCL 750.82 (felonious assault) or MCL 750.529 (armed robbery). MCL 777.31(2)(e).
- Score five points if an offender used an object to suggest that he or she had a weapon. MCL 777.31(2)(c).
- Score five points if an offender used a chemical irritant, a chemical irritant or smoke device, or an imitation harmful substance or device. MCL 777.31(2)(d).
- "Harmful biological substance," "harmful biological device," "harmful chemical substance," "harmful chemical device," "harmful radioactive material," "harmful radioactive device," and "imitation harmful substance or device" are defined in MCL 750.200h. MCL 777.31(3)(a).
- "Incendiary device" includes gasoline or any other flammable substance, a blowtorch, fire bomb, Molotov cocktail, or other similar device. MCL 777.31(3)(b).

OV 3
Degree of Physical Injury to a Victim

Pts		Instructions
100	A victim was killed. MCL 777.33(1)(a).	• In cases involving multiple offenders, if one offender is assessed points for death or physical injury, all offenders must be assessed the same number of points. MCL 777.33(3)(a). • Score 100 points if death results from the commission of the offense and homicide is not the sentencing offense. MCL 777.33(2)(b). Any crime in which the death of a person is an element of the crime is a "homicide." MCL 777.1(c). • Score 50 points under this variable if death results from an offense or attempted offense that involves the operation of a vehicle, vessel, ORV, snowmobile, aircraft, or locomotive and any of the following apply: – the offender was under the influence of or visibly impaired by the use of alcohol, a controlled substance, or a combination of alcohol and a controlled substance, MCL 777.33(2)(c)(i); – the offender had an alcohol content of 0.08 grams* or more per 100 milliliters of blood, per 210 liters of breath, or per 67 milliliters of urine, MCL 777.33(2)(c)(ii); or – the offender's body contained any amount of a controlled substance listed in schedule 1 under MCL 333.7212 or a rule promulgated under that section, or a controlled substance described in MCL 333.7214(a)(iv), MCL 777.33(2)(c)(iii). • Do not score five points if "bodily injury" is an element of the sentencing offense. MCL 777.33(2)(d). • "Requiring medical treatment" refers to an injury's need for treatment not whether a victim was successful in obtaining treatment. MCL 777.33(3). **Effective October 1, 2013, the alcohol content level increases to 0.10 grams or more.*
50	A victim was killed. MCL 777.33(1)(b). (*35 points for offenses committed before September 30, 2003. 2003 PA 134.*)	
25	Life threatening or permanent incapacitating injury occurred to a victim. MCL 777.33(1)(c).	
10	Bodily injury requiring medical treatment occurred to a victim. MCL 777.33(1)(d).	
5	Bodily injury not requiring medical treatment occurred to a victim. MCL 777.33(1)(e).	
0	No physical injury occurred to a victim. MCL 777.33(1)(f).	

OV 4
Degree of Psychological Injury to a Victim

Pts		Instructions
10	Serious psychological injury requiring professional treatment occurred to a victim. MCL 777.34(1)(a).	Ten points may be scored if the victim's serious psychological injury may require professional treatment. Whether the victim has sought treatment for the injury is not conclusive. MCL 777.34(2).
0	No serious psychological injury requiring professional treatment occurred to a victim. MCL 777.34(1)(b).	

PRVs and OVs – Crimes Against Public Order

OV 9
Number of Victims

Pts		Instructions
100	Multiple deaths occurred. MCL 777.39(1)(a).	• A "victim" for purposes of scoring OV 9 is each person placed in danger of injury or loss of life or (effective March 30, 2007)* loss of property. MCL 777.39(2)(a). • 100 points are scored only in homicide cases. MCL 777.39(2)(b). Any crime in which a person's death is an element of the crime is a "homicide." MCL 777.1(c). *2006 PA 548.
25	10 or more victims were placed in danger of physical injury or death. 20 or more victims were placed in danger of property loss (effective March 30, 2007). MCL 777.39(1)(b).	
10	2 to 9 victims were placed in danger of physical injury or death. 4 to 19 victims were placed in danger of property loss (effective March 30, 2007). MCL 777.39(1)(c).	
0	Fewer than 2 victims were placed in danger of physical injury or death. Fewer than 4 victims were placed in danger of property loss (effective March 30, 2007). MCL 777.39(1)(d).	

OV 10
Exploitation of a Victim's Vulnerability

Pts		Instructions
15	Predatory conduct was involved. MCL 777.40(1)(a).	• Do not automatically score points for victim vulnerability just because one or more of the factors addressed by OV 10 are present in the circumstances surrounding the sentencing offense. MCL 777.40(2). • "Predatory conduct" is an offender's preoffense conduct directed at a victim for the primary purpose of victimization. MCL 777.40(3)(a). • To "exploit" a victim is to manipulate a victim for the offender's selfish or unethical purposes. MCL 777.40(3)(b). • A victim's "vulnerability" is the victim's readily apparent susceptibility to injury, physical restraint, persuasion, or temptation. MCL 777.40(3)(c). • "Abuse of authority status" means the offender used a victim's fear of or deference to an authority figure to exploit the victim. Examples of an authority figure include, but are not limited to, a teacher, parent, or physician. MCL 777.40(3)(d).
10	The offender exploited a victim's physical disability, mental disability, youth or agedness, or a domestic relationship or the offender abused his or her authority status. MCL 777.40(1)(b).	
5	The offender exploited a victim by his or her difference in size or strength, or both, or exploited a victim who was intoxicated, under the influence of drugs, asleep, or unconscious. MCL 777.40(1)(c).	
0	The offender did not exploit a victim's vulnerability. MCL 777.40(1)(d).	

PRVs and OVs – Crimes Against Public Order

OV 12
Number of Contemporaneous Felonious Criminal Acts

Pts		Instructions
25	Three or more contemporaneous felonious criminal acts involving crimes against a person were committed. MCL 777.42(1)(a).	• A felonious criminal act is contemporaneous if both of the following circumstances exist: – the criminal act occurred within 24 hours of the sentencing offense, MCL 777.42(2)(a)(i), and – the criminal act has not and will not result in a separate conviction, MCL 777.42(2)(a)(ii). • Conduct scored in OV 11 must not be scored under this variable. MCL 777.42(2)(c). • Violations of MCL 750.227b (possession of a firearm during the commission of a felony) should not be counted when scoring this variable. MCL 777.42(2)(b).
10	Two contemporaneous felonious criminal acts involving crimes against a person were committed. MCL 777.42(1)(b).	
10	Three or more contemporaneous felonious criminal acts involving other crimes were committed. MCL 777.42(1)(c).	
5	One contemporaneous felonious criminal act involving a crime against a person was committed. MCL 777.42(1)(d).	
5	Two contemporaneous felonious criminal acts involving other crimes were committed. MCL 777.42(1)(e).	
1	One contemporaneous felonious criminal act involving any other crime was committed. MCL 777.42(1)(f).	
0	No contemporaneous felonious criminal acts were committed. MCL 777.42(1)(g).	

PRVs and OVs – Crimes Against Public Order

OV 13

Continuing Pattern of Criminal Behavior

Effective March 1, 2003, 2002 PA 666 amended the instructions for OV 13 to include references to specific controlled substance offenses. Language appearing in bold type in the chart below applies to offenses committed on or after March 1, 2003, pursuant to 2002 PA 666.

Pts		Instructions
50	The offense was part of a pattern of felonious criminal activity involving 3 or more sexual penetrations against a person or persons less than 13 years of age. MCL 777.43(1)(a).	• To score this variable, all crimes within a period of five years, including the sentencing offense, must be counted without regard to whether the offense resulted in a conviction. MCL 777.43(2)(a). • The existence of an organized criminal group may be inferred from the facts surrounding the sentencing offense, and the group's existence is more important than the presence or absence of multiple offenders, the age of the offenders, or the degree of sophistication demonstrated by the criminal group. MCL 777.43(2)(b). • Do not consider conduct scored in OVs 11 or 12 unless the offense was related to membership in an organized criminal group. MCL 777.43(2)(c). • Score 50 points only if the sentencing offense is first-degree criminal sexual conduct. MCL 777.43(2)(d). • Only one controlled substance offense arising from the criminal episode for which the offender is being sentenced may be counted when scoring this variable.* MCL 777.43(2)(e). • Only one crime involving the same controlled substance may be counted under this variable.* For example, conspiracy and a substantive offense involving the same amount of controlled substances cannot both be counted under OV 13. Similarly, possession and delivery of the same amount of controlled substances may not be counted as two crimes under OV 13. MCL 777.43(2)(f). **Effective March 1, 2003. 2002 PA 666.*
25	The offense was part of a pattern of felonious criminal activity involving 3 or more crimes against a person. MCL 777.43(1)(b).	
10	The offense was part of a pattern of felonious criminal activity involving a combination of 3 or more crimes against a person or property **or a violation of MCL 333.7401(2)(a)(*i*) to (*iii*) or 333.7403(2)(a)(*i*) to (*iii*)**. MCL 777.43(1)(c).	
10	The offense was part of a pattern of felonious criminal activity directly related to membership in an organized criminal group. MCL 777.43(1)(d).	
10	**The offense was part of a pattern of felonious criminal activity involving a combination of 3 or more violations of MCL 333.7401(2)(a)(i) to (iii) or 333.7403(2)(a)(i) to (iii).** MCL 777.43(1)(e).	
5	The offense was part of a pattern of felonious criminal activity involving 3 or more crimes against property. MCL 777.43(1)(f).	
0	No pattern of felonious criminal activity existed. MCL 777.43(1)(g).	

OV 14

Offender's Role

Pts		Instructions
10	The offender was a leader in a multiple offender situation. MCL 777.44(1)(a).	• Consider the entire criminal transaction in which the sentencing offense occurred when determining the offender's role. MCL 777.44(2)(a). • In cases involving three or more offenders, more than one offender may be considered a leader. MCL 777.44(2)(b).
0	The offender was not a leader in a multiple offender situation. MCL 777.44(1)(b).	

OV 16
Degree of Property Damage

Pts		Instructions
10	Wanton or malicious damage occurred beyond that necessary to commit the crime for which the offender is not charged and will not be charged. MCL 777.46(1)(a).	• In cases involving multiple offenders or multiple victims, the appropriate point total may be determined by aggregating the value of property involved in the offense, including property involved in uncharged offenses or property involved in charges dismissed under a plea agreement. MCL 777.46(2)(a). • Use the value of the property to score this variable in cases where the property was unlawfully obtained, lost to the lawful owner, or destroyed. If the property was damaged, use the amount of money necessary to restore the property to its pre-offense condition. MCL 777.46(2)(b). • Money or property involved in admitted but uncharged offenses or in charges dismissed under a plea agreement may be considered in scoring this variable. MCL 777.46(2)(c).
10	The property had a value of more than $20,000.00 or had significant historical, social, or sentimental value. MCL 777.46(1)(b).	
5	The property had a value of $1,000.00 or more but not more than $20,000.00. MCL 777.46(1)(c).	
1	The property had a value of $200.00 or more but not more than $1,000.00. MCL 777.46(1)(d).	
0	No property was obtained, damaged, lost, or destroyed or the property had a value of less than $200.00. MCL 777.46(1)(e).	

OV 19
Threat to Security or Interference With the Administration of Justice

Pts		Instructions
25	The offender by his or her conduct threatened the security of a penal institution or court. MCL 777.49(a).	
15	The offender used force or the threat of force against another person or the property of another person to interfere with, attempt to interfere with, or that results in the interference with the administration of justice or the rendering of emergency services. MCL 777.49(b).	
10	The offender otherwise interfered with or attempted to interfere with the administration of justice. MCL 777.49(c).	
0	The offender did not threaten the security of a penal institution or court or interfere with or attempt to interfere with the administration of justice or the rendering of emergency services by force or the threat of force. MCL 777.49(d).	

PRVs and OVs – Crimes Against Public Order

OV 20
Terrorism

Pts		Instructions
100	The offender committed an act of terrorism by using or threatening to use a harmful biological substance, harmful biological device, harmful chemical substance, harmful chemical device, harmful radioactive material, harmful radioactive device, incendiary device, or explosive device. MCL 777.49a(1)(a).	• For purposes of scoring this variable, the terms "act of terrorism" and "terrorist" are defined in MCL 750.543b. MCL 777.49a(2)(a). • "Harmful biological substance," "harmful biological device," "harmful chemical substance," "harmful chemical device," "harmful radioactive material," and "harmful radioactive device" are defined in MCL 750.200h. MCL 777.49a(2)(b). • "Incendiary device" includes gasoline or any other flammable substance, a blowtorch, fire bomb, Molotov cocktail, or other similar device. MCL 777.49a(2)(c). • For purposes of OV 20, "terrorist organization" is defined in MCL 750.543c. MCL 777.49a(2)(d).
50	The offender committed an act of terrorism without using or threatening to use a harmful biological substance, harmful biological device, harmful chemical substance, harmful chemical device, harmful radioactive material, harmful radioactive device, incendiary device, or explosive device. MCL 777.49a(1)(b).	
25	The offender supported an act of terrorism, a terrorist, or a terrorist organization. MCL 777.49a(1)(c).	
0	The offender did not commit an act of terrorism or support an act of terrorism, a terrorist, or a terrorist organization. MCL 777.49a(1)(d).	

PRV 1
Prior High Severity Felony Convictions
(All "prior convictions" must satisfy the 10-year gap requirements of MCL 777.50.)

Pts	The offender has:	Instructions
75	3 or more prior high severity convictions.	A **"prior high severity felony conviction"** is a conviction for any of the following crimes if the conviction was entered before the commission date of the sentencing offense: • a crime listed in class M2, A, B, C, or D (or a felony under federal law or the law of another state that corresponds to a crime listed in class M2, A, B, C, or D), or • (effective January 9, 2007)* a felony that is not listed in ***any*** crime class (or a felony under federal law or the law of another state that does not correspond to a crime listed in ***any*** class) that is punishable by a maximum term of imprisonment of 10 years or more. MCL 777.51(2). *2006 PA 655.
50	2 prior high severity convictions.	
25	1 prior high severity conviction.	
0	No prior high severity convictions.	

PRV 2
Prior Low Severity Felony Convictions
(All "prior convictions" must satisfy the 10-year gap requirements of MCL 777.50.)

Pts	The offender has:	Instructions
30	4 or more prior low severity convictions.	A **"prior low severity felony conviction"** is a conviction for any of the following crimes if the conviction was entered before the commission date of the sentencing offense: • a crime listed in class E, F, G, or H (or a felony under federal law or the law of another state that corresponds to a crime listed in class E, F, G, or H), or • (effective January 9, 2007)* a felony that is not listed in ***any*** crime class (or a felony under federal law or the law of another state that does not correspond to a crime listed in ***any*** class) that is punishable by a maximum term of imprisonment of less than 10 years. MCL 777.52(2). *2006 PA 655.
20	3 prior low severity convictions.	
10	2 prior low severity convictions.	
5	1 prior low severity conviction.	
0	No prior low severity convictions.	

PRV 3

Prior High Severity Juvenile Adjudications

(All "prior convictions" must satisfy the 10-year gap requirements of MCL 777.50.)

Pts	The offender has:	Instructions
50	3 or more prior high severity juvenile adjudications.	A **"prior high severity juvenile adjudication"** is an adjudication for conduct that would be any of the following if committed by an adult, if the order of disposition was entered before the commission date of the sentencing offense: • a crime listed in class M2, A, B, C, or D (or a felony under federal law or the law of another state that corresponds to a crime listed in class M2, A, B, C, or D), or • (effective January 9, 2007)* a felony that is not listed in ***any*** crime class (or a felony under federal law or the law of another state that does not correspond to a crime listed in ***any*** class) that is punishable by a maximum term of imprisonment of 10 years or more. MCL 777.53(2). *2006 PA 655.
25	2 prior high severity juvenile adjudications.	
10	1 prior high severity juvenile adjudication.	
0	No prior high severity juvenile adjudications.	

PRV 4

Prior Low Severity Juvenile Adjudications

(All "prior convictions" must satisfy the 10-year gap requirements of MCL 777.50.)

Pts	The offender has:	Instructions
20	6 or more prior low severity juvenile adjudications.	A **"prior low severity juvenile adjudication"** is an adjudication for conduct that would be any of the following if committed by an adult, if the order of disposition was entered before the commission date of the sentencing offense: • a crime listed in class E, F, G, or H (or a felony under federal law or the law of another state that corresponds to a crime listed in class E, F, G, or H), or • (effective January 9, 2007)* a felony that is not listed in ***any*** crime class (or a felony under federal law or the law of another state that does not correspond to a crime listed in ***any*** class) that is punishable by a maximum term of imprisonment of less than 10 years. MCL 777.54(2). *2006 PA 655.
15	5 prior low severity juvenile adjudications.	
10	3 or 4 prior low severity juvenile adjudications.	
5	2 prior low severity juvenile adjudications.	
2	1 prior low severity juvenile adjudication.	
0	No prior low severity juvenile adjudications.	

PRV 5

Prior Misdemeanor Convictions and Prior Misdemeanor Juvenile Adjudications

(All "prior convictions" must satisfy the 10-year gap requirements of MCL 777.50.)

Pts	The offender has:	Instructions
20	7 or more prior misdemeanor convictions or prior misdemeanor juvenile adjudications.	A **"prior misdemeanor conviction"** is a conviction: • for a misdemeanor offense under Michigan law or the law of a political subdivision of Michigan, or under the law of another state or a political subdivision of another state, or under the law of the United States, • if the conviction was entered before the commission date of the sentencing offense. MCL 777.55(3)(a). A **"prior misdemeanor juvenile adjudication"** is a juvenile adjudication: • for conduct that, if committed by an adult, would be a misdemeanor under Michigan law or the law of a political subdivision of Michigan, or under the law of another state or a political subdivision of another state, or under the law of the United States, • if the order of disposition for the juvenile adjudication was entered before the commission date of the sentencing offense. MCL 777.55(3)(b).
15	5 or 6 prior misdemeanor convictions or prior misdemeanor juvenile adjudications.	
10	3 or 4 prior misdemeanor convictions or prior misdemeanor juvenile adjudications.	
5	2 prior misdemeanor convictions or prior misdemeanor juvenile adjudications.	
2	1 prior misdemeanor conviction or prior misdemeanor juvenile adjudication.	
0	No prior misdemeanor convictions or prior misdemeanor juvenile adjudications.	

Special Instructions for PRV 5:

- A prior conviction used to enhance the sentencing offense to a felony may not be counted under PRV 5. MCL 777.55(2)(b).
- Only prior convictions and adjudications for offenses expressly listed in PRV 5 may be counted as "prior misdemeanor convictions" or "prior misdemeanor juvenile adjudications" for purposes of scoring PRV 5:
  - only those prior misdemeanor convictions or prior misdemeanor juvenile adjudications that are offenses against a person or property, weapons offenses, or offenses involving controlled substances, and
  - all prior misdemeanor convictions and juvenile adjudications for operating or attempting to operate a vehicle, vessel, ORV, snowmobile, aircraft, or locomotive while under the influence of or impaired by alcohol, a controlled substance, or a combination of alcohol and a controlled substance. MCL 777.55(2)(a)–(b).

PRVs and OVs – Crimes Against Public Safety

PRV 6
Offender's Relationship to the Criminal Justice System

Pts		Instructions
20	Offender is a prisoner of the department of corrections or serving a sentence in jail (includes an offender who is an escapee from jail or prison). MCL 777.56(3)(b).	PRV 6 assesses points based on an offender's relationship to the criminal justice system at the time the sentencing offense was committed. MCL 777.56.
15	Offender is incarcerated in jail awaiting adjudication or sentencing on a conviction or probation violation.	The scope of PRV 6 includes consideration of an offender's relationship with a criminal justice system outside the state of Michigan. The point values indicated by applicable statements in PRV 6 should be assessed against an offender who is involved with the criminal justice system of another state or the federal criminal justice system.
10	Offender is on parole, probation, or delayed sentence status or on bond awaiting adjudication or sentencing for a felony.	
5	Offender is on probation or delayed sentence status or on bond awaiting adjudication or sentencing for a misdemeanor.	"Delayed sentence status" includes (but is not limited to) an offender assigned or deferred under MCL 333.7411 (deferral for certain controlled substance offenses), MCL 750.350a (deferral under limited circumstances for parental kidnapping), MCL 762.11 to 762.15 (assignment to youthful trainee status), MCL 769.4a (deferral under limited circumstances for domestic assault), MCL 600.1076 (deferral involving drug treatment courts), and MCL 750.430 (deferral for impaired healthcare professionals).
0	Offender has no relationship to the criminal justice system.	

PRV 7
Subsequent or Concurrent Felony Convictions

Pts	The offender has:	Instructions
20	2 or more subsequent or concurrent felony convictions.	• A conviction for felony-firearm may not be counted under PRV 7. MCL 777.57(2)(b). • A concurrent felony conviction that will result in a mandatory consecutive sentence may not be counted under PRV 7. MCL 777.57(2)(c). • A concurrent felony conviction that will result in a consecutive sentence under MCL 333.7401(3)* may not be counted under PRV 7. MCL 777.57(2)(c). *Effective March 1, 2003, 2002 PA 666. Does not apply to offenses committed before March 1, 2003.
10	1 subsequent or concurrent felony conviction.	
0	No subsequent or concurrent felony convictions.	

OV 1
Aggravated Use of a Weapon

<table>
<tr><th>Pts</th><th></th><th>Instructions</th></tr>
<tr><td>25</td><td>A firearm was discharged at or toward a human being or a victim was cut or stabbed with a knife or other cutting or stabbing weapon. MCL 777.31(1)(a).</td><td rowspan="6">• Each person in danger of injury or loss of life is counted as a victim for purposes of scoring OV 1. MCL 777.31(2)(a).
• In cases involving multiple offenders, if one offender is assigned points for the use or the presence of a weapon, all offenders must be assigned the same number of points. MCL 777.31(2)(b).
• Do not score five points if the sentencing offense is a conviction of MCL 750.82 (felonious assault) or MCL 750.529 (armed robbery). MCL 777.31(2)(e).
• Score five points if an offender used an object to suggest that he or she had a weapon. MCL 777.31(2)(c).
• Score five points if an offender used a chemical irritant, a chemical irritant or smoke device, or an imitation harmful substance or device. MCL 777.31(2)(d).
• “Harmful biological substance,” “harmful biological device,” “harmful chemical substance,” “harmful chemical device,” “harmful radioactive material,” “harmful radioactive device,” and “imitation harmful substance or device” are defined in MCL 750.200h. MCL 777.31(3)(a).
• “Incendiary device” includes gasoline or any other flammable substance, a blowtorch, fire bomb, Molotov cocktail, or other similar device. MCL 777.31(3)(b).</td></tr>
<tr><td>20</td><td>The victim was subjected or exposed to a harmful biological substance, harmful biological device, harmful chemical substance, harmful chemical device, harmful radioactive material, harmful radioactive device, incendiary device, or explosive device. MCL 777.31(1)(b).</td></tr>
<tr><td>15</td><td>A firearm was pointed at or toward a victim or the victim had a reasonable apprehension of an immediate battery when threatened with a knife or other cutting or stabbing weapon. MCL 777.31(1)(c).</td></tr>
<tr><td>10</td><td>The victim was touched by any other type of weapon. MCL 777.31(1)(d).</td></tr>
<tr><td>5</td><td>A weapon was displayed or implied. MCL 777.31(1)(e).</td></tr>
<tr><td>0</td><td>No aggravated use of a weapon occurred. MCL 777.31(1)(f).</td></tr>
</table>

OV 3
Degree of Physical Injury to a Victim

Pts		Instructions
100	A victim was killed. MCL 777.33(1)(a).	• In cases involving multiple offenders, if one offender is assessed points for death or physical injury, all offenders must be assessed the same number of points. MCL 777.33(3)(a). • Score 100 points if death results from the commission of the offense and homicide is not the sentencing offense. MCL 777.33(2)(b). Any crime in which the death of a person is an element of the crime is a "homicide." MCL 777.1(c). • Score 50 points under this variable if death results from an offense or attempted offense that involves the operation of a vehicle, vessel, ORV, snowmobile, aircraft, or locomotive and any of the following apply: – the offender was under the influence of or visibly impaired by the use of alcohol, a controlled substance, or a combination of alcohol and a controlled substance, MCL 777.33(2)(c)(i); – the offender had an alcohol content of 0.08 grams* or more per 100 milliliters of blood, per 210 liters of breath, or per 67 milliliters of urine, MCL 777.33(2)(c)(ii); or – the offender's body contained any amount of a controlled substance listed in schedule 1 under MCL 333.7212 or a rule promulgated under that section, or a controlled substance described in MCL 333.7214(a)(iv), MCL 777.33(2)(c)(iii). • Do not score five points if "bodily injury" is an element of the sentencing offense. MCL 777.33(2)(d). • "Requiring medical treatment" refers to an injury's need for treatment not whether a victim was successful in obtaining treatment. MCL 777.33(3). **Effective October 1, 2013, the alcohol content level increases to 0.10 grams or more.*
50	A victim was killed. MCL 777.33(1)(b). *(35 points for offenses committed before September 30, 2003. 2003 PA 134.)*	
25	Life threatening or permanent incapacitating injury occurred to a victim. MCL 777.33(1)(c).	
10	Bodily injury requiring medical treatment occurred to a victim. MCL 777.33(1)(d).	
5	Bodily injury not requiring medical treatment occurred to a victim. MCL 777.33(1)(e).	
0	No physical injury occurred to a victim. MCL 777.33(1)(f).	

OV 4
Degree of Psychological Injury to a Victim

Pts		Instructions
10	Serious psychological injury requiring professional treatment occurred to a victim. MCL 777.34(1)(a).	Ten points may be scored if the victim's serious psychological injury may require professional treatment. Whether the victim has sought treatment for the injury is not conclusive. MCL 777.34(2).
0	No serious psychological injury requiring professional treatment occurred to a victim. MCL 777.34(1)(b).	

OV 9
Number of Victims

Pts		Instructions
100	Multiple deaths occurred. MCL 777.39(1)(a).	• A "victim" for purposes of scoring OV 9 is each person placed in danger of injury or loss of life or (effective March 30, 2007)* loss of property. MCL 777.39(2)(a). • 100 points are scored only in homicide cases. MCL 777.39(2)(b). Any crime in which a person's death is an element of the crime is a "homicide." MCL 777.1(c). *2006 PA 548.
25	10 or more victims were placed in danger of physical injury or death. 20 or more victims were placed in danger of property loss (effective March 30, 2007). MCL 777.39(1)(b).	
10	2 to 9 victims were placed in danger of physical injury or death. 4 to 19 victims were placed in danger of property loss (effective March 30, 2007). MCL 777.39(1)(c).	
0	Fewer than 2 victims were placed in danger of physical injury or death. Fewer than 4 victims were placed in danger of property loss (effective March 30, 2007). MCL 777.39(1)(d).	

OV 10
Exploitation of a Victim's Vulnerability

Pts		Instructions
15	Predatory conduct was involved. MCL 777.40(1)(a).	• Do not automatically score points for victim vulnerability just because one or more of the factors addressed by OV 10 are present in the circumstances surrounding the sentencing offense. MCL 777.40(2). • "Predatory conduct" is an offender's preoffense conduct directed at a victim for the primary purpose of victimization. MCL 777.40(3)(a). • To "exploit" a victim is to manipulate a victim for the offender's selfish or unethical purposes. MCL 777.40(3)(b). • A victim's "vulnerability" is the victim's readily apparent susceptibility to injury, physical restraint, persuasion, or temptation. MCL 777.40(3)(c). • "Abuse of authority status" means the offender used a victim's fear of or deference to an authority figure to exploit the victim. Examples of an authority figure include, but are not limited to, a teacher, parent, or physician. MCL 777.40(3)(d).
10	The offender exploited a victim's physical disability, mental disability, youth or agedness, or a domestic relationship or the offender abused his or her authority status. MCL 777.40(1)(b).	
5	The offender exploited a victim by his or her difference in size or strength, or both, or exploited a victim who was intoxicated, under the influence of drugs, asleep, or unconscious. MCL 777.40(1)(c).	
0	The offender did not exploit a victim's vulnerability. MCL 777.40(1)(d).	

PRVs and OVs – Crimes Against Public Safety

OV 12
Number of Contemporaneous Felonious Criminal Acts

<table>
<tr><th>Pts</th><th></th><th>Instructions</th></tr>
<tr><td>25</td><td>Three or more contemporaneous felonious criminal acts involving crimes against a person were committed. MCL 777.42(1)(a).</td><td rowspan="7">• A felonious criminal act is contemporaneous if both of the following circumstances exist:
– the criminal act occurred within 24 hours of the sentencing offense, MCL 777.42(2)(a)(i), and
– the criminal act has not and will not result in a separate conviction, MCL 777.42(2)(a)(ii).
• Conduct scored in OV 11 must not be scored under this variable. MCL 777.42(2)(c).
• Violations of MCL 750.227b (possession of a firearm during the commission of a felony) should not be counted when scoring this variable. MCL 777.42(2)(b).</td></tr>
<tr><td>10</td><td>Two contemporaneous felonious criminal acts involving crimes against a person were committed. MCL 777.42(1)(b).</td></tr>
<tr><td>10</td><td>Three or more contemporaneous felonious criminal acts involving other crimes were committed. MCL 777.42(1)(c).</td></tr>
<tr><td>5</td><td>One contemporaneous felonious criminal act involving a crime against a person was committed. MCL 777.42(1)(d).</td></tr>
<tr><td>5</td><td>Two contemporaneous felonious criminal acts involving other crimes were committed. MCL 777.42(1)(e).</td></tr>
<tr><td>1</td><td>One contemporaneous felonious criminal act involving any other crime was committed. MCL 777.42(1)(f).</td></tr>
<tr><td>0</td><td>No contemporaneous felonious criminal acts were committed. MCL 777.42(1)(g).</td></tr>
</table>

OV 13
Continuing Pattern of Criminal Behavior

Effective March 1, 2003, 2002 PA 666 amended the instructions for OV 13 to include references to specific controlled substance offenses. Language appearing in bold type in the chart below applies to offenses committed on or after March 1, 2003, pursuant to 2002 PA 666.

Pts		Instructions
50	The offense was part of a pattern of felonious criminal activity involving 3 or more sexual penetrations against a person or persons less than 13 years of age. MCL 777.43(1)(a).	• To score this variable, all crimes within a period of five years, including the sentencing offense, must be counted without regard to whether the offense resulted in a conviction. MCL 777.43(2)(a). • The existence of an organized criminal group may be inferred from the facts surrounding the sentencing offense, and the group's existence is more important than the presence or absence of multiple offenders, the age of the offenders, or the degree of sophistication demonstrated by the criminal group. MCL 777.43(2)(b). • Do not consider conduct scored in OVs 11 or 12 unless the offense was related to membership in an organized criminal group. MCL 777.43(2)(c). • Score 50 points only if the sentencing offense is first-degree criminal sexual conduct. MCL 777.43(2)(d). • Only one controlled substance offense arising from the criminal episode for which the offender is being sentenced may be counted when scoring this variable.* MCL 777.43(2)(e). • Only one crime involving the same controlled substance may be counted under this variable.* For example, conspiracy and a substantive offense involving the same amount of controlled substances cannot both be counted under OV 13. Similarly, possession and delivery of the same amount of controlled substances may not be counted as two crimes under OV 13. MCL 777.43(2)(f). **Effective March 1, 2003. 2002 PA 666.*
25	The offense was part of a pattern of felonious criminal activity involving 3 or more crimes against a person. MCL 777.43(1)(b).	
10	The offense was part of a pattern of felonious criminal activity involving a combination of 3 or more crimes against a person or property **or a violation of MCL 333.7401(2)(a)(*i*) to (*iii*) or 333.7403(2)(a)(*i*) to (*iii*)**. MCL 777.43(1)(c).	
10	The offense was part of a pattern of felonious criminal activity directly related to membership in an organized criminal group. MCL 777.43(1)(d).	
10	**The offense was part of a pattern of felonious criminal activity involving a combination of 3 or more violations of MCL 333.7401(2)(a)(i) to (iii) or 333.7403(2)(a)(i) to (iii).** MCL 777.43(1)(e).	
5	The offense was part of a pattern of felonious criminal activity involving 3 or more crimes against property. MCL 777.43(1)(f).	
0	No pattern of felonious criminal activity existed. MCL 777.43(1)(g).	

OV 14
Offender's Role

Pts		Instructions
10	The offender was a leader in a multiple offender situation. MCL 777.44(1)(a).	• Consider the entire criminal transaction in which the sentencing offense occurred when determining the offender's role. MCL 777.44(2)(a). • In cases involving three or more offenders, more than one offender may be considered a leader. MCL 777.44(2)(b).
0	The offender was not a leader in a multiple offender situation. MCL 777.44(1)(b).	

PRVs and OVs – Crimes Against Public Safety

OV 16
Degree of Property Damage

<table>
<tr><th>Pts</th><th></th><th>Instructions</th></tr>
<tr><td>10</td><td>Wanton or malicious damage occurred beyond that necessary to commit the crime for which the offender is not charged and will not be charged. MCL 777.46(1)(a).</td><td rowspan="5"><ul><li>In cases involving multiple offenders or multiple victims, the appropriate point total may be determined by aggregating the value of property involved in the offense, including property involved in uncharged offenses or property involved in charges dismissed under a plea agreement. MCL 777.46(2)(a).</li><li>Use the value of the property to score this variable in cases where the property was unlawfully obtained, lost to the lawful owner, or destroyed. If the property was damaged, use the amount of money necessary to restore the property to its pre-offense condition. MCL 777.46(2)(b).</li><li>Money or property involved in admitted but uncharged offenses or in charges dismissed under a plea agreement may be considered in scoring this variable. MCL 777.46(2)(c).</li></ul></td></tr>
<tr><td>10</td><td>The property had a value of more than $20,000.00 or had significant historical, social, or sentimental value. MCL 777.46(1)(b).</td></tr>
<tr><td>5</td><td>The property had a value of $1,000.00 or more but not more than $20,000.00. MCL 777.46(1)(c).</td></tr>
<tr><td>1</td><td>The property had a value of $200.00 or more but not more than $1,000.00. MCL 777.46(1)(d).</td></tr>
<tr><td>0</td><td>No property was obtained, damaged, lost, or destroyed or the property had a value of less than $200.00. MCL 777.46(1)(e).</td></tr>
</table>

OV 18

Degree to Which Alcohol or Drugs Affected the Offender

*Score for a crime in the "Public Safety" crime group **only** if the offense or attempted offense involves the operation of a vehicle, vessel, ORV, snowmobile, aircraft, or locomotive.*

Effective September 30, 2003, 2003 PA 134 amended the statute governing point allocations for OV 18. Language appearing in the shaded areas of the chart below represents the variable as it applies to offenses that occurred before September 30, 2003. Unshaded areas contain the instructions for scoring OV 18 for offenses occurring on or after September 30, 2003, the amendment's effective date.

Pts		Instructions
20	The offender operated a vehicle, vessel, ORV, snowmobile, aircraft, or locomotive when his or her bodily alcohol content was 0.20 grams or more per 100 milliliters of blood, per 210 liters of breath, or per 67 milliliters of urine. MCL 777.48(1)(a).	• For purposes of scoring OV 18, "any bodily alcohol content" is either of the following: – an alcohol content of 0.02 grams or more but less than 0.08 grams per 100 milliliters of blood, per 210 liters of breath, or per 67 milliliters of urine,* MCL 777.48(2)(a), or – any presence of alcohol within a person's body from the consumption of alcohol except for alcohol consumption as part of a generally recognized religious service or ceremony, MCL 777.48(2)(b). • Definitions for "aircraft," "ORV," "snowmobile," "vehicle," and "vessel" are referenced in MCL 777.1.
20	The offender operated a vehicle, vessel, ORV, snowmobile, aircraft, or locomotive when his or her bodily alcohol content was 0.20 grams or more per 100 milliliters of blood, per 210 liters of breath, or per 67 milliliters of urine.	
15	The offender operated a vehicle, vessel, ORV, snowmobile, aircraft, or locomotive when his or her bodily alcohol content was 0.15 grams or more but less than 0.20 grams per 100 milliliters of blood, per 210 liters of breath, or per 67 milliliters of urine. MCL 777.48(1)(b).	
15	The offender operated a vehicle, vessel, ORV, snowmobile, aircraft, or locomotive when his or her bodily alcohol content was 0.15 grams or more but less than 0.20 grams per 100 milliliters of blood, per 210 liters of breath, or per 67 milliliters of urine.	
10	The offender operated a vehicle, vessel, ORV, snowmobile, aircraft, or locomotive while the offender was under the influence of alcoholic or intoxicating liquor, a controlled substance, or a combination of alcoholic or intoxicating liquor and a controlled substance; or while the offender's body contained any amount of a controlled substance listed in schedule 1 under MCL 333.7212, or a rule promulgated under that section, or a controlled substance described in MCL 333.7214(a)(iv); or while the offender had an alcohol content of 0.08 grams or more but less than 0.15 grams per 100 milliliters of blood, per 210 liters of breath, or per 67 milliliters of urine or, beginning October 1, 2013, the offender had an alcohol content of 0.10 grams or more but less than 0.15 grams per 100 milliliters of blood, per 210 liters of breath, or per 67 milliliters of urine. MCL 777.48(1)(c).	
10	The offender operated a vehicle, vessel, ORV, snowmobile, aircraft, or locomotive when his or her bodily alcohol content was 0.10 grams or more but less than 0.15 grams per 100 milliliters of blood, per 210 liters of breath, or per 67 milliliters of urine, or while he or she was under the influence of intoxicating liquor or a controlled substance, or a combination of intoxicating liquor and a controlled substance.	
5	The offender operated a vehicle, vessel, ORV, snowmobile, aircraft, or locomotive while he or she was visibly impaired by the use of alcoholic or intoxicating liquor or a controlled substance, or a combination of alcoholic or intoxicating liquor and a controlled substance, or was less than 21 years of age and had any bodily alcohol content. MCL 777.48(1)(d).	**continued on next page**

PRVs and OVs – Crimes Against Public Safety

OV 18

Degree to Which Alcohol or Drugs Affected the Offender

*Score for a crime in the "Public Safety" crime group **only** if the offense or attempted offense involves the operation of a vehicle, vessel, ORV, snowmobile, aircraft, or locomotive.*

Effective September 30, 2003, 2003 PA 134 amended the statute governing point allocations for OV 18. Language appearing in the shaded areas of the chart below represents the variable as it applies to offenses that occurred before September 30, 2003. Unshaded areas contain the instructions for scoring OV 18 for offenses occurring on or after September 30, 2003, the amendment's effective date.

Pts		Instructions
5	The offender operated a vehicle, vessel, ORV, snowmobile, aircraft, or locomotive when his or her bodily alcohol content was 0.07 grams or more but less than 0.10 grams per 100 milliliters of blood, per 210 liters of breath, or per 67 milliliters of urine, or while he or she was visibly impaired by the use of intoxicating liquor or a controlled substance, or a combination of intoxicating liquor and a controlled substance, or was less than 21 years of age and had any bodily alcohol content.	**Beginning October 1, 2013, an alcohol content of 0.02 grams or more but less than 0.10 grams per 100 milliliters of blood, per 210 liters of breath, or per 67 milliliters of urine.*
0	The offender's ability to operate a vehicle, vessel, ORV, snowmobile, aircraft, or locomotive was not affected by an alcoholic or intoxicating liquor or a controlled substance or a combination of alcoholic or intoxicating liquor and a controlled substance. MCL 777.48(1)(e).	
0	The offender's ability to operate a vehicle was not affected by an intoxicating liquor or a controlled substance or a combination of intoxicating liquor and a controlled substance.	

OV 19

Threat to Security or Interference With the Administration of Justice

Pts		Instructions
25	The offender by his or her conduct threatened the security of a penal institution or court. MCL 777.49(a).	
15	The offender used force or the threat of force against another person or the property of another person to interfere with, attempt to interfere with, or that results in the interference with the administration of justice or the rendering of emergency services. MCL 777.49(b).	
10	The offender otherwise interfered with or attempted to interfere with the administration of justice. MCL 777.49(c).	
0	The offender did not threaten the security of a penal institution or court or interfere with or attempt to interfere with the administration of justice or the rendering of emergency services by force or the threat of force. MCL 777.49(d).	

OV 20
Terrorism

Pts		Instructions
100	The offender committed an act of terrorism by using or threatening to use a harmful biological substance, harmful biological device, harmful chemical substance, harmful chemical device, harmful radioactive material, harmful radioactive device, incendiary device, or explosive device. MCL 777.49a(1)(a).	• For purposes of scoring this variable, the terms "act of terrorism" and "terrorist" are defined in MCL 750.543b. MCL 777.49a(2)(a). • "Harmful biological substance," "harmful biological device," "harmful chemical substance," "harmful chemical device," "harmful radioactive material," and "harmful radioactive device" are defined in MCL 750.200h. MCL 777.49a(2)(b). • "Incendiary device" includes gasoline or any other flammable substance, a blowtorch, fire bomb, Molotov cocktail, or other similar device. MCL 777.49a(2)(c). • For purposes of OV 20, "terrorist organization" is defined in MCL 750.543c. MCL 777.49a(2)(d).
50	The offender committed an act of terrorism without using or threatening to use a harmful biological substance, harmful biological device, harmful chemical substance, harmful chemical device, harmful radioactive material, harmful radioactive device, incendiary device, or explosive device. MCL 777.49a(1)(b).	
25	The offender supported an act of terrorism, a terrorist, or a terrorist organization. MCL 777.49a(1)(c).	
0	The offender did not commit an act of terrorism or support an act of terrorism, a terrorist, or a terrorist organization. MCL 777.49a(1)(d).	

PRVs and OVs – Crimes Against Public Trust

PRV 1

Prior High Severity Felony Convictions

(All "prior convictions" must satisfy the 10-year gap requirements of MCL 777.50.)

Pts	The offender has:	Instructions
75	3 or more prior high severity convictions.	A **"prior high severity felony conviction"** is a conviction for any of the following crimes if the conviction was entered before the commission date of the sentencing offense: • a crime listed in class M2, A, B, C, or D (or a felony under federal law or the law of another state that corresponds to a crime listed in class M2, A, B, C, or D), or • (effective January 9, 2007)* a felony that is not listed in ***any*** crime class (or a felony under federal law or the law of another state that does not correspond to a crime listed in ***any*** class) that is punishable by a maximum term of imprisonment of 10 years or more. MCL 777.51(2). *2006 PA 655.
50	2 prior high severity convictions.	
25	1 prior high severity conviction.	
0	No prior high severity convictions.	

PRV 2

Prior Low Severity Felony Convictions

(All "prior convictions" must satisfy the 10-year gap requirements of MCL 777.50.)

Pts	The offender has:	Instructions
30	4 or more prior low severity convictions.	A **"prior low severity felony conviction"** is a conviction for any of the following crimes if the conviction was entered before the commission date of the sentencing offense: • a crime listed in class E, F, G, or H (or a felony under federal law or the law of another state that corresponds to a crime listed in class E, F, G, or H), or • (effective January 9, 2007)* a felony that is not listed in ***any*** crime class (or a felony under federal law or the law of another state that does not correspond to a crime listed in ***any*** class) that is punishable by a maximum term of imprisonment of less than 10 years. MCL 777.52(2). *2006 PA 655.
20	3 prior low severity convictions.	
10	2 prior low severity convictions.	
5	1 prior low severity conviction.	
0	No prior low severity convictions.	

PRV 3

Prior High Severity Juvenile Adjudications

(All "prior convictions" must satisfy the 10-year gap requirements of MCL 777.50.)

<table>
<tr><th>Pts</th><th>The offender has:</th><th>Instructions</th></tr>
<tr><td>50</td><td>3 or more prior high severity juvenile adjudications.</td><td rowspan="4">A "prior high severity juvenile adjudication" is an adjudication for conduct that would be any of the following if committed by an adult, if the order of disposition was entered before the commission date of the sentencing offense:
• a crime listed in class M2, A, B, C, or D (or a felony under federal law or the law of another state that corresponds to a crime listed in class M2, A, B, C, or D), or
• (effective January 9, 2007)* a felony that is not listed in any crime class (or a felony under federal law or the law of another state that does not correspond to a crime listed in any class) that is punishable by a maximum term of imprisonment of 10 years or more. MCL 777.53(2).
*2006 PA 655.</td></tr>
<tr><td>25</td><td>2 prior high severity juvenile adjudications.</td></tr>
<tr><td>10</td><td>1 prior high severity juvenile adjudication.</td></tr>
<tr><td>0</td><td>No prior high severity juvenile adjudications.</td></tr>
</table>

PRV 4

Prior Low Severity Juvenile Adjudications

(All "prior convictions" must satisfy the 10-year gap requirements of MCL 777.50.)

<table>
<tr><th>Pts</th><th>The offender has:</th><th>Instructions</th></tr>
<tr><td>20</td><td>6 or more prior low severity juvenile adjudications.</td><td rowspan="6">A "prior low severity juvenile adjudication" is an adjudication for conduct that would be any of the following if committed by an adult, if the order of disposition was entered before the commission date of the sentencing offense:
• a crime listed in class E, F, G, or H (or a felony under federal law or the law of another state that corresponds to a crime listed in class E, F, G, or H), or
• (effective January 9, 2007)* a felony that is not listed in any crime class (or a felony under federal law or the law of another state that does not correspond to a crime listed in any class) that is punishable by a maximum term of imprisonment of less than 10 years. MCL 777.54(2).
*2006 PA 655.</td></tr>
<tr><td>15</td><td>5 prior low severity juvenile adjudications.</td></tr>
<tr><td>10</td><td>3 or 4 prior low severity juvenile adjudications.</td></tr>
<tr><td>5</td><td>2 prior low severity juvenile adjudications.</td></tr>
<tr><td>2</td><td>1 prior low severity juvenile adjudication.</td></tr>
<tr><td>0</td><td>No prior low severity juvenile adjudications.</td></tr>
</table>

PRVs and OVs – Crimes Against Public Trust

PRV 5

Prior Misdemeanor Convictions and Prior Misdemeanor Juvenile Adjudications

(All "prior convictions" must satisfy the 10-year gap requirements of MCL 777.50.)

Pts	The offender has:	Instructions
20	7 or more prior misdemeanor convictions or prior misdemeanor juvenile adjudications.	A **"prior misdemeanor conviction"** is a conviction: • for a misdemeanor offense under Michigan law or the law of a political subdivision of Michigan, or under the law of another state or a political subdivision of another state, or under the law of the United States, • if the conviction was entered before the commission date of the sentencing offense. MCL 777.55(3)(a). A **"prior misdemeanor juvenile adjudication"** is a juvenile adjudication: • for conduct that, if committed by an adult, would be a misdemeanor under Michigan law or the law of a political subdivision of Michigan, or under the law of another state or a political subdivision of another state, or under the law of the United States, • if the order of disposition for the juvenile adjudication was entered before the commission date of the sentencing offense. MCL 777.55(3)(b).
15	5 or 6 prior misdemeanor convictions or prior misdemeanor juvenile adjudications.	
10	3 or 4 prior misdemeanor convictions or prior misdemeanor juvenile adjudications.	
5	2 prior misdemeanor convictions or prior misdemeanor juvenile adjudications.	
2	1 prior misdemeanor conviction or prior misdemeanor juvenile adjudication.	
0	No prior misdemeanor convictions or prior misdemeanor juvenile adjudications.	

Special Instructions for PRV 5:

- A prior conviction used to enhance the sentencing offense to a felony may not be counted under PRV 5. MCL 777.55(2)(b).
- Only prior convictions and adjudications for offenses expressly listed in PRV 5 may be counted as "prior misdemeanor convictions" or "prior misdemeanor juvenile adjudications" for purposes of scoring PRV 5:
  - only those prior misdemeanor convictions or prior misdemeanor juvenile adjudications that are offenses against a person or property, weapons offenses, or offenses involving controlled substances, and
  - all prior misdemeanor convictions and juvenile adjudications for operating or attempting to operate a vehicle, vessel, ORV, snowmobile, aircraft, or locomotive while under the influence of or impaired by alcohol, a controlled substance, or a combination of alcohol and a controlled substance. MCL 777.55(2)(a)–(b).

PRV 6
Offender's Relationship to the Criminal Justice System

Pts		Instructions
20	Offender is a prisoner of the department of corrections or serving a sentence in jail (includes an offender who is an escapee from jail or prison). MCL 777.56(3)(b).	PRV 6 assesses points based on an offender's relationship to the criminal justice system at the time the sentencing offense was committed. MCL 777.56. The scope of PRV 6 includes consideration of an offender's relationship with a criminal justice system outside the state of Michigan. The point values indicated by applicable statements in PRV 6 should be assessed against an offender who is involved with the criminal justice system of another state or the federal criminal justice system. "Delayed sentence status" includes (but is not limited to) an offender assigned or deferred under MCL 333.7411 (deferral for certain controlled substance offenses), MCL 750.350a (deferral under limited circumstances for parental kidnapping), MCL 762.11 to 762.15 (assignment to youthful trainee status), MCL 769.4a (deferral under limited circumstances for domestic assault), MCL 600.1076 (deferral involving drug treatment courts), and MCL 750.430 (deferral for impaired healthcare professionals).
15	Offender is incarcerated in jail awaiting adjudication or sentencing on a conviction or probation violation.	
10	Offender is on parole, probation, or delayed sentence status or on bond awaiting adjudication or sentencing for a felony.	
5	Offender is on probation or delayed sentence status or on bond awaiting adjudication or sentencing for a misdemeanor.	
0	Offender has no relationship to the criminal justice system.	

PRV 7
Subsequent or Concurrent Felony Convictions

Pts	The offender has:	Instructions
20	2 or more subsequent or concurrent felony convictions.	• A conviction for felony-firearm may not be counted under PRV 7. MCL 777.57(2)(b). • A concurrent felony conviction that will result in a mandatory consecutive sentence may not be counted under PRV 7. MCL 777.57(2)(c). • A concurrent felony conviction that will result in a consecutive sentence under MCL 333.7401(3)* may not be counted under PRV 7. MCL 777.57(2)(c). *Effective March 1, 2003, 2002 PA 666. Does not apply to offenses committed before March 1, 2003.
10	1 subsequent or concurrent felony conviction.	
0	No subsequent or concurrent felony convictions.	

PRVs and OVs – Crimes Against Public Trust

OV 1
Aggravated Use of a Weapon

Pts		Instructions
25	A firearm was discharged at or toward a human being or a victim was cut or stabbed with a knife or other cutting or stabbing weapon. MCL 777.31(1)(a).	• Each person in danger of injury or loss of life is counted as a victim for purposes of scoring OV 1. MCL 777.31(2)(a). • In cases involving multiple offenders, if one offender is assigned points for the use or the presence of a weapon, all offenders must be assigned the same number of points. MCL 777.31(2)(b). • Do not score five points if the sentencing offense is a conviction of MCL 750.82 (felonious assault) or MCL 750.529 (armed robbery). MCL 777.31(2)(e). • Score five points if an offender used an object to suggest that he or she had a weapon. MCL 777.31(2)(c). • Score five points if an offender used a chemical irritant, a chemical irritant or smoke device, or an imitation harmful substance or device. MCL 777.31(2)(d). • "Harmful biological substance," "harmful biological device," "harmful chemical substance," "harmful chemical device," "harmful radioactive material," "harmful radioactive device," and "imitation harmful substance or device" are defined in MCL 750.200h. MCL 777.31(3)(a). • "Incendiary device" includes gasoline or any other flammable substance, a blowtorch, fire bomb, Molotov cocktail, or other similar device. MCL 777.31(3)(b).
20	The victim was subjected or exposed to a harmful biological substance, harmful biological device, harmful chemical substance, harmful chemical device, harmful radioactive material, harmful radioactive device, incendiary device, or explosive device. MCL 777.31(1)(b).	
15	A firearm was pointed at or toward a victim or the victim had a reasonable apprehension of an immediate battery when threatened with a knife or other cutting or stabbing weapon. MCL 777.31(1)(c).	
10	The victim was touched by any other type of weapon. MCL 777.31(1)(d).	
5	A weapon was displayed or implied. MCL 777.31(1)(e).	
0	No aggravated use of a weapon occurred. MCL 777.31(1)(f).	

OV 3
Degree of Physical Injury to a Victim

Pts		Instructions
100	A victim was killed. MCL 777.33(1)(a).	• In cases involving multiple offenders, if one offender is assessed points for death or physical injury, all offenders must be assessed the same number of points. MCL 777.33(3)(a). • Score 100 points if death results from the commission of the offense and homicide is not the sentencing offense. MCL 777.33(2)(b). Any crime in which the death of a person is an element of the crime is a "homicide." MCL 777.1(c). • Score 50 points under this variable if death results from an offense or attempted offense that involves the operation of a vehicle, vessel, ORV, snowmobile, aircraft, or locomotive and any of the following apply: – the offender was under the influence of or visibly impaired by the use of alcohol, a controlled substance, or a combination of alcohol and a controlled substance, MCL 777.33(2)(c)(i); – the offender had an alcohol content of 0.08 grams* or more per 100 milliliters of blood, per 210 liters of breath, or per 67 milliliters of urine, MCL 777.33(2)(c)(ii); or – the offender's body contained any amount of a controlled substance listed in schedule 1 under MCL 333.7212 or a rule promulgated under that section, or a controlled substance described in MCL 333.7214(a)(iv), MCL 777.33(2)(c)(iii). • Do not score five points if "bodily injury" is an element of the sentencing offense. MCL 777.33(2)(d). • "Requiring medical treatment" refers to an injury's need for treatment not whether a victim was successful in obtaining treatment. MCL 777.33(3). *Effective October 1, 2013, the alcohol content level increases to 0.10 grams or more.
50	A victim was killed. MCL 777.33(1)(b). *(35 points for offenses committed before September 30, 2003. 2003 PA 134.)*	
25	Life threatening or permanent incapacitating injury occurred to a victim. MCL 777.33(1)(c).	
10	Bodily injury requiring medical treatment occurred to a victim. MCL 777.33(1)(d).	
5	Bodily injury not requiring medical treatment occurred to a victim. MCL 777.33(1)(e).	
0	No physical injury occurred to a victim. MCL 777.33(1)(f).	

OV 4
Degree of Psychological Injury to a Victim

Pts		Instructions
10	Serious psychological injury requiring professional treatment occurred to a victim. MCL 777.34(1)(a).	Ten points may be scored if the victim's serious psychological injury may require professional treatment. Whether the victim has sought treatment for the injury is not conclusive. MCL 777.34(2).
0	No serious psychological injury requiring professional treatment occurred to a victim. MCL 777.34(1)(b).	

PRVs and OVs – Crimes Against Public Trust

OV 9
Number of Victims

Pts		Instructions
100	Multiple deaths occurred. MCL 777.39(1)(a).	• A "victim" for purposes of scoring OV 9 is each person placed in danger of injury or loss of life or (effective March 30, 2007)* loss of property. MCL 777.39(2)(a). • 100 points are scored only in homicide cases. MCL 777.39(2)(b). Any crime in which a person's death is an element of the crime is a "homicide." MCL 777.1(c). *2006 PA 548.
25	10 or more victims were placed in danger of physical injury or death. 20 or more victims were placed in danger of property loss (effective March 30, 2007). MCL 777.39(1)(b).	
10	2 to 9 victims were placed in danger of physical injury or death. 4 to 19 victims were placed in danger of property loss (effective March 30, 2007). MCL 777.39(1)(c).	
0	Fewer than 2 victims were placed in danger of physical injury or death. Fewer than 4 victims were placed in danger of property loss (effective March 30, 2007). MCL 777.39(1)(d).	

OV 10
Exploitation of a Victim's Vulnerability

Pts		Instructions
15	Predatory conduct was involved. MCL 777.40(1)(a).	• Do not automatically score points for victim vulnerability just because one or more of the factors addressed by OV 10 are present in the circumstances surrounding the sentencing offense. MCL 777.40(2). • "Predatory conduct" is an offender's preoffense conduct directed at a victim for the primary purpose of victimization. MCL 777.40(3)(a). • To "exploit" a victim is to manipulate a victim for the offender's selfish or unethical purposes. MCL 777.40(3)(b). • A victim's "vulnerability" is the victim's readily apparent susceptibility to injury, physical restraint, persuasion, or temptation. MCL 777.40(3)(c). • "Abuse of authority status" means the offender used a victim's fear of or deference to an authority figure to exploit the victim. Examples of an authority figure include, but are not limited to, a teacher, parent, or physician. MCL 777.40(3)(d).
10	The offender exploited a victim's physical disability, mental disability, youth or agedness, or a domestic relationship or the offender abused his or her authority status. MCL 777.40(1)(b).	
5	The offender exploited a victim by his or her difference in size or strength, or both, or exploited a victim who was intoxicated, under the influence of drugs, asleep, or unconscious. MCL 777.40(1)(c).	
0	The offender did not exploit a victim's vulnerability. MCL 777.40(1)(d).	

OV 12
Number of Contemporaneous Felonious Criminal Acts

Pts		Instructions
25	Three or more contemporaneous felonious criminal acts involving crimes against a person were committed. MCL 777.42(1)(a).	• A felonious criminal act is contemporaneous if both of the following circumstances exist: – the criminal act occurred within 24 hours of the sentencing offense, MCL 777.42(2)(a)(i), and – the criminal act has not and will not result in a separate conviction, MCL 777.42(2)(a)(ii). • Conduct scored in OV 11 must not be scored under this variable. MCL 777.42(2)(c). • Violations of MCL 750.227b (possession of a firearm during the commission of a felony) should not be counted when scoring this variable. MCL 777.42(2)(b).
10	Two contemporaneous felonious criminal acts involving crimes against a person were committed. MCL 777.42(1)(b).	
10	Three or more contemporaneous felonious criminal acts involving other crimes were committed. MCL 777.42(1)(c).	
5	One contemporaneous felonious criminal act involving a crime against a person was committed. MCL 777.42(1)(d).	
5	Two contemporaneous felonious criminal acts involving other crimes were committed. MCL 777.42(1)(e).	
1	One contemporaneous felonious criminal act involving any other crime was committed. MCL 777.42(1)(f).	
0	No contemporaneous felonious criminal acts were committed. MCL 777.42(1)(g).	

OV 13
Continuing Pattern of Criminal Behavior

Language appearing in bold type in the chart below applies to offenses committed on or after March 1, 2003. 2002 PA 666.

Pts	
50	The offense was part of a pattern of felonious criminal activity involving 3 or more sexual penetrations against a person or persons less than 13 years of age. MCL 777.43(1)(a).
25	The offense was part of a pattern of felonious criminal activity involving 3 or more crimes against a person. MCL 777.43(1)(b).
10	The offense was part of a pattern of felonious criminal activity involving a combination of 3 or more crimes against a person or property **or a violation of MCL 333.7401(2)(a)(*i*) to (*iii*) or 333.7403(2)(a)(*i*) to (*iii*).** MCL 777.43(1)(c).
10	The offense was part of a pattern of felonious criminal activity directly related to membership in an organized criminal group. MCL 777.43(1)(d).
10	**The offense was part of a pattern of felonious criminal activity involving a combination of 3 or more violations of MCL 333.7401(2)(a)(i) to (iii) or 333.7403(2)(a)(i) to (iii). MCL 777.43(1)(e).**
5	The offense was part of a pattern of felonious criminal activity involving 3 or more crimes against property. MCL 777.43(1)(f).
0	No pattern of felonious criminal activity existed. MCL 777.43(1)(g).

Instructions

- To score this variable, all crimes within a period of five years, including the sentencing offense, must be counted without regard to whether the offense resulted in a conviction. MCL 777.43(2)(a).
- The existence of an organized criminal group may be inferred from the facts surrounding the sentencing offense, and the group's existence is more important than the presence or absence of multiple offenders, the age of the offenders, or the degree of sophistication demonstrated by the criminal group. MCL 777.43(2)(b).
- Do not consider conduct scored in OVs 11 or 12 unless the offense was related to membership in an organized criminal group. MCL 777.43(2)(c).
- Score 50 points only if the sentencing offense is first-degree criminal sexual conduct. MCL 777.43(2)(d).
- Only one controlled substance offense arising from the criminal episode for which the offender is being sentenced may be counted when scoring this variable.* MCL 777.43(2)(e).
- Only one crime involving the same controlled substance may be counted under this variable.* For example, conspiracy and a substantive offense involving the same amount of controlled substances cannot both be counted under OV 13. Similarly, possession and delivery of the same amount of controlled substances may not be counted as two crimes under OV 13. MCL 777.43(2)(f).

**Effective March 1, 2003. 2002 PA 666.*

OV 14
Offender's Role

Pts	
10	The offender was a leader in a multiple offender situation. MCL 777.44(1)(a).
0	The offender was not a leader in a multiple offender situation. MCL 777.44(1)(b).

Instructions

- Consider the entire criminal transaction in which the sentencing offense occurred when determining the offender's role. MCL 777.44(2)(a).
- In cases involving three or more offenders, more than one offender may be considered a leader. MCL 777.44(2)(b).

OV 16
Degree of Property Damage

Pts		Instructions
10	Wanton or malicious damage occurred beyond that necessary to commit the crime for which the offender is not charged and will not be charged. MCL 777.46(1)(a).	• In cases involving multiple offenders or multiple victims, the appropriate point total may be determined by aggregating the value of property involved in the offense, including property involved in uncharged offenses or property involved in charges dismissed under a plea agreement. MCL 777.46(2)(a). • Use the value of the property to score this variable in cases where the property was unlawfully obtained, lost to the lawful owner, or destroyed. If the property was damaged, use the amount of money necessary to restore the property to its pre-offense condition. MCL 777.46(2)(b). • Money or property involved in admitted but uncharged offenses or in charges dismissed under a plea agreement may be considered in scoring this variable. MCL 777.46(2)(c).
10	The property had a value of more than $20,000.00 or had significant historical, social, or sentimental value. MCL 777.46(1)(b).	
5	The property had a value of $1,000.00 or more but not more than $20,000.00. MCL 777.46(1)(c).	
1	The property had a value of $200.00 or more but not more than $1,000.00. MCL 777.46(1)(d).	
0	No property was obtained, damaged, lost, or destroyed or the property had a value of less than $200.00. MCL 777.46(1)(e).	

OV 19
Threat to Security or Interference With the Administration of Justice

Pts		Instructions
25	The offender by his or her conduct threatened the security of a penal institution or court. MCL 777.49(a).	
15	The offender used force or the threat of force against another person or the property of another person to interfere with, attempt to interfere with, or that results in the interference with the administration of justice or the rendering of emergency services. MCL 777.49(b).	
10	The offender otherwise interfered with or attempted to interfere with the administration of justice. MCL 777.49(c).	
0	The offender did not threaten the security of a penal institution or court or interfere with or attempt to interfere with the administration of justice or the rendering of emergency services by force or the threat of force. MCL 777.49(d).	

PRVs and OVs – Crimes Against Public Trust

OV 20
Terrorism

Pts		Instructions
100	The offender committed an act of terrorism by using or threatening to use a harmful biological substance, harmful biological device, harmful chemical substance, harmful chemical device, harmful radioactive material, harmful radioactive device, incendiary device, or explosive device. MCL 777.49a(1)(a).	• For purposes of scoring this variable, the terms "act of terrorism" and "terrorist" are defined in MCL 750.543b. MCL 777.49a(2)(a). • "Harmful biological substance," "harmful biological device," "harmful chemical substance," "harmful chemical device," "harmful radioactive material," and "harmful radioactive device" are defined in MCL 750.200h. MCL 777.49a(2)(b). • "Incendiary device" includes gasoline or any other flammable substance, a blowtorch, fire bomb, Molotov cocktail, or other similar device. MCL 777.49a(2)(c). • For purposes of OV 20, "terrorist organization" is defined in MCL 750.543c. MCL 777.49a(2)(d).
50	The offender committed an act of terrorism without using or threatening to use a harmful biological substance, harmful biological device, harmful chemical substance, harmful chemical device, harmful radioactive material, harmful radioactive device, incendiary device, or explosive device. MCL 777.49a(1)(b).	
25	The offender supported an act of terrorism, a terrorist, or a terrorist organization. MCL 777.49a(1)(c).	
0	The offender did not commit an act of terrorism or support an act of terrorism, a terrorist, or a terrorist organization. MCL 777.49a(1)(d).	

Sentencing Grid for Second-Degree Murder—MCL 777.61

Includes Ranges Calculated for Habitual Offenders (MCL 777.21(3)(a)–(c))

OV Level	PRV Level												Offender Status
	A 0 Points		B 1-9 Points		C 10-24 Points		D 25-49 Points		E 50-74 Points		F 75+ Points		
I 0-49 Points	90	150	144	240	162	270	180	300/L	225	375/L	270	450/L	
		187		300		337		375/L		468/L		562/L	HO2
		225		360		405		450/L		562/L		675/L	HO3
		300		480		540		600/L		750/L		900/L	HO4
II 50-99 Points	144	240	162	270	180	300/L	225	375/L	270	450/L	315	525/L	
		300		337		375/L		468/L		562/L		656/L	HO2
		360		405		450/L		562/L		675/L		787/L	HO3
		480		540		600/L		750/L		900/L		1050/L	HO4
III 100+ Points	162	270/L	180	300/L	225	375/L	270	450/L	315	525/L	365	600/L	
		337/L		375/L		468/L		562/L		656/L		750/L	HO2
		405/L		450/L		562/L		675/L		787/L		900/L	HO3
		540/L		600/L		750/L		900/L		1050/L		1200/L	HO4

The statutory percentage increases for habitual offenders are rounded down to the nearest whole month. The cell range may be less than the maximum possible minimum sentence by a fraction of a month.

Sentencing Grid for Class A Offenses—MCL 777.62

Includes Ranges Calculated for Habitual Offenders (MCL 777.21(3)(a)–(c))

OV Level	PRV Level												Offender Status
	A 0 Points		B 1-9 Points		C 10-24 Points		D 25-49 Points		E 50-74 Points		F 75+ Points		
I 0-19 Points		35		45		70		85		135		180	
	21	43	27	56	42	87	51	106	81	168	108	225	HO2
		52		67		105		127		202		270	HO3
		70		90		140		170		270		360	HO4
II 20-39 Points		45		70		85		135		180		210	
	27	56	42	87	51	106	81	168	108	225	126	262	HO2
		67		105		127		202		270		315	HO3
		90		140		170		270		360		420	HO4
III 40-59 Points		70		85		135		180		210		225	
	42	87	51	106	81	168	108	225	126	262	135	281	HO2
		105		127		202		270		315		337	HO3
		140		170		270		360		420		450	HO4
IV 60-79 Points		85		135		180		210		225		285	
	51	106	81	168	108	225	126	262	135	281	171	356	HO2
		127		202		270		315		337		427	HO3
		170		270		360		420		450		570	HO4
V 80-99 Points		135		180		210		225		285		375/L	
	81	168	108	225	126	262	135	281	171	356	225	468/L	HO2
		202		270		315		337		427		562/L	HO3
		270		360		420		450		570		750/L	HO4
VI 100+ Points		180		210		225		285		375/L		450/L	
	108	225	126	262	135	281	171	356	225	468/L	270	562/L	HO2
		270		315		337		427		562/L		675/L	HO3
		360		420		450		570		750/L		900/L	HO4

The statutory percentage increases for habitual offenders are rounded down to the nearest whole month. The cell range may be less than the maximum possible minimum sentence by a fraction of a month.

Sentencing Grid for Class B Offenses—MCL 777.63

Includes Ranges Calculated for Habitual Offenders (MCL 777.21(3)(a)–(c))

OV Level	PRV Level												Offender Status
	A 0 Points		B 1-9 Points		C 10-24 Points		D 25-49 Points		E 50-74 Points		F 75+ Points		
I 0-9 Points	0	18*	12	20	24	40	36	60	51	85	72	120	
		22		25		50		75		106		150	HO2
		27		30		60		90		127		180	HO3
		36		40		80		120		170		240	HO4
II 10-24 Points	12	20	15	25	30	50	51	85	72	120	78	130	
		25		31		62		106		150		162	HO2
		30		37		75		127		180		195	HO3
		40		50		100		170		240		260	HO4
III 25-34 Points	15	25	21	35	36	60	57	95	78	130	84	140	
		31		43		75		118		162		175	HO2
		37		52		90		142		195		210	HO3
		50		70		120		190		260		280	HO4
IV 35-49 Points	21	35	24	40	45	75	72	120	84	140	87	145	
		43		50		93		150		175		181	HO2
		52		60		112		180		210		217	HO3
		70		80		150		240		280		290	HO4
V 50-74 Points	24	40	36	60	51	85	78	130	87	145	99	160	
		50		75		106		162		181		200	HO2
		60		90		127		195		217		240	HO3
		80		120		170		260		290		320	HO4
VI 75+ Points	36	60	45	75	57	95	84	140	99	160	117	160	
		75		93		118		175		200		200	HO2
		90		112		142		210		240		240	HO3
		120		150		190		280		320		320	HO4

Intermediate sanction cells are marked by asterisks, straddle cells are shaded, and prison cells are unmarked.

The statutory percentage increases for habitual offenders are rounded down to the nearest whole month.
The cell range may be less than the maximum possible minimum sentence by a fraction of a month.

Sentencing Grid for Class C Offenses—MCL 777.64

Includes Ranges Calculated for Habitual Offenders (MCL 777.21(3)(a)–(c))

OV Level	PRV Level												Offender Status
	A 0 Points		B 1-9 Points		C 10-24 Points		D 25-49 Points		E 50-74 Points		F 75+ Points		
I 0-9 Points	0	11*	0	17*	10	19	12	24	19	38	29	57	
		13*		21		23		30		47		71	HO2
		16*		25		28		36		57		85	HO3
		22		34		38		48		76		114	HO4
II 10-24 Points	0	17*	5	17*	12	24	19	38	29	57	36	71	
		21		21		30		47		71		88	HO2
		25		25		36		57		85		106	HO3
		34		34		48		76		114		142	HO4
III 25-34 Points	10	19	12	24	19	38	29	57	36	71	43	86	
		23		30		47		71		88		107	HO2
		28		36		57		85		106		129	HO3
		38		48		76		114		142		172	HO4
IV 35-49 Points	12	24	19	38	29	57	36	71	43	86	50	100	
		30		47		71		88		107		125	HO2
		36		57		85		106		129		150	HO3
		48		76		114		142		172		200	HO4
V 50-74 Points	19	38	29	57	36	71	43	86	50	100	58	114	
		47		71		88		107		125		142	HO2
		57		85		106		129		150		171	HO3
		76		114		142		172		200		228	HO4
VI 75+ Points	29	57	36	71	43	86	50	100	58	114	62	114	
		71		88		107		125		142		142	HO2
		85		106		129		150		171		171	HO3
		114		142		172		200		228		228	HO4

Sentencing Grid for Class D Offenses—MCL 777.65

Includes Ranges Calculated for Habitual Offenders (MCL 777.21(3)(a)–(c))

OV Level	PRV Level												Offender Status
	A 0 Points		B 1-9 Points		C 10-24 Points		D 25-49 Points		E 50-74 Points		F 75+ Points		
I 0-9 Points	0	6*	0	9*	0	11*	0	17*	5	23	10	23	
		7*		11*		13*		21		28		28	HO2
		9*		13*		16*		25		34		34	HO3
		12*		18*		22		34		46		46	HO4
II 10-24 Points	0	9*	0	11*	0	17*	5	23	10	23	19	38	
		11*		13*		21		28		28		47	HO2
		13*		16*		25		34		34		57	HO3
		18*		22		34		46		46		76	HO4
III 25-34 Points	0	11*	0	17*	5	23	10	23	19	38	29	57	
		13*		21		28		28		47		71	HO2
		16*		25		34		34		57		85	HO3
		22		34		46		46		76		114	HO4
IV 35-49 Points	0	17*	5	23	10	23	19	38	29	57	34	67	
		21		28		28		47		71		83	HO2
		25		34		34		57		85		100	HO3
		34		46		46		76		114		134	HO4
V 50-74 Points	5	23	10	23	19	38	29	57	34	67	38	76	
		28		28		47		71		83		95	HO2
		34		34		57		85		100		114	HO3
		46		46		76		114		134		152	HO4
VI 75+ Points	10	23	19	38	29	57	34	67	38	76	43	76	
		28		47		71		83		95		95	HO2
		34		57		85		100		114		114	HO3
		46		76		114		134		152		152	HO4

Sentencing Grid for Class E Offenses—MCL 777.66

Includes Ranges Calculated for Habitual Offenders (MCL 777.21(3)(a)–(c))

OV Level	PRV Level A 0 Points		B 1-9 Points		C 10-24 Points		D 25-49 Points		E 50-74 Points		F 75+ Points		Offender Status
I 0-9 Points	0	3*	0	6*	0	9*	5	23	7	23	9	23	
		3*		7*		11*		28		28		28	HO2
		4*		9*		13*		34		34		34	HO3
		6*		12*		18*		46		46		46	HO4
II 10-24 Points	0	6*	0	9*	0	11*	7	23	10	23	12	24	
		7*		11*		13*		28		28		30	HO2
		9*		13*		16*		34		34		36	HO3
		12*		18*		22		46		46		48	HO4
III 25-34 Points	0	9*	0	11*	0	17*	10	23	12	24	14	29	
		11*		13*		21		28		30		36	HO2
		13*		16*		25		34		36		43	HO3
		18*		22		34		46		48		58	HO4
IV 35-49 Points	0	11*	0	17*	5	23	12	24	14	29	19	38	
		13*		21		28		30		36		47	HO2
		16*		25		34		36		43		57	HO3
		22		34		46		48		58		76	HO4
V 50-74 Points	0	14*	5	23	7	23	14	29	19	38	22	38	
		17*		28		28		36		47		47	HO2
		21		34		34		43		57		57	HO3
		28		46		46		58		76		76	HO4
VI 75+ Points	0	17*	7	23	12	24	19	38	22	38	24	38	
		21		28		30		47		47		47	HO2
		25		34		36		57		57		57	HO3
		34		46		48		76		76		76	HO4

Sentencing Grid for Class F Offenses—MCL 777.67

Includes Ranges Calculated for Habitual Offenders (MCL 777.21(3)(a)–(c))

OV Level	PRV Level												Offender Status
	A 0 Points		B 1-9 Points		C 10-24 Points		D 25-49 Points		E 50-74 Points		F 75+ Points		
I 0-9 Points	0	3*	0	6*	0	9*	2	17*	5	23	10	23	
		3*		7*		11*		21		28		28	HO2
		4*		9*		13*		25		34		34	HO3
		6*		12*		18*		34		46		46	HO4
II 10-34 Points	0	6*	0	9*	0	17*	5	23	10	23	12	24	
		7*		11*		21		28		28		30	HO2
		9*		13*		25		34		34		36	HO3
		12*		18*		34		46		46		48	HO4
III 35-74 Points	0	9*	0	17*	2	17*	10	23	12	24	14	29	
		11*		21		21		28		30		36	HO2
		13*		25		25		34		36		43	HO3
		18*		34		34		46		48		58	HO4
IV 75+ Points	0	17*	2	17*	5	23	12	24	14	29	17	30	
		21		21		28		30		36		37	HO2
		25		25		34		36		43		45	HO3
		34		34		46		48		58		60	HO4

Intermediate sanction cells are marked by asterisks, straddle cells are shaded, and prison cells are unmarked.

The statutory percentage increases for habitual offenders are rounded down to the nearest whole month. The cell range may be less than the maximum possible minimum sentence by a fraction of a month.

Sentencing Grid for Class G Offenses—MCL 777.68

Includes Ranges Calculated for Habitual Offenders (MCL 777.21(3)(a)–(c))

OV Level	PRV Level												Offender Status
	A 0 Points		B 1-9 Points		C 10-24 Points		D 25-49 Points		E 50-74 Points		F 75+ Points		
I 0-9 Points	0	3*	0	6*	0	9*	0	11*	0	17*	2	17*	
		3*		7*		11*		13*		21		21	HO2
		4*		9*		13*		16*		25		25	HO3
		6*		12*		18*		22		34		34	HO4
II 10-15 Points	0	6*	0	9*	0	11*	0	17*	2	17*	5	23	
		7*		11*		13*		21		21		28	HO2
		9*		13*		16*		25		25		34	HO3
		12*		18*		22		34		34		46	HO4
III 16+ Points	0	9*	0	11*	0	17*	2	17*	5	23	7	23	
		11*		13*		21		21		28		28	HO2
		13*		16*		25		25		34		34	HO3
		18*		22		34		34		46		46	HO4

Intermediate sanction cells are marked by asterisks, straddle cells are shaded, and prison cells are unmarked.

The statutory percentage increases for habitual offenders are rounded down to the nearest whole month.
The cell range may be less than the maximum possible minimum sentence by a fraction of a month.

Sentencing Grid for Class H Offenses—MCL 777.69

Includes Ranges Calculated for Habitual Offenders (MCL 777.21(3)(a)–(c))

OV Level	PRV Level												Offender Status
	A 0 Points		B 1-9 Points		C 10-24 Points		D 25-49 Points		E 50-74 Points		F 75+ Points		
I 0-9 Points	0	1*	0	3*	0	6*	0	9*	0	11*	0	17*	
		1*		3*		7*		11*		13*		21	HO2
		1*		4*		9*		13*		16*		25	HO3
		2*		6*		12*		18*		22		34	HO4
II 10-15 Points	0	3*	0	6*	0	9*	0	11*	0	17*	2	17*	
		3*		7*		11*		13*		21		21	HO2
		4*		9*		13*		16*		25		25	HO3
		6*		12*		18*		22		34		34	HO4
III 16+ Points	0	6*	0	9*	0	11*	0	17*	2	17*	5	17*	
		7*		11*		13*		21		21		21	HO2
		9*		13*		16*		25		25		25	HO3
		12*		18*		22		34		34		34	HO4

Intermediate sanction cells are marked by asterisks, straddle cells are shaded, and prison cells are unmarked.

The statutory percentage increases for habitual offenders are rounded down to the nearest whole month. The cell range may be less than the maximum possible minimum sentence by a fraction of a month.

*Unless otherwise noted, the date on which the statutory guidelines were made applicable to the felony offense listed is 1/1/99.

Felonies by MCL #	Group	Class	Description	Stat Max	Effective Date*
MCL 777.11a					
4. 421 (1)	Pub trst	G	Lobbyists – compensation contingent on outcome of action	3	
4. 421 (2)	Pub trst	G	Lobbyists giving gifts	3	
15. 324 (1) (d)	Pub trst	G	Purchase of public residential property by public servant	1	12/16/05
18. 366 (1)	Property	E	False presentation to crime victim services commission to obtain more than $100	10	Deleted, 2001 PA 150 & 154, Eff. 1/1/02
18. 366 (1) (c)	Property	E	False presentation to crime victim services commission to obtain $1,000 - $20,000 or w/ priors	5	1/1/02
18. 366 (1) (d)	Property	D	False presentation to crime victim services commission to obtain $20,000+ or with priors	10	1/1/02
18. 1268 (9)	Pub trst	H	Purposefully submitting false business certification	Fine	Deleted, 2005 PA 265, Eff. 12/16/05
21. 154	Pub trst	E	Public officer – embezzlement	5	
MCL 777.11b					
28. 214	Pub trst	F	Unauthorized disclosure of information from LEIN – subsequent offense	4	1/1/02
28. 214 (4) (b)	Pub trst	F	Unauthorized disclosure of information from LEIN – subsequent offense	4	10/1/00
28. 293 (1)	Pub ord	E	False information when applying for state ID	5	
28. 293 (2)	Pub ord	D	False information when applying for state ID – second offense	7	
28. 293 (3)	Pub ord	C	False information when applying for state ID – third or subsequent offense	15	
28. 295 (1) (a)	Pub ord	H	Forging state ID card to commit felony	4	Replaced, 2004 PA 149, Eff. 9/1/04
28. 295 (1) (a)	Pub ord	D	Counterfeiting/forging/using counterfeited/forged state ID for felony punishable by 10+ years	10	9/1/04
28. 295 (1) (b)	Pub ord	E	Counterfeiting/forging/using state ID for felony punishable by <10 yrs/misdemeanor by >6 mos	5	9/1/04
28. 295 (2)	Pub ord	E	Sell/possess counterfeited/forged state ID w/ intent to deliver or possess 2+ forged ID cards	5	9/1/04
28. 295 (3)	Property	H	Using stolen state ID card to commit felony	Variable	Replaced, 2004 PA 149, Eff. 9/1/04
28. 295 (5)	Property	H	Using stolen state ID card to commit felony	Variable	9/1/04
28. 295 a (1)	Pub ord	H	False representation to obtain or misuse personal information	4	
28. 295 a (2)	Pub ord	G	False representation to obtain or misuse personal information – second offense	7	
28. 295 a (3)	Pub ord	C	False representation to obtain or misuse personal information – third or subsequent offense	15	
28. 422	Pub saf	G	Pistols – license application forgery	4	
28. 422	Pub saf	F	Pistols – license application forgery	4	7/1/01
28. 422 a (4)	Pub saf	F	False statement on pistol sales record	4	7/1/01
28. 425 b (3)	Pub saf	F	False statement on concealed pistol permit application	4	7/1/01
28. 425 j (2)	Pub saf	F	Unlawful granting or presenting of pistol training certificate	4	7/1/01
28. 425 o (5) (c)	Pub saf	F	Carrying concealed pistol in prohibited place – third or subsequent offense	4	7/1/01
28. 435	Pub saf	G	Firearm sale without trigger lock/gun case/storage container – third or subsequent offense	2	7/1/01
28. 729	Pub ord	G	Sex offenders – failure to register	4	Substituted for by 28.729(1)(a)

Lightly shaded lines indicate that the statute governing the felony offense described on that line has been amended, deleted, or replaced.

Updated April 2007

*Unless otherwise noted, the date on which the statutory guidelines were made applicable to the felony offense listed is 1/1/99.

Felonies by MCL #	Group	Class	Description	Stat Max	Effective Date*
28. 729 (1) (a)	Pub ord	F	Failure to register as a sex offender, first offense	4	9/1/99
28. 729 (1) (b)	Pub ord	D	Failure to register as a sex offender, second offense	7	9/1/99
28. 729 (1) (c)	Pub ord	D	Failure to register as a sex offender, third or subsequent offense	10	9/1/99
28. 729 (2) (c)	Pub ord	F	Failure to update sex offender registration information - third or subsequent offense	4	1/1/06
28. 734 (2) (b)	Pub trst	G	Student safety zone violation involving work or loitering - second or subsequent offense	2	1/1/06
28. 735 (2) (b)	Pub trst	G	Student safety zone violation involving residency - second or subsequent violation	2	1/1/06
28. 754	Pub ord	F	False report of a child abduction	4	2/1/06
MCL 777.11c					
35. 929	Pub trst	H	Willful falsification in application for veterans benefits	3	
35. 980	Pub trst	H	False statement in application for Korean veterans benefits	3	
35. 1029	Pub trst	H	False statement in application for Vietnam veterans benefits	3	
38. 412 a (1)	Pub trst	H	County employee providing answers to county civil service exam	1	
38. 516	Pub trst	H	Fire and police civil service – appointment or employment contrary to act	2	
45. 82	Pub trst	E	County purchasing agent – violations in awarding bids or contracts	5	
47. 8	Pub trst	H	Payment of claim against county before audit	2	
47. 56	Pub trst	H	Wayne County treasurer paying claims without appropriate signature	2	
51. 364	Pub trst	H	Appointment or selection contrary to civil service commission rules	2	
110. 28	Pub trst	G	Fourth class cities – misappropriation of money or property	3	
117. 25 (3)	Pub trst	E	Amendment to city electors – willfully affixing another's signature, false representation	15	
125. 1447	Property	G	Michigan state housing development authority – false pretenses over $100	10	Deleted, 2001 PA 154, Eff. 1/1/02
125. 1447 (1) (c)	Property	E	False pretenses under state housing development act involving $1,000 to $20,000 or w/ priors	5	1/1/02
125. 1447 (1) (d)	Property	D	False pretenses under state housing development act involving $20,000+ or w/ priors	10	1/1/02
MCL 777.11d					
168. 731 (4)	Pub trst	G	Election law – filing certain false statements	2	
168. 734	Pub trst	G	Election law – election board refusing to provide challenger conveniences	2	
168. 756	Pub trst	E	Elector's false statement concerning inability to mark ballot	5	
168. 757	Pub trst	E	Election inspector – unlawful conduct	5	
168. 759 (8)	Pub trst	E	Election law – forged signature on absentee ballot	5	
168. 759 b	Pub trst	E	False statement in application for emergency absentee ballot	5	
168. 761 (5)	Pub trst	E	Assisting an absentee voter in making a false statement	5	
168. 769 (4)	Pub trst	E	Voting both in person and by absentee ballot	5	
168. 792 a (11)	Pub trst	E	Disclosing how ballot voted or election results early before polls are closed	5	

Lightly shaded lines indicate that the statute governing the felony offense described on that line has been amended, deleted, or replaced.

Updated April 2007

*Unless otherwise noted, the date on which the statutory guidelines were made applicable to the felony offense listed is 1/1/99.

Felonies by MCL #	Group	Class	Description	Stat Max	Effective Date*
168. 792 a (16)	Pub trst	E	Disclosing election result or how ballot voted	5	
168. 808	Pub trst	E	Untrue statement by member of board of inspectors	4	
168. 873	Pub trst	E	Misconduct of election employee in recount – county and local	5	
168. 887	Pub trst	E	Misconduct of election employee in recount	5	
168. 932 (a)	Pub trst	E	Bribing or intimidating voters	5	
168. 932 (b)	Pub trst	E	Ballot tampering	5	
168. 932 (c)	Pub trst	E	Destroying or falsifying election return or records	5	
168. 932 (d)	Pub trst	E	Disclosing votes or obstructing voter	5	
168. 932 (e)	Pub trst	E	Absentee ballot tampering	5	
168. 932 (f)	Pub trst	E	Election law – possess absent voter ballot delivered to another person	5	
168. 932 (g)	Pub trst	E	Suggesting how a disabled voter should vote	5	
168. 932 (h)	Pub trst	E	Suggesting or influencing how an absentee voter should vote	5	
168. 932 (i)	Pub trst	E	Organizing a meeting where absentee voter ballots are to be voted	5	
168. 932 a	Pub trst	G	Election offenses	4	
168. 933	Pub trst	E	False swearing to register or vote	5	
168. 936	Pub trst	E	Election law – perjury	5	
168. 937	Pub trst	E	Election law – forgery	5	
MCL 777.11e					
169. 254	Pub trst	H	Campaign finance – corporate contributions	3	
169. 255	Pub trst	H	Campaign finance – corporate solicitation for certain funds	3	
169. 266	Pub trst	H	Campaign finance – qualified campaign expenditures	3	
MCL 777.12a					
205. 27 (1) (a)	Pub trst	G	Failure to file or false tax return or payment	5	
205. 27 (1) (b)	Pub trst	G	Aiding and abetting tax evasion or filing false returns	5	
205. 27 (1) (c)	Pub trst	G	Making/permitting false tax returns or payments	5	
205. 27 (3)	Pub trst	G	False tax returns/perjury	15	
205. 28	Pub trst	G	Compromising/unauthorized disclosure of tax information	5	
205. 28 (1) (e)	Pub trst	G	State employee compromising taxes	5	
205. 28 (1) (f)	Pub trst	G	Unauthorized disclosure of tax information	5	
205. 428 (2)	Pub trst	G	Tobacco products tax act violations	5	
205. 428 (3)	Pub trst	G	Illegal sale of cigarettes or other tobacco products with wholesale price of $250 or more	5	10/1/00
205. 428 (6)	Pub trst	F	Illegal tobacco stamp or tobacco stamp device	10	10/1/00

Lightly shaded lines indicate that the statute governing the felony offense described on that line has been amended, deleted, or replaced.

Updated April 2007

*Unless otherwise noted, the date on which the statutory guidelines were made applicable to the felony offense listed is 1/1/99.

	Felonies by MCL #	Group	Class	Description	Stat Max	Effective Date*
	205. 428 (7)	Pub trst	G	Illegal vending machine license, disk, or marker	5	10/1/00
	207. 118 a	Pub ord	G	Gasoline tax – embezzlement over $100	10	Repealed, 2000 PA 403, Eff. 4/1/01
	207. 119	Pub trst	G	Gasoline or motor fuel tax violation	4	Repealed, 2000 PA 403, Eff. 4/1/01
	207. 127 c	Pub ord	G	Diesel fuel tax – embezzlement over $100	10	Repealed, 2000 PA 403, Eff. 4/1/01
	207. 754 (3)	Pub trst	G	State treasurer – municipality tax – divulging confidential information	5	
MCL 777.12b						
	252. 311	Property	H	Destroying a tree or shrub to make a sign more visible	2	10/1/00
MCL 777.12c						
	257. 233 a (7)	Pub ord	G	Odometer tampering	5	
	257. 254	Property	E	Possessing stolen vehicle title	10	
	257. 257 (1)	Property	G	Altering or forging vehicle documents – first offense	5	
	257. 257 (2)	Property	G	Altering or forging vehicle documents – second offense	7	
	257. 257 (3)	Property	E	Altering or forging vehicle documents – third or subsequent offense	15	
MCL 777.12d						
	257. 309 (6)	Pub ord	F	Corrupting an examining officer - see MCL 257.309(7)	5	3/28/01
	257. 309 (7)	Pub ord	F	Deviating from road test criteria - see MCL 257.309(8)	5	3/28/01
	257. 309 (8)	Pub ord	F	Forging, counterfeiting, or altering road test certification - see MCL 257.609(9)	5	3/28/01
	257. 310 (7) (a)	Pub ord	D	Forging driver license with intent to commit crime punishable by 10 years or more	10	4/22/02
	257. 310 (7) (b)	Pub ord	E	Forging driver license w/ intent to commit crime punishable by 6+ months but less than 10 yrs	5	4/22/02
	257. 310 (8)	Pub ord	E	Selling or possessing forged driver license with intent to deliver	5	4/22/02
	257. 310 (9)	Pub ord	E	Possession of 2 or more forged driver licenses	5	4/22/02
	257. 312 b (6)	Pub ord	F	Corrupting a person or agency conducting a motorcycle driving test	5	3/28/01
	257. 312 b (7)	Pub ord	F	Deviating from motorcycle road test criteria	5	3/28/01
	257. 312 b (8)	Pub ord	F	Forging, counterfeiting, or altering motorcycle road test certification	5	3/28/01
	257. 329 (1)	Property	G	Possession/sale of stolen or counterfeit insurance certificates	5	
	257. 329 (2)	Property	E	Possession/sale of stolen or counterfeit insurance certificates – second offense	7	
	257. 329 (3)	Property	E	Possession/sale of stolen or counterfeit insurance certificates – third or subsequent offense	15	
MCL 777.12e						
	257. 601 b (3)	Person	C	Moving violation causing death to construction worker	15	10/1/01
	257. 601 c (2)	Person	C	Moving violation causing death to operator of implement of husbandry	15	10/1/01
	257. 602 a (2)	Pub saf	G	Fleeing and eluding – fourth degree	2	
	257. 602 a (3)	Pub saf	E	Fleeing and eluding – third degree	5	

Lightly shaded lines indicate that the statute governing the felony offense described on that line has been amended, deleted, or replaced.

Updated April 2007

*Unless otherwise noted, the date on which the statutory guidelines were made applicable to the felony offense listed is 1/1/99.

	Felonies by MCL #	Group	Class	Description	Stat Max	Effective Date*
	257. 602 a (4)	Person	D	Fleeing and eluding – second degree	10	
	257. 602 a (5)	Person	C	Fleeing and eluding – first degree	15	
	257. 616 a (2) (b)	Pub saf	G	Using a signal preemption device	2	6/14/04
	257. 616 a (2) (c)	Pub saf	E	Using a signal preemption device causing a traffic accident	5	6/14/04
	257. 616 a (2) (d)	Person	D	Using a signal preemption device causing serious impairment of a body function	10	6/14/04
	257. 616 a (2) (e)	Person	C	Using a signal preemption device causing death	15	6/14/04
	257. 616 a (2) (f)	Pub ord	G	Selling or purchasing a signal preemption device	2	6/14/04
	257. 617	Person	E	Failure to stop at scene of a serious personal injury accident	5	Substituted for by 257.617(2)
	257. 617 (2)	Person	E	Failure to stop at scene of accident resulting in serious impairment or death	5	2/1/02
	257. 617 (3)	Person	C	Failure to stop at scene of accident resulting in death when at fault	15	2/1/02
MCL 777.12f						
	257. 625 (4)	Person	C	OUIL – causing death	15	Substituted for by 257.625(4)(a)
	257. 625 (4) (a)	Person	C	Operating a vehicle under the influence or while impaired causing death	15	3/28/01
	257. 625 (4) (a)	Person	C	Operating a vehicle while intoxicated or impaired causing death	15	9/30/03
	257. 625 (4) (b)	Person	B	OUIL – causing death to emergency personnel	20	3/28/01
	257. 625 (4) (b)	Person	B	Operating a vehicle under the influence or while impaired causing death to certain persons	20	10/1/01
	257. 625 (4) (b)	Person	B	Operating a vehicle while intoxicated or impaired causing death to certain persons	20	9/30/03
	257. 625 (5)	Person	E	OUIL – causing serious impairment of body function	5	
	257. 625 (5)	Person	E	Operating a vehicle under the influence or while impaired causing serious impairment	5	3/28/01
	257. 625 (5)	Person	E	Operating a vehicle while intoxicated or impaired causing serious impairment	5	9/30/03
	257. 625 (7) (a) (ii)	Person	E	Operating under the influence/while impaired with a minor in the vehicle – subsequent offense	5	10/1/00
	257. 625 (7) (a) (ii)	Person	E	Operating while intoxicated or impaired with a minor in the vehicle – subsequent offense	5	9/30/03
	257. 625 (7) (d)	Pub saf	E	OUIL – third offense	5	
	257. 625 (8) (c)	Pub saf	E	Operating a vehicle under the influence – third or subsequent offense	5	Eff. until 9/30/03, replaced by (9)(c)
	257. 625 (9) (b)	Person	E	Allowing a vehicle to be operated while under the influence or impaired causing death	5	Eff. until 9/30/03, replaced by (10)(b)
	257. 625 (9) (c)	Person	G	Allowing a vehicle to be operated while under the influence/impaired - serious impairment	2	Eff. until 9/30/03, replaced by (10)(c)
	257. 625 (9) (c)	Pub saf	E	Operating a vehicle while intoxicated/with presence of drugs – third or subsequent offense	5	9/30/03
	257. 625 (10) (b)	Person	E	Allowing a vehicle to be operated while intoxicated or impaired causing death	5	9/30/03
	257. 625 (10) (c)	Pub saf	E	Impaired driving – third or subsequent offense	5	Eff. until 9/30/03, replaced by (11)(c)
	257. 625 (10) (c)	Person	G	Allowing a vehicle to be operated while intoxicated or impaired causing serious impairment	2	9/30/03
	257. 625 (11) (c)	Pub saf	E	Operating a vehicle while impaired – third or subsequent offense	5	9/30/03
	257. 625 k (7)	Pub saf	D	Knowingly providing false information concerning an ignition interlock device	10	10/1/00

Lightly shaded lines indicate that the statute governing the felony offense described on that line has been amended, deleted, or replaced.

Updated April 2007

*Unless otherwise noted, the date on which the statutory guidelines were made applicable to the felony offense listed is 1/1/99.

Felonies by MCL #	Group	Class	Description	Stat Max	Effective Date*
257. 625 k (9)	Pub saf	D	Failure to report that an ignition interlock device does not meet legal requirements	10	10/1/00
257. 625 k (9)	Pub saf	D	Failure to report illegal ignition interlock device	10	10/1/01
257. 625 m (5)	Pub saf	E	Commercial drunk driving – third or subsequent offense	5	10/1/00
257. 625 n (10)	Pub ord	G	Disposing of vehicle to avoid forfeiture	4	
MCL 777.12g					
257. 626 c	Person	G	Felonious driving	2	2/1/02
257. 653 a (3)	Person	G	Failure to use due care and caution causing injury to emergency personnel	2	3/28/01
257. 653 a (4)	Person	C	Failure to use due care and caution causing death to emergency personnel	15	3/28/01
257. 744 a	Pub saf	D	False statement in citation – perjury	15	
MCL 777.12h					
257. 902	Pub saf	E	Motor vehicle code violations	5	
257. 903 (1)	Property	E	Motor vehicle code – false certification – first offense	5	
257. 903 (2)	Property	E	Motor vehicle code – false certification – second offense	7	
257. 903 (3)	Property	D	Motor vehicle code – false certification – third or subsequent offense	15	
257. 904 (4)	Person	C	Operating a vehicle without a license causing death	15	10/1/00
257. 904 (5)	Person	E	Operating a vehicle without a license causing serious impairment	5	10/1/00
257. 904 (7)	Person	G	Allowing a vehicle to be operated without a license causing serious impairment	2	10/1/00
257. 904 (7)	Person	E	Allowing a vehicle to be operated without a license causing death	5	10/1/00
MCL 777.12j					
257. 1353 (2)	Pub trst	H	Motor vehicle – fail to record material matter – subsequent offense	2	
257. 1354 (2)	Pub trst	H	Motor vehicle – general violations – subsequent offense	2	
257. 1355	Pub trst	H	Motor vehicle – fail to record transaction/falsify records	2	
MCL 777.12k					
259. 80 f (3)	Pub saf	D	Possessing weapon in sterile area of commercial airport	10	3/31/03
259. 83 (2) (b)	Pub saf	G	Aircraft – failure to comply with certification requirements – second violation	2	3/31/03
259. 83 (2) (c)	Pub saf	F	Aircraft – failure to comply with certification requirements – third or subsequent violation	4	3/31/03
259. 83 b (2) (a)	Pub saf	F	Conducting flight operations without certificate	4	3/31/03
259. 83 b (2) (b)	Pub saf	E	Conducting flight operations without certificate – second violation	5	3/31/03
259. 83 b (2) (c)	Pub saf	D	Conducting flight operations without certificate – third or subsequent violation	10	3/31/03
259. 183	Property	E	Aircraft – unlawful taking or tampering	5	
259. 185 (4)	Person	C	Operating or serving as crew of aircraft while under the influence causing death	15	10/1/00
259. 185 (5)	Person	E	Operating or serving as crew of aircraft while under the influence causing serious impairment	5	3/28/01

Lightly shaded lines indicate that the statute governing the felony offense described on that line has been amended, deleted, or replaced.

Updated April 2007

*Unless otherwise noted, the date on which the statutory guidelines were made applicable to the felony offense listed is 1/1/99.

Felonies by MCL #	Group	Class	Description	Stat Max	Effective Date*
259. 185 (8)	Pub saf	G	Operating/serving as crew of aircraft while under the influence – third or subsequent offense	5	
259. 185 (8)	Pub saf	E	Operating/serving as crew of aircraft while under the influence – third or subsequent offense	5	3/28/01
MCL 777.12m					
285. 82	Pub trst	H	Grain dealers act violations	5	Substituted for by 285.83
285. 83	Pub trst	H	Grain dealers act violations	5	3/31/03
285. 279	Pub trst	E	Falsely obtaining money – agricultural land	10	Deleted, 2001 PAs 133, 136 & 160
285. 279 (2) (c)	Property	E	False pretenses under family farm development act involving $1,000 to $20,000 or with priors	5	2/1/02
285. 279 (2) (d)	Property	D	False pretenses under family farm development act involving $20,000 or more or with priors	10	2/1/02
286. 228 (6)	Pub ord	E	Insect pest and plant disease - intentional violation with intent to damage natural resources	5	9/1/05
286. 260 (4)	Pub ord	E	Insect pest and plant disease - intentional violation with intent to damage natural resources	5	9/1/05
286. 455 (2)	Pub saf	G	Agriculture – hazardous substance	5	
286. 929 (4)	Pub trst	G	Organic products act violations	4	3/28/01
287. 77 (1)	Pub saf	H	Agriculture – livestock condemnation	4	
287. 323 (1)	Person	C	Dangerous animal causing death	15	
287. 323 (2)	Person	G	Dangerous animal causing serious injury	4	
287. 679	Pub ord	H	Dead animals	1	
287. 679	Pub ord	H	Dead animals – third or subsequent violation	1	10/1/01
287. 744 (1)	Pub ord	G	Animal industry act violations	5	
287. 855	Pub saf	G	Agriculture – contaminating livestock/false statement/violation of quarantine	5	
287. 967 (5)	Pub ord	G	Cervidae producer violations	4	10/1/00
288. 223	Pub saf	G	Sale or labeling of oleomargarine violations	3	Repealed, 2001 PA 267, Eff. 2/8/02 Deleted, 2005 PA 54, Eff. 9/1/05
288. 257	Pub saf	G	Margarine violations	3	Repealed, 2001 PA 267, Eff. 2/8/02 Deleted, 2005 PA 54, Eff. 9/1/05
288. 284	Pub trst	H	Selling falsely branded cheese	2	Repealed, 2001 PA 267, Eff. 2/8/02 Deleted, 2005 PA 54, Eff. 9/1/05
289. 5107 (2)	Pub saf	F	Adulterated, misbranded, or falsely identified food	4	10/1/00
MCL 777.12n					
290. 629 (1)	Person	G	Weights and measures – assaults enforcement officer	2	
290. 631 (3)	Pub trst	G	Weights and measures	5	
290. 650	Person	G	Motor fuels – assaulting/obstructing director or authorized representative	2	
290. 650 b (3)	Pub trst	H	Motor fuels violations	2	
MCL 777.13b					
324. 1608	Person	G	Resisting and obstructing conservation officer	2	
324. 2157 (1) (c)	Property	E	Damage to state property involving $1,000 to $20,000 or with prior convictions	5	1/1/02

Lightly shaded lines indicate that the statute governing the felony offense described on that line has been amended, deleted, or replaced.

Updated April 2007

*Unless otherwise noted, the date on which the statutory guidelines were made applicable to the felony offense listed is 1/1/99.

Felonies by MCL #	Group	Class	Description	Stat Max	Effective Date*
324. 2157 (1) (d)	Property	D	Damage to state property involving $20,000 or more or with prior convictions	10	1/1/02
324. 2157 (3)	Property	H	State owned property – damages of $1,000 or more	180 days	Deleted, 2001 PA 156, Eff. 1/1/02
MCL 777.13c					
324. 3115 (2)	Pub saf	H	Waste discharge violations – second offense	2	
324. 3115 (2)	Pub saf	H	Waste discharge violations	2	1/1/01
324. 3115 (4)	Pub saf	G	Waste discharge violations – substantial endangerment	5	1/1/01
324. 5531 (4)	Pub saf	H	Knowingly releasing pollutants	2	
324. 5531 (5)	Pub saf	G	Knowingly releasing pollutants – causing death or serious bodily injury	6	
324. 5531 (6)	Pub saf	C	Knowingly releasing pollutants – resulting in death or serious bodily injury	15	
324. 8905 (2)	Pub saf	H	Infectious waste/pathological waste/sharps – littering violation	2	
324. 8905 (3)	Pub saf	G	Infectious waste/pathological waste/sharps – littering violation – subsequent offense	5	
324. 11151 (2)	Pub saf	H	Hazardous waste violations – subsequent offense	2	
324. 11151 (3)	Pub saf	H	Hazardous waste violation – with disregard for human life	2	
324. 11151 (3)	Pub saf	G	Hazardous waste violation – with extreme indifference for human life	5	
324. 11549 (2)	Pub saf	G	Solid waste - importing from foreign country	2	3/13/06
324. 12116 (2)	Pub saf	H	Waste – false statement or entry in a license application	2	
324. 20139 (3)	Pub saf	H	Hazardous waste – knowingly releases or causes the release	2	
324. 21324 (1)	Pub saf	G	Underground storage tanks – false or misleading information	5	
324. 21548 (1)	Pub trst	H	False statement, report, claim, bid, work invoice, or other request for payment	5	
MCL 777.13d					
324. 30316 (3)	Pub saf	H	NREPA violation – subsequent offense	2	
324. 31525	Person	G	NREPA – imminent danger of death or serious injury – subsequent offense	2	
324. 33939 (1)	Pub trst	H	NREPA violation for commercial purposes	2	
MCL 777.13e					
324. 40118 (11)	Pub ord	G	Wildlife conservation – buying or selling protected animals – subsequent offense	4	
324. 41309	Property	E	Possession or release of genetically engineered, nonnative, or prohibited fish	5	Eff. 3/30/04 to 9/1/05, 2005 PA 81
324. 41309 (3) (b)	Property	G	Possession of prohibited species	2	9/1/05
324. 41309 (4) (a)	Property	G	Possession of restricted or nonnative species - intent to damage resources	2	9/1/05
324. 41309 (4) (b)	Property	F	Possession of prohibited or genetically engineered species - intent to damage resources	4	9/1/05
324. 41309 (8)	Property	G	Introduction of prohibited or genetically engineered species - knowing identity of organism	2	9/1/05
324. 41309 (9) (a)	Property	G	Introduction of restricted or nonnative species - knowing introduction is unlawful	2	9/1/05
324. 41309 (9) (b)	Property	F	Introduction of prohibited or genetically engineered species - knowing introduction is unlawful	4	9/1/05

Lightly shaded lines indicate that the statute governing the felony offense described on that line has been amended, deleted, or replaced.

Updated April 2007

*Unless otherwise noted, the date on which the statutory guidelines were made applicable to the felony offense listed is 1/1/99.

Felonies by MCL #	Group	Class	Description	Stat Max	Effective Date*
324. 41309 (10) (a)	Property	F	Introduction of restricted or nonnative species - intent to damage resources	3	9/1/05
324. 41309 (10) (b)	Property	E	Introduction of prohibited or genetically engineered species - intent to damage resources	5	9/1/05
324. 48738 (4)	Property	E	Possession, importation, or planting of genetically engineered fish	5	3/30/04
324. 51120 (2)	Property	H	Removing forest products over $2,500	3	
324. 51512	Pub saf	D	Willfully setting forest fires	10	
324. 52908 (1) (c)	Property	E	Damage to plant involving $1,000 to $20,000 or with prior convictions	5	1/1/02
324. 52908 (1) (d)	Property	D	Damage to plant involving $20,000 or more or with prior convictions	10	1/1/02
324. 52908 (3)	Property	H	Illegally cutting, removing, or transporting tree or other plant involving $1,000 or more	180 days	Eff. 10/1/00 to 1/1/02, 2001 PA 156
MCL 777.13f					
324. 61511	Pub trst	G	False affidavit under NREPA	5	
324. 61521 (1)	Pub trst	G	Evading rule under NREPA	3	
MCL 777.13g					
324. 76107 (3)	Pub ord	D	Removing or mutilating human body from Great Lakes bottomland	10	1/1/02
324. 76107 (4)	Pub trst	G	Recovering abandoned property in Great Lakes without permit	2	Deleted, 2001 PA 156, Eff. 1/1/02
324. 76107 (4) (c)	Property	E	Recovering abandoned property in Great Lakes - value of $1,000 to $20,000 or w/ priors	5	1/1/02
324. 76107 (4) (d)	Property	D	Recovering abandoned property in Great Lakes - value of $20,000+ or with prior convictions	10	1/1/02
324. 80130 d (1)	Pub ord	H	False representation to obtain personal information	4	
324. 80130 d (2)	Pub ord	G	False representation to obtain personal information – second offense	7	
324. 80130 d (3)	Pub ord	C	False representation to obtain personal information – third or subsequent offense	15	
324. 80134 a (2)	Person	E	Failure to stop at scene of marine accident causing serious impairment or death	5	4/1/04
324. 80134 a (3)	Person	C	Failure to stop at scene of marine accident causing death when at fault	15	4/1/04
324. 80172	Person	G	Negligent crippling or homicide by vessel	2	
324. 80173	Person	G	Felonious operation of a vessel	2	
324. 80176 (4)	Person	C	Operating a vessel under the influence causing death	15	
324. 80176 (5)	Person	E	Operating a vessel under the influence causing long-term incapacitating injury	5	
324. 80176 (5)	Person	E	Operating a vessel under the influence causing serious impairment	5	7/1/01
324. 80177 (1) (c)	Pub saf	E	Operating a vessel under the influence – third or subsequent offense	5	
324. 80319 a (1)	Pub ord	H	False representation to obtain personal information	4	
324. 80319 a (2)	Pub ord	G	False representation to obtain personal information – second offense	7	
324. 80319 a (3)	Pub ord	C	False representation to obtain personal information – third or subsequent offense	15	
324. 81120 (1)	Pub ord	H	False representation to obtain personal information	4	
324. 81120 (2)	Pub ord	G	False representation to obtain personal information – second offense	7	

Lightly shaded lines indicate that the statute governing the felony offense described on that line has been amended, deleted, or replaced.

Updated April 2007

*Unless otherwise noted, the date on which the statutory guidelines were made applicable to the felony offense listed is 1/1/99.

Felonies by MCL #	Group	Class	Description	Stat Max	Effective Date*
324. 81120 (3)	Pub ord	C	False representation to obtain personal information – third or subsequent offense	15	
324. 81134 (6)	Pub saf	E	Operating an ORV under the influence – third or subsequent offense	4	
324. 81134 (6)	Pub saf	E	Operating an ORV under the influence – third or subsequent offense	5	7/1/01
324. 81134 (7)	Person	C	Operating an ORV under the influence causing death	15	10/1/00
324. 81134 (8)	Person	E	Operating an ORV under the influence causing serious impairment	5	10/1/00
324. 82126 c (1)	Person	G	Operating a snowmobile carelessly or negligently causing death or serious impairment	2	10/1/00
324. 82126 c (2)	Person	G	Operating a snowmobile without regard to safety causing serious impairment	2	10/1/00
324. 82127 (4)	Person	C	Operating a snowmobile under the influence causing death	15	
324. 82127 (5)	Person	E	Operating a snowmobile under the influence causing long-term incapacitating injury	5	
324. 82127 (5)	Person	E	Operating a snowmobile under the influence causing serious impairment	5	7/1/01
324. 82128 (1) (c)	Pub saf	E	Operating a snowmobile under the influence – third or subsequent offense	5	
324. 82160 (1)	Pub ord	H	False representation to obtain personal information	4	
324. 82160 (2)	Pub ord	G	False representation to obtain personal information – second offense	7	
324. 82160 (3)	Pub ord	C	False representation to obtain personal information – third or subsequent offense	15	
MCL 777.13j					
328. 232	Property	E	Conversion of funeral contracts	5	
330. 1944	Pub saf	F	Criminal sexual psychopath leaving state without permission	4	1/9/07
MCL 777.13k					
333. 2685	Person	E	Use of a live human embryo, fetus for nontherapeutic research	5	See MCL 333.2691
333. 2688	Person	E	Research on dead embryo or fetus without mother's consent	5	See MCL 333.2691
333. 2689	Person	E	Abortion to obtain embryo	5	See MCL 333.2691
333. 2690	Person	E	Sale or delivery of fetus or embryo	5	See MCL 333.2691
333. 2813 (3)	Pub trst	F	Unauthorized disclosure of social security number – subsequent offense	4	10/1/00
333. 2835 (9)	Pub trst	G	Disclosing confidential information – abortion	3	
333. 5210	Person	F	AIDS – sexual penetration with uninformed partner	4	
333. 5661	Person	F	Fraud resulting in patient death	4	
MCL 777.13m					
333. 7340	CS	F	Sale/distribution/delivery of product w/ ephedrine/pseudoephedrine by mail/internet/telephone	4	10/1/06
333. 7341 (8)	CS	G	Delivery or manufacture of imitation controlled substance	2	
333. 7401 (2) (a) (i)	CS	A	Delivery or manufacture of 650 or more grams by juvenile	LIFE	
333. 7401 (2) (a) (i)	CS	A	Delivery/manufacture of 650 or more grams of certain schedule 1 or 2 controlled substances	LIFE	10/1/00
333. 7401 (2) (a) (i)	CS	A	Delivery/manufacture of 1,000 or more grams of certain schedule 1 or 2 substances	LIFE	3/1/03

Lightly shaded lines indicate that the statute governing the felony offense described on that line has been amended, deleted, or replaced.

*Unless otherwise noted, the date on which the statutory guidelines were made applicable to the felony offense listed is 1/1/99.

Felonies by MCL #	Group	Class	Description	Stat Max	Effective Date*
333. 7401 (2) (a) (ii)	CS	A	Delivery/manufacture of 225+ but less than 650 grams of certain schedule 1 or 2 substances	30	10/1/00
333. 7401 (2) (a) (ii)	CS	A	Delivery/manufacture of 450+ but less than 1,000 grams of certain schedule 1 or 2 drugs	30	3/1/03
333. 7401 (2) (a) (iii)	CS	B	Delivery/manufacture of 50+ but less than 225 grams of certain schedule 1 or 2 substances	20	
333. 7401 (2) (a) (iii)	CS	B	Delivery/manufacture of 50+ but less than 450 grams of certain schedule 1 or 2 substances	20	3/1/03
333. 7401 (2) (a) (iv)	CS	D	Delivery/manufacture of less than 50 grams of certain schedule 1 or 2 controlled substances	20	
333. 7401 (2) (b)	CS	E	Delivery or manufacture of schedule 1, 2, or 3 controlled substance except marijuana	7	
333. 7401 (2) (b) (i)	CS	B	Delivery or manufacture of methamphetamine	20	1/1/01
333. 7401 (2) (b) (i)	CS	B	Delivery or manufacture of methamphetamine or 3, 4-methylenedioxymethamphetamine	20	4/1/03
333. 7401 (2) (b) (ii)	CS	E	Delivery or manufacture of certain schedule 1, 2, or 3 controlled substances	7	1/1/01
333. 7401 (2) (c)	CS	F	Delivery or manufacture of schedule 4 controlled substance	4	
333. 7401 (2) (d) (i)	CS	C	Delivery or manufacture of 45 or more kilograms of marijuana	15	
333. 7401 (2) (d) (ii)	CS	D	Delivery or manufacture of 5 or more but less than 45 kilograms of marijuana	7	
333. 7401 (2) (d) (iii)	CS	F	Delivery or manufacture of less than 5 kilograms or 20 plants of marijuana	4	
333. 7401 (2) (e)	CS	G	Delivery or manufacture of schedule 5 controlled substance	2	
333. 7401 (2) (f)	CS	D	Delivery or manufacture of an official or counterfeit prescription form	20	Deleted, 2001 PA 236, Eff. 1/6/03
333. 7401 (2) (f)	CS	D	Delivery or manufacture of prescription or counterfeit form other than official	7	1/6/03
333. 7401 (2) (f)	CS	D	Delivery or manufacture of prescription form or counterfeit prescription form	7	3/1/03
333. 7401 (2) (g)	CS	D	Delivery or manufacture of prescription or counterfeit form (other than official)	7	Rewritten as .7401(2)(f), 2001 PA 236
333. 7401 a	Person	B	Delivering a controlled substance with intent to commit criminal sexual conduct	20	10/1/00
333. 7401 a	Person	B	Delivering a controlled substance or GBL with intent to commit criminal sexual conduct	20	1/1/01
333. 7401 b (3) (a)	CS	E	Delivery or manufacture of GBL	7	1/1/01
333. 7401 b (3) (b)	CS	G	Possession of GBL	2	1/1/01
333. 7401 c (2) (a)	CS	D	Operating or maintaining controlled substance laboratory	10	1/1/01
333. 7401 c (2) (b)	CS	B	Operating or maintaining controlled substance laboratory in presence of minor	20	1/1/01
333. 7401 c (2) (c)	CS	B	Operating or maintaining controlled substance laboratory involving hazardous waste	20	1/1/01
333. 7401 c (2) (d)	CS	B	Operating or maintaining controlled substance laboratory near certain places	20	1/1/01
333. 7401 c (2) (e)	CS	A	Operating/maintaining controlled substance laboratory involving firearm/other harmful device	25	1/1/01
333. 7401 c (2) (f)	CS	B	Operating or maintaining controlled substance laboratory involving methamphetamine	20	4/1/04
333. 7402 (2) (a)	CS	D	Delivery or manufacture of an imitation controlled substance	10	
333. 7402 (2) (a)	CS	D	Delivery or manufacture of certain imitation controlled substances	10	1/1/01
333. 7402 (2) (b)	CS	E	Delivery or manufacture of schedule 1, 2, or 3 imitation controlled substance	5	
333. 7402 (2) (c)	CS	F	Delivery or manufacture of imitation schedule 4 controlled substance	4	

Lightly shaded lines indicate that the statute governing the felony offense described on that line has been amended, deleted, or replaced.

MCL #

Updated April 2007

*Unless otherwise noted, the date on which the statutory guidelines were made applicable to the felony offense listed is 1/1/99.

Felonies by MCL #	Group	Class	Description	Stat Max	Effective Date*
333. 7402 (2) (d)	CS	G	Delivery or manufacture of imitation schedule 5 controlled substance	2	
333. 7402 (2) (e)	CS	C	Delivery or manufacture of controlled substance analogue	15	
333. 7403 (2) (a) (i)	CS	A	Possession of 650 or more grams of certain schedule 1 or 2 controlled substances by juvenile	LIFE	
333. 7403 (2) (a) (i)	CS	A	Possession of 1,000 or more grams of certain schedule 1 or 2 controlled substances	LIFE	3/1/03
333. 7403 (2) (a) (ii)	CS	A	Possession of 225+ but less than 650 grams of certain schedule 1 or 2 controlled substances	30	10/1/00
333. 7403 (2) (a) (ii)	CS	A	Possession of 450+ but less than 1,000 grams of certain schedule 1 or 2 substances	30	3/1/03
333. 7403 (2) (a) (iii)	CS	B	Possession of 50+ but less than 225 grams of certain schedule 1 or 2 controlled substances	20	
333. 7403 (2) (a) (iii)	CS	B	Possession of 50+ but less than 450 grams of certain schedule 1 or 2 controlled substances	20	3/1/03
333. 7403 (2) (a) (iv)	CS	G	Possession of 25+ but less than 50 grams of certain schedule 1 or 2 controlled substances	4	
333. 7403 (2) (a) (v)	CS	G	Possession of less than 25 grams of certain schedule 1 or 2 controlled substances	4	
333. 7403 (2) (b)	CS	G	Possession of certain schedule 1, 2, 3, or 4 controlled substances or analogue	2	
333. 7403 (2) (b) (i)	CS	D	Possession of methamphetamine	10	1/1/01
333. 7403 (2) (b) (i)	CS	D	Possession of methamphetamine or 3, 4-methylenedioxymethamphetamine	10	4/1/03
333. 7403 (2) (b) (ii)	CS	G	Possession of certain schedule 1, 2, 3, or 4 controlled substances or analogue	2	1/1/01
333. 7403 (2) (e)	CS	H	Possession of official prescription form	1	Deleted, 2003 PA 311, Eff. 4/1/04
333. 7405 (a)	CS	G	Controlled substance violations by licensee	2	
333. 7405 (b)	CS	G	Manufacturing or distribution violations by licensee	2	
333. 7405 (c)	CS	G	Refusing lawful inspection	2	
333. 7405 (d)	CS	G	Maintaining drug house	2	
333. 7407 (1) (a)	CS	G	Controlled substance violations by licensee	4	
333. 7407 (1) (b)	CS	G	Use of fictitious, revoked, or suspended license number	4	
333. 7407 (1) (c)	CS	G	Obtaining controlled substance by fraud	4	
333. 7407 (1) (d)	CS	G	False reports under controlled substance article	4	
333. 7407 (1) (e)	CS	G	Possession of counterfeiting implements	4	
333. 7407 (1) (f)	CS	F	Disclosing or obtaining prescription information	4	Deleted, 2001 PA 236, Eff. 1/6/03
333. 7407 (1) (f)	CS	F	Possession of counterfeit prescription form	4	1/6/03
333. 7407 (1) (g)	CS	F	Possession of counterfeit prescription form	4	Rewritten as .7407(1)(f), 2001 PA 236
333. 7407 (2)	CS	G	Refusing to furnish records under controlled substance article	4	
MCL 777.18					
333. 7410	CS	SPEC	Controlled substance delivery or distribution to minors or students	Variable	
333. 7410	CS	SPEC	Controlled substance offense on or near school property	Variable	10/1/00
333. 7410	CS	SPEC	Controlled substance offense or offense involving GBL on or near school property	Variable	1/1/01

Lightly shaded lines indicate that the statute governing the felony offense described on that line has been amended, deleted, or replaced.

MCL #

Updated April 2007

*Unless otherwise noted, the date on which the statutory guidelines were made applicable to the felony offense listed is 1/1/99.

Felonies by MCL #	Group	Class	Description	Stat Max	Effective Date*
333. 7410	CS	SPEC	Controlled substance offense or offense involving GBL on or near school property or library	Variable	As amended, 2006 PA 553, Eff. 3/30/07
MCL 777.13m					
333. 7410 a	CS	G	Controlled substance offense in or near a park	2	10/1/00
333. 7410 a	CS	G	Controlled substance offense or offense involving GBL in or near a park	2	1/1/01
MCL 777.18					
333. 7413 (2)	Pub trst	SPEC	Subsequent controlled substance violations	Variable	
333. 7413 (3)	Pub trst	SPEC	Subsequent controlled substance violations	Variable	
333. 7416 (1) (a)	CS	SPEC	Recruiting or inducing a minor to commit a controlled substance felony	Variable	
MCL 777.13n					
333. 10204 (1)	Pub ord	F	Transferring a human organ for valuable consideration	4	
333. 10204 (4)	Pub saf	F	Removal of a human organ by an unauthorized individual	4	9/1/99
333. 10205	Pub saf	F	Removal of a human organ in an unapproved facility	4	9/1/99
333. 13738 (2)	Pub saf	F	Waste disposal violations – second offense	5	
333. 13738 (3)	Pub saf	F	Disposing of waste – indifference to human life	2	
333. 13738 (3)	Pub saf	B	Disposing of waste – extreme indifference to human life	20	
333. 16170 (3)	Pub trst	F	False representation – health professional recovery program	4	
333. 16294	Pub saf	F	Health profession – unauthorized practice	4	
333. 17764 (3)	Pub saf	F	Adulterate, misbrand, remove, or substitute a drug or device	2	10/12/04
333. 17764 (4)	Pub saf	F	Adulterate, misbrand, remove, or substitute a drug or device causing personal injury	4	10/12/04
333. 17764 (5)	Pub saf	E	Adulterate/misbrand/remove/substitute a drug/device - serious impairment of a body function	5	10/12/04
333. 17764 (6)	Pub saf	C	Adulterate, misbrand, remove, or substitute a drug or device causing death	15	10/12/04
333. 17766 a (2)	CS	F	Possession of steroids – subsequent offense	4	Deleted, 2003 PA 309, Eff. 4/1/04
333. 17766 a (3)	CS	E	Delivery or manufacture of steroids	7	Deleted, 2003 PA 309, Eff. 4/1/04
333. 17766 a (4)	CS	G	Delivery of imitation steroids	7	Deleted, 2003 PA 309, Eff. 4/1/04
333. 17766 c (2)	CS	G	Possession of more than 10 grams ephedrine	2	Eff. 1/1/99 to 4/1/04, 2003 PA 309
333. 17766 c (2)	CS	G	Possession of more than 12 grams ephedrine or pseudoephedrine	2	4/1/04
333. 20142 (5)	Pub trst	F	False statement – application licensure health facility	4	
333. 21792	Pub trst	G	Nursing homes – referral fees/bribing officials/accepting bribes	4	
MCL 777.13p					
338. 823	Pub trst	F	Private detective license act violation	4	10/1/02
338. 1053	Pub trst	F	Private security business and security alarm act violation	4	3/28/01
338. 3434 a (2)	Pub trst	F	Unauthorized disclosure of a social security number – subsequent offense	4	10/1/00

Lightly shaded lines indicate that the statute governing the felony offense described on that line has been amended, deleted, or replaced.

*Unless otherwise noted, the date on which the statutory guidelines were made applicable to the felony offense listed is 1/1/99.

Felonies by MCL #	Group	Class	Description	Stat Max	Effective Date*
338. 3471 (1) (b)	Pub trst	G	Michigan immigration clerical assistant act violation - subsequent offense	2	3/30/05
338. 3621 (1) (b)	Pub trst	G	Michigan immigration clerical assistant act violation - subsequent offense	2	Substituted for by MCL 338.3471(1)(b)
339. 735	Pub trst	E	Unauthorized practice of public accounting	5	12/19/05
380. 1230 d (3) (a)	Pub saf	G	Failure by school employee to report charge or conviction	2	9/29/05
380. 1816	Pub trst	F	Improper use of bond proceeds	4	3/30/05
388. 936	Pub trst	F	Knowingly making false statement – school district loans	4	
388. 962	Pub trst	F	Knowingly making false statement – school district loans	4	Deleted, 2005 PA 125, Eff. 9/29/05
388. 1237	Pub trst	F	Making false statement to obtain qualification of school bond issue/improper use of proceeds	4	Substituted for by MCL 388.1937
388. 1937	Pub trst	F	Making false statement to obtain qualification of school bond issue/improper use of proceeds	4	9/29/05
MCL 777.14a					
400. 60 (2)	Property	H	Welfare – obtaining over $500 by failure to inform	4	
400. 603	Pub trst	G	Medicaid fraud – false statement in benefit/concealing information	4	
400. 604	Pub trst	G	Medicaid fraud – kickback/referral fees	4	
400. 605	Pub trst	G	Medicaid fraud – false statement regarding institutions	4	
400. 606	Property	E	Medicaid fraud – conspiracy	10	
400. 607	Pub trst	G	Medicaid fraud – false claim/medically unnecessary	4	
400. 609	Property	D	Medicaid fraud – fourth offense	10	
400. 713 (13)	Pub saf	H	Adult foster care – unlicensed facility – first offense	2	
400. 713 (13)	Pub saf	H	Adult foster care – unlicensed facility	2	7/1/01
400. 713 (13)	Pub saf	F	Adult foster care – unlicensed facility – second or subsequent violation	5	
400. 713 (13)	Pub saf	F	Adult foster care – unlicensed facility – subsequent violation	5	7/1/01
400. 722 (4)	Pub saf	F	Adult foster care – maintaining operation after refusal of licensure	5	
MCL 777.14b					
408. 1035 (5)	Pub saf	I	MIOSHA violation – first offense	1	
408. 1035 (5)	Person	H	MIOSHA violation causing employee death	1	10/1/00
408. 1035 (5)	Pub saf	G	MIOSHA violation – second offense	3	
408. 1035 (5)	Person	G	MIOSHA violation causing employee death – subsequent offense	3	10/1/00
408. 1035 a (5)	Pub saf	I	MIOSHA – violations/writs of mandamus/assaults – first offense	1	
408. 1035 a (5)	Person	H	MIOSHA violation causing employee death	1	10/1/00
408. 1035 a (5)	Pub saf	G	MIOSHA – violations/writs of mandamus/assaults – second offense	3	
408. 1035 a (5)	Person	G	MIOSHA violation causing employee death – subsequent offense	3	10/1/00
409. 122 (2)	Pub ord	G	Employment of children during certain hours – second offense	2	

Lightly shaded lines indicate that the statute governing the felony offense described on that line has been amended, deleted, or replaced.

Updated April 2007

*Unless otherwise noted, the date on which the statutory guidelines were made applicable to the felony offense listed is 1/1/99.

	Felonies by MCL #	Group	Class	Description	Stat Max	Effective Date*
	409. 122 (2)	Person	G	Employment of children during certain hours – second offense	2	10/1/00
	409. 122 (2)	Person	E	Employment of children during certain hours – third or subsequent offense	10	
	409. 122 (3)	Person	D	Employment of children in child sexually abusive activity	20	
MCL 777.14c						
	421. 54 (a) (ii) (B)	Property	H	Unemployment comp fraud – failure to comply with act/rule $25,000-$100,000	2	
	421. 54 (a) (ii) (C)	Property	G	Unemployment comp fraud – failure to comply with act/rule over $100,000	5	
	421. 54 (a) (iv) (B)	Property	H	Unemployment comp fraud – willful violation of act/rule over $100,000	2	
	421. 54 (b) (ii) (B)	Property	H	Unemployment comp fraud – false statement or misrepresent over $25,000	2	
	421. 54 (b) (ii) (C)	Property	H	Unemployment comp fraud – false statement or misrepresentation without actual loss	2	
	421. 54 (d)	Property	H	Unemployment comp fraud – disclose confidential information for financial gain	1	
	421. 54 a	Property	G	Unemployment comp fraud – false statement as condition of employment	10	
	421. 54 b (b) (i)	Property	H	Unemployment comp fraud – conspiracy with loss of $25,000 or less	2	
	421. 54 b (b) (ii)	Property	G	Unemployment comp fraud – conspiracy with loss over $25,000	5	
	421. 54 b (b) (iii)	Property	H	Unemployment comp fraud – conspiracy with no actual loss	2	
	421. 54 c (b) (ii)	Property	H	Unemployment comp fraud – embezzlement of $25,000 to under $100,000	2	
	421. 54 c (b) (iii)	Property	G	Unemployment comp fraud – embezzlement of $100,000 or more	5	
	421. 54 c (b) (iv)	Property	H	Unemployment comp fraud – embezzlement with no actual loss	2	
	426. 106	Property	E	Marking of logs and timber – forging	5	
MCL 777.14d						
	431. 257	Pub trst	G	Racing, boxing and exhibition racing	2	
	431. 307 (8)	Pub trst	G	Horse racing – testifying falsely to commissioner while under oath	4	
	431. 330 (4)	Pub trst	G	Horse Racing – administering a drug that could affect racing condition	5	
	431. 332	Pub trst	G	Horse Racing – influencing or attempting to influence result of race	5	
	432. 30	Property	G	Lottery – forgery of tickets	5	
	432. 218	Pub ord	D	Casino gaming offenses	10	
MCL 777.14f						
	436. 1701 (2)	Person	D	Selling alcohol to a minor and causing death	10	
	436. 1909 (3)	Pub ord	H	Liquor violation	1	
	436. 1919	Pub ord	H	Fraudulent documents, labels, or stamps	1	
MCL 777.14g						
	438. 41	Property	E	Criminal usury	5	
	440. 9307 (4)	Property	G	Farming – illegal sale of secured products	3	

Lightly shaded lines indicate that the statute governing the felony offense described on that line has been amended, deleted, or replaced.

Updated April 2007

*Unless otherwise noted, the date on which the statutory guidelines were made applicable to the felony offense listed is 1/1/99.

	Felonies by MCL #	Group	Class	Description	Stat Max	Effective Date*
	440. 9320 (8)	Property	G	Farming – illegal sale of secured products	3	7/1/01
	440. 9501	Pub trst	E	Filing a false or fraudulent financing statement with the secretary of state	5	1/1/05
	442. 219	Pub trst	E	Sales – false statement	5	
	443. 50	Pub trst	E	Issuing warehouse receipt for goods not received	5	
	443. 52	Pub trst	E	Issuing duplicate warehouse receipt not so marked	5	
	444. 13	Pub trst	H	Warehousemen and warehouse receipts	2	
	444. 107	Pub trst	E	Warehouse certificates – willfully alter or destroy	5	
MCL 777.14h						
	445. 65	Pub ord	E	Identity theft	5	3/1/05
	445. 67	Pub ord	E	Obtain/possess/sell/transfer identifying info/falsify police report - intent to commit identity theft	5	3/1/05
	445. 408 (2)	Pub ord	F	Buying or selling stolen scrap metal	3	3/30/07
	445. 408 (3)	Pub ord	E	Buying/selling stolen scrap metal from utility pole, telecom corp/govt/utility property or jobsite	5	3/30/07
	445. 487 (2)	Pub ord	H	Precious metal and gem dealer failure to record material matter – subsequent offense	2	
	445. 488 (2)	Pub ord	H	Precious metal and gem dealer violations – subsequent offense	2	
	445. 489	Pub ord	H	Precious metal and gem dealer violations	2	
	445. 490	Pub ord	H	Precious metal and gem dealer failure to obtain a certificate of registration	2	
	445. 779	Pub ord	H	Antitrust violation	2	
	445. 1505	Pub trst	G	Franchise investment law – fraudulent filing/offers	7	
	445. 1508	Pub trst	G	Franchise investment law – sale without proper disclosure	7	
	445. 1513	Pub trst	G	Franchise investment law – illegal offers/sales	7	
	445. 1520	Pub trst	G	Franchise investment law – keeping records	7	
	445. 1521	Pub trst	G	Franchise investment law – false representation	7	
	445. 1523	Pub trst	G	Franchise investment law – false statements of material fact	7	
	445. 1525	Pub trst	G	Franchise investment law – false advertising	7	
	445. 1528	Pub trst	D	Pyramid/chain promotions – offer or sell	7	
	445. 1671	Pub trst	E	Mortgage brokers, lenders – knowingly giving a false statement	15	
	445. 1679	Pub trst	H	Mortgage brokers act – general violations	3	
	445. 2507 (2)	Pub ord	F	Violation of unsolicited commercial e-mail protection act in furtherance of crime	4	9/30/03
MCL 777.14j						
	450. 775	Pub ord	H	Corporations – minority and woman owned businesses	2	
	450. 795	Pub ord	H	Corporations – handicapper business opportunity act	2	
	451. 319	Pub trst	G	Securities, real estate, and debt management – violation	2	

Lightly shaded lines indicate that the statute governing the felony offense described on that line has been amended, deleted, or replaced.

Updated April 2007

*Unless otherwise noted, the date on which the statutory guidelines were made applicable to the felony offense listed is 1/1/99.

Felonies by MCL #	Group	Class	Description	Stat Max	Effective Date*
451. 434	Pub trst	H	Debt management act – licensee violations	2	
451. 501	Pub trst	E	Blue sky laws – fraudulent schemes/statements	10	See MCL 451.809
451. 502	Pub trst	E	Blue sky laws – investment advisor/agent fraud	10	See MCL 451.809
451. 503	Pub trst	E	Blue sky laws – make/sell false bullion/certificates	10	See MCL 451.809
451. 601	Pub trst	E	Blue sky laws – unregistered broker/dealer/agent/advisor	10	See MCL 451.809
451. 603 (h)	Pub trst	E	Blue sky laws – fail to notify administrator of sanctions	10	See MCL 451.809
451. 604 (a) (1) (J)	Pub trst	E	Blue sky laws – various violations	10	See MCL 451.809
451. 604 (a) (1) (K)	Pub trst	E	Blue sky laws – various violations	10	See MCL 451.809
451. 604 (a) (1) (L)	Pub trst	E	Blue sky laws – various violations	10	See MCL 451.809
451. 604 (a) (1) (M)	Pub trst	E	Blue sky laws – various violations	10	See MCL 451.809
451. 604 (a) (1) (N)	Pub trst	E	Blue sky laws – various violations	10	See MCL 451.809
451. 604 (a) (1) (O)	Pub trst	E	Blue sky laws – various violations	10	See MCL 451.809
451. 604 (a) (1) (P)	Pub trst	E	Blue sky laws – various violations	10	See MCL 451.809
451. 604 (a) (1) (Q)	Pub trst	E	Blue sky laws – various violations	10	See MCL 451.809
451. 604 (a) (1) (R)	Pub trst	E	Blue sky laws – various violations	10	See MCL 451.809
451. 604 (a) (1) (S)	Pub trst	E	Blue sky laws – various violations	10	See MCL 451.809
451. 604 (a) (1) (V)	Pub trst	E	Blue sky laws – various violations	10	See MCL 451.809
451. 604 (a) (1) (W)	Pub trst	E	Blue sky laws – various violations	10	See MCL 451.809
451. 604 (a) (1) (X)	Pub trst	E	Blue sky laws – various violations	10	See MCL 451.809
451. 604 (a) (1) (Y)	Pub trst	E	Blue sky laws – various violations	10	See MCL 451.809
451. 604 (a) (1) (Z)	Pub trst	E	Blue sky laws – various violations	10	See MCL 451.809
451. 701	Pub trst	E	Blue sky laws – offer/sell unregistered securities	10	See MCL 451.809
451. 802	Pub trst	E	Blue sky laws – unlawfully selling securities	10	See MCL 451.809
451. 804	Pub trst	E	Blue sky laws – willful false statements	10	See MCL 451.809
451. 805 (b)	Pub trst	E	Blue sky laws – false representation of administrative approval	10	See MCL 451.809
451. 806 (b)	Pub trst	E	Blue sky laws – improper disclosure by cor and sec bur employee	10	See MCL 451.809
MCL 777.14m					
462. 257 (1)	Person	A	Trains – endangering travel	LIFE	
462. 353 (5)	Pub saf	F	Operating a locomotive under the influence – third or subsequent offense	4	
462. 353 (5)	Pub saf	E	Operating a locomotive under the influence – third or subsequent offense	4	7/1/01
462. 353 (5)	Pub saf	E	Operating a locomotive under the influence – third or subsequent offense	5	4/1/03
462. 353 (6)	Person	C	Operating locomotive under the influence or while impaired causing death	15	4/1/03

Lightly shaded lines indicate that the statute governing the felony offense described on that line has been amended, deleted, or replaced.

*Unless otherwise noted, the date on which the statutory guidelines were made applicable to the felony offense listed is 1/1/99.

	Felonies by MCL #	Group	Class	Description	Stat Max	Effective Date*
	462. 353 (7)	Person	E	Operating locomotive under the influence or while impaired causing serious impairment	5	4/1/03
	472. 36	Pub saf	A	Street railways – obstruction of track	LIFE	
MCL 777.14p						
	482. 44	Property	H	Bills of lading – issuance for goods not received	5	
	482. 46	Property	H	Bills of lading – issuance of duplicate not so marked	5	
	482. 46	Property	H	Bills of lading – issuance of duplicate negotiable bill with intent to defraud	5	As amended, 2006 PA 251, Eff. 7/3/06
	482. 48	Property	H	Bills of lading – negotiation when goods not in carriers' possession	5	
	482. 49	Property	H	Bills of lading – inducing carrier to issue when goods have not been received	5	
	482. 50	Property	H	Bills of lading – issuance of non-negotiable bill not so marked	5	
	483. 226	Pub trst	E	Officer of a pipeline company – intent to defraud – stock	10	Deleted, 2006 PA 251, Eff. 7/3/06
	487. 1042 (1)	Pub trst	E	Money transmission - intentional false statement/misrepresentation/certification in record/document	5	7/3/06
	487. 1042 (2)	Pub trst	E	Criminal fraud in the conduct of money transmission services business	5	7/3/06
	487. 1042 (3)	Pub trst	E	Money transmission services act license violation	5	7/3/06
	487. 1505 (6)	Pub trst	E	BIDCO act – knowingly receiving money or property at an interest rate exceeding 25%	5	
	492. 137 (a)	Pub trst	H	Installment sales of motor vehicles	3	
	493. 56 a (13)	Pub trst	C	False statement in reports – secondary mortgage	15	
	493. 77 (2)	Pub trst	H	Regulatory loans	3	
	493. 77 (2)	Pub trst	H	Second mortgage loan act licensing violation	3	As amended, 2006 PA 251, Eff. 7/3/06
MCL 777.15a						
	500. 1325 (3)	Pub trst	E	Insurance code – knowingly misrepresenting false financial condition	5	
	500. 1371	Pub trst	H	Holding companies – violation	2	
	500. 1505 (2)	Pub trst	C	Insurance code – license and regulatory violations	15	
	500. 4511 (1)	Pub trst	F	Insurance code – fraudulent insurance act	4	
	500. 4511 (2)	Pub trst	D	Insurance fraud – agreement or conspiracy to commit	10	
	500. 5252 (4)	Property	G	Insurance – improper personal interest in transactions	5	
	500. 7034 (2)	Pub trst	E	Officer of a MEWA knowingly receive valuables for sale property or loan	10	
	500. 8197 (2)	Pub trst	C	Insurance – knowing or willful false statements in application for insurance	15	
	500. 8197 (3)	Property	E	Consolidation merger – compensation otherwise than expressed in contract	5	
MCL 777.15b						
	551. 6	Person	H	Marriage license – mental or venereal disease	5	Deleted, 2001 PA 10, Eff. 5/29/01
	551. 102 (2)	Pub trst	F	Unauthorized disclosure of social security number – subsequent offense	4	10/1/00
	554. 836	Property	E	Real and property – living care disclosure act	7	

Lightly shaded lines indicate that the statute governing the felony offense described on that line has been amended, deleted, or replaced.

Updated April 2007

*Unless otherwise noted, the date on which the statutory guidelines were made applicable to the felony offense listed is 1/1/99.

	Felonies by MCL #	Group	Class	Description	Stat Max	Effective Date*
	565. 371	Property	G	Fraudulent conveyances – recording with intent to deceive	3	
	565. 827	Pub trst	E	Land sales act – false or fraudulent statement	10	
	570. 152	Property	G	Contractor – fraudulent use of building contract fund	3	
	570. 1110	Property	F	Contractor – false sworn statements over $100	4	Deleted, 2001 PA 152, Eff. 1/1/02
	570. 1110 (c)	Property	E	Contractor – false sworn statement involving $1,000 to $20,000 or with prior convictions	5	1/1/02
	570. 1110 (d)	Property	D	Contractor – false sworn statement involving $20,000 or more or with prior convictions	10	1/1/02
	570. 1207	Property	G	Construction liens – false information	4	
MCL 777.15d						
	600. 908 (8)	Pub trst	E	Immunity to witness – committing perjury	15	
	600. 2136	Pub trst	E	Library record, book, paper – false certification in court	15	
	600. 2907 a	Property	G	Recording documents affecting property without lawful cause	3	
	600. 2916	Pub saf	G	Revised judicature act – lethal gases for fumigation	4	
	600. 8713	Pub trst	G	Revised judicature act – false statement by authorized local officials	15	
	600. 8813	Pub trst	E	Law enforcement officer – knowingly making false statement in a citation	15	
MCL 777.15f						
	710. 54 (11)	Pub trst	F	Offer to give other consideration – adoption – subsequent violation	4	
	710. 55 (1)	Pub trst	F	Adoption – persons not authorized placing child – subsequent violation	4	
	710. 69	Person	F	Michigan adoption law – subsequent offense	4	
	711. 1 (8)	Pub trst	E	Intentional false statement in petition for name change	15	
	712A. 6 b (3)	Pub ord	G	Violation of court order – subsequent conviction	2	10/1/00
MCL 777.15g						
	722. 115 e (2) (a)	Pub saf	G	Failure to report arraignment for criminal charges - child care and day care centers/employees	2	1/1/06
	722. 115 f (8) (a)	Pub saf	G	Failure to report arraignment for criminal charges - family day care and group day care homes	2	1/1/06
	722. 633 (5) (b)	Person	F	Intentional false report of child abuse constituting a felony	4	
	722. 633 (5) (b)	Person	F	Intentional false report of child abuse constituting a felony	Variable	As amended, 2005 PA 106, Eff. 9/14/05, and 2005 PA 134, Eff. 1/1/06
	722. 675	Pub ord	E	Distributing obscene matter to children	2	
	722. 857	Person	E	Surrogate parenting act – contracts involving minors, mentally retarded, etc.	5	
	722. 857	Person	E	Surrogate parenting contracts involving minors, mentally retarded, etc.	5	As amended, 2005 PA 106, Eff. 9/14/05, and 2005 PA 134, Eff. 1/1/06
	722. 859 (3)	Person	E	Surrogate parenting act – contracts for compensation	5	
	722. 859 (3)	Person	E	Surrogate parenting contracts for compensation	5	As amended, 2005 PA 106, Eff. 9/14/05, and 2005 PA 134, Eff. 1/1/06
MCL 777.16a						
	750. 11	Person	A	Taking a woman and compelling her to marry	LIFE	

Lightly shaded lines indicate that the statute governing the felony offense described on that line has been amended, deleted, or replaced.

Updated April 2007

*Unless otherwise noted, the date on which the statutory guidelines were made applicable to the felony offense listed is 1/1/99.

Felonies by MCL #	Group	Class	Description	Stat Max	Effective Date*
750. 12	Person	H	Taking a woman with intent to compel her to marry	10	
750. 13	Person	D	Enticing female under 16 for immoral purposes	10	
750. 14	Person	C	Abortion resulting in death of female	15	
750. 14	Person	G	Abortion	4	
750. 16 (1)	Person	G	Adulterate, misbrand, remove, or substitute a drug or medicine	2	10/12/04
750. 16 (2)	Person	F	Adulterate, misbrand, remove, or substitute a drug or medicine causing personal injury	4	10/12/04
750. 16 (3)	Person	E	Adulterate/misbrand/remove/substitute a drug/medicine - serious impairment of body function	5	10/12/04
750. 16 (4)	Person	C	Adulterate, misbrand, remove, or substitute a drug or medicine resulting in death	15	10/12/04
750. 18 (3)	Person	G	Mix/color/stain/powder a drug/medicine with an ingredient/material affecting quality/potency	2	10/12/04
750. 18 (4)	Person	F	Mix/color/stain/powder a drug/medicine w/ ingredient/material resulting in personal injury	4	10/12/04
750. 18 (5)	Person	E	Mix/color/stain/powder a drug/medicine resulting in serious impairment of body function	5	10/12/04
750. 18 (6)	Person	C	Mix/color/stain/powder a drug/medicine w/ ingredient/material resulting in death	15	10/12/04
750. 30	Pub ord	H	Adultery	4	
750. 32	Pub ord	H	Cohabitation of divorced parties	4	
MCL 777.16b					
750. 49 (2) (a)	Pub ord	F	Fighting animals or providing facilities for animal fights	4	
750. 49 (2) (b)	Pub ord	F	Fighting animals or providing facilities for animal fights	4	
750. 49 (2) (c)	Pub ord	F	Fighting animals or providing facilities for animal fights	4	
750. 49 (2) (d)	Pub ord	F	Fighting animals or providing facilities for animal fights	4	
750. 49 (2) (e)	Pub ord	F	Organizing or promoting animal fights	4	
750. 49 (2) (f)	Pub ord	H	Attending animal fight	4	
750. 49 (2) (g)	Pub ord	F	Breeding or selling fighting animals	4	
750. 49 (2) (h)	Pub ord	F	Selling or possessing equipment for animal fights	4	
750. 49 (8)	Person	A	Inciting fighting animal resulting in death	LIFE	
750. 49 (9)	Person	F	Inciting fighting animal to attack	4	
750. 49 (10)	Person	D	Fighting animal attacking without provocation and death resulting	15	
750. 50 (4)	Pub ord	G	Animal neglect or cruelty – second offense	2	
750. 50 (4)	Pub ord	F	Animal neglect or cruelty – third or subsequent offense	4	
750. 50 b (2)	Property	F	Killing or torturing animals	4	
750. 50 c (5)	Pub ord	E	Killing or causing serious physical harm to law enforcement animal	5	
750. 50 c (5)	Pub ord	E	Killing or causing serious physical harm to law enforcement animal or search and rescue dog	5	As amended, 2006 PA 518, Eff. 12/29/06
750. 50 c (7)	Pub saf	H	Harassing or causing harm to law enforcement animal while committing crime	2	

Lightly shaded lines indicate that the statute governing the felony offense described on that line has been amended, deleted, or replaced.

MCL #

Updated April 2007

*Unless otherwise noted, the date on which the statutory guidelines were made applicable to the felony offense listed is 1/1/99.

	Felonies by MCL #	Group	Class	Description	Stat Max	Effective Date*
	750. 50 c (7)	Pub saf	H	Harassing/harming law enforcement animal or search and rescue dog while committing crime	2	As amended, 2006 PA 518, Eff. 12/29/06
	750. 68	Property	G	Changing brands with intent to steal	4	
MCL 777.16c						
	750. 72	Person	B	Arson of dwelling house	20	
	750. 73	Property	D	Arson of real property	10	
	750. 74	Person	F	Arson of personal property greater than $50	4	
	750. 74	Person	E	Arson of personal property having a value of $1,000 to $20,000 or with prior convictions	5	10/1/00
	750. 74 (1) (d)	Person	D	Arson of personal property of $20,000 or more or with prior convictions	10	10/1/00
	750. 75	Property	D	Arson of insured property	10	
	750. 77	Person	F	Preparing to burn personal property greater than $50	4	
	750. 77 (1) (c)	Person	E	Preparing to burn personal property having value of $1,000 to $20,000 or w/ prior convictions	5	10/1/00
	750. 77 (1) (d)	Person	D	Preparing to burn personal property of $20,000 or more or with prior convictions	10	10/1/00
	750. 78	Pub saf	F	Arson of woods and prairies	4	
	750. 79	Pub saf	F	Violating township rules concerning clearing of land and burning	4	
	750. 80	Property	D	Arson of mines	LIFE	
MCL 777.16d						
	750. 81 (4)	Person	G	Domestic assault – third offense	2	
	750. 81 (4)	Person	G	Domestic assault with prior convictions	2	10/1/00
	750. 81 a (3)	Person	G	Aggravated domestic assault – second offense	2	
	750. 81 a (3)	Person	G	Aggravated domestic assault with prior convictions	2	10/1/00
	750. 81 c (2)	Person	G	Assault and battery of an FIA employee	2	9/1/01
	750. 81 c (3)	Person	E	Assault and battery of an FIA employee causing serious impairment	5	9/1/01
	750. 81 d (1)	Person	G	Assaulting, resisting, or obstructing certain persons	2	7/15/02
	750. 81 d (2)	Person	F	Assaulting, resisting, or obstructing certain persons causing injury	4	7/15/02
	750. 81 d (3)	Person	C	Assaulting, resisting, or obstructing certain persons causing serious impairment	15	7/15/02
	750. 81 d (4)	Person	B	Assaulting, resisting, or obstructing certain persons causing death	20	7/15/02
	750. 82 (1)	Person	F	Felonious assault	4	
	750. 82 (2)	Person	F	Felonious assault – weapon-free school zone	4	
	750. 83	Person	A	Assault with intent to murder	LIFE	
	750. 84	Person	D	Assault with intent to do great bodily harm less than murder	10	
	750. 85	Person	A	Torture	LIFE	3/1/06
	750. 86	Person	D	Assault with intent to maim	10	

Lightly shaded lines indicate that the statute governing the felony offense described on that line has been amended, deleted, or replaced.

MCL #

Updated April 2007

*Unless otherwise noted, the date on which the statutory guidelines were made applicable to the felony offense listed is 1/1/99.

Felonies by MCL #	Group	Class	Description	Stat Max	Effective Date*
750. 87	Person	D	Assault with intent to commit a felony	10	
750. 88	Person	C	Assault with intent to commit unarmed robbery	15	
750. 89	Person	A	Assault with intent to commit armed robbery	LIFE	
750. 90	Person	D	Sexual intercourse under pretext of medical treatment	10	
750. 90 a	Person	A	Assault against a pregnant individual causing miscarriage/stillbirth with intent or recklessness	LIFE	10/1/00
750. 90 a	Person	A	Assault causing miscarriage/stillbirth/death to embryo/fetus w/ intent or recklessness	LIFE	6/1/01
750. 90 b (a)	Person	C	Assault against a pregnant individual resulting in miscarriage or stillbirth	15	10/1/00
750. 90 b (a)	Person	C	Assault against a pregnant individual resulting in miscarriage/stillbirth/death to embryo or fetus	15	6/1/01
750. 90 b (b)	Person	D	Assault against a pregnant individual resulting in great bodily harm to embryo or fetus	10	10/1/00
750. 90 c (a)	Person	C	Gross negligence against a pregnant individual resulting in miscarriage or stillbirth	15	10/1/00
750. 90 c (a)	Person	C	Gross negligence resulting in miscarriage/stillbirth/death to embryo or fetus	15	6/1/01
750. 90 c (b)	Person	E	Gross negligence resulting in great bodily harm to embryo or fetus	5	10/1/00
750. 90 d (a)	Person	C	OUIL causing miscarriage or stillbirth	15	10/1/00
750. 90 d (a)	Person	C	Operating under the influence/impaired causing miscarriage/stillbirth/death to embryo or fetus	15	6/1/01
750. 90 d (b)	Person	E	Operating under the influence/impaired causing serious or aggravated injury to embryo/fetus	5	10/1/00
750. 90 e	Person	G	Careless or reckless driving causing miscarriage or stillbirth	2	10/1/00
750. 90 e	Person	G	Careless or reckless driving causing miscarriage, stillbirth, or death to embryo or fetus	2	6/1/01
750. 90 g (3)	Person	A	Performance of procedure on live infant with intent to cause death	LIFE	3/10/00
750. 91	Person	A	Attempted murder	LIFE	
MCL 777.16e					
750. 93	Property	G	Removing or destroying bonds in state treasury	10	
750. 94	Property	G	Issuing bank notes without complying with requirements	10	
750. 95	Property	G	Fraudulent bank notes	10	
750. 96	Property	G	Fraudulent disposal of bank property	4	
750. 97	Property	H	Statements derogatory to financial condition of bank	4	
750. 98	Pub ord	G	Private banking	4	
750. 99	Pub trst	G	Certifying checks without sufficient funds	4	
750. 100	Pub trst	E	Banks – conducting business when insolvent	5	
750. 101	Pub trst	E	Violating financial institutions act	5	
750. 104	Property	F	Fitting boat with intent to destroy	4	
750. 105	Property	G	Making false cargo invoice for boat	4	
750. 106	Property	G	Boats – making or procuring false protest	4	

Lightly shaded lines indicate that the statute governing the felony offense described on that line has been amended, deleted, or replaced.

MCL #

Updated April 2007

*Unless otherwise noted, the date on which the statutory guidelines were made applicable to the felony offense listed is 1/1/99.

Felonies by MCL #	Group	Class	Description	Stat Max	Effective Date*
MCL 777.16f					
750. 110	Property	D	Breaking and entering with intent to commit felony or larceny	10	
750. 110 a (2)	Person	B	Home invasion – first degree	20	10/1/00
750. 110 a (3)	Person	C	Home invasion – second degree	15	10/1/00
750. 110 a (4)	Person	B	Home invasion – first degree	20	
750. 110 a (4)	Person	E	Home invasion – third degree	5	10/1/00
750. 110 a (5)	Person	C	Home invasion – second degree	15	
750. 111	Property	E	Entering without breaking with intent to commit felony or larceny	5	
750. 112	Person	A	Burglary with explosives		
750. 116	Property	E	Possession of burglar's tools	10	
750. 117	Pub trst	F	Bribing a public officer	4	
750. 118	Pub trst	D	Public officer accepting bribe	10	
750. 119	Pub trst	F	Bribing a juror or other person	4	Substituted for by 750.119(1)(a)
750. 119 (1) (a)	Pub trst	F	Bribing a juror or other person	4	3/28/01
750. 119 (1) (b)	Pub trst	D	Bribing a juror or other person in case punishable by more than 10 years	10	3/28/01
750. 120	Pub trst	F	Juror or other person accepting a bribe	4	
750. 120 a (2) (a)	Pub ord	F	Juror intimidation	4	3/28/01
750. 120 a (2) (b)	Pub ord	D	Juror intimidation in case punishable by more than 10 years	10	3/28/01
750. 120 a (2) (c)	Person	C	Juror intimidation by committing crime or threatening to kill or injure	15	3/28/01
750. 120 a (4)	Person	D	Retaliating against juror	10	3/28/01
750. 121	Pub trst	F	Bribing a public officer to influence contract	4	
750. 122 (7) (a)	Pub ord	F	Bribing or intimidating witness	4	3/28/01
750. 122 (7) (b)	Pub ord	D	Bribing or intimidating witness in case punishable by more than 10 years	10	3/28/01
750. 122 (7) (c)	Person	C	Intimidating witness by committing crime or threatening to kill or injure	15	3/28/01
750. 122 (8)	Person	D	Retaliating against witness	10	3/28/01
750. 124	Pub trst	G	Bribing an athlete	4	
750. 128	Pub ord	H	Bucket shop violation	2	
750. 131 (3) (a) (iv)	Property	H	NSF checks – $50 or less – fourth offense	13 mos.	
750. 131 (3) (b) (ii)	Property	H	NSF checks – $50 to $200 – third offense	13 mos.	
750. 131 (3) (b) (ii)	Property	G	NSF checks – $100 to $500 – third or subsequent offense	2	10/1/00
750. 131 (3) (c)	Property	H	NSF checks – over $200	13 mos.	
750. 131 (3) (c)	Property	G	NSF checks – $500 or more	2	10/1/00

Lightly shaded lines indicate that the statute governing the felony offense described on that line has been amended, deleted, or replaced.

MCL #

MCL #

Updated April 2007

*Unless otherwise noted, the date on which the statutory guidelines were made applicable to the felony offense listed is 1/1/99.

Felonies by MCL #	Group	Class	Description	Stat Max	Effective Date*
750. 131 a (1)	Property	H	No account checks	2	
750. 131 a (2)	Property	H	NSF checks – 3 or more within 10 days	2	
MCL 777.16g					
750. 135	Person	D	Exposing children with intent to injure or abandon	10	
750. 136 b (2)	Person	C	Child abuse – first degree	15	
750. 136 b (2)	Person	B	Child abuse – first degree	15	10/1/00
750. 136 b (4)	Person	F	Child abuse – second degree	4	
750. 136 b (5)	Person	G	Child abuse – third degree	2	
750. 136 c	Person	B	Buying or selling an individual	20	10/1/00
750. 145 a	Person	F	Soliciting child to commit an immoral act	4	6/1/02
750. 145 b	Person	F	Accosting children for immoral purposes – subsequent offense	4	
750. 145 b	Person	D	Accosting children for immoral purposes with prior conviction	10	6/1/02
750. 145 c (2)	Person	B	Child sexually abusive activity or materials – active involvement	20	
750. 145 c (3)	Person	D	Child sexually abusive activity or materials – distributing, promoting or financing	7	
750. 145 c (4)	Person	F	Child sexually abusive activities or materials – possession	4	6/1/02
750. 145 d (2)	Person	G	Using internet or computer for certain crimes	2	8/1/99
750. 145 d (2) (b)	Variable	G	Using internet/computer for crime punishable by max term at least 1 yr but less than 2 yrs	2	10/1/00
750. 145 d (2) (c)	Variable	F	Using internet/computerfor crime punishable by max term at least 2 yrs but less than 4 yrs	4	10/1/00
750. 145 d (2) (d)	Variable	D	Using internet/computer for crime punishable by max term at least 4 yrs but less than 10 yrs	10	10/1/00
750. 145 d (2) (e)	Variable	C	Using internet/computer for crime punishable by max term at least 10 yrs but less than 15 yrs	15	10/1/00
750. 145 d (2) (f)	Variable	B	Using internet/computer to commit crime punishable by max term of at least 15 yrs or for life	20	10/1/00
750. 145 d (3)	Person	E	Using internet or computer for certain crimes or second or subsequent offense	5	8/1/99
750. 145 n (1)	Person	C	Vulnerable adult abuse – first degree	15	
750. 145 n (2)	Person	F	Vulnerable adult abuse – second degree	4	
750. 145 n (3)	Person	G	Vulnerable adult abuse – third degree	2	
750. 145 o	Person	E	Death of vulnerable adult caused by unlicensed caretaker	5	
750. 145 p (1)	Person	G	Vulnerable adult – commingling funds, obstructing investigation, or filing false information	2	
750. 145 p (2)	Person	G	Retaliation or discrimination by caregiver against vulnerable adult	2	
750. 145 p (5)	Person	E	Vulnerable adult – caregiver violations – subsequent offense	5	
750. 147 b	Person	G	Ethnic intimidation	2	
MCL 777.16h					
750. 149	Pub saf	F	Concealing an offense punishable by life	4	

Lightly shaded lines indicate that the statute governing the felony offense described on that line has been amended, deleted, or replaced.

MCL #

MCL #

Updated April 2007

*Unless otherwise noted, the date on which the statutory guidelines were made applicable to the felony offense listed is 1/1/99.

	Felonies by MCL #	Group	Class	Description	Stat Max	Effective Date*
MCL 777.18						
	750. 157 a (a)	Pub saf	SPEC	Conspiracy	Variable	
MCL 777.16h						
	750. 157 a (b)	Pub ord	H	Conspiracy – gambling	5	
	750. 157 a (d)	Pub ord	G	Conspiracy to commit legal act in illegal manner	5	
	750. 157 b (2)	Person	A	Solicitation of murder	LIFE	
	750. 157 b (3) (a)	Pub ord	E	Solicitation of felony punishable by life or 5 or more years	5	
	750. 157 b (3) (b)	Pub ord	G	Solicitation of felony punishable by less than 5 years	2	
MCL 777.18						
	750. 157 c	Person	SPEC	Inducing minor to commit a felony	Variable	
MCL 777.16h						
	750. 157 n (1)	Property	H	Financial transaction device – stealing, retaining, or using without consent	4	
	750. 157 n (2)	Property	H	Possessing fraudulent or altered financial transaction device	4	
	750. 157 p	Property	H	Possessing financial transaction device without permission and with intent to use or sell	4	
	750. 157 q	Property	H	Delivery or sale of fraudulent financial transaction device	4	
	750. 157 r	Property	H	Financial transaction device – forgery, alteration, or counterfeiting	4	
	750. 157 s	Property	H	Financial transaction device – use of revoked or canceled financial device over $100	1	
	750. 157 s (1) (b) (ii)	Property	H	Using revoked/canceled financial transaction device involving $100 to $500 w/ priors	2	10/1/00
	750. 157 s (1) (c)	Property	H	Use of revoked or canceled financial transaction device involving $500 or more	2	10/1/00
	750. 157 t	Property	H	Furnishing goods or services to person committing violation with financial transaction device	4	
	750. 157 u	Property	H	Overcharging person using financial transaction device	4	
	750. 157 v	Property	H	False statement of identity to obtain financial transaction device	4	
	750. 157 w	Property	H	Fraudulently withdrawing or transferring more than $500 with financial transaction device	4	
	750. 157 w (1) (c)	Property	E	Fraudulently withdrawing or transferring $1,000 to $20,000 with financial transaction device	5	10/1/00
	750. 157 w (1) (d)	Property	D	Fraudulently withdrawing or transferring $20,000 or more with financial transaction device	10	10/1/00
MCL 777.16i						
	750. 158	Pub ord	E	Sodomy	15	
	750. 159 j	Pub saf	B	Racketeering	20	
	750. 160	Pub ord	D	Disinterring or mutilating dead human bodies	10	
	750. 160	Pub ord	D	Disinterring or mutilating dead human body	10	4/1/04
	750. 160 a	Pub ord	H	Photographing dead human bodies	2	
	750. 160 a	Pub ord	H	Photographing dead human body	2	4/1/04

Lightly shaded lines indicate that the statute governing the felony offense described on that line has been amended, deleted, or replaced.

MCL #

Updated April 2007

*Unless otherwise noted, the date on which the statutory guidelines were made applicable to the felony offense listed is 1/1/99.

Felonies by MCL #	Group	Class	Description	Stat Max	Effective Date*
750. 160 c	Pub ord	D	Improper disposal of dead human body after more than 180 days	10	4/1/04
750. 161	Pub ord	G	Desertion/abandonment/nonsupport	3	
750. 164	Pub ord	F	Desertion to escape prosecution	4	
750. 165	Pub ord	F	Failing to pay support and leaving state	4	
750. 168 (2) (a)	Pub ord	G	Disorderly conduct at a funeral	2	8/22/06
750. 168 (2) (b)	Pub ord	F	Disorderly conduct at a funeral - subsequent offense	4	8/22/06
750. 171	Person	E	Duelling	10	
750. 174	Property	D	Embezzlement by agent over $100	10	
750. 174 (4)	Property	E	Embezzlement by agent of $1,000 to $20,000 [or] with prior convictions	5	10/1/00
750. 174 (4)	Property	E	Embezzlement by agent of $200-$1K from nonprofit/charitable org, or $1K-$20K, or with priors	5	As amended, 2006 PA 574, Eff. 3/30/07
750. 174 (5)	Property	D	Embezzlement by agent of $20,000 or more or $1,000 to $20,000 with prior convictions	10	10/1/00
750. 174 (5)	Property	D	Embezzlement by agent of $1K-$20K from nonprofit/charitable org, or $20K-$50K, or $1K-$20K with priors	10	As amended, 2006 PA 574, Eff. 3/30/07
750. 174 (6)	Property	C	Embezzlement by agent of $50,000 or more but less than $100,000	15	3/30/07
750. 174 (7)	Property	B	Embezzlement by agent of $100,000 or more	20	3/30/07
750. 175	Pub trst	D	Embezzlement by public official over $50	10	
750. 176	Pub trst	E	Embezzlement by administrator/executor/guardian	10	
750. 177	Property	H	Embezzlement by chattel mortgagor over $100	2	
750. 177 (2)	Property	D	Embezzlement by chattel mortgagor of $20,000 or more or $1,000 to $20,000 with priors	10	10/1/00
750. 177 (3)	Property	E	Embezzlement by chattel mortgagor of $1,000 to $20,000 or with prior convictions	5	10/1/00
750. 178	Property	G	Embezzlement of mortgaged or leased property – over $100	2	
750. 178 (2)	Property	D	Embezzlement of mortgaged or leased property of $20,000+ or $1,000 to $20,000 with priors	10	10/1/00
750. 178 (3)	Property	E	Embezzling mortgaged or leased property with value of $1,000 to $20,000 or with priors	5	10/1/00
750. 179	Property	G	Embezzlement of railroad tickets	4	Deleted, 2002 PA 278, Eff. 5/9/02
750. 180	Property	D	Embezzlement by financial institutions	20	
750. 181	Property	E	Embezzlement of jointly held property over $100	10	
750. 181 (4)	Property	E	Embezzling jointly held property with value of $1,000 to $20,000 or with prior convictions	5	10/1/00
750. 181 (5)	Property	D	Embezzling jointly held property with value of $20,000+ or $1,000 to $20,000 with priors	10	10/1/00
750. 182	Property	G	Embezzlement by warehouses	4	
750. 182 a	Pub trst	H	Falsifying school records	2	
MCL 777.16j					
750. 183	Pub saf	E	Aiding escaping prisoner	7	
750. 186 a (1)	Pub saf	F	Escape from a juvenile facility	4	

Lightly shaded lines indicate that the statute governing the felony offense described on that line has been amended, deleted, or replaced.

Updated April 2007

*Unless otherwise noted, the date on which the statutory guidelines were made applicable to the felony offense listed is 1/1/99.

Felonies by MCL #	Group	Class	Description	Stat Max	Effective Date*
MCL 777.18					
750. 188	Pub ord	SPEC	Voluntarily suffering prisoner to escape	Variable	
MCL 777.16j					
750. 189	Pub saf	H	Officer negligently allowing prisoner to escape or refusing to receive prisoner	2	
750. 190	Pub saf	G	Officer receiving a reward to assist or permit escape	2	
750. 193	Pub saf	E	Escape from prison	5	
750. 195 (1)	Pub saf	H	Escape from a misdemeanor jail sentence	2	
750. 195 (2)	Pub saf	F	Escape from a felony jail sentence	4	
750. 197 (1)	Pub saf	H	Escape while awaiting trial for misdemeanor	2	
750. 197 (2)	Pub saf	F	Escape while awaiting trial for felony	4	
750. 197 c	Pub saf	F	Escape from jail through violence	4	Eff. until 12/29/06, 2006 PA 536
750. 197 c	Pub saf	E	Escape from jail through violence	5	As amended, 2006 PA 536, Eff. 12/29/06
750. 199 (3)	Pub saf	F	Harboring a person for whom felony warrant has been issued	4	6/30/06
750. 199 a	Pub ord	F	Absconding on or forfeiting bond	4	
MCL 777.16k					
750. 200	Pub saf	F	Explosives – transport by common carriers	4	
750. 200	Pub saf	E	Transporting an explosive by common carrier	5	10/1/00
750. 200 i (2) (a)	Pub saf	C	Manufacturing or using a harmful device	15	10/1/00
750. 200 i (2) (b)	Property	B	Harmful device causing property damage	20	10/1/00
750. 200 i (2) (c)	Person	A	Harmful device causing personal injury	25	10/1/00
750. 200 i (2) (d)	Person	A	Harmful device causing serious impairment	LIFE	10/1/00
750. 200 j (2) (a)	Person	E	Irritant or irritant device	5	10/23/01
750. 200 j (2) (b)	Property	F	Irritant or irritant device causing property damage	4	10/1/00
750. 200 j (2) (b)	Property	E	Irritant or irritant device causing property damage	7	10/23/01
750. 200 j (2) (c)	Person	D	Irritant or irritant device causing personal injury	10	10/1/00
750. 200 j (2) (d)	Person	A	Irritant or irritant device causing serious impairment	25	10/1/00
750. 200 j (2) (e)	Person	A	Irritant or irritant device causing death	LIFE	10/1/00
750. 200 l	Person	E	Falsely exposing person to harmful substance or device	5	10/23/01
750. 201	Pub saf	F	Transportation of concussion or friction type explosives	4	
750. 201	Pub saf	E	Transporting certain types of explosives	5	10/1/00
750. 202	Pub saf	F	Shipping an explosive with false markings or invoice	4	
750. 204	Pub saf	E	Sending explosives with intent to injure persons	5	

Lightly shaded lines indicate that the statute governing the felony offense described on that line has been amended, deleted, or replaced.

Updated April 2007

*Unless otherwise noted, the date on which the statutory guidelines were made applicable to the felony offense listed is 1/1/99.

Felonies by MCL #	Group	Class	Description	Stat Max	Effective Date*
750. 204 (2) (a)	Pub saf	C	Sending an explosive with malicious intent	15	10/1/00
750. 204 (2) (b)	Property	B	Sending an explosive causing property damage	20	10/1/00
750. 204 (2) (c)	Person	A	Sending an explosive causing physical injury	25	10/1/00
750. 204 (2) (d)	Person	A	Sending an explosive causing serious impairment	LIFE	10/1/00
750. 204 a	Pub saf	F	Sending or transporting imitation explosive device with malicious intent	4	
750. 204 a	Pub saf	E	Sending or transporting an imitation explosive device with malicious intent	5	10/1/00
750. 205	Pub saf	C	Placing explosives with the intent to destroy property	15	
750. 205 a	Pub saf	F	Intimidation or harassment by device represented as an explosive	4	
750. 206	Person	B	Placing explosives with damage to property resulting	25	
750. 207 (2) (a)	Pub saf	C	Placing an explosive with malicious intent	15	10/1/00
750. 207 (2) (b)	Property	B	Placing an explosive causing property damage	20	10/1/00
750. 207 (2) (c)	Person	A	Placing an explosive causing physical injury	25	10/1/00
750. 207 (2) (d)	Person	A	Placing an explosive causing serious impairment	LIFE	10/1/00
750. 208	Pub saf	C	Aiding or abetting explosives placement with intent to destroy property	15	
750. 209	Pub saf	C	Placing foul or offensive substance to injure	15	
750. 209	Pub saf	F	Placing foul or offensive substance to alarm	4	
750. 209 (1) (a)	Pub saf	C	Placing an offensive or injurious substance with intent to injure	15	10/1/00
750. 209 (1) (b)	Property	B	Placing an offensive or injurious substance causing property damage	20	10/1/00
750. 209 (1) (c)	Person	A	Placing an offensive or injurious substance causing physical injury	25	10/1/00
750. 209 (1) (d)	Person	A	Placing an offensive or injurious substance causing serious impairment	LIFE	10/1/00
750. 209 (2)	Pub saf	E	Placing an offensive or injurious substance with intent to alarm or annoy	5	10/1/00
750. 209 a	Pub saf	D	Possessing an explosive device in public place	10	10/1/00
750. 210	Pub saf	E	Possession of bombs with unlawful intent	5	
750. 210 (2) (a)	Pub saf	C	Possessing or carrying an explosive or combustible substance with malicious intent	15	10/1/00
750. 210 (2) (b)	Property	B	Possessing or carrying an explosive or combustible substance causing property damage	20	10/1/00
750. 210 (2) (c)	Person	A	Possessing or carrying an explosive or combustible substance causing physical injury	25	10/1/00
750. 210 (2) (d)	Person	A	Possessing or carrying an explosive or combustible substance causing serious impairment	LIFE	10/1/00
750. 210 a	Pub saf	H	Sale of valerium	5	
750. 211	Pub saf	E	Manufacture of explosives with unlawful intent	5	
750. 211 a	Pub saf	F	Possessing or manufacturing device designed to explode upon impact or heating	4	
750. 211 a (2) (a)	Pub saf	F	Manufacturing/possessing a Molotov cocktail/similar device designed to explode on impact	4	4/1/05
750. 211 a (2) (a)	Pub saf	C	Manufacturing or possessing an explosive or incendiary device with malicious intent	15	Eff. 10/1/00 to 4/1/05

Lightly shaded lines indicate that the statute governing the felony offense described on that line has been amended, deleted, or replaced.

Updated April 2007

*Unless otherwise noted, the date on which the statutory guidelines were made applicable to the felony offense listed is 1/1/99.

Felonies by MCL #	Group	Class	Description	Stat Max	Effective Date*
750. 211 a (2) (b)	Pub saf	C	Manufacturing or possessing an explosive or incendiary device with malicious intent	15	Relettered, 2004 PA 524, Eff. 4/1/05
750. 211 a (2) (b)	Property	B	Manufacturing or possessing an explosive or incendiary device causing property damage	20	Eff. 10/1/00 to 4/1/05
750. 211 a (2) (c)	Property	B	Manufacturing or possessing an explosive or incendiary device causing property damage	20	Relettered, 2004 PA 524, Eff. 4/1/05
750. 211 a (2) (c)	Person	A	Manufacturing or possessing an explosive or incendiary device causing physical injury	25	Eff. 10/1/00 to 4/1/05
750. 211 a (2) (d)	Person	A	Manufacturing or possessing an explosive or incendiary device causing physical injury	25	Relettered, 2004 PA 524, Eff. 4/1/05
750. 211 a (2) (d)	Person	A	Manufacturing or possessing an explosive or incendiary device causing serious impairment	LIFE	Eff. 10/1/00 to 4/1/05
750. 211 a (2) (e)	Person	A	Manufacturing or possessing an explosive or incendiary device causing serious impairment	LIFE	Relettered, 2004 PA 524, Eff. 4/1/05
750. 212 a	Person	B	Explosives violation involving a vulnerable target causing death or injury	20	10/1/00
MCL 777.16l					
750. 213	Person	B	Threats to extort money	20	
750. 215 (3)	Pub saf	F	Impersonating peace officer	4	9/1/03
750. 217 b	Pub saf	G	Impersonating public utility employee	2	
750. 217 c (3)	Pub ord	H	Impersonating public officer or employee	2	10/1/00
750. 217 c (4)	Pub ord	G	Impersonating public officer or employee – third or subsequent conviction	4	10/1/00
750. 217 d	Pub saf	C	False representation or practice as health professional	15	10/1/00
750. 217 e	Pub ord	G	Impersonating an FIA employee	2	9/1/01
750. 217 e	Pub ord	G	Impersonating a DHS employee	2	As amended, 2005 PA 171, Eff. 1/1/06
750. 217 f	Pub saf	G	Impersonating a firefighter or emergency medical service personnel	2	1/1/06
750. 218	Property	E	False pretenses over $100	10	
750. 218 (4)	Property	E	False pretenses involving $1,000 to $20,000 or with prior convictions	5	10/1/00
750. 218 (5)	Property	D	False pretenses involving $20,000 or more or $1,000 to $20,000 with prior convictions	10	10/1/00
750. 219 a (2) (c)	Property	E	Telecommunications fraud – 2 prior convictions or value between $1,000-$20,000	5	
750. 219 a (2) (c)	Property	E	Telecommunications fraud - 1 or more prior convictions or value of $1,000 to $20,000	5	10/1/00
750. 219 a (2) (d)	Property	D	Telecommunications fraud – 3 or more prior convictions or value over $20,000	10	
750. 219 a (2) (d)	Property	D	Telecommunications fraud - 2 or more prior convictions or value of $20,000 or more	10	10/1/00
750. 219 e	Property	F	Receive/possess/prepare/submit or receive/possess proceeds from unauthorized credit app	4	3/10/00
750. 219 e	Property	F	Receive/possess/prepare/submit unauthorized credit application or receive/possess proceeds	4	9/1/01
750. 219 f	Property	F	Receive/possess w/ intent to forward/forwarding unauthorized credit application/proceeds	4	3/10/00
750. 219 f	Property	F	Receive/possess w/ intent to forward/forwarding unauthorized credit application or proceeds	4	9/1/01
MCL 777.16m					
750. 223 (2)	Pub saf	F	Sale of firearm to minor – subsequent offense	4	
750. 223 (3)	Pub ord	D	Sale of firearm to person prohibited from possessing	10	

Lightly shaded lines indicate that the statute governing the felony offense described on that line has been amended, deleted, or replaced.

*Unless otherwise noted, the date on which the statutory guidelines were made applicable to the felony offense listed is 1/1/99.

Felonies by MCL #	Group	Class	Description	Stat Max	Effective Date*
750. 224	Pub saf	E	Manufacture or sale of silencer, bomb, blackjack, automatic weapon, gas spray, etc.	5	
750. 224 a	Pub saf	F	Possession or sale of electrical current weapons	4	
750. 224 b	Pub saf	E	Possession of short barreled shotgun or rifle	5	
750. 224 c	Pub saf	F	Armor piercing ammunition	4	
750. 224 d (2)	Person	G	Using self-defense spray device	2	
750. 224 e	Pub saf	F	Manufacture/sale/possession of devices to convert semiautomatic weapons	4	
750. 224 f	Pub saf	E	Possession or sale of firearm by felon	5	
750. 226	Pub saf	E	Carrying firearm or dangerous weapon with unlawful intent	5	
750. 227	Pub saf	E	Carrying a concealed weapon	5	
750. 227 a	Pub saf	F	Unlawful possession of pistol	4	
750. 227 c	Pub saf	G	Possessing a loaded firearm in or upon a vehicle	2	
750. 227 f	Pub saf	F	Wearing body armor during commission of violent crime	4	
750. 227 f	Pub saf	F	Wearing body armor during commission of certain crimes	4	As amended, 2005 PA 106, Eff. 9/14/05
750. 227 g (1)	Pub saf	F	Felon purchasing, owning, possessing, or using body armor	4	10/1/00
750. 230	Pub saf	G	Altering ID mark on firearm	2	
750. 232 a (3)	Pub saf	G	False statement in a pistol application	4	
750. 234 a	Pub saf	F	Discharging firearm from vehicle	4	
750. 234 b	Pub saf	F	Discharging firearm in or at a building	4	
750. 234 c	Pub saf	F	Discharging firearm at emergency/police vehicle	4	
750. 236	Person	C	Setting spring gun – death resulting	15	
750. 237 (3)	Person	E	Using firearm while under the influence or impaired causing serious impairment	5	2/1/02
750. 237 (4)	Person	C	Using firearm while under the influence or impaired causing death	15	2/1/02
MCL 777.18					
750. 237 a	Pub saf	SPEC	Felony committed in a weapon-free school zone	Variable	10/1/00
750. 237 a (1)	Pub saf	F	Weapon-free school zones – general felony violations	Variable	
MCL 777.16n					
750. 241 (1)	Pub saf	F	Obstructing firefighter	4	Deleted, 2002 PA 272, Eff. 7/15/02
750. 241 (2)	Pub saf	F	Obstructing public service facility personnel in civil disturbance	4	7/15/02
750. 241 (3)	Pub saf	F	Obstructing public service facility personnel in civil disturbance	4	Substituted for by 750.241(2)
750. 248	Property	E	Forgery	14	
750. 248 a	Property	F	Uttering and publishing financial transaction device	4	
750. 249	Property	E	Uttering and publishing forged records	14	

Lightly shaded lines indicate that the statute governing the felony offense described on that line has been amended, deleted, or replaced.

Updated April 2007

*Unless otherwise noted, the date on which the statutory guidelines were made applicable to the felony offense listed is 1/1/99.

Felonies by MCL #	Group	Class	Description	Stat Max	Effective Date*
750. 249 a	Property	H	Molds or dies to forge financial transaction device	4	
750. 250	Property	E	Forgery of treasury notes	7	
750. 251	Property	E	Forgery of bank bills	7	
750. 252	Property	E	Possessing counterfeit notes	7	
750. 253	Property	G	Uttering counterfeit notes	5	
750. 254	Property	E	Possession of counterfeit notes or bills	5	
750. 255	Property	E	Possession of counterfeiting tools	10	
750. 260	Property	E	Counterfeiting coins or possession of 5 or more counterfeit coins	LIFE	
750. 261	Property	E	Possession of 5 or fewer counterfeit coins	10	
750. 262	Property	E	Manufacture or possession of tools to counterfeit coins	10	
750. 263 (3)	Property	E	Delivery/use/display items w/ counterfeit mark – subsequent offense or $1000+ or 100+ items	5	
750. 263 (4)	Property	E	Manufacturing items with counterfeit mark	5	
750. 266	Property	G	Counterfeiting railroad tickets	4	Deleted, 2002 PA 321, Eff. 7/15/02
MCL 777.16o					
750. 271	Property	E	Fraudulently issuing or selling domestic securities	10	
750. 272	Property	G	Sale of fraudulent stock of foreign corporations	10	
750. 273	Property	E	Obtaining signature to financial document with intent to defraud	10	
750. 274	Property	E	Fraud – purchasing/collecting on fraudulent financial document	10	
750. 276	Property	G	Fraud – promise to vendee of grain at fictitious price	4	
750. 277	Pub trst	G	Promise to vendee of grain to sell at a fictitious price – sale and transfer	4	
750. 278	Property	G	Fraud – warehouse receipts	5	
750. 279	Property	G	Fraud – disposition of exhausted property	4	
750. 280	Property	E	Gross frauds/cheats at common law	10	
750. 282	Pub ord	G	Public utility – fraudulent use over $500	4	
750. 285	Property	E	Obtaining personal ID information without authorization	5	Eff. 4/1/01 to 3/1/05, 2004 PA 457
750. 300	Pub ord	G	Animals – killing/injuring to defraud insurance company	2	
750. 300 a (1) (a)	Property	G	Food stamp fraud – $250 or less – second offense	5	
750. 300 a (1) (a)	Property	G	Food stamp fraud – $250 or less – third or subsequent offense	10	
750. 300 a (1) (b)	Property	E	Food stamp fraud – more than $250 to $1,000	5	
750. 300 a (1) (b)	Property	E	Food stamp fraud – more than $250 to $1,000 – subsequent offense	10	
750. 300 a (1) (c)	Property	E	Food stamp fraud – over $1,000	10	
750. 303	Pub ord	H	Gambling	2	

Lightly shaded lines indicate that the statute governing the felony offense described on that line has been amended, deleted, or replaced.

MCL #

Updated April 2007

*Unless otherwise noted, the date on which the statutory guidelines were made applicable to the felony offense listed is 1/1/99.

	Felonies by MCL #	Group	Class	Description	Stat Max	Effective Date*
	750. 303	Pub ord	H	Gaming	2	As amended, 2004 PA 457, Eff. 3/1/05
	750. 313	Pub ord	H	Gambling – stocks/bonds/commodities	2	
MCL 777.16p						
	750. 317	Person	M2	Second degree murder	LIFE	
	750. 317 a	Person	A	Delivery of controlled substance causing death	LIFE	1/1/06
	750. 321	Person	C	Manslaughter	15	
	750. 322	Person	C	Willful killing of unborn quick child	15	
	750. 323	Person	C	Abortion resulting in death	15	
	750. 324	Person	G	Negligent homicide	2	
	750. 327	Person	A	Death by explosives on vehicle or vessel	LIFE	
	750. 328	Person	A	Death by explosives in or near building	LIFE	
	750. 329	Person	C	Homicide – weapon aimed with intent but not malice	15	
	750. 329 a	Person	E	Assisting a suicide	5	10/1/00
MCL 777.16q						
	750. 332	Property	H	Entering horse in race under false name	4	
	750. 335 a	Person	A	Indecent exposure by sexually delinquent person	LIFE	Relettered, 2005 PA 302, Eff. 2/1/06
	750. 335 a (2) (b)	Person	G	Aggravated indecent exposure	2	2/1/06
	750. 335 a (2) (c)	Person	A	Indecent exposure by sexually delinquent person	LIFE	Formerly MCL 750.335a, Eff. 2/1/06
	750. 338	Pub ord	G	Gross indecency between males	5	
	750. 338	Pub ord	A	Gross indecency between males involving sexually delinquent person	LIFE	8/24/06
	750. 338 a	Pub ord	G	Gross indecency between females	5	
	750. 338 a	Pub ord	A	Gross indecency between females involving sexually delinquent person	LIFE	8/24/06
	750. 338 b	Pub ord	G	Gross indecency between males and females	5	
	750. 338 b	Pub ord	A	Gross indecency between males and females involving sexually delinquent person	LIFE	8/24/06
	750. 348	Pub saf	H	Inciting Indians to violate a treaty	4	Deleted, 2002 PA 261, Eff. 5/1/02
	750. 349	Person	A	Kidnapping	LIFE	
	750. 349 a	Person	A	Prisoner taking a hostage	LIFE	
	750. 349 b	Person	C	Unlawful imprisonment	15	8/24/06
	750. 350	Person	A	Kidnapping – child enticement	LIFE	
	750. 350 a	Person	H	Kidnapping – custodial interference	1	
MCL 777.16r						
	750. 356	Property	E	Larceny over $100	5	

Lightly shaded lines indicate that the statute governing the felony offense described on that line has been amended, deleted, or replaced.

MCL #

Updated April 2007

*Unless otherwise noted, the date on which the statutory guidelines were made applicable to the felony offense listed is 1/1/99.

Felonies by MCL #	Group	Class	Description	Stat Max	Effective Date*
750. 356 (2)	Property	D	Larceny involving $20,000 or more or with prior convictions	10	10/1/00
750. 356 (3)	Property	E	Larceny involving $1,000 to $20,000 or with prior convictions	5	10/1/00
750. 356 a	Property	G	Larceny from a motor vehicle	5	
750. 356 a (1)	Property	G	Larceny from a motor vehicle	5	10/1/00
750. 356 a (2) (c)	Property	E	Breaking and entering a vehicle to steal $1,000 to $20,000 or with prior convictions	5	10/1/00
750. 356 a (2) (d)	Property	D	Breaking and entering a vehicle to steal $20,000 or more or with prior convictions	10	10/1/00
750. 356 a (3)	Property	G	Breaking and entering a vehicle to steal causing damage	5	10/1/00
750. 356 b	Property	G	Breaking and entering a coin telephone	4	
750. 356 c	Property	H	Retail fraud – first degree	2	
750. 356 c	Property	E	Retail fraud – first degree	5	10/1/00
750. 357	Person	D	Larceny from the person	10	
750. 357 a	Property	G	Larceny of livestock	4	
750. 357 b	Property	E	Larceny – stealing firearms of another	5	
750. 358	Property	G	Larceny from burning building	5	
750. 360	Property	G	Larceny in a building	4	
750. 360 a (2) (b)	Property	F	Theft detection device offense with prior conviction	4	7/1/02
750. 361	Property	H	Trains – stealing/maliciously removing parts	2	
750. 362	Property	E	Larceny by conversion over $100	5	
750. 362	Property	E	Larceny by conversion involving $1,000 to $20,000 or with prior convictions	5	10/1/00
750. 362	Property	D	Larceny by conversion involving $20,000 or more or with prior convictions	10	10/1/00
750. 362 a	Property	H	Larceny of rental property	2	
750. 362 a (2)	Property	D	Larceny of rental property involving $20,000 or more or with prior convictions	10	10/1/00
750. 362 a (3)	Property	E	Larceny of rental property involving $1,000 to $20,000 or with prior convictions	5	10/1/00
750. 363	Property	E	Larceny by false personation over $100	5	
750. 363	Property	E	Larceny by false personation involving $1,000 to $20,000 or with prior convictions	5	10/1/00
750. 363	Property	D	Larceny by false personation involving $20,000 or more	10	10/1/00
750. 365	Person	D	Larceny from car or persons detained or injured by accident	20	
750. 366	Property	G	Larceny of railroad tickets	4	Deleted, 2002 PA 279, Eff. 5/9/02
750. 367	Property	G	Larceny of trees & shrubs over $100	5	
750. 367	Property	E	Larceny of trees or shrubs involving $1,000 to $20,000 or with prior convictions	5	10/1/00
750. 367	Property	D	Larceny of a tree or shrub involving $20,000 or more or with prior convictions	10	10/1/00

Lightly shaded lines indicate that the statute governing the felony offense described on that line has been amended, deleted, or replaced.

Updated April 2007

*Unless otherwise noted, the date on which the statutory guidelines were made applicable to the felony offense listed is 1/1/99.

Felonies by MCL #	Group	Class	Description	Stat Max	Effective Date*
MCL 777.18					
750. 367 a	Property	SPEC	Larceny of rationed goods	Variable	
MCL 777.16r					
750. 367 b	Property	E	Airplanes – taking possession	5	
750. 368 (5)	Pub ord	G	Preparing, serving, or executing unauthorized process – third or subsequent offense	4	10/1/00
750. 372	Pub ord	H	Running or allowing lottery	2	
750. 373	Pub ord	H	Selling or possessing lottery tickets	2	
750. 374	Pub ord	H	Lottery violations – subsequent offense	4	
MCL 777.16s					
750. 377 a	Property	G	Malicious destruction of personal property over $100	4	
750. 377 a (1) (a)	Property	D	Malicious destruction of personal property involving $20,000 or more or with prior convictions	10	10/1/00
750. 377 a (1) (b)	Property	E	Malicious destruction of personal property involving $1,000 to $20,000 or with priors	5	10/1/00
750. 377 b	Property	F	Malicious destruction of fire/police property	4	
750. 377 c	Property	E	School bus – intentional damage	5	
750. 378	Property	F	Malicious destruction of property – dams/canals/mills	4	
750. 379	Property	F	Malicious destruction of property – bridges/railroads/locks	4	
750. 380	Property	F	Malicious destruction of building over $100	4	
750. 380 (2)	Property	D	Malicious destruction of building involving $20,000 or more or with prior convictions	10	10/1/00
750. 380 (3)	Property	E	Malicious destruction of a building involving $1,000 to $20,000 or with prior convictions	5	10/1/00
750. 382 (1) (c)	Property	E	Malicious destruction of plants or turf involving $1,000 to $20,000 or with prior convictions	5	10/1/00
750. 382 (1) (d)	Property	D	Malicious destruction of plants or turf involving $20,000 or more or with prior convictions	10	10/1/00
750. 383 a	Property	F	Malicious destruction of utility equipment	4	
750. 385 (2) (c)	Property	E	Damaging/destroying research property-between $1,000 and $20,000 or w/ prior convictions	5	Eff. 4/1/05 to 9/14/05
750. 385 (2) (d)	Property	E	Damaging/destroying research property - $20,000 or more or 2 or more prior convictions	5	Eff. 4/1/05 to 9/14/05
750. 385 (2) (e)	Person	E	Damaging or destroying research property resulting in physical injury	5	Eff. 4/1/05 to 9/14/05
750. 385 (2) (f)	Person	D	Damaging or destroying research property resulting in serious impairment of body function	10	Eff. 4/1/05 to 9/14/05
750. 385 (2) (g)	Person	C	Damaging or destroying research property resulting in death	15	Eff. 4/1/05 to 9/14/05
750. 386	Property	E	Malicious destruction of mine property	20	
750. 387	Property	G	Malicious destruction of tombs & memorials	5	
750. 387 (5)	Property	E	Malicious destruction of a tomb or memorial involving $1,000 to $20,000 or with priors	5	10/1/00
750. 387 (6)	Property	D	Malicious destruction of a tomb or memorial involving $20,000 or more or with prior convictions	10	10/1/00
750. 392	Property	E	Malicious destruction of property – vessels	10	

Lightly shaded lines indicate that the statute governing the felony offense described on that line has been amended, deleted, or replaced.

Updated April 2007

*Unless otherwise noted, the date on which the statutory guidelines were made applicable to the felony offense listed is 1/1/99.

Felonies by MCL #	Group	Class	Description	Stat Max	Effective Date*
750. 394 (2) (c)	Person	F	Throwing or dropping dangerous object at vehicle causing injury	4	1/1/04
750. 394 (2) (d)	Person	D	Throwing or dropping dangerous object at vehicle causing serious impairment	10	1/1/04
750. 394 (2) (e)	Person	C	Throwing or dropping dangerous object at vehicle causing death	15	1/1/04
750. 395 (2) (c)	Property	E	Damaging/destroying research property-between $1,000 and $20,000 or w/ prior convictions	5	Replaced MCL 750.385(2)(c), 2005 PA 106, Eff. 9/14/05
750. 395 (2) (d)	Property	E	Damaging/destroying research property - $20,000 or more or 2 or more prior convictions	5	Replaced MCL 750.385(2)(d), 2005 PA 106, Eff. 9/14/05
750. 395 (2) (e)	Person	E	Damaging or destroying research property resulting in physical injury	5	Replaced MCL 750.385(2)(e), 2005 PA 106, Eff. 9/14/05
750. 395 (2) (f)	Person	D	Damaging or destroying research property resulting in serious impairment of body function	10	Replaced MCL 750.385(2)(f), 2005 PA 106, Eff. 9/14/05
750. 395 (2) (g)	Person	C	Damaging or destroying research property resulting in death	15	Replaced MCL 750.385(2)(g), 2005 PA 106, Eff. 9/14/05
750. 397	Person	D	Mayhem	10	
750. 397 a	Person	D	Placing harmful objects in food	10	
750. 405	Pub saf	E	Inciting soldiers to desert	5	
750. 406	Pub saf	E	Military stores – larceny, embezzlement or destruction	5	
MCL 777.16t					
750. 410 a	Person	G	Conspiracy to commit a person to state hospital unjustly	4	
750. 411 a (1) (b)	Pub ord	F	False report of a felony	4	
750. 411 a (2)	Pub ord	F	False report of a bombing or threat to bomb	4	Substituted for by 750.411a(3)(a)
750. 411 a (3) (a)	Pub ord	F	Threat or false report of an explosive or harmful device, substance, or material	4	4/1/01
750. 411 a (3) (b)	Pub ord	D	Threat/false report of explosive or harmful device/substance/material – subsequent offense	10	4/1/01
750. 411 b	Pub trst	G	Excess fees to members of legislature	4	
750. 411 h (2) (b)	Person	E	Stalking of a minor	5	
750. 411 i (3) (a)	Person	E	Aggravated stalking	5	10/1/00
750. 411 i (3) (b)	Person	D	Aggravated stalking of a minor	10	
750. 411 l	Pub ord	H	Money laundering – fourth degree	2	
750. 411 m	Pub ord	E	Money laundering – third degree	5	
750. 411 n	Pub ord	D	Money laundering – second degree	10	
750. 411 o	Pub ord	B	Money laundering – first degree	20	
750. 411 p (2) (a)	Property	B	Money laundering of proceeds from controlled substance offense involving $10,000 or more	20	
750. 411 p (2) (b)	Property	D	Money laundering proceeds from controlled substance offense/other proceeds of $10,000+	10	
750. 411 p (2) (c)	Property	E	Money laundering – transactions involving represented proceeds	5	
750. 411 s (2) (a)	Person	G	Unlawful posting of message	2	4/1/01
750. 411 s (2) (b)	Person	E	Unlawful posting of message with aggravating circumstances	5	4/1/01
750. 411 t (2) (b)	Person	E	Hazing resulting in serious impairment	5	8/18/04

Lightly shaded lines indicate that the statute governing the felony offense described on that line has been amended, deleted, or replaced.

*Unless otherwise noted, the date on which the statutory guidelines were made applicable to the felony offense listed is 1/1/99.

	Felonies by MCL #	Group	Class	Description	Stat Max	Effective Date*
	750. 411 t (2) (c)	Person	C	Hazing resulting in death	15	8/18/04
MCL 777.16u						
	750. 413	Property	E	Unlawful driving away of an automobile	5	
	750. 414	Property	H	Unlawful use of an automobile	2	
	750. 415 (2)	Property	G	Motor vehicles – conceal/misrepresent identity with intent to mislead	4	
	750. 415 (5)	Property	G	Motor vehicles – buy/sell/exchange/give paraphernalia capable of changing/misrepresenting ID	4	10/1/00
	750. 415 (6)	Property	E	Motor vehicles – buy/receive/obtain w/ intent to sell/dispose knowing VIN was altered	10	10/1/00
	750. 417	Property	H	Motor vehicle – mortgaged – removal from state	4	
	750. 418	Property	H	Removing a vehicle out of state without vendor's consent	4	
	750. 420	Pub saf	H	Motor vehicle – equipping to release smoke/gas	4	
	750. 421	Pub saf	H	Motor vehicle – designed for attack	5	
	750. 421 b	Pub saf	H	Hinder transport of farm/commercial products – subsequent offense	2	
MCL 777.16v						
	750. 422	Pub trst	G	Perjury committed in court/noncapital crime	15	
	750. 422	Pub trst	C	Perjury committed in court – noncapital crime	15	10/1/00
	750. 422	Pub trst	G	Perjury – committed in court/capital crime	LIFE	
	750. 422	Pub trst	B	Perjury committed in court – capital crime	LIFE	10/1/00
	750. 423	Pub trst	E	Perjury	15	
	750. 423	Pub trst	E	Perjury by falsely swearing	15	10/1/00
	750. 424	Pub trst	E	Subornation of perjury	15	
	750. 424	Pub trst	C	Subornation of perjury	15	10/1/00
	750. 425	Pub trst	E	Inciting or procuring perjury	5	
	750. 425	Pub trst	E	Inciting or procuring perjury but perjury not committed	5	10/1/00
	750. 430 a	Person	D	Human cloning	10	10/1/00
	750. 436 (1)	Person	E	Poisoning food/drink/wells	5	Deleted, 2002 PA 123, Eff. 4/22/02
	750. 436 (2)	Person	A	Poison – food/drink/medicine/wells – large amounts/injury	LIFE	Deleted, 2002 PA 123, Eff. 4/22/02
	750. 436 (2) (a)	Pub saf	C	Poisoning food, drink, medicine, or water supply	15	4/22/02
	750. 436 (2) (b)	Property	B	Poisoning food, drink, medicine, or water supply causing property damage	20	4/22/02
	750. 436 (2) (c)	Person	A	Poisoning food, drink, medicine, or water supply causing injury	25	4/22/02
	750. 436 (2) (d)	Person	A	Poisoning food, drink, medicine, or water supply causing serious impairment	LIFE	4/22/02
	750. 436 (3)	Pub saf	H	Poison – malicious false statement of poisoning	2	Deleted, 2002 PA 123, Eff. 4/22/02
	750. 436 (3) (a)	Pub ord	F	False report of poisoning food, drink, medicine, or water supply	4	4/22/02

Lightly shaded lines indicate that the statute governing the felony offense described on that line has been amended, deleted, or replaced.

Updated April 2007

*Unless otherwise noted, the date on which the statutory guidelines were made applicable to the felony offense listed is 1/1/99.

Felonies by MCL #	Group	Class	Description	Stat Max	Effective Date*
750. 436 (3) (b)	Pub ord	D	False report of poisoning food, drink, medicine, or water supply with prior conviction	10	4/22/02
750. 439	Pub ord	G	Polygamy	4	
750. 440	Pub ord	G	Polygamy – knowingly entering a prohibited marriage	4	
750. 441	Pub ord	G	Teaching or advocating polygamy	4	
750. 442	Pub ord	G	Participating in prizefights	4	
750. 443	Pub ord	G	Prizefights – training	4	
MCL 777.16w					
750. 451	Pub ord	G	Prostitution – various offenses – third or subsequent offense	2	
750. 452	Pub ord	E	Keeping a house of prostitution	5	
750. 455	Pub ord	G	Pandering	20	
750. 456	Person	B	Placing spouse into prostitution	20	
750. 457	Pub ord	G	Accepting earnings of a prostitute	20	
750. 458	Person	B	Prostitution – detaining female for debt	20	
750. 459	Person	B	Transporting a female for prostitution	20	
750. 462 b (1)	Person	D	Human trafficking - forced labor through physical harm	10	8/24/06
750. 462 b (2)	Person	C	Human trafficking - forced labor through physical harm causing injury	15	8/24/06
750. 462 b (3)	Person	A	Human trafficking - forced labor through physical harm causing death	LIFE	8/24/06
750. 462 c (1)	Person	D	Human trafficking - forced labor through physical restraint	10	8/24/06
750. 462 c (2)	Person	C	Human trafficking - forced labor through physical restraint causing injury	15	8/24/06
750. 462 c (3)	Person	A	Human trafficking - forced labor through physical restraint causing death	LIFE	8/24/06
750. 462 d (1)	Person	D	Human trafficking - forced labor through abuse of legal process	10	8/24/06
750. 462 d (2)	Person	C	Human trafficking - forced labor through abuse of legal process causing injury	15	8/24/06
750. 462 d (3)	Person	A	Human trafficking - forced labor through abuse of legal process causing death	LIFE	8/24/06
750. 462 e (1)	Person	D	Human trafficking - forced labor through destruction of ID document	10	8/24/06
750. 462 e (2)	Person	C	Human trafficking - forced labor through destruction of ID document causing injury	15	8/24/06
750. 462 e (3)	Person	A	Human trafficking - forced labor through destruction of ID document causing death	LIFE	8/24/06
750. 462 f (1)	Person	D	Human trafficking - forced labor through blackmail	10	8/24/06
750. 462 f (2)	Person	C	Human trafficking - forced labor through blackmail causing injury	15	8/24/06
750. 462 f (3)	Person	A	Human trafficking - forced labor through blackmail causing death	LIFE	8/24/06
750. 462 g (1)	Person	B	Human trafficking - obtain minor for child sexual abusive activity	20	8/24/06
750. 462 h (2)	Person	D	Human trafficking - recruit minor for forced labor	10	8/24/06
750. 462 h (3)	Person	C	Human trafficking - recruit minor for forced labor causing injury	15	8/24/06

Lightly shaded lines indicate that the statute governing the felony offense described on that line has been amended, deleted, or replaced.

*Unless otherwise noted, the date on which the statutory guidelines were made applicable to the felony offense listed is 1/1/99.

Felonies by MCL #	Group	Class	Description	Stat Max	Effective Date*
750. 462 h (4)	Person	A	Human trafficking - recruit minor for forced labor causing death	LIFE	8/24/06
750. 462 i	Person	A	Human trafficking - compound felony	LIFE	8/24/06
750. 465 a (1) (b)	Property	G	Operating audiovisual recording device in a theatrical facility - second offense	2	12/15/04
750. 465 a (1) (c)	Property	F	Operating audiovisual recording device in a theatrical facility - third or subsequent offense	40	38336
MCL 777.16x					
750. 478 a (2)	Pub ord	H	Unauthorized process to obstruct a public officer or employee	2	10/1/00
750. 478 a (3)	Pub ord	G	Unauthorized process to obstruct a public officer or employee – subsequent offense	4	10/1/00
750. 479	Person	G	Resisting or obstructing a peace officer	2	Substituted for by 750.479(2)
750. 479 (2)	Person	G	Assaulting or obstructing certain officials	2	7/15/02
750. 479 (3)	Person	G	Assaulting or obstructing certain officials causing injury	4	7/15/02
750. 479 (4)	Person	D	Assaulting or obstructing certain officials causing serious impairment	10	7/15/02
750. 479 (5)	Person	B	Assaulting or obstructing certain officials causing death	20	7/15/02
750. 479 a (2)	Pub saf	G	Fleeing and eluding – fourth degree	2	
750. 479 a (3)	Pub saf	E	Fleeing and eluding – third degree	5	
750. 479 a (4)	Person	D	Fleeing and eluding – second degree	10	
750. 479 a (5)	Person	C	Fleeing and eluding – first degree	15	
750. 479 a (6)	Person	H	Assaulting peace officer	2	Deleted, 2002 PA 271, Eff. 7/15/02
750. 479 b (1)	Person	F	Disarming peace officer – nonfirearm	4	
750. 479 b (2)	Person	D	Disarming peace officer – firearm	10	
750. 480	Pub trst	F	Public officers – refusing to turn over books/money to successor	4	
750. 483 a (2) (b)	Person	D	Retaliating for reporting crime	10	3/28/01
750. 483 a (2) (b)	Person	D	Retaliating for reporting crime punishable by more than 10 years	10	7/15/02
750. 483 a (2) (b)	Person	D	Withholding evidence/preventing/retaliating for reporting crime punishable by more than 10 yrs	10	As amended, 2006 PA 40, Eff. 3/2/06
750. 483 a (4) (b)	Person	F	Interfering with police investigation by committing crime or threatening to kill or injure	10	3/28/01
750. 483 a (4) (b)	Person	D	Interfering with police investigation by committing crime or threatening to kill or injure	10	7/15/02
750. 483 a (6) (a)	Pub ord	F	Tampering with evidence	4	3/28/01
750. 483 a (6) (a)	Pub ord	F	Tampering with evidence or offering false evidence	4	As amended, 2006 PA 40, Eff. 3/2/06
750. 483 a (6) (b)	Pub ord	D	Tampering with evidence in case punishable by more than 10 years	10	3/28/01
750. 483 a (6) (b)	Pub ord	D	Tampering with evidence/offering false evidence in case punishable by more than 10 years	10	As amended, 2006 PA 40, Eff. 3/2/06
750. 488	Pub trst	H	Public officers – state official – retaining fees	2	
750. 490	Pub trst	H	Public money – safekeeping	2	
750. 491	Pub trst	H	Public records – removal/mutilation/destruction	2	

Lightly shaded lines indicate that the statute governing the felony offense described on that line has been amended, deleted, or replaced.

MCL #

Updated April 2007

*Unless otherwise noted, the date on which the statutory guidelines were made applicable to the felony offense listed is 1/1/99.

	Felonies by MCL #	Group	Class	Description	Stat Max	Effective Date*
	750. 492 a (1) (a)	Pub trst	G	Medical record – intentional[ly] place false information – health care provider	4	
	750. 492 a (2)	Pub trst	G	Medical record – health care provider alter conceal injury/death	4	
	750. 492 a (2)	Pub trst	G	Medical record – health care provider - altering to conceal injury/death	4	As amended, 2006 PA 40, Eff. 3/2/06
	750. 495 a (2)	Person	F	Concealing objects in trees or wood products – causing injury	4	
	750. 495 a (3)	Person	C	Concealing objects in trees or wood products – causing death	15	
	750. 498 b (2) (a)	Person	E	Tampering/taking/removing marine safety device without authority causing serious impairment	5	7/1/06
	750. 498 b (2) (b)	Person	C	Tampering/taking/removing marine safety device without authority causing death	15	7/1/06
	750. 502 d	Pub saf	F	Unlawfully possessing or transporting anhydrous ammonia or tampering with containers	4	4/1/04
	750. 505	Pub ord	E	Common law offenses	5	
	750. 508 (2) (b)	Pub ord	G	Carrying or possessing a scanner in the commission of a crime	2	3/2/06
	750. 511	Person	A	Blocking or wrecking railroad track	LIFE	
	750. 512	Property	E	Uncoupling railroad cars	10	
	750. 513	Property	H	Issuing fraudulent railroad securities	10	Deleted, 2002 PA 320, Eff. 7/15/02
	750. 514	Property	H	Seizing locomotive with mail car	10	Deleted, 2002 PA 320, Eff. 7/15/02
	750. 516	Person	C	Stopping train to rob	LIFE	Deleted, 2002 PA 320, Eff. 7/15/02
	750. 517	Person	C	Boarding train to rob	LIFE	Deleted, 2002 PA 320, Eff. 7/15/02
MCL 777.16y						
	750. 520 b	Person	A	Criminal sexual conduct – first degree	LIFE	
	750. 520 b (2)	Person	A	Criminal sexual conduct -- first degree	LIFE	As amended, 2006 PA 166, Eff. 8/28/06 and 2006 PA 655, Eff. 1/9/07
	750. 520 c	Person	C	Criminal sexual conduct – second degree	15	
	750. 520 d	Person	C	Criminal sexual conduct – third degree	15	
	750. 520 d	Person	B	Criminal sexual conduct – third degree	15	10/1/00
	750. 520 e	Person	G	Criminal sexual conduct – fourth degree	2	
	750. 520 g (1)	Person	D	Assault with intent to commit sexual penetration	10	
	750. 520 g (2)	Person	E	Assault with intent to commit sexual contact	5	
	750. 520 n	Pub saf	G	Electronic monitoring device violation	2	8/28/06
	750. 528	Pub saf	F	Destroying dwelling house or other property	4	
	750. 528	Pub saf	F	Destroying dwelling house or other property during riot or unlawful assembly	4	As amended, 2006 PA 166, Eff. 8/28/06
	750. 528 a	Pub saf	F	Civil disorders – firearms/explosives	4	
	750. 529	Person	A	Armed robbery	LIFE	
	750. 529 a	Person	A	Carjacking	LIFE	
	750. 530	Person	C	Unarmed robbery	15	

Lightly shaded lines indicate that the statute governing the felony offense described on that line has been amended, deleted, or replaced.

MCL #

Updated April 2007

*Unless otherwise noted, the date on which the statutory guidelines were made applicable to the felony offense listed is 1/1/99.

Felonies by MCL #	Group	Class	Description	Stat Max	Effective Date*
750. 531	Person	C	Bank robbery/safebreaking	LIFE	
750. 532	Person	H	Seduction	5	
MCL 777.16z					
750. 535	Property	E	Receiving or concealing stolen property over $100	5	
750. 535 (2)	Property	D	Receiving/concealing stolen property having a value of $20,000 or more or with priors	10	10/1/00
750. 535 (3)	Property	E	Receiving or concealing stolen property having a value of $1,000 to $20,000 or with priors	5	10/1/00
750. 535 (7)	Property	E	Receiving or concealing stolen motor vehicle	5	2/12/04
750. 535 a	Pub ord	E	Operating a chop shop	5	Substituted for by 750.535a(2)
750. 535 a (2)	Pub ord	D	Operating a chop shop	10	10/1/00
750. 535 a (3)	Pub ord	D	Operating a chop shop – subsequent violation	10	10/1/00
750. 535 b	Pub saf	E	Stolen firearms or ammunition	10	
750. 539 c	Pub ord	H	Eavesdropping	2	
750. 539 d	Pub ord	H	Installing eavesdropping device	2	Replaced, 2004 PA 157, Eff. 6/16/04
750. 539 d (3) (a) (i)	Pub ord	H	Installing, placing, or using eavesdropping device	2	6/16/04
750. 539 d (3) (a) (ii)	Pub ord	E	Installing, placing, or using eavesdropping device – subsequent offense	5	6/16/04
750. 539 d (3) (b)	Pub ord	E	Distributing, disseminating, or transmitting recording or image obtained by eavesdropping	5	6/16/04
750. 539 e	Pub ord	H	Divulging or using information obtained by eavesdropping	2	
750. 539 f	Pub ord	H	Manufacture or possession of eavesdropping device	2	
750. 539 j (2) (a) (i)	Pub ord	H	Lewd surveillance or capturing lewd image	2	6/16/04
750. 539 j (2) (a) (ii)	Pub ord	E	Lewd surveillance or capturing lewd image – subsequent offense	5	6/16/04
750. 539 j (2) (b)	Pub ord	E	Distributing, disseminating, or transmitting visual image obtained by surveillance	5	6/16/04
750. 540	Pub ord	H	Tapping or cutting telephone lines	2	
750. 540 (5) (a)	Pub ord	H	Damaging, destroying, using, or obstructing use of electronic medium of communication	2	As amended, 2006 PA 62, Eff. 6/1/06
750. 540 (5) (b)	Person	F	Damaging/destroying/using/obstructing electronic communication resulting in injury/death	4	6/1/06
750. 540 c (3)	Property	F	Telecommunications and computer – manufacture or deliver counterfeit communications	4	
750. 540 c (3)	Property	F	Manufacturing or delivering a counterfeit communications device	4	Eff. 10/1/00 to 2/12/04, 2004 PA 2
750. 540 c (4)	Property	F	Telecommunication violation	4	2/12/04
750. 540 f (2)	Property	E	Telecommunications and computer–knowingly publishing counterfeit devices–2nd conviction	5	
750. 540 f (2)	Property	E	Knowingly publishing a communications access device with prior convictions	5	10/1/00
750. 540 g (1) (c)	Property	E	Diverting telecommunications services having a value of $1,000 - $20,000 or with priors	5	
750. 540 g (1) (d)	Property	D	Diverting telecommunications services having a value of $20,000 or more or with priors	10	
750. 543 f	Person	A	Terrorism without causing death	LIFE	4/22/02

Lightly shaded lines indicate that the statute governing the felony offense described on that line has been amended, deleted, or replaced.

Updated April 2007

*Unless otherwise noted, the date on which the statutory guidelines were made applicable to the felony offense listed is 1/1/99.

Felonies by MCL #	Group	Class	Description	Stat Max	Effective Date*
750. 543 h	Pub ord	A	Hindering prosecution of terrorism	LIFE	Eff. 4/22/02 to 7/15/02, 2002 PA 271
750. 543 h (3) (a)	Pub ord	B	Hindering prosecution of terrorism – certain terrorist acts	20	7/15/02
750. 543 h (3) (b)	Pub ord	A	Hindering prosecution of terrorism – act of terrorism	LIFE	7/15/02
750. 543 k	Pub saf	B	Soliciting material support for terrorism or terrorist acts	20	4/22/02
750. 543 k	Pub saf	B	Soliciting or providing material support for terrorism or terrorist acts	20	7/15/02
750. 543 m	Pub ord	B	Threat or false report of terrorism	20	4/22/02
750. 543 p	Pub saf	B	Use of internet or telecommunications to commit terrorism	20	4/22/02
750. 543 p	Pub saf	B	Use of internet or telecommunications to commit certain terrorist acts	20	7/15/02
750. 543 r	Pub saf	B	Surveillance of vulnerable target with intent to commit terrorism	20	4/22/02
750. 543 r	Pub saf	B	Possession of vulnerable target information with intent to commit certain terrorist acts	20	7/15/02
750. 545	Pub ord	E	Misprision of treason	5	
750. 552 b	Property	F	Trespassing on correctional facility property	4	
750. 552 c	Pub saf	F	Trespass upon key facility	4	4/15/06
MCL 777.17b					
752. 191	Pub saf	G	Felonious driving	2	Deleted, 2001 PA 136, Eff. 2/1/02
752. 272 (2) (c)	Pub saf	F	Sale or distribution of nitrous oxide device – 2 or more prior convictions	4	1/1/01
752. 365 (3)	Pub ord	G	Obscenity – subsequent offense	2	
752. 541	Pub saf	D	Riot	10	
752. 542	Pub saf	D	Incitement to riot	10	
752. 542 a	Pub saf	D	Riot in state correctional facilities	10	
752. 543	Pub saf	G	Unlawful assembly	5	
752. 701	Property	H	Destruction or removal of timber	1	
MCL 777.17c					
752. 797 (1) (c)	Property	E	Computer fraud – 2 prior convictions or value of $1,000 to $20,000	5	
752. 797 (1) (d)	Property	D	Computer fraud – 3 or more prior convictions or value of $20,000 or more	10	
752. 797 (2) (a)	Property	E	Unlawfully accessing computer, computer system, or computer program	5	10/1/00
752. 797 (2) (b)	Property	D	Unlawfully accessing computer, computer system, or computer program, with prior conviction	10	10/1/00
752. 797 (3) (b)	Variable	G	Using computer for crime punishable by maximum term of more than 1 yr but less than 2 yrs	2	10/1/00
752. 797 (3) (c)	Variable	F	Using computer for crime punishable by maximum term of at least 2 yrs but less than 4 yrs	4	10/1/00
752. 797 (3) (d)	Variable	D	Using computer for crime punishable by maximum term of at least 4 yrs but less than 10 yrs	7	10/1/00
752. 797 (3) (e)	Variable	D	Using computer for crime punishable by maximum term of at least 10 yrs but less than 20 yrs	10	10/1/00
752. 797 (3) (f)	Variable	B	Using computerfor crime punishable by maximum term of at least 20 yrs or for life	20	10/1/00

Lightly shaded lines indicate that the statute governing the felony offense described on that line has been amended, deleted, or replaced.

Updated April 2007

*Unless otherwise noted, the date on which the statutory guidelines were made applicable to the felony offense listed is 1/1/99.

Felonies by MCL #	Group	Class	Description	Stat Max	Effective Date*
MCL 777.17d					
752. 802	Property	H	Vending machines – manufacture/sale of slugs	5	
752. 811	Property	H	Breaking and entering a coin operated device	3	
752. 861	Person	G	Careless discharge of firearm causing injury or death	2	
752. 881	Person	G	Reckless use of bow and arrow resulting in injury or death	2	
752. 1003	Property	F	Health care fraud – false claim/state, unnecessary, conceal information	4	
752. 1004	Property	F	Health care fraud – kickbacks/referral fees	4	
752. 1005	Property	H	Health care fraud – conspiracy	10	
752. 1006	Property	D	Health care fraud – subsequent offense	20	
752. 1027	Person	F	Assisted suicide	4	
752. 1054 (2)	Property	G	Copying audio/video recordings for gain	5	
MCL 777.17f					
764. 1 e	Pub trst	C	Peace officer – false statement in a complaint	15	
767. 4 a	Pub trst	F	Disclosing or possessing grand jury information	4	
767A. 9 (a)	Pub trst	C	Perjury committed in prosecutor's investigative hearing – noncapital crime	15	Eff. 10/1/00 then replaced by .9(1)(a)
767A. 9 (1) (a)	Pub trst	C	Perjury committed in prosecutor's investigative hearing – noncapital crime	15	2/1/02
767A. 9 (b)	Pub trst	B	Perjury committed in prosecutor's investigative hearing – capital crime	LIFE	Eff. 10/1/00, then replaced by .9(1)(b)
767A. 9 (1) (b)	Pub trst	B	Perjury committed in prosecutor's investigative hearing – capital crime	LIFE	2/1/02
791. 236 (17)	Pub ord	F	Failure to provide correct notice of proposed domicile by sex offender	4	12/1/06
MCL 777.17g					
800. 281 (1)	Pub saf	H	Furnishing prisoner with contraband	5	
800. 281 (2)	Pub saf	H	Furnishing prisoner with contraband outside	5	
800. 281 (3)	Pub saf	H	Bringing contraband into prisons	5	
800. 281 (4)	Pub saf	E	Prisoner possessing contraband	5	
800. 283 (1)	Pub saf	E	Furnishing weapon to prisoner in prison	5	
800. 283 (2)	Pub saf	E	Prisons – knowledge of a weapon in a correctional facility	5	
800. 283 (3)	Pub saf	E	Bringing weapon into prison	5	
800. 283 (4)	Pub saf	E	Prisoner possessing weapon	5	
800. 283 a	Pub saf	E	Furnishing cell phone to prisoner	5	12/29/06
801. 262 (1) (a)	Pub saf	E	Bringing weapon into jail	5	8/1/99
801. 262 (1) (b)	Pub saf	E	Furnishing weapon to prisoner in jail	5	8/1/99
801. 262 (2)	Pub saf	E	Prisoner in jail possessing weapon	5	8/1/99

Lightly shaded lines indicate that the statute governing the felony offense described on that line has been amended, deleted, or replaced.

Updated April 2007

*Unless otherwise noted, the date on which the statutory guidelines were made applicable to the felony offense listed is 1/1/99.

Felonies by MCL #	Group	Class	Description	Stat Max	Effective Date*
801. 263 (1)	Pub saf	H	Furnishing contraband to prisoner in jail	5	8/1/99
801. 263 (2)	Pub saf	H	Prisoner in jail possessing contraband	5	8/1/99

Lightly shaded lines indicate that the statute governing the felony offense described on that line has been amended, deleted, or replaced.

*Unless otherwise noted, the date on which the statutory guidelines were made applicable to the felony offense listed is 1/1/99.

MCL #	Group	Class	Description	Stat Max	Effective Date*
750. 14	Person	G	Abortion	4	
750. 323	Person	C	Abortion resulting in death	15	
750. 14	Person	C	Abortion resulting in death of female	15	
333. 2689	Person	E	Abortion to obtain embryo	5	See MCL 333.2691
750. 199 a	Pub ord	F	Absconding on or forfeiting bond	4	
168. 932 (e)	Pub trst	E	Absentee ballot tampering	5	
750. 457	Pub ord	G	Accepting earnings of a prostitute	20	
750. 145 b	Person	F	Accosting children for immoral purposes – subsequent offense	4	
750. 145 b	Person	D	Accosting children for immoral purposes with prior conviction	10	6/1/02
710. 55 (1)	Pub trst	F	Adoption – persons not authorized placing child – subsequent violation	4	
400. 722 (4)	Pub saf	F	Adult foster care – maintaining operation after refusal of licensure	5	
400. 713 (13)	Pub saf	H	Adult foster care – unlicensed facility	2	7/1/01
400. 713 (13)	Pub saf	H	Adult foster care – unlicensed facility – first offense	2	
400. 713 (13)	Pub saf	F	Adult foster care – unlicensed facility – second or subsequent violation	5	
400. 713 (13)	Pub saf	F	Adult foster care – unlicensed facility – subsequent violation	5	7/1/01
333. 17764 (3)	Pub saf	F	Adulterate, misbrand, remove, or substitute a drug or device	2	10/12/04
333. 17764 (6)	Pub saf	C	Adulterate, misbrand, remove, or substitute a drug or device causing death	15	10/12/04
333. 17764 (4)	Pub saf	F	Adulterate, misbrand, remove, or substitute a drug or device causing personal injury	4	10/12/04
750. 16 (1)	Person	G	Adulterate, misbrand, remove, or substitute a drug or medicine	2	10/12/04
750. 16 (2)	Person	F	Adulterate, misbrand, remove, or substitute a drug or medicine causing personal injury	4	10/12/04
750. 16 (4)	Person	C	Adulterate, misbrand, remove, or substitute a drug or medicine resulting in death	15	10/12/04
333. 17764 (5)	Pub saf	E	Adulterate/misbrand/remove/substitute a drug/device - serious impairment of a body function	5	10/12/04
750. 16 (3)	Person	E	Adulterate/misbrand/remove/substitute a drug/medicine - serious impairment of body function	5	10/12/04
289. 5107 (2)	Pub saf	F	Adulterated, misbranded, or falsely identified food	4	10/1/00
750. 30	Pub ord	H	Adultery	4	
750. 81 a (3)	Person	G	Aggravated domestic assault – second offense	2	
750. 81 a (3)	Person	G	Aggravated domestic assault with prior convictions	2	10/1/00
750. 335 a (2) (b)	Person	G	Aggravated indecent exposure	2	2/1/06
750. 411 i (3) (a)	Person	E	Aggravated stalking	5	10/1/00
750. 411 i (3) (b)	Person	D	Aggravated stalking of a minor	10	
287. 855	Pub saf	G	Agriculture – contaminating livestock/false statement/violation of quarantine	5	
286. 455 (2)	Pub saf	G	Agriculture – hazardous substance	5	

Lightly shaded lines indicate that the statute governing the felony offense described on that line has been amended, deleted, or replaced.

Updated April 2007

*Unless otherwise noted, the date on which the statutory guidelines were made applicable to the felony offense listed is 1/1/99.

MCL #	Group	Class	Description	Stat Max	Effective Date*
287. 77 (1)	Pub saf	H	Agriculture – livestock condemnation	4	
205. 27 (1) (b)	Pub trst	G	Aiding and abetting tax evasion or filing false returns	5	
750. 183	Pub saf	E	Aiding escaping prisoner	7	
750. 208	Pub saf	C	Aiding or abetting explosives placement with intent to destroy property	15	
333. 5210	Person	F	AIDS – sexual penetration with uninformed partner	4	
259. 83 (2) (b)	Pub saf	G	Aircraft – failure to comply with certification requirements – second violation	2	3/31/03
259. 83 (2) (c)	Pub saf	F	Aircraft – failure to comply with certification requirements – third or subsequent violation	4	3/31/03
259. 183	Property	E	Aircraft – unlawful taking or tampering	5	
750. 367 b	Property	E	Airplanes – taking possession	5	
257. 625 (10) (b)	Person	E	Allowing a vehicle to be operated while intoxicated or impaired causing death	5	9/30/03
257. 625 (10) (c)	Person	G	Allowing a vehicle to be operated while intoxicated or impaired causing serious impairment	2	9/30/03
257. 625 (9) (b)	Person	E	Allowing a vehicle to be operated while under the influence or impaired causing death	5	Eff. until 9/30/03, replaced by (10)(b)
257. 625 (9) (c)	Person	G	Allowing a vehicle to be operated while under the influence/impaired - serious impairment	2	Eff. until 9/30/03, replaced by (10)(c)
257. 904 (7)	Person	E	Allowing a vehicle to be operated without a license causing death	5	10/1/00
257. 904 (7)	Person	G	Allowing a vehicle to be operated without a license causing serious impairment	2	10/1/00
750. 230	Pub saf	G	Altering ID mark on firearm	2	
257. 257 (1)	Property	G	Altering or forging vehicle documents – first offense	5	
257. 257 (2)	Property	G	Altering or forging vehicle documents – second offense	7	
257. 257 (3)	Property	E	Altering or forging vehicle documents – third or subsequent offense	15	
117. 25 (3)	Pub trst	E	Amendment to city electors – willfully affixing another's signature, false representation	15	
287. 744 (1)	Pub ord	G	Animal industry act violations	5	
750. 50 (4)	Pub ord	G	Animal neglect or cruelty – second offense	2	
750. 50 (4)	Pub ord	F	Animal neglect or cruelty – third or subsequent offense	4	
750. 300	Pub ord	G	Animals – killing/injuring to defraud insurance company	2	
445. 779	Pub ord	H	Antitrust violation	2	
51. 364	Pub trst	H	Appointment or selection contrary to civil service commission rules	2	
750. 529	Person	A	Armed robbery	LIFE	
750. 224 c	Pub saf	F	Armor piercing ammunition	4	
750. 72	Person	B	Arson of dwelling house	20	
750. 75	Property	D	Arson of insured property	10	
750. 80	Property	D	Arson of mines	LIFE	
750. 74	Person	F	Arson of personal property greater than $50	4	

Lightly shaded lines indicate that the statute governing the felony offense described on that line has been amended, deleted, or replaced.

*Unless otherwise noted, the date on which the statutory guidelines were made applicable to the felony offense listed is 1/1/99.

MCL #	Group	Class	Description	Stat Max	Effective Date*
750. 74	Person	E	Arson of personal property having a value of $1,000 to $20,000 or with prior convictions	5	10/1/00
750. 74 (1) (d)	Person	D	Arson of personal property of $20,000 or more or with prior convictions	10	10/1/00
750. 73	Property	D	Arson of real property	10	
750. 78	Pub saf	F	Arson of woods and prairies	4	
750. 90 a	Person	A	Assault against a pregnant individual causing miscarriage/stillbirth with intent or recklessness	LIFE	10/1/00
750. 90 b (b)	Person	D	Assault against a pregnant individual resulting in great bodily harm to embryo or fetus	10	10/1/00
750. 90 b (a)	Person	C	Assault against a pregnant individual resulting in miscarriage or stillbirth	15	10/1/00
750. 90 b (a)	Person	C	Assault against a pregnant individual resulting in miscarriage/stillbirth/death to embryo or fetus	15	6/1/01
750. 81 c (2)	Person	G	Assault and battery of an FIA employee	2	9/1/01
750. 81 c (3)	Person	E	Assault and battery of an FIA employee causing serious impairment	5	9/1/01
750. 90 a	Person	A	Assault causing miscarriage/stillbirth/death to embryo/fetus w/ intent or recklessness	LIFE	6/1/01
750. 87	Person	D	Assault with intent to commit a felony	10	
750. 89	Person	A	Assault with intent to commit armed robbery	LIFE	
750. 520 g (2)	Person	E	Assault with intent to commit sexual contact	5	
750. 520 g (1)	Person	D	Assault with intent to commit sexual penetration	10	
750. 88	Person	C	Assault with intent to commit unarmed robbery	15	
750. 84	Person	D	Assault with intent to do great bodily harm less than murder	10	
750. 86	Person	D	Assault with intent to maim	10	
750. 83	Person	A	Assault with intent to murder	LIFE	
750. 479 (2)	Person	G	Assaulting or obstructing certain officials	2	7/15/02
750. 479 (5)	Person	B	Assaulting or obstructing certain officials causing death	20	7/15/02
750. 479 (3)	Person	G	Assaulting or obstructing certain officials causing injury	4	7/15/02
750. 479 (4)	Person	D	Assaulting or obstructing certain officials causing serious impairment	10	7/15/02
750. 479 a (6)	Person	H	Assaulting peace officer	2	Deleted, 2002 PA 271, Eff. 7/15/02
750. 81 d (1)	Person	G	Assaulting, resisting, or obstructing certain persons	2	7/15/02
750. 81 d (4)	Person	B	Assaulting, resisting, or obstructing certain persons causing death	20	7/15/02
750. 81 d (2)	Person	F	Assaulting, resisting, or obstructing certain persons causing injury	4	7/15/02
750. 81 d (3)	Person	C	Assaulting, resisting, or obstructing certain persons causing serious impairment	15	7/15/02
752. 1027	Person	F	Assisted suicide	4	
750. 329 a	Person	E	Assisting a suicide	5	10/1/00
168. 761 (5)	Pub trst	E	Assisting an absentee voter in making a false statement	5	
750. 91	Person	A	Attempted murder	LIFE	

Lightly shaded lines indicate that the statute governing the felony offense described on that line has been amended, deleted, or replaced.

*Unless otherwise noted, the date on which the statutory guidelines were made applicable to the felony offense listed is 1/1/99.

MCL #	Group	Class	Description	Stat Max	Effective Date*
750. 49 (2) (f)	Pub ord	H	Attending animal fight	4	
168. 932 (b)	Pub trst	E	Ballot tampering	5	
750. 531	Person	C	Bank robbery/safebreaking	LIFE	
750. 100	Pub trst	E	Banks – conducting business when insolvent	5	
487. 1505 (6)	Pub trst	E	BIDCO act – knowingly receiving money or property at an interest rate exceeding 25%	5	
482. 49	Property	H	Bills of lading – inducing carrier to issue when goods have not been received	5	
482. 44	Property	H	Bills of lading – issuance for goods not received	5	
482. 46	Property	H	Bills of lading – issuance of duplicate negotiable bill with intent to defraud	5	As amended, 2006 PA 251, Eff. 7/3/06
482. 46	Property	H	Bills of lading – issuance of duplicate not so marked	5	
482. 50	Property	H	Bills of lading – issuance of non-negotiable bill not so marked	5	
482. 48	Property	H	Bills of lading – negotiation when goods not in carriers' possession	5	
750. 511	Person	A	Blocking or wrecking railroad track	LIFE	
451. 603 (h)	Pub trst	E	Blue sky laws – fail to notify administrator of sanctions	10	See MCL 451.809
451. 805 (b)	Pub trst	E	Blue sky laws – false representation of administrative approval	10	See MCL 451.809
451. 501	Pub trst	E	Blue sky laws – fraudulent schemes/statements	10	See MCL 451.809
451. 806 (b)	Pub trst	E	Blue sky laws – improper disclosure by cor and sec bur employee	10	See MCL 451.809
451. 502	Pub trst	E	Blue sky laws – investment advisor/agent fraud	10	See MCL 451.809
451. 503	Pub trst	E	Blue sky laws – make/sell false bullion/certificates	10	See MCL 451.809
451. 701	Pub trst	E	Blue sky laws – offer/sell unregistered securities	10	See MCL 451.809
451. 802	Pub trst	E	Blue sky laws – unlawfully selling securities	10	See MCL 451.809
451. 601	Pub trst	E	Blue sky laws – unregistered broker/dealer/agent/advisor	10	See MCL 451.809
451. 604 (a) (1) (J)	Pub trst	E	Blue sky laws – various violations	10	See MCL 451.809
451. 604 (a) (1) (K)	Pub trst	E	Blue sky laws – various violations	10	See MCL 451.809
451. 604 (a) (1) (L)	Pub trst	E	Blue sky laws – various violations	10	See MCL 451.809
451. 604 (a) (1) (M)	Pub trst	E	Blue sky laws – various violations	10	See MCL 451.809
451. 604 (a) (1) (N)	Pub trst	E	Blue sky laws – various violations	10	See MCL 451.809
451. 604 (a) (1) (O)	Pub trst	E	Blue sky laws – various violations	10	See MCL 451.809
451. 604 (a) (1) (P)	Pub trst	E	Blue sky laws – various violations	10	See MCL 451.809
451. 604 (a) (1) (Q)	Pub trst	E	Blue sky laws – various violations	10	See MCL 451.809
451. 604 (a) (1) (R)	Pub trst	E	Blue sky laws – various violations	10	See MCL 451.809
451. 604 (a) (1) (S)	Pub trst	E	Blue sky laws – various violations	10	See MCL 451.809
451. 604 (a) (1) (V)	Pub trst	E	Blue sky laws – various violations	10	See MCL 451.809

Lightly shaded lines indicate that the statute governing the felony offense described on that line has been amended, deleted, or replaced.

Updated April 2007

*Unless otherwise noted, the date on which the statutory guidelines were made applicable to the felony offense listed is 1/1/99.

MCL #	Group	Class	Description	Stat Max	Effective Date*
451. 604 (a) (1) (W)	Pub trst	E	Blue sky laws – various violations	10	See MCL 451.809
451. 604 (a) (1) (X)	Pub trst	E	Blue sky laws – various violations	10	See MCL 451.809
451. 604 (a) (1) (Y)	Pub trst	E	Blue sky laws – various violations	10	See MCL 451.809
451. 604 (a) (1) (Z)	Pub trst	E	Blue sky laws – various violations	10	See MCL 451.809
451. 804	Pub trst	E	Blue sky laws – willful false statements	10	See MCL 451.809
750. 517	Person	C	Boarding train to rob	LIFE	Deleted, 2002 PA 320, Eff. 7/15/02
750. 106	Property	G	Boats – making or procuring false protest	4	
752. 811	Property	H	Breaking and entering a coin operated device	3	
750. 356 b	Property	G	Breaking and entering a coin telephone	4	
750. 356 a (2) (c)	Property	E	Breaking and entering a vehicle to steal $1,000 to $20,000 or with prior convictions	5	10/1/00
750. 356 a (2) (d)	Property	D	Breaking and entering a vehicle to steal $20,000 or more or with prior convictions	10	10/1/00
750. 356 a (3)	Property	G	Breaking and entering a vehicle to steal causing damage	5	10/1/00
750. 110	Property	D	Breaking and entering with intent to commit felony or larceny	10	
750. 49 (2) (g)	Pub ord	F	Breeding or selling fighting animals	4	
750. 119	Pub trst	F	Bribing a juror or other person	4	Substituted for by 750.119(1)(a)
750. 119 (1) (a)	Pub trst	F	Bribing a juror or other person	4	3/28/01
750. 119 (1) (b)	Pub trst	D	Bribing a juror or other person in case punishable by more than 10 years	10	3/28/01
750. 117	Pub trst	F	Bribing a public officer	4	
750. 121	Pub trst	F	Bribing a public officer to influence contract	4	
750. 124	Pub trst	G	Bribing an athlete	4	
168. 932 (a)	Pub trst	E	Bribing or intimidating voters	5	
750. 122 (7) (a)	Pub ord	F	Bribing or intimidating witness	4	3/28/01
750. 122 (7) (b)	Pub ord	D	Bribing or intimidating witness in case punishable by more than 10 years	10	3/28/01
800. 281 (3)	Pub saf	H	Bringing contraband into prisons	5	
801. 262 (1) (a)	Pub saf	E	Bringing weapon into jail	5	8/1/99
800. 283 (3)	Pub saf	E	Bringing weapon into prison	5	
750. 128	Pub ord	H	Bucket shop violation	2	
750. 112	Person	A	Burglary with explosives		
750. 136 c	Person	B	Buying or selling an individual	20	10/1/00
445. 408 (2)	Pub ord	F	Buying or selling stolen scrap metal	3	3/30/07
445. 408 (3)	Pub ord	E	Buying/selling stolen scrap metal from utility pole, telecom corp/govt/utility property or jobsite	5	3/30/07
169. 254	Pub trst	H	Campaign finance – corporate contributions	3	

Lightly shaded lines indicate that the statute governing the felony offense described on that line has been amended, deleted, or replaced.

*Unless otherwise noted, the date on which the statutory guidelines were made applicable to the felony offense listed is 1/1/99.

MCL #	Group	Class	Description	Stat Max	Effective Date*
169. 255	Pub trst	H	Campaign finance – corporate solicitation for certain funds	3	
169. 266	Pub trst	H	Campaign finance – qualified campaign expenditures	3	
752. 861	Person	G	Careless discharge of firearm causing injury or death	2	
750. 90 e	Person	G	Careless or reckless driving causing miscarriage or stillbirth	2	10/1/00
750. 90 e	Person	G	Careless or reckless driving causing miscarriage, stillbirth, or death to embryo or fetus	2	6/1/01
750. 529 a	Person	A	Carjacking	LIFE	
750. 227	Pub saf	E	Carrying a concealed weapon	5	
28. 425 o (5) (c)	Pub saf	F	Carrying concealed pistol in prohibited place – third or subsequent offense	4	7/1/01
750. 226	Pub saf	E	Carrying firearm or dangerous weapon with unlawful intent	5	
750. 508 (2) (b)	Pub ord	G	Carrying or possessing a scanner in the commission of a crime	2	3/2/06
432. 218	Pub ord	D	Casino gaming offenses	10	
750. 99	Pub trst	G	Certifying checks without sufficient funds	4	
287. 967 (5)	Pub ord	G	Cervidae producer violations	4	10/1/00
750. 68	Property	G	Changing brands with intent to steal	4	
750. 136 b (2)	Person	C	Child abuse – first degree	15	
750. 136 b (2)	Person	B	Child abuse – first degree	15	10/1/00
750. 136 b (4)	Person	F	Child abuse – second degree	4	
750. 136 b (5)	Person	G	Child abuse – third degree	2	
750. 145 c (4)	Person	F	Child sexually abusive activities or materials – possession	4	6/1/02
750. 145 c (2)	Person	B	Child sexually abusive activity or materials – active involvement	20	
750. 145 c (3)	Person	D	Child sexually abusive activity or materials – distributing, promoting or financing	7	
750. 528 a	Pub saf	F	Civil disorders – firearms/explosives	4	
750. 32	Pub ord	H	Cohabitation of divorced parties	4	
257. 625 m (5)	Pub saf	E	Commercial drunk driving – third or subsequent offense	5	10/1/00
750. 505	Pub ord	E	Common law offenses	5	
205. 28	Pub trst	G	Compromising/unauthorized disclosure of tax information	5	
752. 797 (1) (c)	Property	E	Computer fraud – 2 prior convictions or value of $1,000 to $20,000	5	
752. 797 (1) (d)	Property	D	Computer fraud – 3 or more prior convictions or value of $20,000 or more	10	
750. 149	Pub saf	F	Concealing an offense punishable by life	4	
750. 495 a (3)	Person	C	Concealing objects in trees or wood products – causing death	15	
750. 495 a (2)	Person	F	Concealing objects in trees or wood products – causing injury	4	
259. 83 b (2) (a)	Pub saf	F	Conducting flight operations without certificate	4	3/31/03

Lightly shaded lines indicate that the statute governing the felony offense described on that line has been amended, deleted, or replaced.

*Unless otherwise noted, the date on which the statutory guidelines were made applicable to the felony offense listed is 1/1/99.

MCL #	Group	Class	Description	Stat Max	Effective Date*
259. 83 b (2) (b)	Pub saf	E	Conducting flight operations without certificate – second violation	5	3/31/03
259. 83 b (2) (c)	Pub saf	D	Conducting flight operations without certificate – third or subsequent violation	10	3/31/03
500. 8197 (3)	Property	E	Consolidation merger – compensation otherwise than expressed in contract	5	
750. 157 a (a)	Pub saf	SPEC	Conspiracy	Variable	
750. 157 a (b)	Pub ord	H	Conspiracy – gambling	5	
750. 410 a	Person	G	Conspiracy to commit a person to state hospital unjustly	4	
750. 157 a (d)	Pub ord	G	Conspiracy to commit legal act in illegal manner	5	
570. 1207	Property	G	Construction liens – false information	4	
570. 1110 (c)	Property	E	Contractor – false sworn statement involving $1,000 to $20,000 or with prior convictions	5	1/1/02
570. 1110 (d)	Property	D	Contractor – false sworn statement involving $20,000 or more or with prior convictions	10	1/1/02
570. 1110	Property	F	Contractor – false sworn statements over $100	4	Deleted, 2001 PA 152, Eff. 1/1/02
570. 152	Property	G	Contractor – fraudulent use of building contract fund	3	
333. 7410	CS	SPEC	Controlled substance delivery or distribution to minors or students	Variable	
333. 7410 a	CS	G	Controlled substance offense in or near a park	2	10/1/00
333. 7410	CS	SPEC	Controlled substance offense on or near school property	Variable	10/1/00
333. 7410 a	CS	G	Controlled substance offense or offense involving GBL in or near a park	2	1/1/01
333. 7410	CS	SPEC	Controlled substance offense or offense involving GBL on or near school property	Variable	1/1/01
333. 7410	CS	SPEC	Controlled substance offense or offense involving GBL on or near school property or library	Variable	As amended, 2006 PA 553, Eff. 3/30/07
333. 7405 (a)	CS	G	Controlled substance violations by licensee	2	
333. 7407 (1) (a)	CS	G	Controlled substance violations by licensee	4	
328. 232	Property	E	Conversion of funeral contracts	5	
752. 1054 (2)	Property	G	Copying audio/video recordings for gain	5	
450. 795	Pub ord	H	Corporations – handicapper business opportunity act	2	
450. 775	Pub ord	H	Corporations – minority and woman owned businesses	2	
257. 312 b (6)	Pub ord	F	Corrupting a person or agency conducting a motorcycle driving test	5	3/28/01
257. 309 (6)	Pub ord	F	Corrupting an examining officer - see MCL 257.309(7)	5	3/28/01
750. 260	Property	E	Counterfeiting coins or possession of 5 or more counterfeit coins	LIFE	
750. 266	Property	G	Counterfeiting railroad tickets	4	Deleted, 2002 PA 321, Eff. 7/15/02
28. 295 (1) (a)	Pub ord	D	Counterfeiting/forging/using counterfeited/forged state ID for felony punishable by 10+ years	10	9/1/04
28. 295 (1) (b)	Pub ord	E	Counterfeiting/forging/using state ID for felony punishable by <10 yrs/misdemeanor by >6 mos	5	9/1/04
38. 412 a (1)	Pub trst	H	County employee providing answers to county civil service exam	1	
45. 82	Pub trst	E	County purchasing agent – violations in awarding bids or contracts	5	

Lightly shaded lines indicate that the statute governing the felony offense described on that line has been amended, deleted, or replaced.

Updated April 2007

*Unless otherwise noted, the date on which the statutory guidelines were made applicable to the felony offense listed is 1/1/99.

MCL #	Group	Class	Description	Stat Max	Effective Date*
487. 1042 (2)	Pub trst	E	Criminal fraud in the conduct of money transmission services business	5	7/3/06
750. 520 b (2)	Person	A	Criminal sexual conduct -- first degree	LIFE	As amended, 2006 PA 166, Eff. 8/28/06 and 2006 PA 655, Eff. 1/9/07
750. 520 b	Person	A	Criminal sexual conduct – first degree	LIFE	
750. 520 e	Person	G	Criminal sexual conduct – fourth degree	2	
750. 520 c	Person	C	Criminal sexual conduct – second degree	15	
750. 520 d	Person	C	Criminal sexual conduct – third degree	15	
750. 520 d	Person	B	Criminal sexual conduct – third degree	15	10/1/00
330. 1944	Pub saf	F	Criminal sexual psychopath leaving state without permission	4	1/9/07
438. 41	Property	E	Criminal usury	5	
324. 52908 (1) (c)	Property	E	Damage to plant involving $1,000 to $20,000 or with prior convictions	5	1/1/02
324. 52908 (1) (d)	Property	D	Damage to plant involving $20,000 or more or with prior convictions	10	1/1/02
324. 2157 (1) (c)	Property	E	Damage to state property involving $1,000 to $20,000 or with prior convictions	5	1/1/02
324. 2157 (1) (d)	Property	D	Damage to state property involving $20,000 or more or with prior convictions	10	1/1/02
750. 385 (2) (g)	Person	C	Damaging or destroying research property resulting in death	15	Eff. 4/1/05 to 9/14/05
750. 395 (2) (g)	Person	C	Damaging or destroying research property resulting in death	15	Replaced MCL 750.385(2)(g), 2005 PA 106, Eff. 9/14/05
750. 385 (2) (e)	Person	E	Damaging or destroying research property resulting in physical injury	5	Eff. 4/1/05 to 9/14/05
750. 395 (2) (e)	Person	E	Damaging or destroying research property resulting in physical injury	5	Replaced MCL 750.385(2)(e), 2005 PA 106, Eff. 9/14/05
750. 385 (2) (f)	Person	D	Damaging or destroying research property resulting in serious impairment of body function	10	Eff. 4/1/05 to 9/14/05
750. 395 (2) (f)	Person	D	Damaging or destroying research property resulting in serious impairment of body function	10	Replaced MCL 750.385(2)(f), 2005 PA 106, Eff. 9/14/05
750. 540 (5) (a)	Pub ord	H	Damaging, destroying, using, or obstructing use of electronic medium of communication	2	As amended, 2006 PA 62, Eff. 6/1/06
750. 385 (2) (d)	Property	E	Damaging/destroying research property - $20,000 or more or 2 or more prior convictions	5	Eff. 4/1/05 to 9/14/05
750. 395 (2) (d)	Property	E	Damaging/destroying research property - $20,000 or more or 2 or more prior convictions	5	Replaced MCL 750.385(2)(d), 2005 PA 106, Eff. 9/14/05
750. 385 (2) (c)	Property	E	Damaging/destroying research property-between $1,000 and $20,000 or w/ prior convictions	5	Eff. 4/1/05 to 9/14/05
750. 395 (2) (c)	Property	E	Damaging/destroying research property-between $1,000 and $20,000 or w/ prior convictions	5	Replaced MCL 750.385(2)(c), 2005 PA 106, Eff. 9/14/05
750. 540 (5) (b)	Person	F	Damaging/destroying/using/obstructing electronic communication resulting in injury/death	4	6/1/06
287. 323 (1)	Person	C	Dangerous animal causing death	15	
287. 323 (2)	Person	G	Dangerous animal causing serious injury	4	
287. 679	Pub ord	H	Dead animals	1	
287. 679	Pub ord	H	Dead animals – third or subsequent violation	1	10/1/01
750. 328	Person	A	Death by explosives in or near building	LIFE	
750. 327	Person	A	Death by explosives on vehicle or vessel	LIFE	
750. 145 o	Person	E	Death of vulnerable adult caused by unlicensed caretaker	5	

Lightly shaded lines indicate that the statute governing the felony offense described on that line has been amended, deleted, or replaced.

*Unless otherwise noted, the date on which the statutory guidelines were made applicable to the felony offense listed is 1/1/99.

MCL #	Group	Class	Description	Stat Max	Effective Date*
451. 434	Pub trst	H	Debt management act – licensee violations	2	
333. 7401 a	Person	B	Delivering a controlled substance or GBL with intent to commit criminal sexual conduct	20	1/1/01
333. 7401 a	Person	B	Delivering a controlled substance with intent to commit criminal sexual conduct	20	10/1/00
750. 317 a	Person	A	Delivery of controlled substance causing death	LIFE	1/1/06
333. 17766 a (4)	CS	G	Delivery of imitation steroids	7	Deleted, 2003 PA 309, Eff. 4/1/04
333. 7401 (2) (d) (i)	CS	C	Delivery or manufacture of 45 or more kilograms of marijuana	15	
333. 7401 (2) (d) (ii)	CS	D	Delivery or manufacture of 5 or more but less than 45 kilograms of marijuana	7	
333. 7401 (2) (a) (i)	CS	A	Delivery or manufacture of 650 or more grams by juvenile	LIFE	
333. 7402 (2) (a)	CS	D	Delivery or manufacture of an imitation controlled substance	10	
333. 7401 (2) (f)	CS	D	Delivery or manufacture of an official or counterfeit prescription form	20	Deleted, 2001 PA 236, Eff. 1/6/03
333. 7402 (2) (a)	CS	D	Delivery or manufacture of certain imitation controlled substances	10	1/1/01
333. 7401 (2) (b) (ii)	CS	E	Delivery or manufacture of certain schedule 1, 2, or 3 controlled substances	7	1/1/01
333. 7402 (2) (e)	CS	C	Delivery or manufacture of controlled substance analogue	15	
333. 7401 b (3) (a)	CS	E	Delivery or manufacture of GBL	7	1/1/01
333. 7341 (8)	CS	G	Delivery or manufacture of imitation controlled substance	2	
333. 7402 (2) (c)	CS	F	Delivery or manufacture of imitation schedule 4 controlled substance	4	
333. 7402 (2) (d)	CS	G	Delivery or manufacture of imitation schedule 5 controlled substance	2	
333. 7401 (2) (d) (iii)	CS	F	Delivery or manufacture of less than 5 kilograms or 20 plants of marijuana	4	
333. 7401 (2) (b) (i)	CS	B	Delivery or manufacture of methamphetamine	20	1/1/01
333. 7401 (2) (b) (i)	CS	B	Delivery or manufacture of methamphetamine or 3, 4-methylenedioxymethamphetamine	20	4/1/03
333. 7401 (2) (f)	CS	D	Delivery or manufacture of prescription form or counterfeit prescription form	7	3/1/03
333. 7401 (2) (g)	CS	D	Delivery or manufacture of prescription or counterfeit form (other than official)	7	Rewritten as .7401(2)(f), 2001 PA 236
333. 7401 (2) (f)	CS	D	Delivery or manufacture of prescription or counterfeit form other than official	7	1/6/03
333. 7401 (2) (b)	CS	E	Delivery or manufacture of schedule 1, 2, or 3 controlled substance except marijuana	7	
333. 7402 (2) (b)	CS	E	Delivery or manufacture of schedule 1, 2, or 3 imitation controlled substance	5	
333. 7401 (2) (c)	CS	F	Delivery or manufacture of schedule 4 controlled substance	4	
333. 7401 (2) (e)	CS	G	Delivery or manufacture of schedule 5 controlled substance	2	
333. 17766 a (3)	CS	E	Delivery or manufacture of steroids	7	Deleted, 2003 PA 309, Eff. 4/1/04
750. 157 q	Property	H	Delivery or sale of fraudulent financial transaction device	4	
333. 7401 (2) (a) (i)	CS	A	Delivery/manufacture of 1,000 or more grams of certain schedule 1 or 2 substances	LIFE	3/1/03
333. 7401 (2) (a) (ii)	CS	A	Delivery/manufacture of 225+ but less than 650 grams of certain schedule 1 or 2 substances	30	10/1/00
333. 7401 (2) (a) (ii)	CS	A	Delivery/manufacture of 450+ but less than 1,000 grams of certain schedule 1 or 2 drugs	30	3/1/03

Lightly shaded lines indicate that the statute governing the felony offense described on that line has been amended, deleted, or replaced.

*Unless otherwise noted, the date on which the statutory guidelines were made applicable to the felony offense listed is 1/1/99.

MCL #	Group	Class	Description	Stat Max	Effective Date*
333. 7401 (2) (a) (iii)	CS	B	Delivery/manufacture of 50+ but less than 225 grams of certain schedule 1 or 2 substances	20	
333. 7401 (2) (a) (iii)	CS	B	Delivery/manufacture of 50+ but less than 450 grams of certain schedule 1 or 2 substances	20	3/1/03
333. 7401 (2) (a) (i)	CS	A	Delivery/manufacture of 650 or more grams of certain schedule 1 or 2 controlled substances	LIFE	10/1/00
333. 7401 (2) (a) (iv)	CS	D	Delivery/manufacture of less than 50 grams of certain schedule 1 or 2 controlled substances	20	
750. 263 (3)	Property	E	Delivery/use/display items w/ counterfeit mark – subsequent offense or $1000+ or 100+ items	5	
750. 164	Pub ord	F	Desertion to escape prosecution	4	
750. 161	Pub ord	G	Desertion/abandonment/nonsupport	3	
252. 311	Property	H	Destroying a tree or shrub to make a sign more visible	2	10/1/00
750. 528	Pub saf	F	Destroying dwelling house or other property	4	
750. 528	Pub saf	F	Destroying dwelling house or other property during riot or unlawful assembly	4	As amended, 2006 PA 166, Eff. 8/28/06
168. 932 (c)	Pub trst	E	Destroying or falsifying election return or records	5	
752. 701	Property	H	Destruction or removal of timber	1	
257. 312 b (7)	Pub ord	F	Deviating from motorcycle road test criteria	5	3/28/01
257. 309 (7)	Pub ord	F	Deviating from road test criteria - see MCL 257.309(8)	5	3/28/01
207. 127 c	Pub ord	G	Diesel fuel tax – embezzlement over $100	10	Repealed, 2000 PA 403, Eff. 4/1/01
750. 479 b (2)	Person	D	Disarming peace officer – firearm	10	
750. 479 b (1)	Person	F	Disarming peace officer – nonfirearm	4	
750. 234 c	Pub saf	F	Discharging firearm at emergency/police vehicle	4	
750. 234 a	Pub saf	F	Discharging firearm from vehicle	4	
750. 234 b	Pub saf	F	Discharging firearm in or at a building	4	
333. 2835 (9)	Pub trst	G	Disclosing confidential information – abortion	3	
168. 792 a (16)	Pub trst	E	Disclosing election result or how ballot voted	5	
168. 792 a (11)	Pub trst	E	Disclosing how ballot voted or election results early before polls are closed	5	
333. 7407 (1) (f)	CS	F	Disclosing or obtaining prescription information	4	Deleted, 2001 PA 236, Eff. 1/6/03
767. 4 a	Pub trst	F	Disclosing or possessing grand jury information	4	
168. 932 (d)	Pub trst	E	Disclosing votes or obstructing voter	5	
750. 160	Pub ord	D	Disinterring or mutilating dead human bodies	10	
750. 160	Pub ord	D	Disinterring or mutilating dead human body	10	4/1/04
750. 168 (2) (a)	Pub ord	G	Disorderly conduct at a funeral	2	8/22/06
750. 168 (2) (b)	Pub ord	F	Disorderly conduct at a funeral - subsequent offense	4	8/22/06
257. 625 n (10)	Pub ord	G	Disposing of vehicle to avoid forfeiture	4	
333. 13738 (3)	Pub saf	B	Disposing of waste – extreme indifference to human life	20	

Lightly shaded lines indicate that the statute governing the felony offense described on that line has been amended, deleted, or replaced.

*Unless otherwise noted, the date on which the statutory guidelines were made applicable to the felony offense listed is 1/1/99.

MCL #	Group	Class	Description	Stat Max	Effective Date*
333. 13738 (3)	Pub saf	F	Disposing of waste – indifference to human life	2	
722. 675	Pub ord	E	Distributing obscene matter to children	2	
750. 539 d (3) (b)	Pub ord	E	Distributing, disseminating, or transmitting recording or image obtained by eavesdropping	5	6/16/04
750. 539 j (2) (b)	Pub ord	E	Distributing, disseminating, or transmitting visual image obtained by surveillance	5	6/16/04
750. 540 g (1) (c)	Property	E	Diverting telecommunications services having a value of $1,000 - $20,000 or with priors	5	
750. 540 g (1) (d)	Property	D	Diverting telecommunications services having a value of $20,000 or more or with priors	10	
750. 539 e	Pub ord	H	Divulging or using information obtained by eavesdropping	2	
750. 81 (4)	Person	G	Domestic assault – third offense	2	
750. 81 (4)	Person	G	Domestic assault with prior convictions	2	10/1/00
750. 171	Person	E	Duelling	10	
750. 539 c	Pub ord	H	Eavesdropping	2	
168. 757	Pub trst	E	Election inspector – unlawful conduct	5	
168. 734	Pub trst	G	Election law – election board refusing to provide challenger conveniences	2	
168. 731 (4)	Pub trst	G	Election law – filing certain false statements	2	
168. 759 (8)	Pub trst	E	Election law – forged signature on absentee ballot	5	
168. 937	Pub trst	E	Election law – forgery	5	
168. 936	Pub trst	E	Election law – perjury	5	
168. 932 (f)	Pub trst	E	Election law – possess absent voter ballot delivered to another person	5	
168. 932 a	Pub trst	G	Election offenses	4	
168. 756	Pub trst	E	Elector's false statement concerning inability to mark ballot	5	
750. 520 n	Pub saf	G	Electronic monitoring device violation	2	8/28/06
750. 176	Pub trst	E	Embezzlement by administrator/executor/guardian	10	
750. 174 (4)	Property	E	Embezzlement by agent of $1,000 to $20,000 [or] with prior convictions	5	10/1/00
750. 174 (7)	Property	B	Embezzlement by agent of $100,000 or more	20	3/30/07
750. 174 (5)	Property	D	Embezzlement by agent of $1K-$20K from nonprofit/charitable org, or $20K-$50K, or $1K-$20K with priors	10	As amended, 2006 PA 574, Eff. 3/30/07
750. 174 (5)	Property	D	Embezzlement by agent of $20,000 or more or $1,000 to $20,000 with prior convictions	10	10/1/00
750. 174 (4)	Property	E	Embezzlement by agent of $200-$1K from nonprofit/charitable org, or $1K-$20K, or with priors	5	As amended, 2006 PA 574, Eff. 3/30/07
750. 174 (6)	Property	C	Embezzlement by agent of $50,000 or more but less than $100,000	15	3/30/07
750. 174	Property	D	Embezzlement by agent over $100	10	
750. 177 (3)	Property	E	Embezzlement by chattel mortgagor of $1,000 to $20,000 or with prior convictions	5	10/1/00
750. 177 (2)	Property	D	Embezzlement by chattel mortgagor of $20,000 or more or $1,000 to $20,000 with priors	10	10/1/00
750. 177	Property	H	Embezzlement by chattel mortgagor over $100	2	

Lightly shaded lines indicate that the statute governing the felony offense described on that line has been amended, deleted, or replaced.

*Unless otherwise noted, the date on which the statutory guidelines were made applicable to the felony offense listed is 1/1/99.

MCL #	Group	Class	Description	Stat Max	Effective Date*
750. 180	Property	D	Embezzlement by financial institutions	20	
750. 175	Pub trst	D	Embezzlement by public official over $50	10	
750. 182	Property	G	Embezzlement by warehouses	4	
750. 181	Property	E	Embezzlement of jointly held property over $100	10	
750. 178	Property	G	Embezzlement of mortgaged or leased property – over $100	2	
750. 178 (2)	Property	D	Embezzlement of mortgaged or leased property of $20,000+ or $1,000 to $20,000 with priors	10	10/1/00
750. 179	Property	G	Embezzlement of railroad tickets	4	Deleted, 2002 PA 278, Eff. 5/9/02
750. 181 (4)	Property	E	Embezzling jointly held property with value of $1,000 to $20,000 or with prior convictions	5	10/1/00
750. 181 (5)	Property	D	Embezzling jointly held property with value of $20,000+ or $1,000 to $20,000 with priors	10	10/1/00
750. 178 (3)	Property	E	Embezzling mortgaged or leased property with value of $1,000 to $20,000 or with priors	5	10/1/00
409. 122 (2)	Pub ord	G	Employment of children during certain hours – second offense	2	
409. 122 (2)	Person	G	Employment of children during certain hours – second offense	2	10/1/00
409. 122 (2)	Person	E	Employment of children during certain hours – third or subsequent offense	10	
409. 122 (3)	Person	D	Employment of children in child sexually abusive activity	20	
750. 332	Property	H	Entering horse in race under false name	4	
750. 111	Property	E	Entering without breaking with intent to commit felony or larceny	5	
750. 13	Person	D	Enticing female under 16 for immoral purposes	10	
750. 195 (2)	Pub saf	F	Escape from a felony jail sentence	4	
750. 186 a (1)	Pub saf	F	Escape from a juvenile facility	4	
750. 195 (1)	Pub saf	H	Escape from a misdemeanor jail sentence	2	
750. 197 c	Pub saf	F	Escape from jail through violence	4	Eff. until 12/29/06, 2006 PA 536
750. 197 c	Pub saf	E	Escape from jail through violence	5	As amended, 2006 PA 536, Eff. 12/29/06
750. 193	Pub saf	E	Escape from prison	5	
750. 197 (2)	Pub saf	F	Escape while awaiting trial for felony	4	
750. 197 (1)	Pub saf	H	Escape while awaiting trial for misdemeanor	2	
750. 147 b	Person	G	Ethnic intimidation	2	
324. 61521 (1)	Pub trst	G	Evading rule under NREPA	3	
750. 411 b	Pub trst	G	Excess fees to members of legislature	4	
750. 200	Pub saf	F	Explosives – transport by common carriers	4	
750. 212 a	Person	B	Explosives violation involving a vulnerable target causing death or injury	20	10/1/00
750. 135	Person	D	Exposing children with intent to injure or abandon	10	
750. 165	Pub ord	F	Failing to pay support and leaving state	4	

Lightly shaded lines indicate that the statute governing the felony offense described on that line has been amended, deleted, or replaced.

*Unless otherwise noted, the date on which the statutory guidelines were made applicable to the felony offense listed is 1/1/99.

MCL #	Group	Class	Description	Stat Max	Effective Date*
380. 1230 d (3) (a)	Pub saf	G	Failure by school employee to report charge or conviction	2	9/29/05
205. 27 (1) (a)	Pub trst	G	Failure to file or false tax return or payment	5	
791. 236 (17)	Pub ord	F	Failure to provide correct notice of proposed domicile by sex offender	4	12/1/06
28. 729 (1) (a)	Pub ord	F	Failure to register as a sex offender, first offense	4	9/1/99
28. 729 (1) (b)	Pub ord	D	Failure to register as a sex offender, second offense	7	9/1/99
28. 729 (1) (c)	Pub ord	D	Failure to register as a sex offender, third or subsequent offense	10	9/1/99
722. 115 e (2) (a)	Pub saf	G	Failure to report arraignment for criminal charges - child care and day care centers/employees	2	1/1/06
722. 115 f (8) (a)	Pub saf	G	Failure to report arraignment for criminal charges - family day care and group day care homes	2	1/1/06
257. 625 k (9)	Pub saf	D	Failure to report illegal ignition interlock device	10	10/1/01
257. 625 k (9)	Pub saf	D	Failure to report that an ignition interlock device does not meet legal requirements	10	10/1/00
257. 617	Person	E	Failure to stop at scene of a serious personal injury accident	5	Substituted for by 257.617(2)
257. 617 (3)	Person	C	Failure to stop at scene of accident resulting in death when at fault	15	2/1/02
257. 617 (2)	Person	E	Failure to stop at scene of accident resulting in serious impairment or death	5	2/1/02
324. 80134 a (3)	Person	C	Failure to stop at scene of marine accident causing death when at fault	15	4/1/04
324. 80134 a (2)	Person	E	Failure to stop at scene of marine accident causing serious impairment or death	5	4/1/04
28. 729 (2) (c)	Pub ord	F	Failure to update sex offender registration information - third or subsequent offense	4	1/1/06
257. 653 a (4)	Person	C	Failure to use due care and caution causing death to emergency personnel	15	3/28/01
257. 653 a (3)	Person	G	Failure to use due care and caution causing injury to emergency personnel	2	3/28/01
324. 61511	Pub trst	G	False affidavit under NREPA	5	
28. 293 (1)	Pub ord	E	False information when applying for state ID	5	
28. 293 (2)	Pub ord	D	False information when applying for state ID – second offense	7	
28. 293 (3)	Pub ord	C	False information when applying for state ID – third or subsequent offense	15	
18. 366 (1) (c)	Property	E	False presentation to crime victim services commission to obtain $1,000 - $20,000 or w/ priors	5	1/1/02
18. 366 (1) (d)	Property	D	False presentation to crime victim services commission to obtain $20,000+ or with priors	10	1/1/02
18. 366 (1)	Property	E	False presentation to crime victim services commission to obtain more than $100	10	Deleted, 2001 PA 150 & 154, Eff. 1/1/02
750. 218 (4)	Property	E	False pretenses involving $1,000 to $20,000 or with prior convictions	5	10/1/00
750. 218 (5)	Property	D	False pretenses involving $20,000 or more or $1,000 to $20,000 with prior convictions	10	10/1/00
750. 218	Property	E	False pretenses over $100	10	
285. 279 (2) (c)	Property	E	False pretenses under family farm development act involving $1,000 to $20,000 or with priors	5	2/1/02
285. 279 (2) (d)	Property	D	False pretenses under family farm development act involving $20,000 or more or with priors	10	2/1/02
125. 1447 (1) (c)	Property	E	False pretenses under state housing development act involving $1,000 to $20,000 or w/ priors	5	1/1/02
125. 1447 (1) (d)	Property	D	False pretenses under state housing development act involving $20,000+ or w/ priors	10	1/1/02

Lightly shaded lines indicate that the statute governing the felony offense described on that line has been amended, deleted, or replaced.

Updated April 2007

*Unless otherwise noted, the date on which the statutory guidelines were made applicable to the felony offense listed is 1/1/99.

MCL #	Group	Class	Description	Stat Max	Effective Date*
750. 411 a (2)	Pub ord	F	False report of a bombing or threat to bomb	4	Substituted for by 750.411a(3)(a)
28. 754	Pub ord	F	False report of a child abduction	4	2/1/06
750. 411 a (1) (b)	Pub ord	F	False report of a felony	4	
750. 436 (3) (a)	Pub ord	F	False report of poisoning food, drink, medicine, or water supply	4	4/22/02
750. 436 (3) (b)	Pub ord	D	False report of poisoning food, drink, medicine, or water supply with prior conviction	10	4/22/02
333. 7407 (1) (d)	CS	G	False reports under controlled substance article	4	
333. 16170 (3)	Pub trst	F	False representation – health professional recovery program	4	
750. 217 d	Pub saf	C	False representation or practice as health professional	15	10/1/00
28. 295 a (1)	Pub ord	H	False representation to obtain or misuse personal information	4	
28. 295 a (2)	Pub ord	G	False representation to obtain or misuse personal information – second offense	7	
28. 295 a (3)	Pub ord	C	False representation to obtain or misuse personal information – third or subsequent offense	15	
324. 80130 d (1)	Pub ord	H	False representation to obtain personal information	4	
324. 80319 a (1)	Pub ord	H	False representation to obtain personal information	4	
324. 81120 (1)	Pub ord	H	False representation to obtain personal information	4	
324. 82160 (1)	Pub ord	H	False representation to obtain personal information	4	
324. 80130 d (2)	Pub ord	G	False representation to obtain personal information – second offense	7	
324. 80319 a (2)	Pub ord	G	False representation to obtain personal information – second offense	7	
324. 81120 (2)	Pub ord	G	False representation to obtain personal information – second offense	7	
324. 82160 (2)	Pub ord	G	False representation to obtain personal information – second offense	7	
324. 80130 d (3)	Pub ord	C	False representation to obtain personal information – third or subsequent offense	15	
324. 80319 a (3)	Pub ord	C	False representation to obtain personal information – third or subsequent offense	15	
324. 81120 (3)	Pub ord	C	False representation to obtain personal information – third or subsequent offense	15	
324. 82160 (3)	Pub ord	C	False representation to obtain personal information – third or subsequent offense	15	
333. 20142 (5)	Pub trst	F	False statement – application licensure health facility	4	
750. 232 a (3)	Pub saf	G	False statement in a pistol application	4	
168. 759 b	Pub trst	E	False statement in application for emergency absentee ballot	5	
35. 980	Pub trst	H	False statement in application for Korean veterans benefits	3	
35. 1029	Pub trst	H	False statement in application for Vietnam veterans benefits	3	
257. 744 a	Pub saf	D	False statement in citation – perjury	15	
493. 56 a (13)	Pub trst	C	False statement in reports – secondary mortgage	15	
750. 157 v	Property	H	False statement of identity to obtain financial transaction device	4	
28. 425 b (3)	Pub saf	F	False statement on concealed pistol permit application	4	7/1/01

Lightly shaded lines indicate that the statute governing the felony offense described on that line has been amended, deleted, or replaced.

*Unless otherwise noted, the date on which the statutory guidelines were made applicable to the felony offense listed is 1/1/99.

MCL #	Group	Class	Description	Stat Max	Effective Date*
28. 422 a (4)	Pub saf	F	False statement on pistol sales record	4	7/1/01
324. 21548 (1)	Pub trst	H	False statement, report, claim, bid, work invoice, or other request for payment	5	
168. 933	Pub trst	E	False swearing to register or vote	5	
205. 27 (3)	Pub trst	G	False tax returns/perjury	15	
750. 200 l	Person	E	Falsely exposing person to harmful substance or device	5	10/23/01
285. 279	Pub trst	E	Falsely obtaining money – agricultural land	10	Deleted, 2001 PAs 133, 136 & 160
750. 182 a	Pub trst	H	Falsifying school records	2	
440. 9307 (4)	Property	G	Farming – illegal sale of secured products	3	
440. 9320 (8)	Property	G	Farming – illegal sale of secured products	3	7/1/01
750. 227 g (1)	Pub saf	F	Felon purchasing, owning, possessing, or using body armor	4	10/1/00
750. 82 (1)	Person	F	Felonious assault	4	
750. 82 (2)	Person	F	Felonious assault – weapon-free school zone	4	
257. 626 c	Person	G	Felonious driving	2	2/1/02
752. 191	Pub saf	G	Felonious driving	2	Deleted, 2001 PA 136, Eff. 2/1/02
324. 80173	Person	G	Felonious operation of a vessel	2	
750. 237 a	Pub saf	SPEC	Felony committed in a weapon-free school zone	Variable	10/1/00
750. 49 (10)	Person	D	Fighting animal attacking without provocation and death resulting	15	
750. 49 (2) (a)	Pub ord	F	Fighting animals or providing facilities for animal fights	4	
750. 49 (2) (b)	Pub ord	F	Fighting animals or providing facilities for animal fights	4	
750. 49 (2) (c)	Pub ord	F	Fighting animals or providing facilities for animal fights	4	
750. 49 (2) (d)	Pub ord	F	Fighting animals or providing facilities for animal fights	4	
440. 9501	Pub trst	E	Filing a false or fraudulent financing statement with the secretary of state	5	1/1/05
750. 157 r	Property	H	Financial transaction device – forgery, alteration, or counterfeiting	4	
750. 157 n (1)	Property	H	Financial transaction device – stealing, retaining, or using without consent	4	
750. 157 s	Property	H	Financial transaction device – use of revoked or canceled financial device over $100	1	
38. 516	Pub trst	H	Fire and police civil service – appointment or employment contrary to act	2	
28. 435	Pub saf	G	Firearm sale without trigger lock/gun case/storage container – third or subsequent offense	2	7/1/01
750. 104	Property	F	Fitting boat with intent to destroy	4	
257. 602 a (5)	Person	C	Fleeing and eluding – first degree	15	
750. 479 a (5)	Person	C	Fleeing and eluding – first degree	15	
257. 602 a (2)	Pub saf	G	Fleeing and eluding – fourth degree	2	
750. 479 a (2)	Pub saf	G	Fleeing and eluding – fourth degree	2	

Lightly shaded lines indicate that the statute governing the felony offense described on that line has been amended, deleted, or replaced.

*Unless otherwise noted, the date on which the statutory guidelines were made applicable to the felony offense listed is 1/1/99.

MCL #	Group	Class	Description	Stat Max	Effective Date*
257. 602 a (4)	Person	D	Fleeing and eluding – second degree	10	
750. 479 a (4)	Person	D	Fleeing and eluding – second degree	10	
257. 602 a (3)	Pub saf	E	Fleeing and eluding – third degree	5	
750. 479 a (3)	Pub saf	E	Fleeing and eluding – third degree	5	
750. 300 a (1) (a)	Property	G	Food stamp fraud – $250 or less – second offense	5	
750. 300 a (1) (a)	Property	G	Food stamp fraud – $250 or less – third or subsequent offense	10	
750. 300 a (1) (b)	Property	E	Food stamp fraud – more than $250 to $1,000	5	
750. 300 a (1) (b)	Property	E	Food stamp fraud – more than $250 to $1,000 – subsequent offense	10	
750. 300 a (1) (c)	Property	E	Food stamp fraud – over $1,000	10	
750. 248	Property	E	Forgery	14	
750. 251	Property	E	Forgery of bank bills	7	
750. 250	Property	E	Forgery of treasury notes	7	
257. 310 (7) (b)	Pub ord	E	Forging driver license w/ intent to commit crime punishable by 6+ months but less than 10 yrs	5	4/22/02
257. 310 (7) (a)	Pub ord	D	Forging driver license with intent to commit crime punishable by 10 years or more	10	4/22/02
28. 295 (1) (a)	Pub ord	H	Forging state ID card to commit felony	4	Replaced, 2004 PA 149, Eff. 9/1/04
257. 312 b (8)	Pub ord	F	Forging, counterfeiting, or altering motorcycle road test certification	5	3/28/01
257. 309 (8)	Pub ord	F	Forging, counterfeiting, or altering road test certification - see MCL 257.609(9)	5	3/28/01
110. 28	Pub trst	G	Fourth class cities – misappropriation of money or property	3	
445. 1525	Pub trst	G	Franchise investment law – false advertising	7	
445. 1521	Pub trst	G	Franchise investment law – false representation	7	
445. 1523	Pub trst	G	Franchise investment law – false statements of material fact	7	
445. 1505	Pub trst	G	Franchise investment law – fraudulent filing/offers	7	
445. 1513	Pub trst	G	Franchise investment law – illegal offers/sales	7	
445. 1520	Pub trst	G	Franchise investment law – keeping records	7	
445. 1508	Pub trst	G	Franchise investment law – sale without proper disclosure	7	
750. 279	Property	G	Fraud – disposition of exhausted property	4	
750. 276	Property	G	Fraud – promise to vendee of grain at fictitious price	4	
750. 274	Property	E	Fraud – purchasing/collecting on fraudulent financial document	10	
750. 278	Property	G	Fraud – warehouse receipts	5	
333. 5661	Person	F	Fraud resulting in patient death	4	
750. 95	Property	G	Fraudulent bank notes	10	
565. 371	Property	G	Fraudulent conveyances – recording with intent to deceive	3	

Lightly shaded lines indicate that the statute governing the felony offense described on that line has been amended, deleted, or replaced.

*Unless otherwise noted, the date on which the statutory guidelines were made applicable to the felony offense listed is 1/1/99.

MCL #	Group	Class	Description	Stat Max	Effective Date*
750. 96	Property	G	Fraudulent disposal of bank property	4	
436. 1919	Pub ord	H	Fraudulent documents, labels, or stamps	1	
750. 271	Property	E	Fraudulently issuing or selling domestic securities	10	
750. 157 w (1) (c)	Property	E	Fraudulently withdrawing or transferring $1,000 to $20,000 with financial transaction device	5	10/1/00
750. 157 w (1) (d)	Property	D	Fraudulently withdrawing or transferring $20,000 or more with financial transaction device	10	10/1/00
750. 157 w	Property	H	Fraudulently withdrawing or transferring more than $500 with financial transaction device	4	
800. 283 a	Pub saf	E	Furnishing cell phone to prisoner	5	12/29/06
801. 263 (1)	Pub saf	H	Furnishing contraband to prisoner in jail	5	8/1/99
750. 157 t	Property	H	Furnishing goods or services to person committing violation with financial transaction device	4	
800. 281 (1)	Pub saf	H	Furnishing prisoner with contraband	5	
800. 281 (2)	Pub saf	H	Furnishing prisoner with contraband outside	5	
801. 262 (1) (b)	Pub saf	E	Furnishing weapon to prisoner in jail	5	8/1/99
800. 283 (1)	Pub saf	E	Furnishing weapon to prisoner in prison	5	
750. 303	Pub ord	H	Gambling	2	
750. 313	Pub ord	H	Gambling – stocks/bonds/commodities	2	
750. 303	Pub ord	H	Gaming	2	As amended, 2004 PA 457, Eff. 3/1/05
207. 119	Pub trst	G	Gasoline or motor fuel tax violation	4	Repealed, 2000 PA 403, Eff. 4/1/01
207. 118 a	Pub ord	G	Gasoline tax – embezzlement over $100	10	Repealed, 2000 PA 403, Eff. 4/1/01
285. 82	Pub trst	H	Grain dealers act violations	5	Substituted for by 285.83
285. 83	Pub trst	H	Grain dealers act violations	5	3/31/03
750. 280	Property	E	Gross frauds/cheats at common law	10	
750. 338 a	Pub ord	G	Gross indecency between females	5	
750. 338 a	Pub ord	A	Gross indecency between females involving sexually delinquent person	LIFE	8/24/06
750. 338	Pub ord	G	Gross indecency between males	5	
750. 338 b	Pub ord	G	Gross indecency between males and females	5	
750. 338 b	Pub ord	A	Gross indecency between males and females involving sexually delinquent person	LIFE	8/24/06
750. 338	Pub ord	A	Gross indecency between males involving sexually delinquent person	LIFE	8/24/06
750. 90 c (a)	Person	C	Gross negligence against a pregnant individual resulting in miscarriage or stillbirth	15	10/1/00
750. 90 c (b)	Person	E	Gross negligence resulting in great bodily harm to embryo or fetus	5	10/1/00
750. 90 c (a)	Person	C	Gross negligence resulting in miscarriage/stillbirth/death to embryo or fetus	15	6/1/01
750. 50 c (7)	Pub saf	H	Harassing or causing harm to law enforcement animal while committing crime	2	
750. 50 c (7)	Pub saf	H	Harassing/harming law enforcement animal or search and rescue dog while committing crime	2	As amended, 2006 PA 518, Eff. 12/29/06

Lightly shaded lines indicate that the statute governing the felony offense described on that line has been amended, deleted, or replaced.

*Unless otherwise noted, the date on which the statutory guidelines were made applicable to the felony offense listed is 1/1/99.

MCL #	Group	Class	Description	Stat Max	Effective Date*
750. 199 (3)	Pub saf	F	Harboring a person for whom felony warrant has been issued	4	6/30/06
750. 200 i (2) (c)	Person	A	Harmful device causing personal injury	25	10/1/00
750. 200 i (2) (b)	Property	B	Harmful device causing property damage	20	10/1/00
750. 200 i (2) (d)	Person	A	Harmful device causing serious impairment	LIFE	10/1/00
324. 20139 (3)	Pub saf	H	Hazardous waste – knowingly releases or causes the release	2	
324. 11151 (3)	Pub saf	H	Hazardous waste violation – with disregard for human life	2	
324. 11151 (3)	Pub saf	G	Hazardous waste violation – with extreme indifference for human life	5	
324. 11151 (2)	Pub saf	H	Hazardous waste violations – subsequent offense	2	
750. 411 t (2) (c)	Person	C	Hazing resulting in death	15	8/18/04
750. 411 t (2) (b)	Person	E	Hazing resulting in serious impairment	5	8/18/04
752. 1005	Property	H	Health care fraud – conspiracy	10	
752. 1003	Property	F	Health care fraud – false claim/state, unnecessary, conceal information	4	
752. 1004	Property	F	Health care fraud – kickbacks/referral fees	4	
752. 1006	Property	D	Health care fraud – subsequent offense	20	
333. 16294	Pub saf	F	Health profession – unauthorized practice	4	
750. 421 b	Pub saf	H	Hinder transport of farm/commercial products – subsequent offense	2	
750. 543 h	Pub ord	A	Hindering prosecution of terrorism	LIFE	Eff. 4/22/02 to 7/15/02, 2002 PA 271
750. 543 h (3) (b)	Pub ord	A	Hindering prosecution of terrorism – act of terrorism	LIFE	7/15/02
750. 543 h (3) (a)	Pub ord	B	Hindering prosecution of terrorism – certain terrorist acts	20	7/15/02
500. 1371	Pub trst	H	Holding companies – violation	2	
750. 110 a (2)	Person	B	Home invasion – first degree	20	10/1/00
750. 110 a (4)	Person	B	Home invasion – first degree	20	
750. 110 a (3)	Person	C	Home invasion – second degree	15	10/1/00
750. 110 a (5)	Person	C	Home invasion – second degree	15	
750. 110 a (4)	Person	E	Home invasion – third degree	5	10/1/00
750. 329	Person	C	Homicide – weapon aimed with intent but not malice	15	
431. 330 (4)	Pub trst	G	Horse Racing – administering a drug that could affect racing condition	5	
431. 332	Pub trst	G	Horse Racing – influencing or attempting to influence result of race	5	
431. 307 (8)	Pub trst	G	Horse racing – testifying falsely to commissioner while under oath	4	
750. 430 a	Person	D	Human cloning	10	10/1/00
750. 462 i	Person	A	Human trafficking - compound felony	LIFE	8/24/06
750. 462 d (1)	Person	D	Human trafficking - forced labor through abuse of legal process	10	8/24/06

Lightly shaded lines indicate that the statute governing the felony offense described on that line has been amended, deleted, or replaced.

*Unless otherwise noted, the date on which the statutory guidelines were made applicable to the felony offense listed is 1/1/99.

MCL #	Group	Class	Description	Stat Max	Effective Date*
750. 462 d (3)	Person	A	Human trafficking - forced labor through abuse of legal process causing death	LIFE	8/24/06
750. 462 d (2)	Person	C	Human trafficking - forced labor through abuse of legal process causing injury	15	8/24/06
750. 462 f (1)	Person	D	Human trafficking - forced labor through blackmail	10	8/24/06
750. 462 f (3)	Person	A	Human trafficking - forced labor through blackmail causing death	LIFE	8/24/06
750. 462 f (2)	Person	C	Human trafficking - forced labor through blackmail causing injury	15	8/24/06
750. 462 e (1)	Person	D	Human trafficking - forced labor through destruction of ID document	10	8/24/06
750. 462 e (3)	Person	A	Human trafficking - forced labor through destruction of ID document causing death	LIFE	8/24/06
750. 462 e (2)	Person	C	Human trafficking - forced labor through destruction of ID document causing injury	15	8/24/06
750. 462 b (1)	Person	D	Human trafficking - forced labor through physical harm	10	8/24/06
750. 462 b (3)	Person	A	Human trafficking - forced labor through physical harm causing death	LIFE	8/24/06
750. 462 b (2)	Person	C	Human trafficking - forced labor through physical harm causing injury	15	8/24/06
750. 462 c (1)	Person	D	Human trafficking - forced labor through physical restraint	10	8/24/06
750. 462 c (3)	Person	A	Human trafficking - forced labor through physical restraint causing death	LIFE	8/24/06
750. 462 c (2)	Person	C	Human trafficking - forced labor through physical restraint causing injury	15	8/24/06
750. 462 g (1)	Person	B	Human trafficking - obtain minor for child sexual abusive activity	20	8/24/06
750. 462 h (2)	Person	D	Human trafficking - recruit minor for forced labor	10	8/24/06
750. 462 h (4)	Person	A	Human trafficking - recruit minor for forced labor causing death	LIFE	8/24/06
750. 462 h (3)	Person	C	Human trafficking - recruit minor for forced labor causing injury	15	8/24/06
445. 65	Pub ord	E	Identity theft	5	3/1/05
205. 428 (3)	Pub trst	G	Illegal sale of cigarettes or other tobacco products with wholesale price of $250 or more	5	10/1/00
205. 428 (6)	Pub trst	F	Illegal tobacco stamp or tobacco stamp device	10	10/1/00
205. 428 (7)	Pub trst	G	Illegal vending machine license, disk, or marker	5	10/1/00
324. 52908 (3)	Property	H	Illegally cutting, removing, or transporting tree or other plant involving $1,000 or more	180 days	Eff. 10/1/00 to 1/1/02, 2001 PA 156
600. 908 (8)	Pub trst	E	Immunity to witness – committing perjury	15	
257. 625 (10) (c)	Pub saf	E	Impaired driving – third or subsequent offense	5	Eff. until 9/30/03, replaced by (11)(c)
750. 217 e	Pub ord	G	Impersonating a DHS employee	2	As amended, 2005 PA 171, Eff. 1/1/06
750. 217 f	Pub saf	G	Impersonating a firefighter or emergency medical service personnel	2	1/1/06
750. 217 e	Pub ord	G	Impersonating an FIA employee	2	9/1/01
750. 215 (3)	Pub saf	F	Impersonating peace officer	4	9/1/03
750. 217 c (3)	Pub ord	H	Impersonating public officer or employee	2	10/1/00
750. 217 c (4)	Pub ord	G	Impersonating public officer or employee – third or subsequent conviction	4	10/1/00
750. 217 b	Pub saf	G	Impersonating public utility employee	2	

Lightly shaded lines indicate that the statute governing the felony offense described on that line has been amended, deleted, or replaced.

*Unless otherwise noted, the date on which the statutory guidelines were made applicable to the felony offense listed is 1/1/99.

MCL #	Group	Class	Description	Stat Max	Effective Date*
750. 160 c	Pub ord	D	Improper disposal of dead human body after more than 180 days	10	4/1/04
380. 1816	Pub trst	F	Improper use of bond proceeds	4	3/30/05
752. 542	Pub saf	D	Incitement to riot	10	
750. 49 (8)	Person	A	Inciting fighting animal resulting in death	LIFE	
750. 49 (9)	Person	F	Inciting fighting animal to attack	4	
750. 348	Pub saf	H	Inciting Indians to violate a treaty	4	Deleted, 2002 PA 261, Eff. 5/1/02
750. 425	Pub trst	E	Inciting or procuring perjury	5	
750. 425	Pub trst	E	Inciting or procuring perjury but perjury not committed	5	10/1/00
750. 405	Pub saf	E	Inciting soldiers to desert	5	
750. 335 a	Person	A	Indecent exposure by sexually delinquent person	LIFE	Relettered, 2005 PA 302, Eff. 2/1/06
750. 335 a (2) (c)	Person	A	Indecent exposure by sexually delinquent person	LIFE	Formerly MCL 750.335a, Eff. 2/1/06
750. 157 c	Person	SPEC	Inducing minor to commit a felony	Variable	
324. 8905 (2)	Pub saf	H	Infectious waste/pathological waste/sharps – littering violation	2	
324. 8905 (3)	Pub saf	G	Infectious waste/pathological waste/sharps – littering violation – subsequent offense	5	
286. 228 (6)	Pub ord	E	Insect pest and plant disease - intentional violation with intent to damage natural resources	5	9/1/05
286. 260 (4)	Pub ord	E	Insect pest and plant disease - intentional violation with intent to damage natural resources	5	9/1/05
750. 539 d	Pub ord	H	Installing eavesdropping device	2	Replaced, 2004 PA 157, Eff. 6/16/04
750. 539 d (3) (a) (i)	Pub ord	H	Installing, placing, or using eavesdropping device	2	6/16/04
750. 539 d (3) (a) (ii)	Pub ord	E	Installing, placing, or using eavesdropping device – subsequent offense	5	6/16/04
492. 137 (a)	Pub trst	H	Installment sales of motor vehicles	3	
500. 5252 (4)	Property	G	Insurance – improper personal interest in transactions	5	
500. 8197 (2)	Pub trst	C	Insurance – knowing or willful false statements in application for insurance	15	
500. 4511 (1)	Pub trst	F	Insurance code – fraudulent insurance act	4	
500. 1325 (3)	Pub trst	E	Insurance code – knowingly misrepresenting false financial condition	5	
500. 1505 (2)	Pub trst	C	Insurance code – license and regulatory violations	15	
500. 4511 (2)	Pub trst	D	Insurance fraud – agreement or conspiracy to commit	10	
722. 633 (5) (b)	Person	F	Intentional false report of child abuse constituting a felony	4	
722. 633 (5) (b)	Person	F	Intentional false report of child abuse constituting a felony	Variable	As amended, 2005 PA 106, Eff. 9/14/05, and 2005 PA 134, Eff. 1/1/06
711. 1 (8)	Pub trst	E	Intentional false statement in petition for name change	15	
750. 483 a (4) (b)	Person	F	Interfering with police investigation by committing crime or threatening to kill or injure	10	3/28/01
750. 483 a (4) (b)	Person	D	Interfering with police investigation by committing crime or threatening to kill or injure	10	7/15/02
750. 122 (7) (c)	Person	C	Intimidating witness by committing crime or threatening to kill or injure	15	3/28/01

Lightly shaded lines indicate that the statute governing the felony offense described on that line has been amended, deleted, or replaced.

*Unless otherwise noted, the date on which the statutory guidelines were made applicable to the felony offense listed is 1/1/99.

MCL #	Group	Class	Description	Stat Max	Effective Date*
750. 205 a	Pub saf	F	Intimidation or harassment by device represented as an explosive	4	
324. 41309 (10) (b)	Property	E	Introduction of prohibited or genetically engineered species - intent to damage resources	5	9/1/05
324. 41309 (8)	Property	G	Introduction of prohibited or genetically engineered species - knowing identity of organism	2	9/1/05
324. 41309 (9) (b)	Property	F	Introduction of prohibited or genetically engineered species - knowing introduction is unlawful	4	9/1/05
324. 41309 (10) (a)	Property	F	Introduction of restricted or nonnative species - intent to damage resources	3	9/1/05
324. 41309 (9) (a)	Property	G	Introduction of restricted or nonnative species - knowing introduction is unlawful	2	9/1/05
750. 200 j (2) (a)	Person	E	Irritant or irritant device	5	10/23/01
750. 200 j (2) (e)	Person	A	Irritant or irritant device causing death	LIFE	10/1/00
750. 200 j (2) (c)	Person	D	Irritant or irritant device causing personal injury	10	10/1/00
750. 200 j (2) (b)	Property	F	Irritant or irritant device causing property damage	4	10/1/00
750. 200 j (2) (b)	Property	E	Irritant or irritant device causing property damage	7	10/23/01
750. 200 j (2) (d)	Person	A	Irritant or irritant device causing serious impairment	25	10/1/00
750. 94	Property	G	Issuing bank notes without complying with requirements	10	
443. 52	Pub trst	E	Issuing duplicate warehouse receipt not so marked	5	
750. 513	Property	H	Issuing fraudulent railroad securities	10	Deleted, 2002 PA 320, Eff. 7/15/02
443. 50	Pub trst	E	Issuing warehouse receipt for goods not received	5	
750. 120 a (2) (a)	Pub ord	F	Juror intimidation	4	3/28/01
750. 120 a (2) (c)	Person	C	Juror intimidation by committing crime or threatening to kill or injure	15	3/28/01
750. 120 a (2) (b)	Pub ord	D	Juror intimidation in case punishable by more than 10 years	10	3/28/01
750. 120	Pub trst	F	Juror or other person accepting a bribe	4	
750. 452	Pub ord	E	Keeping a house of prostitution	5	
750. 349	Person	A	Kidnapping	LIFE	
750. 350	Person	A	Kidnapping – child enticement	LIFE	
750. 350 a	Person	H	Kidnapping – custodial interference	1	
750. 50 c (5)	Pub ord	E	Killing or causing serious physical harm to law enforcement animal	5	
750. 50 c (5)	Pub ord	E	Killing or causing serious physical harm to law enforcement animal or search and rescue dog	5	As amended, 2006 PA 518, Eff. 12/29/06
750. 50 b (2)	Property	F	Killing or torturing animals	4	
388. 936	Pub trst	F	Knowingly making false statement – school district loans	4	
388. 962	Pub trst	F	Knowingly making false statement – school district loans	4	Deleted, 2005 PA 125, Eff. 9/29/05
257. 625 k (7)	Pub saf	D	Knowingly providing false information concerning an ignition interlock device	10	10/1/00
750. 540 f (2)	Property	E	Knowingly publishing a communications access device with prior convictions	5	10/1/00
324. 5531 (4)	Pub saf	H	Knowingly releasing pollutants	2	

Lightly shaded lines indicate that the statute governing the felony offense described on that line has been amended, deleted, or replaced.

Updated April 2007

*Unless otherwise noted, the date on which the statutory guidelines were made applicable to the felony offense listed is 1/1/99.

MCL #	Group	Class	Description	Stat Max	Effective Date*
324. 5531 (5)	Pub saf	G	Knowingly releasing pollutants – causing death or serious bodily injury	6	
324. 5531 (6)	Pub saf	C	Knowingly releasing pollutants – resulting in death or serious bodily injury	15	
565. 827	Pub trst	E	Land sales act – false or fraudulent statement	10	
750. 357 b	Property	E	Larceny – stealing firearms of another	5	
750. 362	Property	E	Larceny by conversion involving $1,000 to $20,000 or with prior convictions	5	10/1/00
750. 362	Property	D	Larceny by conversion involving $20,000 or more or with prior convictions	10	10/1/00
750. 362	Property	E	Larceny by conversion over $100	5	
750. 363	Property	E	Larceny by false personation involving $1,000 to $20,000 or with prior convictions	5	10/1/00
750. 363	Property	D	Larceny by false personation involving $20,000 or more	10	10/1/00
750. 363	Property	E	Larceny by false personation over $100	5	
750. 356 a	Property	G	Larceny from a motor vehicle	5	
750. 356 a (1)	Property	G	Larceny from a motor vehicle	5	10/1/00
750. 358	Property	G	Larceny from burning building	5	
750. 365	Person	D	Larceny from car or persons detained or injured by accident	20	
750. 357	Person	D	Larceny from the person	10	
750. 360	Property	G	Larceny in a building	4	
750. 356 (3)	Property	E	Larceny involving $1,000 to $20,000 or with prior convictions	5	10/1/00
750. 356 (2)	Property	D	Larceny involving $20,000 or more or with prior convictions	10	10/1/00
750. 367	Property	D	Larceny of a tree or shrub involving $20,000 or more or with prior convictions	10	10/1/00
750. 357 a	Property	G	Larceny of livestock	4	
750. 366	Property	G	Larceny of railroad tickets	4	Deleted, 2002 PA 279, Eff. 5/9/02
750. 367 a	Property	SPEC	Larceny of rationed goods	Variable	
750. 362 a	Property	H	Larceny of rental property	2	
750. 362 a (3)	Property	E	Larceny of rental property involving $1,000 to $20,000 or with prior convictions	5	10/1/00
750. 362 a (2)	Property	D	Larceny of rental property involving $20,000 or more or with prior convictions	10	10/1/00
750. 367	Property	G	Larceny of trees & shrubs over $100	5	
750. 367	Property	E	Larceny of trees or shrubs involving $1,000 to $20,000 or with prior convictions	5	10/1/00
750. 356	Property	E	Larceny over $100	5	
600. 8813	Pub trst	E	Law enforcement officer – knowingly making false statement in a citation	15	
750. 539 j (2) (a) (i)	Pub ord	H	Lewd surveillance or capturing lewd image	2	6/16/04
750. 539 j (2) (a) (ii)	Pub ord	E	Lewd surveillance or capturing lewd image – subsequent offense	5	6/16/04
600. 2136	Pub trst	E	Library record, book, paper – false certification in court	15	

Lightly shaded lines indicate that the statute governing the felony offense described on that line has been amended, deleted, or replaced.

*Unless otherwise noted, the date on which the statutory guidelines were made applicable to the felony offense listed is 1/1/99.

MCL #	Group	Class	Description	Stat Max	Effective Date*
436. 1909 (3)	Pub ord	H	Liquor violation	1	
4. 421 (1)	Pub trst	G	Lobbyists – compensation contingent on outcome of action	3	
4. 421 (2)	Pub trst	G	Lobbyists giving gifts	3	
432. 30	Property	G	Lottery – forgery of tickets	5	
750. 374	Pub ord	H	Lottery violations – subsequent offense	4	
333. 7405 (d)	CS	G	Maintaining drug house	2	
750. 105	Property	G	Making false cargo invoice for boat	4	
388. 1237	Pub trst	F	Making false statement to obtain qualification of school bond issue/improper use of proceeds	4	Substituted for by MCL 388.1937
388. 1937	Pub trst	F	Making false statement to obtain qualification of school bond issue/improper use of proceeds	4	9/29/05
205. 27 (1) (c)	Pub trst	G	Making/permitting false tax returns or payments	5	
750. 380 (3)	Property	E	Malicious destruction of a building involving $1,000 to $20,000 or with prior convictions	5	10/1/00
750. 387 (5)	Property	E	Malicious destruction of a tomb or memorial involving $1,000 to $20,000 or with priors	5	10/1/00
750. 387 (6)	Property	D	Malicious destruction of a tomb or memorial involving $20,000 or more or with prior convictions	10	10/1/00
750. 380 (2)	Property	D	Malicious destruction of building involving $20,000 or more or with prior convictions	10	10/1/00
750. 380	Property	F	Malicious destruction of building over $100	4	
750. 377 b	Property	F	Malicious destruction of fire/police property	4	
750. 386	Property	E	Malicious destruction of mine property	20	
750. 377 a (1) (b)	Property	E	Malicious destruction of personal property involving $1,000 to $20,000 or with priors	5	10/1/00
750. 377 a (1) (a)	Property	D	Malicious destruction of personal property involving $20,000 or more or with prior convictions	10	10/1/00
750. 377 a	Property	G	Malicious destruction of personal property over $100	4	
750. 382 (1) (c)	Property	E	Malicious destruction of plants or turf involving $1,000 to $20,000 or with prior convictions	5	10/1/00
750. 382 (1) (d)	Property	D	Malicious destruction of plants or turf involving $20,000 or more or with prior convictions	10	10/1/00
750. 379	Property	F	Malicious destruction of property – bridges/railroads/locks	4	
750. 378	Property	F	Malicious destruction of property – dams/canals/mills	4	
750. 392	Property	E	Malicious destruction of property – vessels	10	
750. 387	Property	G	Malicious destruction of tombs & memorials	5	
750. 383 a	Property	F	Malicious destruction of utility equipment	4	
750. 321	Person	C	Manslaughter	15	
750. 211	Pub saf	E	Manufacture of explosives with unlawful intent	5	
750. 539 f	Pub ord	H	Manufacture or possession of eavesdropping device	2	
750. 262	Property	E	Manufacture or possession of tools to counterfeit coins	10	
750. 224	Pub saf	E	Manufacture or sale of silencer, bomb, blackjack, automatic weapon, gas spray, etc.	5	

Lightly shaded lines indicate that the statute governing the felony offense described on that line has been amended, deleted, or replaced.

*Unless otherwise noted, the date on which the statutory guidelines were made applicable to the felony offense listed is 1/1/99.

MCL #	Group	Class	Description	Stat Max	Effective Date*
750. 224 e	Pub saf	F	Manufacture/sale/possession of devices to convert semiautomatic weapons	4	
750. 263 (4)	Property	E	Manufacturing items with counterfeit mark	5	
750. 540 c (3)	Property	F	Manufacturing or delivering a counterfeit communications device	4	Eff. 10/1/00 to 2/12/04, 2004 PA 2
333. 7405 (b)	CS	G	Manufacturing or distribution violations by licensee	2	
750. 211 a (2) (c)	Person	A	Manufacturing or possessing an explosive or incendiary device causing physical injury	25	Eff. 10/1/00 to 4/1/05
750. 211 a (2) (d)	Person	A	Manufacturing or possessing an explosive or incendiary device causing physical injury	25	Relettered, 2004 PA 524, Eff. 4/1/05
750. 211 a (2) (b)	Property	B	Manufacturing or possessing an explosive or incendiary device causing property damage	20	Eff. 10/1/00 to 4/1/05
750. 211 a (2) (c)	Property	B	Manufacturing or possessing an explosive or incendiary device causing property damage	20	Relettered, 2004 PA 524, Eff. 4/1/05
750. 211 a (2) (d)	Person	A	Manufacturing or possessing an explosive or incendiary device causing serious impairment	LIFE	Eff. 10/1/00 to 4/1/05
750. 211 a (2) (e)	Person	A	Manufacturing or possessing an explosive or incendiary device causing serious impairment	LIFE	Relettered, 2004 PA 524, Eff. 4/1/05
750. 211 a (2) (a)	Pub saf	C	Manufacturing or possessing an explosive or incendiary device with malicious intent	15	Eff. 10/1/00 to 4/1/05
750. 211 a (2) (b)	Pub saf	C	Manufacturing or possessing an explosive or incendiary device with malicious intent	15	Relettered, 2004 PA 524, Eff. 4/1/05
750. 200 i (2) (a)	Pub saf	C	Manufacturing or using a harmful device	15	10/1/00
750. 211 a (2) (a)	Pub saf	F	Manufacturing/possessing a Molotov cocktail/similar device designed to explode on impact	4	4/1/05
288. 257	Pub saf	G	Margarine violations	3	Repealed, 2001 PA 267, Eff. 2/8/02 Deleted, 2005 PA 54, Eff. 9/1/05
426. 106	Property	E	Marking of logs and timber – forging	5	
551. 6	Person	H	Marriage license – mental or venereal disease	5	Deleted, 2001 PA 10, Eff. 5/29/01
750. 397	Person	D	Mayhem	10	
400. 606	Property	E	Medicaid fraud – conspiracy	10	
400. 607	Pub trst	G	Medicaid fraud – false claim/medically unnecessary	4	
400. 603	Pub trst	G	Medicaid fraud – false statement in benefit/concealing information	4	
400. 605	Pub trst	G	Medicaid fraud – false statement regarding institutions	4	
400. 609	Property	D	Medicaid fraud – fourth offense	10	
400. 604	Pub trst	G	Medicaid fraud – kickback/referral fees	4	
750. 492 a (2)	Pub trst	G	Medical record – health care provider - altering to conceal injury/death	4	As amended, 2006 PA 40, Eff. 3/2/06
750. 492 a (2)	Pub trst	G	Medical record – health care provider alter conceal injury/death	4	
750. 492 a (1) (a)	Pub trst	G	Medical record – intentional[ly] place false information – health care provider	4	
710. 69	Person	F	Michigan adoption law – subsequent offense	4	
338. 3471 (1) (b)	Pub trst	G	Michigan immigration clerical assistant act violation - subsequent offense	2	3/30/05
338. 3621 (1) (b)	Pub trst	G	Michigan immigration clerical assistant act violation - subsequent offense	2	Substituted for by MCL 338.3471(1)(b)
125. 1447	Property	G	Michigan state housing development authority – false pretenses over $100	10	Deleted, 2001 PA 154, Eff. 1/1/02
750. 406	Pub saf	E	Military stores – larceny, embezzlement or destruction	5	

Lightly shaded lines indicate that the statute governing the felony offense described on that line has been amended, deleted, or replaced.

*Unless otherwise noted, the date on which the statutory guidelines were made applicable to the felony offense listed is 1/1/99.

MCL #	Group	Class	Description	Stat Max	Effective Date*
408. 1035 a (5)	Person	H	MIOSHA violation causing employee death	1	10/1/00
408. 1035 a (5)	Pub saf	I	MIOSHA – violations/writs of mandamus/assaults – first offense	1	
408. 1035 a (5)	Pub saf	G	MIOSHA – violations/writs of mandamus/assaults – second offense	3	
408. 1035 (5)	Pub saf	I	MIOSHA violation – first offense	1	
408. 1035 (5)	Pub saf	G	MIOSHA violation – second offense	3	
408. 1035 (5)	Person	H	MIOSHA violation causing employee death	1	10/1/00
408. 1035 (5)	Person	G	MIOSHA violation causing employee death – subsequent offense	3	10/1/00
408. 1035 a (5)	Person	G	MIOSHA violation causing employee death – subsequent offense	3	10/1/00
168. 887	Pub trst	E	Misconduct of election employee in recount	5	
168. 873	Pub trst	E	Misconduct of election employee in recount – county and local	5	
750. 545	Pub ord	E	Misprision of treason	5	
750. 18 (5)	Person	E	Mix/color/stain/powder a drug/medicine resulting in serious impairment of body function	5	10/12/04
750. 18 (6)	Person	C	Mix/color/stain/powder a drug/medicine w/ ingredient/material resulting in death	15	10/12/04
750. 18 (4)	Person	F	Mix/color/stain/powder a drug/medicine w/ ingredient/material resulting in personal injury	4	10/12/04
750. 18 (3)	Person	G	Mix/color/stain/powder a drug/medicine with an ingredient/material affecting quality/potency	2	10/12/04
750. 249 a	Property	H	Molds or dies to forge financial transaction device	4	
750. 411 o	Pub ord	B	Money laundering – first degree	20	
750. 411 l	Pub ord	H	Money laundering – fourth degree	2	
750. 411 n	Pub ord	D	Money laundering – second degree	10	
750. 411 m	Pub ord	E	Money laundering – third degree	5	
750. 411 p (2) (c)	Property	E	Money laundering – transactions involving represented proceeds	5	
750. 411 p (2) (a)	Property	B	Money laundering of proceeds from controlled substance offense involving $10,000 or more	20	
750. 411 p (2) (b)	Property	D	Money laundering proceeds from controlled substance offense/other proceeds of $10,000+	10	
487. 1042 (1)	Pub trst	E	Money transmission - intentional false statement/misrepresentation/certification in record/document	5	7/3/06
487. 1042 (3)	Pub trst	E	Money transmission services act license violation	5	7/3/06
445. 1679	Pub trst	H	Mortgage brokers act – general violations	3	
445. 1671	Pub trst	E	Mortgage brokers, lenders – knowingly giving a false statement	15	
290. 650	Person	G	Motor fuels – assaulting/obstructing director or authorized representative	2	
290. 650 b (3)	Pub trst	H	Motor fuels violations	2	
750. 421	Pub saf	H	Motor vehicle – designed for attack	5	
750. 420	Pub saf	H	Motor vehicle – equipping to release smoke/gas	4	
257. 1353 (2)	Pub trst	H	Motor vehicle – fail to record material matter – subsequent offense	2	

Lightly shaded lines indicate that the statute governing the felony offense described on that line has been amended, deleted, or replaced.

*Unless otherwise noted, the date on which the statutory guidelines were made applicable to the felony offense listed is 1/1/99.

MCL #	Group	Class	Description	Stat Max	Effective Date*
257. 1355	Pub trst	H	Motor vehicle – fail to record transaction/falsify records	2	
257. 1354 (2)	Pub trst	H	Motor vehicle – general violations – subsequent offense	2	
750. 417	Property	H	Motor vehicle – mortgaged – removal from state	4	
257. 903 (1)	Property	E	Motor vehicle code – false certification – first offense	5	
257. 903 (2)	Property	E	Motor vehicle code – false certification – second offense	7	
257. 903 (3)	Property	D	Motor vehicle code – false certification – third or subsequent offense	15	
257. 902	Pub saf	E	Motor vehicle code violations	5	
750. 415 (6)	Property	E	Motor vehicles – buy/receive/obtain w/ intent to sell/dispose knowing VIN was altered	10	10/1/00
750. 415 (5)	Property	G	Motor vehicles – buy/sell/exchange/give paraphernalia capable of changing/misrepresenting ID	4	10/1/00
750. 415 (2)	Property	G	Motor vehicles – conceal/misrepresent identity with intent to mislead	4	
257. 601 b (3)	Person	C	Moving violation causing death to construction worker	15	10/1/01
257. 601 c (2)	Person	C	Moving violation causing death to operator of implement of husbandry	15	10/1/01
324. 80172	Person	G	Negligent crippling or homicide by vessel	2	
750. 324	Person	G	Negligent homicide	2	
750. 131 a (1)	Property	H	No account checks	2	
324. 31525	Person	G	NREPA – imminent danger of death or serious injury – subsequent offense	2	
324. 30316 (3)	Pub saf	H	NREPA violation – subsequent offense	2	
324. 33939 (1)	Pub trst	H	NREPA violation for commercial purposes	2	
750. 131 (3) (b) (ii)	Property	G	NSF checks – $100 to $500 – third or subsequent offense	2	10/1/00
750. 131 (3) (a) (iv)	Property	H	NSF checks – $50 or less – fourth offense	13 mos.	
750. 131 (3) (b) (ii)	Property	H	NSF checks – $50 to $200 – third offense	13 mos.	
750. 131 (3) (c)	Property	G	NSF checks – $500 or more	2	10/1/00
750. 131 a (2)	Property	H	NSF checks – 3 or more within 10 days	2	
750. 131 (3) (c)	Property	H	NSF checks – over $200	13 mos.	
333. 21792	Pub trst	G	Nursing homes – referral fees/bribing officials/accepting bribes	4	
752. 365 (3)	Pub ord	G	Obscenity – subsequent offense	2	
750. 241 (1)	Pub saf	F	Obstructing firefighter	4	Deleted, 2002 PA 272, Eff. 7/15/02
750. 241 (2)	Pub saf	F	Obstructing public service facility personnel in civil disturbance	4	7/15/02
750. 241 (3)	Pub saf	F	Obstructing public service facility personnel in civil disturbance	4	Substituted for by 750.241(2)
445. 67	Pub ord	E	Obtain/possess/sell/transfer identifying info/falsify police report - intent to commit identity theft	5	3/1/05
333. 7407 (1) (c)	CS	G	Obtaining controlled substance by fraud	4	
750. 285	Property	E	Obtaining personal ID information without authorization	5	Eff. 4/1/01 to 3/1/05, 2004 PA 457

Lightly shaded lines indicate that the statute governing the felony offense described on that line has been amended, deleted, or replaced.

*Unless otherwise noted, the date on which the statutory guidelines were made applicable to the felony offense listed is 1/1/99.

MCL #	Group	Class	Description	Stat Max	Effective Date*
750. 273	Property	E	Obtaining signature to financial document with intent to defraud	10	
257. 233 a (7)	Pub ord	G	Odometer tampering	5	
710. 54 (11)	Pub trst	F	Offer to give other consideration – adoption – subsequent violation	4	
750. 189	Pub saf	H	Officer negligently allowing prisoner to escape or refusing to receive prisoner	2	
500. 7034 (2)	Pub trst	E	Officer of a MEWA knowingly receive valuables for sale property or loan	10	
483. 226	Pub trst	E	Officer of a pipeline company – intent to defraud – stock	10	Deleted, 2006 PA 251, Eff. 7/3/06
750. 190	Pub saf	G	Officer receiving a reward to assist or permit escape	2	
750. 535 a	Pub ord	E	Operating a chop shop	5	Substituted for by 750.535a(2)
750. 535 a (2)	Pub ord	D	Operating a chop shop	10	10/1/00
750. 535 a (3)	Pub ord	D	Operating a chop shop – subsequent violation	10	10/1/00
462. 353 (5)	Pub saf	F	Operating a locomotive under the influence – third or subsequent offense	4	
462. 353 (5)	Pub saf	E	Operating a locomotive under the influence – third or subsequent offense	4	7/1/01
462. 353 (5)	Pub saf	E	Operating a locomotive under the influence – third or subsequent offense	5	4/1/03
324. 82126 c (1)	Person	G	Operating a snowmobile carelessly or negligently causing death or serious impairment	2	10/1/00
324. 82128 (1) (c)	Pub saf	E	Operating a snowmobile under the influence – third or subsequent offense	5	
324. 82127 (4)	Person	C	Operating a snowmobile under the influence causing death	15	
324. 82127 (5)	Person	E	Operating a snowmobile under the influence causing long-term incapacitating injury	5	
324. 82127 (5)	Person	E	Operating a snowmobile under the influence causing serious impairment	5	7/1/01
324. 82126 c (2)	Person	G	Operating a snowmobile without regard to safety causing serious impairment	2	10/1/00
257. 625 (8) (c)	Pub saf	E	Operating a vehicle under the influence – third or subsequent offense	5	Eff. until 9/30/03, replaced by (9)(c)
257. 625 (4) (a)	Person	C	Operating a vehicle under the influence or while impaired causing death	15	3/28/01
257. 625 (4) (b)	Person	B	Operating a vehicle under the influence or while impaired causing death to certain persons	20	10/1/01
257. 625 (5)	Person	E	Operating a vehicle under the influence or while impaired causing serious impairment	5	3/28/01
257. 625 (11) (c)	Pub saf	E	Operating a vehicle while impaired – third or subsequent offense	5	9/30/03
257. 625 (4) (a)	Person	C	Operating a vehicle while intoxicated or impaired causing death	15	9/30/03
257. 625 (4) (b)	Person	B	Operating a vehicle while intoxicated or impaired causing death to certain persons	20	9/30/03
257. 625 (5)	Person	E	Operating a vehicle while intoxicated or impaired causing serious impairment	5	9/30/03
257. 625 (9) (c)	Pub saf	E	Operating a vehicle while intoxicated/with presence of drugs – third or subsequent offense	5	9/30/03
257. 904 (4)	Person	C	Operating a vehicle without a license causing death	15	10/1/00
257. 904 (5)	Person	E	Operating a vehicle without a license causing serious impairment	5	10/1/00
324. 80177 (1) (c)	Pub saf	E	Operating a vessel under the influence – third or subsequent offense	5	
324. 80176 (4)	Person	C	Operating a vessel under the influence causing death	15	

Lightly shaded lines indicate that the statute governing the felony offense described on that line has been amended, deleted, or replaced.

*Unless otherwise noted, the date on which the statutory guidelines were made applicable to the felony offense listed is 1/1/99.

MCL #	Group	Class	Description	Stat Max	Effective Date*
324. 80176 (5)	Person	E	Operating a vessel under the influence causing long-term incapacitating injury	5	
324. 80176 (5)	Person	E	Operating a vessel under the influence causing serious impairment	5	7/1/01
324. 81134 (6)	Pub saf	E	Operating an ORV under the influence – third or subsequent offense	4	
324. 81134 (6)	Pub saf	E	Operating an ORV under the influence – third or subsequent offense	5	7/1/01
324. 81134 (7)	Person	C	Operating an ORV under the influence causing death	15	10/1/00
324. 81134 (8)	Person	E	Operating an ORV under the influence causing serious impairment	5	10/1/00
750. 465 a (1) (b)	Property	G	Operating audiovisual recording device in a theatrical facility - second offense	2	12/15/04
750. 465 a (1) (c)	Property	F	Operating audiovisual recording device in a theatrical facility - third or subsequent offense	40	38336
462. 353 (6)	Person	C	Operating locomotive under the influence or while impaired causing death	15	4/1/03
462. 353 (7)	Person	E	Operating locomotive under the influence or while impaired causing serious impairment	5	4/1/03
333. 7401 c (2) (a)	CS	D	Operating or maintaining controlled substance laboratory	10	1/1/01
333. 7401 c (2) (b)	CS	B	Operating or maintaining controlled substance laboratory in presence of minor	20	1/1/01
333. 7401 c (2) (c)	CS	B	Operating or maintaining controlled substance laboratory involving hazardous waste	20	1/1/01
333. 7401 c (2) (f)	CS	B	Operating or maintaining controlled substance laboratory involving methamphetamine	20	4/1/04
333. 7401 c (2) (d)	CS	B	Operating or maintaining controlled substance laboratory near certain places	20	1/1/01
259. 185 (4)	Person	C	Operating or serving as crew of aircraft while under the influence causing death	15	10/1/00
259. 185 (5)	Person	E	Operating or serving as crew of aircraft while under the influence causing serious impairment	5	3/28/01
750. 90 d (a)	Person	C	Operating under the influence/impaired causing miscarriage/stillbirth/death to embryo or fetus	15	6/1/01
750. 90 d (b)	Person	E	Operating under the influence/impaired causing serious or aggravated injury to embryo/fetus	5	10/1/00
257. 625 (7) (a) (ii)	Person	E	Operating under the influence/while impaired with a minor in the vehicle – subsequent offense	5	10/1/00
257. 625 (7) (a) (ii)	Person	E	Operating while intoxicated or impaired with a minor in the vehicle – subsequent offense	5	9/30/03
333. 7401 c (2) (e)	CS	A	Operating/maintaining controlled substance laboratory involving firearm/other harmful device	25	1/1/01
259. 185 (8)	Pub saf	G	Operating/serving as crew of aircraft while under the influence – third or subsequent offense	5	
259. 185 (8)	Pub saf	E	Operating/serving as crew of aircraft while under the influence – third or subsequent offense	5	3/28/01
286. 929 (4)	Pub trst	G	Organic products act violations	4	3/28/01
168. 932 (i)	Pub trst	E	Organizing a meeting where absentee voter ballots are to be voted	5	
750. 49 (2) (e)	Pub ord	F	Organizing or promoting animal fights	4	
257. 625 (4)	Person	C	OUIL – causing death	15	Substituted for by 257.625(4)(a)
257. 625 (4) (b)	Person	B	OUIL – causing death to emergency personnel	20	3/28/01
257. 625 (5)	Person	E	OUIL – causing serious impairment of body function	5	
257. 625 (7) (d)	Pub saf	E	OUIL – third offense	5	
750. 90 d (a)	Person	C	OUIL causing miscarriage or stillbirth	15	10/1/00

Lightly shaded lines indicate that the statute governing the felony offense described on that line has been amended, deleted, or replaced.

*Unless otherwise noted, the date on which the statutory guidelines were made applicable to the felony offense listed is 1/1/99.

MCL #	Group	Class	Description	Stat Max	Effective Date*
750. 157 u	Property	H	Overcharging person using financial transaction device	4	
750. 455	Pub ord	G	Pandering	20	
750. 442	Pub ord	G	Participating in prizefights	4	
47. 8	Pub trst	H	Payment of claim against county before audit	2	
764. 1 e	Pub trst	C	Peace officer – false statement in a complaint	15	
750. 90 g (3)	Person	A	Performance of procedure on live infant with intent to cause death	LIFE	3/10/00
750. 423	Pub trst	E	Perjury	15	
750. 422	Pub trst	G	Perjury – committed in court/capital crime	LIFE	
750. 423	Pub trst	E	Perjury by falsely swearing	15	10/1/00
750. 422	Pub trst	B	Perjury committed in court – capital crime	LIFE	10/1/00
750. 422	Pub trst	C	Perjury committed in court – noncapital crime	15	10/1/00
750. 422	Pub trst	G	Perjury committed in court/noncapital crime	15	
767A. 9 (b)	Pub trst	B	Perjury committed in prosecutor's investigative hearing – capital crime	LIFE	Eff. 10/1/00, then replaced by .9(1)(b)
767A. 9 (1) (b)	Pub trst	B	Perjury committed in prosecutor's investigative hearing – capital crime	LIFE	2/1/02
767A. 9 (a)	Pub trst	C	Perjury committed in prosecutor's investigative hearing – noncapital crime	15	Eff. 10/1/00 then replaced by .9(1)(a)
767A. 9 (1) (a)	Pub trst	C	Perjury committed in prosecutor's investigative hearing – noncapital crime	15	2/1/02
750. 160 a	Pub ord	H	Photographing dead human bodies	2	
750. 160 a	Pub ord	H	Photographing dead human body	2	4/1/04
28. 422	Pub saf	G	Pistols – license application forgery	4	
28. 422	Pub saf	F	Pistols – license application forgery	4	7/1/01
750. 207 (2) (c)	Person	A	Placing an explosive causing physical injury	25	10/1/00
750. 207 (2) (b)	Property	B	Placing an explosive causing property damage	20	10/1/00
750. 207 (2) (d)	Person	A	Placing an explosive causing serious impairment	LIFE	10/1/00
750. 207 (2) (a)	Pub saf	C	Placing an explosive with malicious intent	15	10/1/00
750. 209 (1) (c)	Person	A	Placing an offensive or injurious substance causing physical injury	25	10/1/00
750. 209 (1) (b)	Property	B	Placing an offensive or injurious substance causing property damage	20	10/1/00
750. 209 (1) (d)	Person	A	Placing an offensive or injurious substance causing serious impairment	LIFE	10/1/00
750. 209 (2)	Pub saf	E	Placing an offensive or injurious substance with intent to alarm or annoy	5	10/1/00
750. 209 (1) (a)	Pub saf	C	Placing an offensive or injurious substance with intent to injure	15	10/1/00
750. 206	Person	B	Placing explosives with damage to property resulting	25	
750. 205	Pub saf	C	Placing explosives with the intent to destroy property	15	
750. 209	Pub saf	F	Placing foul or offensive substance to alarm	4	

Lightly shaded lines indicate that the statute governing the felony offense described on that line has been amended, deleted, or replaced.

*Unless otherwise noted, the date on which the statutory guidelines were made applicable to the felony offense listed is 1/1/99.

MCL #	Group	Class	Description	Stat Max	Effective Date*
750. 209	Pub saf	C	Placing foul or offensive substance to injure	15	
750. 397 a	Person	D	Placing harmful objects in food	10	
750. 456	Person	B	Placing spouse into prostitution	20	
750. 436 (2)	Person	A	Poison – food/drink/medicine/wells – large amounts/injury	LIFE	Deleted, 2002 PA 123, Eff. 4/22/02
750. 436 (3)	Pub saf	H	Poison – malicious false statement of poisoning	2	Deleted, 2002 PA 123, Eff. 4/22/02
750. 436 (2) (a)	Pub saf	C	Poisoning food, drink, medicine, or water supply	15	4/22/02
750. 436 (2) (c)	Person	A	Poisoning food, drink, medicine, or water supply causing injury	25	4/22/02
750. 436 (2) (b)	Property	B	Poisoning food, drink, medicine, or water supply causing property damage	20	4/22/02
750. 436 (2) (d)	Person	A	Poisoning food, drink, medicine, or water supply causing serious impairment	LIFE	4/22/02
750. 436 (1)	Person	E	Poisoning food/drink/wells	5	Deleted, 2002 PA 123, Eff. 4/22/02
750. 439	Pub ord	G	Polygamy	4	
750. 440	Pub ord	G	Polygamy – knowingly entering a prohibited marriage	4	
750. 227 c	Pub saf	G	Possessing a loaded firearm in or upon a vehicle	2	
750. 209 a	Pub saf	D	Possessing an explosive device in public place	10	10/1/00
750. 252	Property	E	Possessing counterfeit notes	7	
750. 157 p	Property	H	Possessing financial transaction device without permission and with intent to use or sell	4	
750. 157 n (2)	Property	H	Possessing fraudulent or altered financial transaction device	4	
750. 210 (2) (c)	Person	A	Possessing or carrying an explosive or combustible substance causing physical injury	25	10/1/00
750. 210 (2) (b)	Property	B	Possessing or carrying an explosive or combustible substance causing property damage	20	10/1/00
750. 210 (2) (d)	Person	A	Possessing or carrying an explosive or combustible substance causing serious impairment	LIFE	10/1/00
750. 210 (2) (a)	Pub saf	C	Possessing or carrying an explosive or combustible substance with malicious intent	15	10/1/00
750. 211 a	Pub saf	F	Possessing or manufacturing device designed to explode upon impact or heating	4	
257. 254	Property	E	Possessing stolen vehicle title	10	
259. 80 f (3)	Pub saf	D	Possessing weapon in sterile area of commercial airport	10	3/31/03
333. 7403 (2) (a) (i)	CS	A	Possession of 1,000 or more grams of certain schedule 1 or 2 controlled substances	LIFE	3/1/03
257. 310 (9)	Pub ord	E	Possession of 2 or more forged driver licenses	5	4/22/02
333. 7403 (2) (a) (ii)	CS	A	Possession of 225+ but less than 650 grams of certain schedule 1 or 2 controlled substances	30	10/1/00
333. 7403 (2) (a) (iv)	CS	G	Possession of 25+ but less than 50 grams of certain schedule 1 or 2 controlled substances	4	
333. 7403 (2) (a) (ii)	CS	A	Possession of 450+ but less than 1,000 grams of certain schedule 1 or 2 substances	30	3/1/03
750. 261	Property	E	Possession of 5 or fewer counterfeit coins	10	
333. 7403 (2) (a) (iii)	CS	B	Possession of 50+ but less than 225 grams of certain schedule 1 or 2 controlled substances	20	
333. 7403 (2) (a) (iii)	CS	B	Possession of 50+ but less than 450 grams of certain schedule 1 or 2 controlled substances	20	3/1/03

Lightly shaded lines indicate that the statute governing the felony offense described on that line has been amended, deleted, or replaced.

*Unless otherwise noted, the date on which the statutory guidelines were made applicable to the felony offense listed is 1/1/99.

MCL #	Group	Class	Description	Stat Max	Effective Date*
333. 7403 (2) (a) (i)	CS	A	Possession of 650 or more grams of certain schedule 1 or 2 controlled substances by juvenile	LIFE	
750. 210	Pub saf	E	Possession of bombs with unlawful intent	5	
750. 116	Property	E	Possession of burglar's tools	10	
333. 7403 (2) (b)	CS	G	Possession of certain schedule 1, 2, 3, or 4 controlled substances or analogue	2	
333. 7403 (2) (b) (ii)	CS	G	Possession of certain schedule 1, 2, 3, or 4 controlled substances or analogue	2	1/1/01
750. 254	Property	E	Possession of counterfeit notes or bills	5	
333. 7407 (1) (f)	CS	F	Possession of counterfeit prescription form	4	1/6/03
333. 7407 (1) (g)	CS	F	Possession of counterfeit prescription form	4	Rewritten as .7407(1)(f), 2001 PA 236
333. 7407 (1) (e)	CS	G	Possession of counterfeiting implements	4	
750. 255	Property	E	Possession of counterfeiting tools	10	
333. 7401 b (3) (b)	CS	G	Possession of GBL	2	1/1/01
333. 7403 (2) (a) (v)	CS	G	Possession of less than 25 grams of certain schedule 1 or 2 controlled substances	4	
333. 7403 (2) (b) (i)	CS	D	Possession of methamphetamine	10	1/1/01
333. 7403 (2) (b) (i)	CS	D	Possession of methamphetamine or 3, 4-methylenedioxymethamphetamine	10	4/1/03
333. 17766 c (2)	CS	G	Possession of more than 10 grams ephedrine	2	Eff. 1/1/99 to 4/1/04, 2003 PA 309
333. 17766 c (2)	CS	G	Possession of more than 12 grams ephedrine or pseudoephedrine	2	4/1/04
333. 7403 (2) (e)	CS	H	Possession of official prescription form	1	Deleted, 2003 PA 311, Eff. 4/1/04
324. 41309 (4) (b)	Property	F	Possession of prohibited or genetically engineered species - intent to damage resources	4	9/1/05
324. 41309 (3) (b)	Property	G	Possession of prohibited species	2	9/1/05
324. 41309 (4) (a)	Property	G	Possession of restricted or nonnative species - intent to damage resources	2	9/1/05
750. 224 b	Pub saf	E	Possession of short barreled shotgun or rifle	5	
333. 17766 a (2)	CS	F	Possession of steroids – subsequent offense	4	Deleted, 2003 PA 309, Eff. 4/1/04
750. 543 r	Pub saf	B	Possession of vulnerable target information with intent to commit certain terrorist acts	20	7/15/02
324. 41309	Property	E	Possession or release of genetically engineered, nonnative, or prohibited fish	5	Eff. 3/30/04 to 9/1/05, 2005 PA 81
750. 224 a	Pub saf	F	Possession or sale of electrical current weapons	4	
750. 224 f	Pub saf	E	Possession or sale of firearm by felon	5	
324. 48738 (4)	Property	E	Possession, importation, or planting of genetically engineered fish	5	3/30/04
257. 329 (1)	Property	G	Possession/sale of stolen or counterfeit insurance certificates	5	
257. 329 (2)	Property	E	Possession/sale of stolen or counterfeit insurance certificates – second offense	7	
257. 329 (3)	Property	E	Possession/sale of stolen or counterfeit insurance certificates – third or subsequent offense	15	
445. 490	Pub ord	H	Precious metal and gem dealer failure to obtain a certificate of registration	2	
445. 487 (2)	Pub ord	H	Precious metal and gem dealer failure to record material matter – subsequent offense	2	

Lightly shaded lines indicate that the statute governing the felony offense described on that line has been amended, deleted, or replaced.

*Unless otherwise noted, the date on which the statutory guidelines were made applicable to the felony offense listed is 1/1/99.

MCL #	Group	Class	Description	Stat Max	Effective Date*
445. 489	Pub ord	H	Precious metal and gem dealer violations	2	
445. 488 (2)	Pub ord	H	Precious metal and gem dealer violations – subsequent offense	2	
750. 77	Person	F	Preparing to burn personal property greater than $50	4	
750. 77 (1) (c)	Person	E	Preparing to burn personal property having value of $1,000 to $20,000 or w/ prior convictions	5	10/1/00
750. 77 (1) (d)	Person	D	Preparing to burn personal property of $20,000 or more or with prior convictions	10	10/1/00
750. 368 (5)	Pub ord	G	Preparing, serving, or executing unauthorized process – third or subsequent offense	4	10/1/00
801. 263 (2)	Pub saf	H	Prisoner in jail possessing contraband	5	8/1/99
801. 262 (2)	Pub saf	E	Prisoner in jail possessing weapon	5	8/1/99
800. 281 (4)	Pub saf	E	Prisoner possessing contraband	5	
800. 283 (4)	Pub saf	E	Prisoner possessing weapon	5	
750. 349 a	Person	A	Prisoner taking a hostage	LIFE	
800. 283 (2)	Pub saf	E	Prisons – knowledge of a weapon in a correctional facility	5	
750. 98	Pub ord	G	Private banking	4	
338. 823	Pub trst	F	Private detective license act violation	4	10/1/02
338. 1053	Pub trst	F	Private security business and security alarm act violation	4	3/28/01
750. 443	Pub ord	G	Prizefights – training	4	
750. 277	Pub trst	G	Promise to vendee of grain to sell at a fictitious price – sale and transfer	4	
750. 458	Person	B	Prostitution – detaining female for debt	20	
750. 451	Pub ord	G	Prostitution – various offenses – third or subsequent offense	2	
750. 490	Pub trst	H	Public money – safekeeping	2	
21. 154	Pub trst	E	Public officer – embezzlement	5	
750. 118	Pub trst	D	Public officer accepting bribe	10	
750. 480	Pub trst	F	Public officers – refusing to turn over books/money to successor	4	
750. 488	Pub trst	H	Public officers – state official – retaining fees	2	
750. 491	Pub trst	H	Public records – removal/mutilation/destruction	2	
750. 282	Pub ord	G	Public utility – fraudulent use over $500	4	
15. 324 (1) (d)	Pub trst	G	Purchase of public residential property by public servant	1	12/16/05
18. 1268 (9)	Pub trst	H	Purposefully submitting false business certification	Fine	Deleted, 2005 PA 265, Eff. 12/16/05
445. 1528	Pub trst	D	Pyramid/chain promotions – offer or sell	7	
431. 257	Pub trst	G	Racing, boxing and exhibition racing	2	
750. 159 j	Pub saf	B	Racketeering	20	
554. 836	Property	E	Real and property – living care disclosure act	7	

Lightly shaded lines indicate that the statute governing the felony offense described on that line has been amended, deleted, or replaced.

*Unless otherwise noted, the date on which the statutory guidelines were made applicable to the felony offense listed is 1/1/99.

MCL #	Group	Class	Description	Stat Max	Effective Date*
750. 219 f	Property	F	Receive/possess w/ intent to forward/forwarding unauthorized credit application or proceeds	4	9/1/01
750. 219 f	Property	F	Receive/possess w/ intent to forward/forwarding unauthorized credit application/proceeds	4	3/10/00
750. 219 e	Property	F	Receive/possess/prepare/submit or receive/possess proceeds from unauthorized credit app	4	3/10/00
750. 219 e	Property	F	Receive/possess/prepare/submit unauthorized credit application or receive/possess proceeds	4	9/1/01
750. 535 (7)	Property	E	Receiving or concealing stolen motor vehicle	5	2/12/04
750. 535 (3)	Property	E	Receiving or concealing stolen property having a value of $1,000 to $20,000 or with priors	5	10/1/00
750. 535	Property	E	Receiving or concealing stolen property over $100	5	
750. 535 (2)	Property	D	Receiving/concealing stolen property having a value of $20,000 or more or with priors	10	10/1/00
752. 881	Person	G	Reckless use of bow and arrow resulting in injury or death	2	
600. 2907 a	Property	G	Recording documents affecting property without lawful cause	3	
324. 76107 (4) (c)	Property	E	Recovering abandoned property in Great Lakes - value of $1,000 to $20,000 or w/ priors	5	1/1/02
324. 76107 (4) (d)	Property	D	Recovering abandoned property in Great Lakes - value of $20,000+ or with prior convictions	10	1/1/02
324. 76107 (4)	Pub trst	G	Recovering abandoned property in Great Lakes without permit	2	Deleted, 2001 PA 156, Eff. 1/1/02
333. 7416 (1) (a)	CS	SPEC	Recruiting or inducing a minor to commit a controlled substance felony	Variable	
333. 7405 (c)	CS	G	Refusing lawful inspection	2	
333. 7407 (2)	CS	G	Refusing to furnish records under controlled substance article	4	
493. 77 (2)	Pub trst	H	Regulatory loans	3	
333. 10204 (4)	Pub saf	F	Removal of a human organ by an unauthorized individual	4	9/1/99
333. 10205	Pub saf	F	Removal of a human organ in an unapproved facility	4	9/1/99
750. 418	Property	H	Removing a vehicle out of state without vendor's consent	4	
324. 51120 (2)	Property	H	Removing forest products over $2,500	3	
750. 93	Property	G	Removing or destroying bonds in state treasury	10	
324. 76107 (3)	Pub ord	D	Removing or mutilating human body from Great Lakes bottomland	10	1/1/02
333. 2688	Person	E	Research on dead embryo or fetus without mother's consent	5	See MCL 333.2691
324. 1608	Person	G	Resisting and obstructing conservation officer	2	
750. 479	Person	G	Resisting or obstructing a peace officer	2	Substituted for by 750.479(2)
750. 356 c	Property	H	Retail fraud – first degree	2	
750. 356 c	Property	E	Retail fraud – first degree	5	10/1/00
750. 120 a (4)	Person	D	Retaliating against juror	10	3/28/01
750. 122 (8)	Person	D	Retaliating against witness	10	3/28/01
750. 483 a (2) (b)	Person	D	Retaliating for reporting crime	10	3/28/01

Lightly shaded lines indicate that the statute governing the felony offense described on that line has been amended, deleted, or replaced.

*Unless otherwise noted, the date on which the statutory guidelines were made applicable to the felony offense listed is 1/1/99.

MCL #	Group	Class	Description	Stat Max	Effective Date*
750. 483 a (2) (b)	Person	D	Retaliating for reporting crime punishable by more than 10 years	10	7/15/02
750. 145 p (2)	Person	G	Retaliation or discrimination by caregiver against vulnerable adult	2	
600. 8713	Pub trst	G	Revised judicature act – false statement by authorized local officials	15	
600. 2916	Pub saf	G	Revised judicature act – lethal gases for fumigation	4	
752. 541	Pub saf	D	Riot	10	
752. 542 a	Pub saf	D	Riot in state correctional facilities	10	
750. 372	Pub ord	H	Running or allowing lottery	2	
750. 223 (2)	Pub saf	F	Sale of firearm to minor – subsequent offense	4	
750. 223 (3)	Pub ord	D	Sale of firearm to person prohibited from possessing	10	
750. 272	Property	G	Sale of fraudulent stock of foreign corporations	10	
750. 210 a	Pub saf	H	Sale of valerium	5	
333. 2690	Person	E	Sale or delivery of fetus or embryo	5	See MCL 333.2691
752. 272 (2) (c)	Pub saf	F	Sale or distribution of nitrous oxide device – 2 or more prior convictions	4	1/1/01
288. 223	Pub saf	G	Sale or labeling of oleomargarine violations	3	Repealed, 2001 PA 267, Eff. 2/8/02 Deleted, 2005 PA 54, Eff. 9/1/05
333. 7340	CS	F	Sale/distribution/delivery of product w/ ephedrine/pseudoephedrine by mail/internet/telephone	4	10/1/06
442. 219	Pub trst	E	Sales – false statement	5	
750. 377 c	Property	E	School bus – intentional damage	5	
750. 317	Person	M2	Second degree murder	LIFE	
493. 77 (2)	Pub trst	H	Second mortgage loan act licensing violation	3	As amended, 2006 PA 251, Eff. 7/3/06
451. 319	Pub trst	G	Securities, real estate, and debt management – violation	2	
750. 532	Person	H	Seduction	5	
750. 514	Property	H	Seizing locomotive with mail car	10	Deleted, 2002 PA 320, Eff. 7/15/02
28. 295 (2)	Pub ord	E	Sell/possess counterfeited/forged state ID w/ intent to deliver or possess 2+ forged ID cards	5	9/1/04
436. 1701 (2)	Person	D	Selling alcohol to a minor and causing death	10	
288. 284	Pub trst	H	Selling falsely branded cheese	2	Repealed, 2001 PA 267, Eff. 2/8/02 Deleted, 2005 PA 54, Eff. 9/1/05
750. 49 (2) (h)	Pub ord	F	Selling or possessing equipment for animal fights	4	
257. 310 (8)	Pub ord	E	Selling or possessing forged driver license with intent to deliver	5	4/22/02
750. 373	Pub ord	H	Selling or possessing lottery tickets	2	
257. 616 a (2) (f)	Pub ord	G	Selling or purchasing a signal preemption device	2	6/14/04
750. 204 (2) (c)	Person	A	Sending an explosive causing physical injury	25	10/1/00
750. 204 (2) (b)	Property	B	Sending an explosive causing property damage	20	10/1/00
750. 204 (2) (d)	Person	A	Sending an explosive causing serious impairment	LIFE	10/1/00

Lightly shaded lines indicate that the statute governing the felony offense described on that line has been amended, deleted, or replaced.

*Unless otherwise noted, the date on which the statutory guidelines were made applicable to the felony offense listed is 1/1/99.

MCL #	Group	Class	Description	Stat Max	Effective Date*
750. 204 (2) (a)	Pub saf	C	Sending an explosive with malicious intent	15	10/1/00
750. 204	Pub saf	E	Sending explosives with intent to injure persons	5	
750. 204 a	Pub saf	E	Sending or transporting an imitation explosive device with malicious intent	5	10/1/00
750. 204 a	Pub saf	F	Sending or transporting imitation explosive device with malicious intent	4	
750. 236	Person	C	Setting spring gun – death resulting	15	
28. 729	Pub ord	G	Sex offenders – failure to register	4	Substituted for by 28.729(1)(a)
750. 90	Person	D	Sexual intercourse under pretext of medical treatment	10	
750. 202	Pub saf	F	Shipping an explosive with false markings or invoice	4	
750. 158	Pub ord	E	Sodomy	15	
750. 157 b (3) (b)	Pub ord	G	Solicitation of felony punishable by less than 5 years	2	
750. 157 b (3) (a)	Pub ord	E	Solicitation of felony punishable by life or 5 or more years	5	
750. 157 b (2)	Person	A	Solicitation of murder	LIFE	
750. 145 a	Person	F	Soliciting child to commit an immoral act	4	6/1/02
750. 543 k	Pub saf	B	Soliciting material support for terrorism or terrorist acts	20	4/22/02
750. 543 k	Pub saf	B	Soliciting or providing material support for terrorism or terrorist acts	20	7/15/02
324. 11549 (2)	Pub saf	G	Solid waste - importing from foreign country	2	3/13/06
750. 411 h (2) (b)	Person	E	Stalking of a minor	5	
205. 28 (1) (e)	Pub trst	G	State employee compromising taxes	5	
324. 2157 (3)	Property	H	State owned property – damages of $1,000 or more	180 days	Deleted, 2001 PA 156, Eff. 1/1/02
207. 754 (3)	Pub trst	G	State treasurer – municipality tax – divulging confidential information	5	
750. 97	Property	H	Statements derogatory to financial condition of bank	4	
750. 535 b	Pub saf	E	Stolen firearms or ammunition	10	
750. 516	Person	C	Stopping train to rob	LIFE	Deleted, 2002 PA 320, Eff. 7/15/02
472. 36	Pub saf	A	Street railways – obstruction of track	LIFE	
28. 735 (2) (b)	Pub trst	G	Student safety zone violation involving residency - second or subsequent violation	2	1/1/06
28. 734 (2) (b)	Pub trst	G	Student safety zone violation involving work or loitering - second or subsequent offense	2	1/1/06
750. 424	Pub trst	E	Subornation of perjury	15	
750. 424	Pub trst	C	Subornation of perjury	15	10/1/00
333. 7413 (2)	Pub trst	SPEC	Subsequent controlled substance violations	Variable	
333. 7413 (3)	Pub trst	SPEC	Subsequent controlled substance violations	Variable	
168. 932 (g)	Pub trst	E	Suggesting how a disabled voter should vote	5	
168. 932 (h)	Pub trst	E	Suggesting or influencing how an absentee voter should vote	5	

Lightly shaded lines indicate that the statute governing the felony offense described on that line has been amended, deleted, or replaced.

*Unless otherwise noted, the date on which the statutory guidelines were made applicable to the felony offense listed is 1/1/99.

MCL #	Group	Class	Description	Stat Max	Effective Date*
722. 859 (3)	Person	E	Surrogate parenting act – contracts for compensation	5	
722. 857	Person	E	Surrogate parenting act – contracts involving minors, mentally retarded, etc.	5	
722. 859 (3)	Person	E	Surrogate parenting contracts for compensation	5	As amended, 2005 PA 106, Eff. 9/14/05, and 2005 PA 134, Eff. 1/1/06
722. 857	Person	E	Surrogate parenting contracts involving minors, mentally retarded, etc.	5	As amended, 2005 PA 106, Eff. 9/14/05, and 2005 PA 134, Eff. 1/1/06
750. 543 r	Pub saf	B	Surveillance of vulnerable target with intent to commit terrorism	20	4/22/02
750. 11	Person	A	Taking a woman and compelling her to marry	LIFE	
750. 12	Person	H	Taking a woman with intent to compel her to marry	10	
750. 483 a (6) (a)	Pub ord	F	Tampering with evidence	4	3/28/01
750. 483 a (6) (b)	Pub ord	D	Tampering with evidence in case punishable by more than 10 years	10	3/28/01
750. 483 a (6) (a)	Pub ord	F	Tampering with evidence or offering false evidence	4	As amended, 2006 PA 40, Eff. 3/2/06
750. 483 a (6) (b)	Pub ord	D	Tampering with evidence/offering false evidence in case punishable by more than 10 years	10	As amended, 2006 PA 40, Eff. 3/2/06
750. 498 b (2) (b)	Person	C	Tampering/taking/removing marine safety device without authority causing death	15	7/1/06
750. 498 b (2) (a)	Person	E	Tampering/taking/removing marine safety device without authority causing serious impairment	5	7/1/06
750. 540	Pub ord	H	Tapping or cutting telephone lines	2	
750. 441	Pub ord	G	Teaching or advocating polygamy	4	
750. 540 c (4)	Property	F	Telecommunication violation	4	2/12/04
750. 540 c (3)	Property	F	Telecommunications and computer – manufacture or deliver counterfeit communications	4	
750. 540 f (2)	Property	E	Telecommunications and computer–knowingly publishing counterfeit devices–2nd conviction	5	
750. 219 a (2) (c)	Property	E	Telecommunications fraud - 1 or more prior convictions or value of $1,000 to $20,000	5	10/1/00
750. 219 a (2) (d)	Property	D	Telecommunications fraud - 2 or more prior convictions or value of $20,000 or more	10	10/1/00
750. 219 a (2) (c)	Property	E	Telecommunications fraud – 2 prior convictions or value between $1,000-$20,000	5	
750. 219 a (2) (d)	Property	D	Telecommunications fraud – 3 or more prior convictions or value over $20,000	10	
750. 543 f	Person	A	Terrorism without causing death	LIFE	4/22/02
750. 360 a (2) (b)	Property	F	Theft detection device offense with prior conviction	4	7/1/02
750. 411 a (3) (a)	Pub ord	F	Threat or false report of an explosive or harmful device, substance, or material	4	4/1/01
750. 543 m	Pub ord	B	Threat or false report of terrorism	20	4/22/02
750. 411 a (3) (b)	Pub ord	D	Threat/false report of explosive or harmful device/substance/material – subsequent offense	10	4/1/01
750. 213	Person	B	Threats to extort money	20	
750. 394 (2) (e)	Person	C	Throwing or dropping dangerous object at vehicle causing death	15	1/1/04
750. 394 (2) (c)	Person	F	Throwing or dropping dangerous object at vehicle causing injury	4	1/1/04
750. 394 (2) (d)	Person	D	Throwing or dropping dangerous object at vehicle causing serious impairment	10	1/1/04
205. 428 (2)	Pub trst	G	Tobacco products tax act violations	5	

Lightly shaded lines indicate that the statute governing the felony offense described on that line has been amended, deleted, or replaced.

Updated April 2007

*Unless otherwise noted, the date on which the statutory guidelines were made applicable to the felony offense listed is 1/1/99.

MCL #	Group	Class	Description	Stat Max	Effective Date*
750. 85	Person	A	Torture	LIFE	3/1/06
462. 257 (1)	Person	A	Trains – endangering travel	LIFE	
750. 361	Property	H	Trains – stealing/maliciously removing parts	2	
333. 10204 (1)	Pub ord	F	Transferring a human organ for valuable consideration	4	
750. 201	Pub saf	F	Transportation of concussion or friction type explosives	4	
750. 459	Person	B	Transporting a female for prostitution	20	
750. 200	Pub saf	E	Transporting an explosive by common carrier	5	10/1/00
750. 201	Pub saf	E	Transporting certain types of explosives	5	10/1/00
750. 552 c	Pub saf	F	Trespass upon key facility	4	4/15/06
750. 552 b	Property	F	Trespassing on correctional facility property	4	
750. 530	Person	C	Unarmed robbery	15	
338. 3434 a (2)	Pub trst	F	Unauthorized disclosure of a social security number – subsequent offense	4	10/1/00
28. 214	Pub trst	F	Unauthorized disclosure of information from LEIN – subsequent offense	4	1/1/02
28. 214 (4) (b)	Pub trst	F	Unauthorized disclosure of information from LEIN – subsequent offense	4	10/1/00
333. 2813 (3)	Pub trst	F	Unauthorized disclosure of social security number – subsequent offense	4	10/1/00
551. 102 (2)	Pub trst	F	Unauthorized disclosure of social security number – subsequent offense	4	10/1/00
205. 28 (1) (f)	Pub trst	G	Unauthorized disclosure of tax information	5	
339. 735	Pub trst	E	Unauthorized practice of public accounting	5	12/19/05
750. 478 a (2)	Pub ord	H	Unauthorized process to obstruct a public officer or employee	2	10/1/00
750. 478 a (3)	Pub ord	G	Unauthorized process to obstruct a public officer or employee – subsequent offense	4	10/1/00
750. 512	Property	E	Uncoupling railroad cars	10	
324. 21324 (1)	Pub saf	G	Underground storage tanks – false or misleading information	5	
421. 54 b (b) (i)	Property	H	Unemployment comp fraud – conspiracy with loss of $25,000 or less	2	
421. 54 b (b) (ii)	Property	G	Unemployment comp fraud – conspiracy with loss over $25,000	5	
421. 54 b (b) (iii)	Property	H	Unemployment comp fraud – conspiracy with no actual loss	2	
421. 54 (d)	Property	H	Unemployment comp fraud – disclose confidential information for financial gain	1	
421. 54 c (b) (iii)	Property	G	Unemployment comp fraud – embezzlement of $100,000 or more	5	
421. 54 c (b) (ii)	Property	H	Unemployment comp fraud – embezzlement of $25,000 to under $100,000	2	
421. 54 c (b) (iv)	Property	H	Unemployment comp fraud – embezzlement with no actual loss	2	
421. 54 (a) (ii) (B)	Property	H	Unemployment comp fraud – failure to comply with act/rule $25,000-$100,000	2	
421. 54 (a) (ii) (C)	Property	G	Unemployment comp fraud – failure to comply with act/rule over $100,000	5	
421. 54 a	Property	G	Unemployment comp fraud – false statement as condition of employment	10	

Lightly shaded lines indicate that the statute governing the felony offense described on that line has been amended, deleted, or replaced.

*Unless otherwise noted, the date on which the statutory guidelines were made applicable to the felony offense listed is 1/1/99.

MCL #	Group	Class	Description	Stat Max	Effective Date*
421. 54 (b) (ii) (B)	Property	H	Unemployment comp fraud – false statement or misrepresent over $25,000	2	
421. 54 (b) (ii) (C)	Property	H	Unemployment comp fraud – false statement or misrepresentation without actual loss	2	
421. 54 (a) (iv) (B)	Property	H	Unemployment comp fraud – willful violation of act/rule over $100,000	2	
752. 543	Pub saf	G	Unlawful assembly	5	
750. 413	Property	E	Unlawful driving away of an automobile	5	
28. 425 j (2)	Pub saf	F	Unlawful granting or presenting of pistol training certificate	4	7/1/01
750. 349 b	Person	C	Unlawful imprisonment	15	8/24/06
750. 227 a	Pub saf	F	Unlawful possession of pistol	4	
750. 411 s (2) (a)	Person	G	Unlawful posting of message	2	4/1/01
750. 411 s (2) (b)	Person	E	Unlawful posting of message with aggravating circumstances	5	4/1/01
750. 414	Property	H	Unlawful use of an automobile	2	
752. 797 (2) (a)	Property	E	Unlawfully accessing computer, computer system, or computer program	5	10/1/00
752. 797 (2) (b)	Property	D	Unlawfully accessing computer, computer system, or computer program, with prior conviction	10	10/1/00
750. 502 d	Pub saf	F	Unlawfully possessing or transporting anhydrous ammonia or tampering with containers	4	4/1/04
168. 808	Pub trst	E	Untrue statement by member of board of inspectors	4	
333. 2685	Person	E	Use of a live human embryo, fetus for nontherapeutic research	5	See MCL 333.2691
333. 7407 (1) (b)	CS	G	Use of fictitious, revoked, or suspended license number	4	
750. 543 p	Pub saf	B	Use of internet or telecommunications to commit certain terrorist acts	20	7/15/02
750. 543 p	Pub saf	B	Use of internet or telecommunications to commit terrorism	20	4/22/02
750. 157 s (1) (c)	Property	H	Use of revoked or canceled financial transaction device involving $500 or more	2	10/1/00
257. 616 a (2) (b)	Pub saf	G	Using a signal preemption device	2	6/14/04
257. 616 a (2) (c)	Pub saf	E	Using a signal preemption device causing a traffic accident	5	6/14/04
257. 616 a (2) (e)	Person	C	Using a signal preemption device causing death	15	6/14/04
257. 616 a (2) (d)	Person	D	Using a signal preemption device causing serious impairment of a body function	10	6/14/04
752. 797 (3) (e)	Variable	D	Using computer for crime punishable by maximum term of at least 10 yrs but less than 20 yrs	10	10/1/00
752. 797 (3) (c)	Variable	F	Using computer for crime punishable by maximum term of at least 2 yrs but less than 4 yrs	4	10/1/00
752. 797 (3) (d)	Variable	D	Using computer for crime punishable by maximum term of at least 4 yrs but less than 10 yrs	7	10/1/00
752. 797 (3) (b)	Variable	G	Using computer for crime punishable by maximum term of more than 1 yr but less than 2 yrs	2	10/1/00
752. 797 (3) (f)	Variable	B	Using computerfor crime punishable by maximum term of at least 20 yrs or for life	20	10/1/00
750. 237 (4)	Person	C	Using firearm while under the influence or impaired causing death	15	2/1/02
750. 237 (3)	Person	E	Using firearm while under the influence or impaired causing serious impairment	5	2/1/02
750. 145 d (2)	Person	G	Using internet or computer for certain crimes	2	8/1/99

Lightly shaded lines indicate that the statute governing the felony offense described on that line has been amended, deleted, or replaced.

*Unless otherwise noted, the date on which the statutory guidelines were made applicable to the felony offense listed is 1/1/99.

MCL #	Group	Class	Description	Stat Max	Effective Date*
750. 145 d (3)	Person	E	Using internet or computer for certain crimes or second or subsequent offense	5	8/1/99
750. 145 d (2) (b)	Variable	G	Using internet/computer for crime punishable by max term at least 1 yr but less than 2 yrs	2	10/1/00
750. 145 d (2) (e)	Variable	C	Using internet/computer for crime punishable by max term at least 10 yrs but less than 15 yrs	15	10/1/00
750. 145 d (2) (d)	Variable	D	Using internet/computer for crime punishable by max term at least 4 yrs but less than 10 yrs	10	10/1/00
750. 145 d (2) (f)	Variable	B	Using internet/computer to commit crime punishable by max term of at least 15 yrs or for life	20	10/1/00
750. 145 d (2) (c)	Variable	F	Using internet/computerfor crime punishable by max term at least 2 yrs but less than 4 yrs	4	10/1/00
750. 157 s (1) (b) (ii)	Property	H	Using revoked/canceled financial transaction device involving $100 to $500 w/ priors	2	10/1/00
750. 224 d (2)	Person	G	Using self-defense spray device	2	
28. 295 (3)	Property	H	Using stolen state ID card to commit felony	Variable	Replaced, 2004 PA 149, Eff. 9/1/04
28. 295 (5)	Property	H	Using stolen state ID card to commit felony	Variable	9/1/04
750. 248 a	Property	F	Uttering and publishing financial transaction device	4	
750. 249	Property	E	Uttering and publishing forged records	14	
750. 253	Property	G	Uttering counterfeit notes	5	
752. 802	Property	H	Vending machines – manufacture/sale of slugs	5	
750. 101	Pub trst	E	Violating financial institutions act	5	
750. 79	Pub saf	F	Violating township rules concerning clearing of land and burning	4	
712A. 6 b (3)	Pub ord	G	Violation of court order – subsequent conviction	2	10/1/00
445. 2507 (2)	Pub ord	F	Violation of unsolicited commercial e-mail protection act in furtherance of crime	4	9/30/03
750. 188	Pub ord	SPEC	Voluntarily suffering prisoner to escape	Variable	
168. 769 (4)	Pub trst	E	Voting both in person and by absentee ballot	5	
750. 145 p (5)	Person	E	Vulnerable adult – caregiver violations – subsequent offense	5	
750. 145 p (1)	Person	G	Vulnerable adult – commingling funds, obstructing investigation, or filing false information	2	
750. 145 n (1)	Person	C	Vulnerable adult abuse – first degree	15	
750. 145 n (2)	Person	F	Vulnerable adult abuse – second degree	4	
750. 145 n (3)	Person	G	Vulnerable adult abuse – third degree	2	
444. 107	Pub trst	E	Warehouse certificates – willfully alter or destroy	5	
444. 13	Pub trst	H	Warehousemen and warehouse receipts	2	
324. 12116 (2)	Pub saf	H	Waste – false statement or entry in a license application	2	
324. 3115 (2)	Pub saf	H	Waste discharge violations	2	1/1/01
324. 3115 (2)	Pub saf	H	Waste discharge violations – second offense	2	
324. 3115 (4)	Pub saf	G	Waste discharge violations – substantial endangerment	5	1/1/01
333. 13738 (2)	Pub saf	F	Waste disposal violations – second offense	5	

Lightly shaded lines indicate that the statute governing the felony offense described on that line has been amended, deleted, or replaced.

*Unless otherwise noted, the date on which the statutory guidelines were made applicable to the felony offense listed is 1/1/99.

MCL #	Group	Class	Description	Stat Max	Effective Date*
47. 56	Pub trst	H	Wayne County treasurer paying claims without appropriate signature	2	
750. 237 a (1)	Pub saf	F	Weapon-free school zones – general felony violations	Variable	
750. 227 f	Pub saf	F	Wearing body armor during commission of certain crimes	4	As amended, 2005 PA 106, Eff. 9/14/05
750. 227 f	Pub saf	F	Wearing body armor during commission of violent crime	4	
290. 631 (3)	Pub trst	G	Weights and measures	5	
290. 629 (1)	Person	G	Weights and measures – assaults enforcement officer	2	
400. 60 (2)	Property	H	Welfare – obtaining over $500 by failure to inform	4	
324. 40118 (11)	Pub ord	G	Wildlife conservation – buying or selling protected animals – subsequent offense	4	
35. 929	Pub trst	H	Willful falsification in application for veterans benefits	3	
750. 322	Person	C	Willful killing of unborn quick child	15	
324. 51512	Pub saf	D	Willfully setting forest fires	10	
750. 483 a (2) (b)	Person	D	Withholding evidence/preventing/retaliating for reporting crime punishable by more than 10 yrs	10	As amended, 2006 PA 40, Eff. 3/2/06

Lightly shaded lines indicate that the statute governing the felony offense described on that line has been amended, deleted, or replaced.

MICHIGAN COMPILED LAWS

CHAPTER 769

CODE OF CRIMINAL PROCEDURE—JUDGMENT AND SENTENCE

Analysis of Sections

[Chapter in part]

CHAPTER IX. JUDGMENT AND SENTENCE

CHAPTER IX. JUDGMENT AND SENTENCE

769.8. Indeterminate sentence; first conviction

Sec. 8. (1) When a person is convicted for the first time for committing a felony and the punishment prescribed by law for that offense may be imprisonment in a state prison, the court imposing sentence shall not fix a definite term of imprisonment, but shall fix a minimum term, except as otherwise provided in this chapter. The maximum penalty provided by law shall be the maximum sentence in all cases except as provided in this chapter and shall be stated by the judge in imposing the sentence.

(2) Before or at the time of imposing sentence, the judge shall ascertain by examining the defendant under oath, or otherwise, and by other evidence as can be obtained tending to indicate briefly the causes of the defendant's criminal character or conduct, which facts and other facts that appear to be pertinent in the case the judge shall cause to be entered upon the minutes of the court.

Amended by P.A.1994, No. 322, § 1; P.A.1998, No. 317, Eff. Dec. 15, 1998.

769.9. Indeterminate sentence; life imprisonment; major controlled substance offenses

Sec. 9. (1) The provisions of this chapter relative to indeterminate sentences shall not apply to a person convicted for the commission of an offense for which the only punishment prescribed by law is imprisonment for life.

(2) In all cases where the maximum sentence in the discretion of the court may be imprisonment for life or any number or term of years, the court may impose a sentence for life or may impose a sentence for any term of years. If the

sentence imposed by the court is for any term of years, the court shall fix both the minimum and the maximum of that sentence in terms of years or fraction thereof, and sentences so imposed shall be considered indeterminate sentences. The court shall not impose a sentence in which the maximum penalty is life imprisonment with a minimum for a term of years included in the same sentence.

(3) In cases involving a major controlled substance offense for which the court is directed by law to impose a sentence which cannot be less than a specified term of years nor more than a specified term of years, the court in imposing the sentence shall fix the length of both the minimum and maximum sentence within those specified limits, in terms of years or fraction thereof, and the sentence so imposed shall be considered an indeterminate sentence.

769.10. Subsequent felony

Sec. 10. (1) If a person has been convicted of a felony or an attempt to commit a felony, whether the conviction occurred in this state or would have been for a felony or attempt to commit a felony in this state if obtained in this state, and that person commits a subsequent felony within this state, the person shall be punished upon conviction of the subsequent felony and sentencing under section 13 [1] of this chapter as follows:

(a) If the subsequent felony is punishable upon a first conviction by imprisonment for a term less than life, the court, except as otherwise provided in this section or section 1 [2] of chapter XI, may place the person on probation or sentence the person to imprisonment for a maximum term that is not more than 1–½ times the longest term prescribed for a first conviction of that offense or for a lesser term.

(b) If the subsequent felony is punishable upon a first conviction by imprisonment for life, the court, except as otherwise provided in this section or section 1 of chapter XI, may place the person on probation or sentence the person to imprisonment for life or for a lesser term.

(c) If the subsequent felony is a major controlled substance offense, the person shall be punished as provided by part 74 of the public health code, 1978 PA 368, MCL 333.7401 to 333.7461.

(2) If the court pursuant to this section imposes a sentence of imprisonment for any term of years, the court shall fix the length of both the minimum and maximum sentence within any specified limits in terms of years or a fraction of a year and the sentence so imposed shall be considered an indeterminate sentence. The court shall not fix a maximum sentence that is less than the maximum term for a first conviction.

(3) A conviction shall not be used to enhance a sentence under this section if that conviction is used to enhance a sentence under a statute that prohibits use of the conviction for further enhancement under this section.

Amended by P.A.1988, No. 90, § 1, Imd. Eff. March 30; P.A.1998, No. 317, Eff. Dec. 15, 1998; P.A.2006, No. 655, Imd. Eff. Jan. 9, 2007.

[1] M.C.L.A. § 769.13.

[2] M.C.L.A. § 771.1.

769.11. Punishment for subsequent felony of person convicted of 2 or more felonies; sentence for term of years as indeterminate sentence; restrictions upon use of conviction to enhance sentence

Sec. 11. (1) If a person has been convicted of any combination of 2 or more felonies or attempts to commit felonies, whether the convictions occurred in this state or would have been for felonies or attempts to commit felonies in this state if obtained in this state, and that person commits a subsequent felony within this state, the person shall be punished upon conviction of the subsequent felony and sentencing under section 13 [1] of this chapter as follows:

(a) If the subsequent felony is punishable upon a first conviction by imprisonment for a term less than life, the court, except as otherwise provided in this section or section 1 [2] of chapter XI, may sentence the person to imprisonment for a maximum term that is not more than twice the longest term prescribed by law for a first conviction of that offense or for a lesser term.

(b) If the subsequent felony is punishable upon a first conviction by imprisonment for life, the court, except as otherwise provided in this section or section 1 of chapter XI, may sentence the person to imprisonment for life or for a lesser term.

(c) If the subsequent felony is a major controlled substance offense, the person shall be punished as provided by part 74 of the public health code, 1978 PA 368, MCL 333.7401 to 333.7461.

(2) If the court pursuant to this section imposes a sentence of imprisonment for any term of years, the court shall fix the length of both the minimum and maximum sentence within any specified limits in terms of years or a fraction of a year, and the sentence so imposed shall be considered an indeterminate sentence. The court shall not fix a maximum sentence that is less than the maximum term for a first conviction.

(3) A conviction shall not be used to enhance a sentence under this section if that conviction is used to enhance a sentence under a statute that prohibits use of the conviction for further enhancement under this section.

Amended by P.A.1988, No. 90, § 1, Imd. Eff. March 30; P.A.1998, No. 317, Eff. Dec. 15, 1998; P.A.2006, No. 655, Imd. Eff. Jan. 9, 2007.

[1] M.C.L.A. § 769.13.

[2] M.C.L.A. § 771.1.

769.11a. Sentencing credit; time served under void sentence

Sec. 11a. Whenever any person has been heretofore or hereafter convicted of any crime within this state and has served any time upon a void sentence, the trial court, in imposing sentence upon conviction or acceptance of a plea of guilty based upon facts arising out of the earlier void conviction, shall in imposing the sentence specifically grant or allow the defendant credit against and by reduction of the statutory maximum by the time already served by such defendant on the sentence imposed for the prior erroneous conviction. Failure of the corrections commission to carry out the terms of said sentence shall be cause for the issuance of a writ of habeas corpus to have the prisoner brought before the court for the taking of such further action as the court may again determine.

769.11b. Sentencing credit; time served prior due to denial of or inability to furnish bond

Sec. 11b. Whenever any person is hereafter convicted of any crime within this state and has served any time in jail prior to sentencing because of being denied or unable to furnish bond for the offense of which he is convicted, the trial court in imposing sentence shall specifically grant credit against the sentence for such time served in jail prior to sentencing.

769.12. Punishment for subsequent felony of person convicted of 3 or more felonies; sentence for term of years as indeterminate sentence; restrictions upon use of conviction to enhance sentence; eligibility for parole; imposition of consecutive sentence for subsequent felony

Sec. 12. (1) If a person has been convicted of any combination of 3 or more felonies or attempts to commit felonies, whether the convictions occurred in this state or would have been for felonies or attempts to commit felonies in this state if obtained in this state, and that person commits a subsequent felony within this state, the person shall be punished upon conviction of the subsequent felony and sentencing under section 13 [1] of this chapter as follows:

(a) If the subsequent felony is punishable upon a first conviction by imprisonment for a maximum term of 5 years or more or for life, the court, except as otherwise provided in this section or section 1 [2] of chapter XI, may sentence the person to imprisonment for life or for a lesser term.

(b) If the subsequent felony is punishable upon a first conviction by imprisonment for a maximum term that is less than 5 years, the court, except as otherwise provided in this section or section 1 of chapter XI, may sentence the person to imprisonment for a maximum term of not more than 15 years.

(c) If the subsequent felony is a major controlled substance offense, the person shall be punished as provided by part 74 of the public health code, 1978 PA 368, MCL 333.7401 to 333.7461.

(2) If the court pursuant to this section imposes a sentence of imprisonment for any term of years, the court shall fix the length of both the minimum and maximum sentence within any specified limits in terms of years or a fraction of a year, and the sentence so imposed shall be considered an indeterminate sentence. The court shall not fix a maximum sentence that is

less than the maximum term for a first conviction.

(3) A conviction shall not be used to enhance a sentence under this section if that conviction is used to enhance a sentence under a statute that prohibits use of the conviction for further enhancement under this section.

(4) An offender sentenced under this section or section 10 or 11 [3] of this chapter for an offense other than a major controlled substance offense is not eligible for parole until expiration of the following:

(a) For a prisoner other than a prisoner subject to disciplinary time, the minimum term fixed by the sentencing judge at the time of sentence unless the sentencing judge or a successor gives written approval for parole at an earlier date authorized by law.

(b) For a prisoner subject to disciplinary time, the minimum term fixed by the sentencing judge.

(5) This section and sections 10 and 11 of this chapter are not in derogation of other provisions of law that permit or direct the imposition of a consecutive sentence for a subsequent felony.

(6) As used in this section, "prisoner subject to disciplinary time" means that term as defined in section 34 of 1893 PA 118, MCL 800.34.

Amended by P.A.1988, No. 90, § 1, Imd. Eff. March 30; P.A.1994, No. 445, § 1, Imd. Eff. Jan. 10, 1995; P.A.1998, No. 317, Eff. Dec. 15, 1998; P.A.2006, No. 655, Imd. Eff. Jan. 9, 2007.

[1] M.C.L.A. § 769.13.

[2] M.C.L.A. § 771.1.

[3] M.C.L.A. §§ 769.10 or 769.11.

769.13. Notice of intent to seek enhanced sentence; contents, filing, service, time, challenge, existence of prior convictions

Sec. 13. (1) In a criminal action, the prosecuting attorney may seek to enhance the sentence of the defendant as provided under section 10, 11, or 12 [1] of this chapter, by filing a written notice of his or her intent to do so within 21 days after the defendant's arraignment on the information charging the underlying offense or, if arraignment is waived, within 21 days after the filing of the information charging the underlying offense.

(2) A notice of intent to seek an enhanced sentence filed under subsection (1) shall list the prior conviction or convictions that will or may be relied upon for purposes of sentence enhancement. The notice shall be filed with the court and served upon the defendant or his or her attorney within the time provided in subsection (1). The notice may be personally served upon the defendant or his or her attorney at the arraignment on the information charging the underlying offense, or may be served in the manner provided by law or court rule for service of written pleadings. The prosecuting attorney shall file a written proof of service with the clerk of the court.

(3) The prosecuting attorney may file notice of intent to seek an enhanced sentence after the defendant has been convicted of the underlying offense or a lesser offense, upon his or her plea of guilty or nolo contendere if the defendant pleads guilty or nolo contendere at the arraignment on the information charging the underlying offense, or within the time allowed for filing of the notice under subsection (1).

(4) A defendant who has been given notice that the prosecuting attorney will seek to enhance his or her sentence as provided under section 10, 11, or 12 of this chapter, may challenge the accuracy or constitutional validity of 1 or more of the prior convictions listed in the notice by filing a written motion with the court and by serving a copy of the motion upon the prosecuting attorney in accordance with rules of the supreme court.

(5) The existence of the defendant's prior conviction or convictions shall be determined by the court, without a jury, at sentencing, or at a separate hearing scheduled for that purpose before sentencing. The existence of a prior conviction may be established by any evidence that is relevant for that purpose, including, but not limited to, 1 or more of the following:

(a) A copy of a judgment of conviction.

(b) A transcript of a prior trial or a plea-taking or sentencing proceeding.

(c) A copy of a court register of actions.

(d) Information contained in a presentence report.

(e) A statement of the defendant.

(6) The court shall resolve any challenges to the accuracy or constitutional validity of a prior

conviction or convictions that have been raised in a motion filed under subsection (4) at sentencing or at a separate hearing scheduled for that purpose before sentencing. The defendant, or his or her attorney, shall be given an opportunity to deny, explain, or refute any evidence or information pertaining to the defendant's prior conviction or convictions before sentence is imposed, and shall be permitted to present relevant evidence for that purpose. The defendant shall bear the burden of establishing a prima facie showing that an alleged prior conviction is inaccurate or constitutionally invalid. If the defendant establishes a prima facie showing that information or evidence concerning an alleged prior conviction is inaccurate, the prosecuting attorney shall bear the burden of proving, by a preponderance of the evidence, that the information or evidence is accurate. If the defendant establishes a prima facie showing that an alleged prior conviction is constitutionally invalid, the prosecuting attorney shall bear the burden of proving, by a preponderance of the evidence, that the prior conviction is constitutionally valid.

Amended by P.A.1994, No. 110, § 1, Eff. May 1, 1994; P.A.2006, No. 655, Imd. Eff. Jan. 9, 2007.

[1] M.C.L.A. §§ 769.10, 769.11, or 769.12.

769.31. Sentencing guidelines; definitions

Sec. 31. As used in this section and section 34 of this chapter: [1]

(a) "Departure" means a sentence imposed that is not within the appropriate minimum sentence range established under the sentencing guidelines set forth in chapter XVII. [2]

(b) "Intermediate sanction" means probation or any sanction, other than imprisonment in a state prison or state reformatory, that may lawfully be imposed. Intermediate sanction includes, but is not limited to, 1 or more of the following:

(*i*) Inpatient or outpatient drug treatment or participation in a drug treatment court under chapter 10A of the revised judicature act of 1961, 1961 PA 236, MCL 600.1060 to 600.1082.

(*ii*) Probation with any probation conditions required or authorized by law.

(*iii*) Residential probation.

(*iv*) Probation with jail.

(*v*) Probation with special alternative incarceration.

(*vi*) Mental health treatment.

(*vii*) Mental health or substance abuse counseling.

(*viii*) Jail.

(*ix*) Jail with work or school release.

(*x*) Jail, with or without authorization for day parole under 1962 PA 60, MCL 801.251 to 801.258.

(*xi*) Participation in a community corrections program.

(*xii*) Community service.

(*xiii*) Payment of a fine.

(*xiv*) House arrest.

(*xv*) Electronic monitoring.

(c) "Offender characteristics" means only the prior criminal record of an offender.

(d) "Offense characteristics" means the elements of the crime and the aggravating and mitigating factors relating to the offense that the legislature determines are appropriate. For purposes of this subdivision, an offense described in section 33b of the corrections code of 1953, 1953 PA 232, MCL 791.233b, that resulted in a conviction and that arose out of the same transaction as the offense for which the sentencing guidelines are being scored shall be considered as an aggravating factor.

(e) "Prior criminal record" means all of the following:

(*i*) Misdemeanor and felony convictions.

(*ii*) Probation and parole violations involving criminal activity.

(*iii*) Dispositions entered under section 18 of chapter XIIA of 1939 PA 288, MCL 712A.18, for acts that would have been crimes if committed by an adult.

(*iv*) Assignment to youthful trainee status under sections 11 to 15 of chapter II. [3]

(*v*) A conviction set aside under 1965 PA 213, MCL 780.621 to 780.624.

(*vi*) Dispositions described in subparagraph (*iii*) that have been set aside under section 18e of chapter XIIA of 1939 PA 288, MCL 712A.18e, or expunged.

P.A.1927, No. 175, c. IX, § 31, added by P.A.1994, No. 445, § 1, Imd. Eff. Jan. 10, 1995. Amended by P.A. 1998, No. 317, Eff. Dec. 15, 1998; P.A.2002, No. 31, Eff. April 1, 2002; P.A.2004, No. 220, Eff. Jan. 1, 2005.

[1] M.C.L.A. § 769.34.
[2] M.C.L.A. § 777.1 et seq.
[3] M.C.L.A. §§ 762.11 to 762.15.

769.34. Sentencing guidelines; application; minimum sentence; departure from sentencing range; intermediate sanctions; mandatory penalty; fines, costs, or assessments; appeal; review; time served

Sec. 34. (1) The sentencing guidelines promulgated by order of the Michigan supreme court do not apply to felonies enumerated in part 2 of chapter XVII [1] committed on or after January 1, 1999.

(2) Except as otherwise provided in this subsection or for a departure from the appropriate minimum sentence range provided for under subsection (3), the minimum sentence imposed by a court of this state for a felony enumerated in part 2 of chapter XVII committed on or after January 1, 1999 shall be within the appropriate sentence range under the version of those sentencing guidelines in effect on the date the crime was committed. Both of the following apply to minimum sentences under this subsection:

(a) If a statute mandates a minimum sentence for an individual sentenced to the jurisdiction of the department of corrections, the court shall impose sentence in accordance with that statute. Imposing a mandatory minimum sentence is not a departure under this section. If a statute mandates a minimum sentence for an individual sentenced to the jurisdiction of the department of corrections and the statute authorizes the sentencing judge to depart from that minimum sentence, imposing a sentence that exceeds the recommended sentence range but is less than the mandatory minimum sentence is not a departure under this section. If the Michigan vehicle code, 1949 PA 300, MCL 257.1 to 257.923, mandates a minimum sentence for an individual sentenced to the jurisdiction of the department of corrections and the Michigan vehicle code, 1949 PA 300, MCL 257.1 to 257.923, authorizes the sentencing judge to impose a sentence that is less than that minimum sentence, imposing a sentence that exceeds the recommended sentence range but is less than the mandatory minimum sentence is not a departure under this section.

(b) The court shall not impose a minimum sentence, including a departure, that exceeds 2/3 of the statutory maximum sentence.

(3) A court may depart from the appropriate sentence range established under the sentencing guidelines set forth in chapter XVII [2] if the court has a substantial and compelling reason for that departure and states on the record the reasons for departure. All of the following apply to a departure:

(a) The court shall not use an individual's gender, race, ethnicity, alienage, national origin, legal occupation, lack of employment, representation by appointed legal counsel, representation by retained legal counsel, appearance in propria persona, or religion to depart from the appropriate sentence range.

(b) The court shall not base a departure on an offense characteristic or offender characteristic already taken into account in determining the appropriate sentence range unless the court finds from the facts contained in the court record, including the presentence investigation report, that the characteristic has been given inadequate or disproportionate weight.

(4) Intermediate sanctions shall be imposed under this chapter as follows:

(a) If the upper limit of the recommended minimum sentence range for a defendant determined under the sentencing guidelines set forth in chapter XVII is 18 months or less, the court shall impose an intermediate sanction unless the court states on the record a substantial and compelling reason to sentence the individual to the jurisdiction of the department of corrections. An intermediate sanction may include a jail term that does not exceed the upper limit of the recommended minimum sentence range or 12 months, whichever is less.

(b) If an attempt to commit a felony designated in offense class H in part 2 of chapter XVII is punishable by imprisonment for more than 1 year, the court shall impose an intermediate sanction upon conviction of that offense absent a departure.

(c) If the upper limit of the recommended minimum sentence exceeds 18 months and the lower limit of the recommended minimum sentence is 12 months or less, the court shall sentence the offender as follows absent a departure:

(*i*) To imprisonment with a minimum term within that range.

(*ii*) To an intermediate sanction that may include a term of imprisonment of not more than 12 months.

(5) If a crime has a mandatory determinant penalty or a mandatory penalty of life imprisonment, the court shall impose that penalty. This section does not apply to sentencing for that crime.

(6) As part of the sentence, the court may also order the defendant to pay any combination of a fine, costs, or applicable assessments. The court shall order payment of restitution as provided by law.

(7) If the trial court imposes on a defendant a minimum sentence that is longer or more severe than the appropriate sentence range, as part of the court's advice of the defendant's rights concerning appeal, the court shall advise the defendant orally and in writing that he or she may appeal the sentence as provided by law on grounds that it is longer or more severe than the appropriate sentence range.

(8) All of the following shall be part of the record filed for an appeal of a sentence under this section:

(a) An entire record of the sentencing proceedings.

(b) The presentence investigation report. Any portion of the presentence investigation report exempt from disclosure by law shall not be a public record.

(c) Any other reports or documents the sentencing court used in imposing sentence.

(9) An appeal of a sentence under this section does not stay execution of the sentence.

(10) If a minimum sentence is within the appropriate guidelines sentence range, the court of appeals shall affirm that sentence and shall not remand for resentencing absent an error in scoring the sentencing guidelines or inaccurate information relied upon in determining the defendant's sentence. A party shall not raise on appeal an issue challenging the scoring of the sentencing guidelines or challenging the accuracy of information relied upon in determining a sentence that is within the appropriate guidelines sentence range unless the party has raised the issue at sentencing, in a proper motion for resentencing, or in a proper motion to remand filed in the court of appeals.

(11) If, upon a review of the record, the court of appeals finds the trial court did not have a substantial and compelling reason for departing from the appropriate sentence range, the court shall remand the matter to the sentencing judge or another trial court judge for resentencing under this chapter.

(12) Time served on the sentence appealed under this section is considered time served on any sentence imposed after remand.

P.A.1927, No. 175, c. IX, § 34, added by P.A.1994, No. 445, § 1. Amended by P.A.1998, No. 317, Eff. Dec. 15, 1998; P.A.1999, No. 227, Imd. Eff. Dec. 28, 1999; P.A.2000, No. 279, Eff. Oct. 1, 2000; P.A.2002, No. 666, Eff. March 1, 2003.

[1] M.C.L.A. § 777.11 et seq.

[2] M.C.L.A. § 777.1 et seq.

769.35. Jail reimbursement program; operation; criteria for reimbursement

Sec. 35. The department of corrections shall operate a jail reimbursement program that provides funding to counties for housing offenders in county jails who otherwise would have been sentenced to prison. The criteria for reimbursement, including but not limited to criteria for determining those offenders who otherwise would have been sentenced to prison, and the rate of reimbursement shall be established in the annual appropriations acts for the department of corrections.

P.A.1927, No. 175, c. IX, § 35, added by P.A.1998, No. 317, Eff. Dec. 15, 1998.

CHAPTER 771

CODE OF CRIMINAL PROCEDURE—PROBATION

Analysis of Sections

[Chapter in part]

CHAPTER XI. PROBATION

CHAPTER XI. PROBATION

771.14. Presentence investigation report; requirement, contents, disclosure, modification, review, challenges, filing, copies, generally

Sec. 14. (1) Before the court sentences a person charged with a felony or a person who is a licensee or registrant under article 15 of the public health code, 1978 PA 368, MCL 333.16101 to 333.18838, as described in section 1(11) of chapter IX, [1] and, if directed by the court, in any other case in which a person is charged with a misdemeanor within the jurisdiction of the court, the probation officer shall inquire into the antecedents, character, and circumstances of the person, and shall report in writing to the court.

(2) A presentence investigation report prepared under subsection (1) shall include all of the following:

(a) An evaluation of and a prognosis for the person's adjustment in the community based on factual information contained in the report.

(b) If requested by a victim, any written impact statement submitted by the victim under the crime victim's rights act, 1985 PA 87, MCL 780.751 to 780.834.

(c) A specific written recommendation for disposition based on the evaluation and other information as prescribed by the assistant director of the department of corrections in charge of probation.

(d) A statement prepared by the prosecuting attorney as to whether consecutive sentencing is required or authorized by law.

(e) For a person to be sentenced under the sentencing guidelines set forth in chapter XVII, [2] all of the following:

(*i*) For each conviction for which a consecutive sentence is authorized or required, the sentence grid in part 6 of chapter XVII that contains the recommended minimum sentence range.

(*ii*) Unless otherwise provided in subparagraph (*i*), for each crime having the highest crime class, the sentence grid in part 6 of chapter XVII [3] that contains the recommended minimum sentence range.

(*iii*) Unless otherwise provided in subparagraph (*i*), the computation that determines the recommended minimum sentence range for the crime having the highest crime class.

(*iv*) A specific statement as to the applicability of intermediate sanctions, as defined in section 31 of chapter IX. [4]

(*v*) The recommended sentence.

(f) If a person is to be sentenced for a felony or for a misdemeanor involving the illegal delivery, possession, or use of alcohol or a controlled substance, a statement that the person is licensed or registered under article 15 of the public health code, 1978 PA 368, MCL 333.16101 to 333.18838, if applicable.

(g) Diagnostic opinions that are available and not exempted from disclosure under subsection (3).

(3) The court may exempt from disclosure in the presentence investigation report information or a diagnostic opinion that might seriously disrupt a program of rehabilitation or sources of information obtained on a promise of confidentiality. If a part of the presentence investigation report is not disclosed, the court shall state on the record the reasons for its action and inform

the defendant and his or her attorney that information has not been disclosed. The action of the court in exempting information from disclosure is subject to appellate review. Information or a diagnostic opinion exempted from disclosure pursuant to this subsection shall be specifically noted in the presentence investigation report.

(4) If a prepared presentence investigation report is amended or altered before sentencing by the supervisor of the probation officer who prepared the report or by any other person who has the authority to amend or alter a presentence investigation report, the probation officer may request that the court strike his or her name from the report and the court shall comply with that request.

(5) The court shall permit the prosecutor, the defendant's attorney, and the defendant to review the presentence investigation report before sentencing.

(6) At the time of sentencing, either party may challenge, on the record, the accuracy or relevancy of any information contained in the presentence investigation report. The court may order an adjournment to permit the parties to prepare a challenge or a response to a challenge. If the court finds on the record that the challenged information is inaccurate or irrelevant, that finding shall be made a part of the record, the presentence investigation report shall be amended, and the inaccurate or irrelevant information shall be stricken accordingly before the report is transmitted to the department of corrections.

(7) On appeal, the defendant's attorney, or the defendant if proceeding pro se, shall be provided with a copy of the presentence investigation report and any attachments to the report with the exception of any information exempted from disclosure by the court under subsection (3).

(8) If the person is committed to a state penal institution, a copy or amended copy of the presentence investigation report and, if a psychiatric examination of the person has been made for the court, a copy of the psychiatric report shall accompany the commitment papers. If the person is sentenced by fine or imprisonment or placed on probation or other disposition of his or her case is made by the court, a copy or amended copy of the presentence investigation report, including a psychiatric examination report made in the case, shall be filed with the department of corrections.

(9) A prisoner under the jurisdiction of the department of corrections shall be provided with a copy of any presentence investigation report in the department's possession about that prisoner, except for information exempted from disclosure under subsection (3), not less than 30 days before a parole interview is conducted under section 35 of 1953 PA 232, MCL 791.235.

Amended by P.A.1982, No. 61, § 1, Eff. March 30, 1983; P.A.1985, No. 88, § 1, Imd. Eff. July 10, 1985; P.A.1993, No. 85, § 1, Eff. April 1, 1994; P.A.1994, No. 445, § 1, Eff. Feb. 1, 1995; P.A.1998, No. 317, Eff. Dec. 15, 1998; P.A.2000, No. 279, Eff. Oct. 1, 2000.

[1] M.C.L.A. § 769.1.

[2] M.C.L.A. § 777.1 et seq.

[3] M.C.L.A. § 777.61 et seq.

[4] M.C.L.A. § 769.31.

CHAPTER 777

CODE OF CRIMINAL PROCEDURE—SENTENCING GUIDELINES

Analysis of Sections

CHAPTER XVII. SENTENCING GUIDELINES

PART 1. GENERAL PROVISIONS

CHAPTER XVII. SENTENCING GUIDELINES

Caption editorially supplied

Chapter XVII of P.A.1927, No. 175, relating to sentencing guidelines, comprising §§ 777.1 to 777.69, was added by P.A.1998, No. 317, Eff. Dec. 15, 1998.

The Michigan Supreme Court, in People v. Claypool, 470 Mich. 715, 684 N.W.2d 278 (2004), held that the United States Supreme Court's decision in Blakely v. Washington, 542 U.S. 2531, 124 S.Ct. 2531, 159 L.Ed.2d 403 (2004), which involved Washington sentencing guidelines, did not affect Michigan's sentencing guidelines since they involved an indeterminate sentencing scheme. In People v. Green, 2006 WL 234887 (2006)(unpublished), the Michigan Court of Appeals stated that the United States Supreme Court's decision in United States v. Booker, 543 U.S. 220, 125 S.Ct. 738, 160 L.Ed.2d 621 (2005), which involved the federal sentencing guidelines, did not affect the Michigan guidelines for the same reasons that the decision in Blakely was inapplicable.

A former Chapter XVII, entitled "Repeals", derived from P.A.1927, No. 175, c. XVII, §§ 1 to 3, and providing as indicated below, was repealed by P.A. 1945, No. 267, Imd. Eff. May 25, 1945.

PART 1. GENERAL PROVISIONS

777.1. Definitions

Sec. 1. As used in this chapter:

(a) "Aircraft" means that term as defined in section 2 of the aeronautics code of the state of Michigan, 1945 PA 327, MCL 259.2.

(b) "Departure" means that term as defined in section 31 of chapter IX.[1]

(c) "Homicide" means any crime in which the death of a human being is an element of that crime.

(d) "Intermediate sanction" means that term as defined in section 31 of chapter IX.

(e) "ORV" means that term as defined in section 81101 of the natural resources and environmental protection act, 1994 PA 451, MCL 324.81101.

(f) "Snowmobile" means that term as defined in section 82101 of the natural resources and environmental protection act, 1994 PA 451, MCL 324.82101.

(g) "Vehicle" means that term as defined in section 79 of the Michigan vehicle code, 1949 PA 300, MCL 257.79.

(h) "Vessel" means that term as defined in section 80104 of the natural resources and environmental protection act, 1994 PA 451, MCL 324.80104.

P.A.1927, No. 175, c. XVII, § 1, added by P.A.1998, No. 317, Eff. Dec. 15, 1998. Amended by P.A.2000, No. 279, Eff. Oct. 1, 2000; P.A.2002, No. 34, Eff. May 15, 2002.

[1] M.C.L.A. § 769.31.

777.5. Designation of offense categories

Sec. 5. The offense categories are designated in part 2 of this chapter [1] as follows:

(a) Crimes against a person are designated "person".

(b) Crimes against property are designated "property".

(c) Crimes involving a controlled substance are designated "CS".

(d) Crimes against public order are designated "pub ord".

(e) Crimes against public trust are designated "pub trst".

(f) Crimes against public safety are designated "pub saf".

P.A.1927, No. 175, c. XVII, § 5, added by P.A.1998, No. 317, Eff. Dec. 15, 1998.

[1] M.C.L.A. § 777.11 et seq.

777.6. Construction of offense descriptions

Sec. 6. The offense descriptions in part 2 of this chapter [1] are for assistance only and the statutes listed govern application of the sentencing guidelines.

P.A.1927, No. 175, c. XVII, § 6, added by P.A.1998, No. 317, Eff. Dec. 15, 1998.

[1] M.C.L.A. § 777.11 et seq.

PART 2. APPLICATION OF CHAPTER TO PARTICULAR FELONIES

Caption editorially supplied

777.11. Application of chapter to Michigan Compiled Laws chapters 1 to 199

Sec. 11. This chapter applies to felonies enumerated in chapters 1 to 199 of the Michigan Compiled Laws as set forth in sections 11a to 11e of this chapter. [1]

P.A.1927, No. 175, c. XVII, § 11, added by P.A.1998, No. 317, Eff. Dec. 15, 1998. Amended by P.A.1999, No. 90, Eff. Sept. 1, 1999; P.A.2000, No. 279, Eff. Oct. 1, 2000; P.A.2000, No. 492, Eff. July 1, 2001; P.A.2001, No. 150, Eff. Jan. 1, 2002; P.A.2001, No. 154, Eff. Jan. 1, 2002; P.A.2002, No. 31, Eff. April 1, 2002.

[1] M.C.L.A. §§ 777.11a to 777.11e.

777.11a. Application of chapter to Michigan Compiled Laws chapters 1 to 27; enumerated felonies

Sec. 11a. This chapter applies to the following felonies enumerated in chapters 1 to 27 of the Michigan Compiled Laws:

M.C.L.	Category	Class	Description	Stat Max
4.421(1)	Pub trst	G	Lobbyists —compensation contingent on outcome of action	3
4.421(2)	Pub trst	G	Lobbyists giving gifts	3
15.324(1)(d)	Pub trst	G	Purchase of public residential property by public servant	1
18.366(1)(c)	Property	E	False presentation to crime victim services commission to obtain $1,000 to $20,000 or with prior convictions	5
18.366(1)(d)	Property	D	False presentation to crime victim services commission to obtain $20,000 or more or with prior convictions	10
21.154	Pub trst	E	Public officer —embezzlement	5

P.A.1927, No. 175, c. XVII, § 11a, added by P.A.2002, No. 31, Eff. April 1, 2002. Amended by P.A.2005, No. 265, Imd. Eff. Dec. 16, 2005.

777.11b. Application of chapter to Michigan Compiled Laws chapter 28; enumerated felonies

Sec. 11b. This chapter applies to the following felonies enumerated in chapter 28 of the Michigan Compiled Laws:

M.C.L.	Category	Class	Description	Stat Max
28.214	Pub trst	F	Unauthorized disclosure of information from LEIN —subsequent offense	4
28.293(1)	Pub ord	E	False information when applying for state ID	5
28.293(2)	Pub ord	D	False information when applying for state ID — second offense	7
28.293(3)	Pub ord	C	False information when applying for state ID — third or subsequent offense	15
28.295(1)(a)	Pub ord	D	Counterfeiting or forging state ID card or using counterfeited or forged state ID card to commit felony punishable by imprisonment for 10 years or more	10
28.295(1)(b)	Pub ord	E	Counterfeiting or forging state ID card or using counterfeited or forged state ID card to commit felony punishable by imprisonment for less than 10 years or a misdemeanor punishable by more than 6 months	5

M.C.L.	Category	Class	Description	Stat Max
28.295(2)	Pub ord	E	Selling counterfeited or forged state ID card or possessing counterfeited or forged state ID card with intent to deliver to another person or possessing 2 or more counterfeited or forged state ID cards	5
28.295(5)	Property	H	Using stolen state ID card to commit felony	Variable
28.295a(1)	Pub ord	H	False representation to obtain or misuse personal information	4
28.295a(2)	Pub ord	G	False representation to obtain or misuse personal information —second offense	7
28.295a(3)	Pub ord	C	False representation to obtain or misuse personal information —third or subsequent offense	15
28.422	Pub saf	F	Pistols —license application forgery	4
28.422a(4)	Pub saf	F	False statement on pistol sales record	4
28.425b(3)	Pub saf	F	False statement on concealed pistol permit application	4
28.425j(2)	Pub saf	F	Unlawful granting or presenting of pistol training certificate	4
28.425o(5)(c)	Pub saf	F	Carrying concealed pistol in prohibited place —third or subsequent offense	4
28.435(14)(c)	Pub saf	G	Firearm sale without trigger lock, gun case, or storage container —third or subsequent offense	2
28.729(1)(a)	Pub ord	F	Failure to register as a sex offender, first offense	4
28.729(1)(b)	Pub ord	D	Failure to register as a sex offender, second offense	7
28.729(1)(c)	Pub ord	D	Failure to register as a sex offender, third or subsequent offense	10
28.729(2)(c)	Pub ord	F	Failure to update sex offender registration information —third or subsequent offense	4
28.734(2)(b)	Pub trst	G	Student safety zone violation involving work or loitering —second or subsequent offense	2
28.735(2)(b)	Pub trst	G	Student safety zone violation involving residency —second or subsequent violation	2
28.754	Pub ord	F	False report of a child abduction	4

P.A.1927, No. 175, c. XVII, § 11b, added by P.A.2002, No. 31, Eff. April 1, 2002. Amended by P.A.2004, No. 150, Eff. Sept. 1, 2004; P.A.2005, No. 122, Eff. Jan. 1, 2006; P.A.2005, No. 139, Eff. Jan. 1, 2006; P.A.2005, No. 207, Eff. Feb. 1, 2006.

777.11c. Application of chapter to Michigan Compiled Laws chapters 29 to 167; enumerated felonies

Sec. 11c. This chapter applies to the following felonies enumerated in chapters 29 to 167 of the Michigan Compiled Laws:

M.C.L.	Category	Class	Description	Stat Max
35.929	Pub trst	H	Willful falsification in application for veterans benefits	3
35.980	Pub trst	H	False statement in application for Korean veterans benefits	3
35.1029	Pub trst	H	False statement in application for Vietnam veterans benefits	3
38.412a(1)	Pub trst	H	County employee providing answers to county civil service exam	1
38.516	Pub trst	H	Fire and police civil service —appointment or employment contrary to act	2
45.82	Pub trst	E	County purchasing agent —violations in awarding bids or contracts	5
47.8	Pub trst	H	Payment of claim against county before audit	2
47.56	Pub trst	H	Wayne county treasurer paying claims without appropriate signature	2
51.364	Pub trst	H	Appointment or selection contrary to civil service commission rules	2
110.28	Pub trst	G	Fourth class cities —misappropriation of money or property	3
117.25(3)	Pub trst	E	Amendment to city electors —willfully affixing another's signature, false representation	15
125.1447(1)(c)	Property	E	False pretenses under state housing development act involving $1,000 to $20,000 or with prior convictions	5
125.1447(1)(d)	Property	D	False pretenses under state housing development authority act involving $20,000 or more or with prior convictions	10

P.A.1927, No. 175, c. XVII, § 11c, added by P.A.2002, No. 31, Eff. April 1, 2002.

777.11d. Application of chapter to Michigan Compiled Laws chapter 168; enumerated felonies

Sec. 11d. This chapter applies to the following felonies enumerated in chapter 168 of the Michigan Compiled Laws:

M.C.L.	Category	Class	Description	Stat Max
168.731(4)	Pub trst	G	Election law —filing certain false statements	2
168.734	Pub trst	G	Election law —election board refusing to provide challenger conveniences	2
168.756	Pub trst	E	Elector's false statement concerning inability to mark ballot	5

M.C.L.	Category	Class	Description	Stat Max
168.757	Pub trst	E	Election inspector —unlawful conduct	5
168.759(8)	Pub trst	E	Forged signature on absentee ballot	5
168.759b	Pub trst	E	False statement in application for emergency absentee ballot	5
168.761(5)	Pub trst	E	Assisting an absentee voter in making a false statement	5
168.769(4)	Pub trst	E	Voting both in person and by absentee ballot	5
168.792a(11)	Pub trst	E	Disclosing how ballot voted or election results early before polls are closed	5
168.792a(16)	Pub trst	E	Disclosing election result or how ballot voted	5
168.808	Pub trst	E	Untrue statement by member of board of inspectors	4
168.873	Pub trst	E	Misconduct of election employee in recount —county and local	5
168.887	Pub trst	E	Misconduct of election employee in recount	5
168.932(a)	Pub trst	E	Bribing or intimidating voters	5
168.932(b)	Pub trst	E	Ballot tampering	5
168.932(c)	Pub trst	E	Destroying or falsifying election return or records	5
168.932(d)	Pub trst	E	Disclosing votes or obstructing voter	5
168.932(e)	Pub trst	E	Absentee ballot tampering	5
168.932(f)	Pub trst	E	Election law —possess absent voter ballot delivered to another person	5
168.932(g)	Pub trst	E	Suggesting how a disabled voter should vote	5
168.932(h)	Pub trst	E	Suggesting or influencing how an absentee voter should vote	5
168.932(i)	Pub trst	E	Organizing a meeting where absentee voter ballots are to be voted	5
168.932a	Pub trst	G	Election offenses	4
168.933	Pub trst	E	False swearing to register or vote	5
168.936	Pub trst	E	Election law —perjury	5
168.937	Pub trst	E	Election law —forgery	5

P.A.1927, No. 175, c. XVII, § 11d, added by P.A.2002, No. 31, Eff. April 1, 2002.

777.11e. Application of chapter to Michigan Compiled Laws chapters 169 to 199; enumerated felonies

Sec. 11e. This chapter applies to the following felonies enumerated in chapters 169 to 199 of the Michigan Compiled Laws:

M.C.L.	Category	Class	Description	Stat Max
169.254	Pub trst	H	Campaign finance —corporate contributions	3
169.255	Pub trst	H	Campaign finance —corporate solicitation for certain funds	3
169.266	Pub trst	H	Campaign finance —qualified campaign expenditures	3

P.A.1927, No. 175, c. XVII, § 11e, added by P.A.2002, No. 31, Eff. April 1, 2002.

777.12. Application of chapter to Michigan Compiled Laws chapters 200 to 299

Sec. 12. This chapter applies to felonies enumerated in chapters 200 to 299 of the Michigan Compiled Laws as set forth in sections 12a to 12n of this chapter [1].

P.A.1927, No. 175, c. XVII, § 12, added by P.A.1998, No. 317, Eff. Dec. 15, 1998. Amended by P.A.2000, No. 279, Eff. Oct. 1, 2000; P.A.2000, No. 457, Eff. March 28, 2001; P.A.2000, No. 459, Eff. March 28, 2001; P.A.2001, No. 104, Eff. Oct. 1, 2001; P.A.2001, No. 133, Eff. Jan. 1, 2002; P.A.2001, No. 136, Eff. Feb. 1, 2002; P.A.2001, No. 160, Eff. Feb. 1, 2002; P.A.2002, No. 24, Eff. March 31, 2003; P.A.2002, No. 34, Eff. April 1, 2002.

[1] M.C.L.A. §§ 779.12a to 779.12n.

777.12a. Application of chapter to Michigan Compiled Laws chapters 200 to 219; enumerated felonies

Sec. 12a. This chapter applies to the following felonies enumerated in chapters 200 to 219 of the Michigan Compiled Laws:

M.C.L.	Category	Class	Description	Stat Max
205.27(1)(a)	Pub trst	G	Failure to file or false tax return or payment	5
205.27(1)(b)	Pub trst	G	Aiding and abetting tax evasion or filing false returns	5
205.27(1)(c)	Pub trst	G	Making/permitting false tax returns or payments	5
205.27(3)	Pub trst	G	False tax returns/perjury	15
205.28(1)(e)	Pub trst	G	State employee compromising taxes	5
205.28(1)(f)	Pub trst	G	Unauthorized disclosure of tax information	5
205.428(2)	Pub trst	G	Tobacco products tax act violations	5
205.428(3)	Pub trst	G	Illegal sale of cigarettes or other tobacco products with wholesale price of $250.00 or more	5
205.428(6)	Pub trst	F	Illegal tobacco stamp or tobacco stamp device	10
205.428(7)	Pub trst	G	Illegal vending machine license, disk, or marker	5
207.118a	Pub ord	G	Gasoline tax —embezzlement over $100	10
207.119	Pub trst	G	Gasoline or motor fuel tax violation	4
207.127c	Pub ord	G	Diesel fuel tax —embezzlement over $100	10
207.754(3)	Pub trst	G	State treasurer —municipality tax —divulging confidential information	5

P.A.1927, No. 175, c. XVII, § 12a, added by P.A.2002, No. 34, Eff. April 1, 2002.

777.12b. Application of chapter to Michigan Compiled Laws chapters 220 to 256; enumerated felonies

Sec. 12b. This chapter applies to the following felonies enumerated in chapters 220 to 256 of the Michigan Compiled Laws:

M.C.L.	Category	Class	Description	Stat Max
252.311	Property	H	Destroying a tree or shrub to make a sign more visible	2

P.A.1927, No. 175, c. XVII, § 12b, added by P.A.2002, No. 34, Eff. April 1, 2002.

777.12c. Application of chapter to Michigan Compiled Laws chapter 257, Michigan vehicle code chapters I and II; enumerated felonies

Sec. 12c. This chapter applies to the following felonies enumerated in chapters I and II of the Michigan vehicle code, 1949 PA 300, within chapter 257 of the Michigan Compiled Laws:

M.C.L.	Category	Class	Description	Stat Max
257.233a(7)	Pub ord	G	Odometer tampering	5
257.254	Property	E	Possessing stolen vehicle title	10
257.257(1)	Property	G	Altering or forging vehicle documents —first offense	5
257.257(2)	Property	G	Altering or forging vehicle documents —second offense	7
257.257(3)	Property	E	Altering or forging vehicle documents —third or subsequent offense	15

P.A.1927, No. 175, c. XVII, § 12c, added by P.A.2002, No. 34, Eff. April 1, 2002.

777.12d. Application of chapter to Michigan Compiled Laws chapter 257, Michigan vehicle code chapters III, IV, and V; enumerated felonies

Sec. 12d. This chapter applies to the following felonies enumerated in chapters III, IV, and V of the Michigan vehicle code, 1949 PA 300, within chapter 257 of the Michigan Compiled Laws:

M.C.L.	Category	Class	Description	Stat Max
257.309(6)	Pub ord	F	Corrupting an examining officer	5
257.309(7)	Pub ord	F	Deviating from road test criteria	5
257.309(8)	Pub ord	F	Forging, counterfeiting, or altering road test certification	5
257.310(7)(a)	Pub ord	D	Forging driver license with intent to commit crime punishable by 10 years or more	10
257.310(7)(b)	Pub ord	E	Forging driver license with intent to commit crime punishable by 6 months or more but less than 10 years	5
257.310(8)	Pub ord	E	Selling or possessing forged driver license with intent to deliver	5
257.310(9)	Pub ord	E	Possession of 2 or more forged driver licenses	5
257.312b(6)	Pub ord	F	Corrupting a person or agency conducting a motorcycle driving test	5
257.312b(7)	Pub ord	F	Deviating from motorcycle road test criteria	5
257.312b(8)	Pub ord	F	Forging, counterfeiting, or altering motorcycle road test certification	5
257.329(1)	Property	G	Possession/sale of stolen or counterfeit insurance certificates	5
257.329(2)	Property	E	Possession/sale of stolen or counterfeit insurance certificates — second offense	7
257.329(3)	Property	E	Possession/sale of stolen or counterfeit insurance certificates — third or subsequent offense	15

P.A.1927, No. 175, c. XVII, § 12d, added by P.A.2002, No. 34, Eff. April 1, 2002. Amended by P.A.2002, No. 127, Eff. April 22, 2002.

777.12e. Application of chapter to Michigan Compiled Laws chapter 257, Michigan vehicle code chapter VI, sections 601 to 624b; enumerated felonies

Sec. 12e. This chapter applies to the following felonies enumerated in sections 601 to 624b of chapter VI of the Michigan vehicle code, 1949 PA 300, within chapter 257 of the Michigan Compiled Laws:

M.C.L.	Category	Class	Description	Stat Max
257.601b(3)	Person	C	Moving violation causing death to construction worker	15
257.601c(2)	Person	C	Moving violation causing death to operator of implement of husbandry	15
257.602a(2)	Pub saf	G	Fleeing and eluding — fourth degree	2
257.602a(3)	Pub saf	E	Fleeing and eluding — third degree	5
257.602a(4)	Person	D	Fleeing and eluding —second degree	10
257.602a(5)	Person	C	Fleeing and eluding —first degree	15
257.616a(2)(b)	Pub saf	G	Using a signal preemption device	2
257.616a(2)(c)	Pub saf	E	Using a signal preemption device causing a traffic accident	5
257.616a(2)(d)	Person	D	Using a signal preemption device causing serious impairment of a body function	10
257.616a(2)(e)	Person	C	Using a signal preemption device causing death	15
257.616a(2)(f)	Pub ord	G	Selling or purchasing a signal preemption device	2
257.617(2)	Person	E	Failure to stop at scene of accident resulting in serious impairment or death	5
257.617(3)	Person	C	Failure to stop at scene of accident resulting in death when at fault	15

P.A.1927, No. 175, c. XVII, § 12e, added by P.A.2002, No. 34, Eff. April 1, 2002. Amended by P.A.2004, No. 26, Eff. June 14, 2004.

777.12f. Application of chapter to Michigan Compiled Laws chapter 257, Michigan vehicle code chapter VI, sections 625 to 625o; enumerated felonies

Sec. 12f. This chapter applies to the following felonies enumerated in sections 625 to 625o of chapter VI of the Michigan vehicle code, 1949 PA 300, within chapter 257 of the Michigan Compiled Laws:

M.C.L.	Category	Class	Description	Stat Max
257.625(4)(a)	Person	C	Operating a vehicle while intoxicated or impaired causing death	15
257.625(4)(b)	Person	B	Operating a vehicle while intoxicated or impaired causing death to certain persons	20
257.625(5)	Person	E	Operating a vehicle while intoxicated or impaired causing serious impairment	5
257.625(7)(a)(*ii*)	Person	E	Operating a vehicle while intoxicated or impaired with a minor in the vehicle —subsequent offense	5
257.625(9)(c)	Pub saf	E	Operating a vehicle while intoxicated or with the presence of a controlled substance —third or subsequent offense	5
257.625(10)(b)	Person	E	Allowing a vehicle to be operated while intoxicated or impaired causing death	5
257.625(10)(c)	Person	G	Allowing a vehicle to be operated while intoxicated or impaired causing serious impairment	2
257.625(11)(c)	Pub saf	E	Operating a vehicle while impaired —third or subsequent offense	5
257.625k(7)	Pub saf	D	Knowingly providing false information concerning an ignition interlock device	10
257.625k(9)	Pub saf	D	Failure to report illegal ignition interlock device	10
257.625m(5)	Pub saf	E	Commercial drunk driving —third or subsequent offense	5

P.A.1927, No. 175, c. XVII, § 12f, added by P.A.2002, No. 34, Eff. April 1, 2002. Amended by P.A.2003, No. 134, Eff. Sept. 30, 2003.

777.12g. Application of chapter to Michigan Compiled Laws chapter 257, Michigan vehicle code chapter VI, sections 626 to 750; enumerated felonies

Sec. 12g. This chapter applies to the following felonies enumerated in sections 626 to 750 of chapter VI of the Michigan vehicle code, 1949 PA 300, within chapter 257 of the Michigan Compiled Laws:

M.C.L.	Category	Class	Description	Stat Max
257.626c	Person	G	Felonious driving	2
257.653a(3)	Person	G	Failure to use due care and caution causing injury to emergency personnel	2
257.653a(4)	Person	C	Failure to use due care and caution causing death to emergency personnel	15
257.744a	Pub saf	D	False statement in citation —perjury	15

P.A.1927, No. 175, c. XVII, § 12g, added by P.A.2002, No. 34, Eff. April 1, 2002.

777.12h. Application of chapter to Michigan Compiled Laws chapter 257, Michigan vehicle code chapters VII, VIII, and IX; enumerated felonies

Sec. 12h. This chapter applies to the following felonies enumerated in chapters VII, VIII, and IX of the Michigan vehicle code, 1949 PA 300, within chapter 257 of the Michigan Compiled Laws:

M.C.L.	Category	Class	Description	Stat Max
257.902	Pub saf	E	Motor vehicle code violations	5
257.903(1)	Property	E	Motor vehicle code —false certification —first offense	5
257.903(2)	Property	E	Motor vehicle code —false certification —second offense	7
257.903(3)	Property	D	Motor vehicle code —false certification —third or subsequent offense	15
257.904(4)	Person	C	Operating a vehicle without a license causing death	15
257.904(5)	Person	E	Operating a vehicle without a license causing serious impairment	5
257.904(7)	Person	G	Allowing a vehicle to be operated without a license causing serious impairment	2
	Person	E	Allowing a vehicle to be operated without a license causing death	5

P.A.1927, No. 175, c. XVII, § 12h, added by P.A.2002, No. 34, Eff. April 1, 2002.

777.12j. Application of chapter to Michigan Compiled Laws chapter 257, beginning with section 257.941; enumerated felonies

Sec. 12j. This chapter applies to the following felonies enumerated in chapter 257 of the Michigan Compiled Laws beginning with MCL 257.941:

M.C.L.	Category	Class	Description	Stat Max
257.1353(2)	Pub trst	H	Motor vehicle —fail to record material matter —subsequent offense	2
257.1354(2)	Pub trst	H	Motor vehicle —general violations —subsequent offense	2
257.1355	Pub trst	H	Motor vehicle —fail to record transaction/falsify records	2

P.A.1927, No. 175, c. XVII, § 12j, added by P.A.2002, No. 34, Eff. April 1, 2002.

777.12k. Application of chapter to Michigan Compiled Laws chapters 258 to 260; enumerated felonies

Sec. 12k. This chapter applies to the following felonies enumerated in chapters 258 to 260 of the Michigan Compiled Laws:

M.C.L.	Category	Class	Description	Stat Max
259.80f(3)	Pub saf	D	Possessing weapon in sterile area of commercial airport	10
259.83(2)(b)	Pub saf	G	Aircraft —failure to comply with certification requirements —second violation	2
259.83(2)(c)	Pub saf	F	Aircraft —failure to comply with certification requirements —third or subsequent violation	4
259.83b(2)(a)	Pub saf	F	Conducting flight operations without certificate	4
259.83b(2)(b)	Pub saf	E	Conducting flight operations without certificate —second violation	5
259.83b(2)(c)	Pub saf	D	Conducting flight operations without certificate —third or subsequent violation	10
259.183	Property	E	Aircraft —unlawful taking or tampering	5
259.185(4)	Person	C	Operating or serving as crew of aircraft while under the influence causing death	15
259.185(5)	Person	E	Operating or serving as crew of aircraft while under the influence causing serious impairment	5
259.185(8)	Pub saf	E	Operating or serving as crew of aircraft while under the influence —third or subsequent offense	5

P.A.1927, No. 175, c. XVII, § 12k, added by P.A.2002, No. 34, Eff. April 1, 2002.

777.12m. Application of chapter to Michigan Compiled Laws chapters 285 to 289; enumerated felonies

Sec. 12m. This chapter applies to the following felonies enumerated in chapters 285 to 289 of the Michigan Compiled Laws:

M.C.L.	Category	Class	Description	Stat Max
285.83	Pub trst	H	Grain dealers act violations	5
285.279(2)(c)	Property	E	False pretenses under Michigan family farm development act involving $1,000 to $20,000 or with prior convictions	5
285.279(2)(d)	Property	D	False pretenses under Michigan family farm development act involving $20,000 or more or with prior convictions	10
286.228(6)	Pub ord	E	Insect pest and plant disease —intentional violation with intent to damage natural resources	5
286.260(4)	Pub ord	E	Insect pest and plant disease —intentional violation with intent to damage natural resources	5
286.455(2)	Pub saf	G	Agriculture—hazardous substance	5
286.929(4)	Pub trst	G	Organic products act violations	4
287.323(1)	Person	C	Dangerous animal causing death	15
287.323(2)	Person	G	Dangerous animal causing serious injury	4
287.679	Pub ord	H	Dead animals—third or subsequent violation	1
287.744(1)	Pub ord	G	Animal industry act violations	5
287.855	Pub saf	G	Agriculture—contaminating livestock/false statement/violation of quarantine	5
287.967(5)	Pub ord	G	Cervidae producer violations	4
289.5107(2)	Pub saf	F	Adulterated, misbranded, or falsely identified food	4

P.A.1927, No. 175, c. XVII, § 12m, added by P.A. 2002, No. 34, Eff. April 1, 2002. Amended by P.A. 2002, No. 421, Eff. March 31, 2003; P.A.2005, No. 54, Eff. Sept. 1, 2005.

777.12n. Application of chapter to Michigan Compiled Laws chapters 290 to 299; enumerated felonies

Sec. 12n. This chapter applies to the following felonies enumerated in chapters 290 to 299 of the Michigan Compiled Laws:

M.C.L.	Category	Class	Description	Stat Max
290.629(1)	Person	G	Weights and measures —assaults enforcement officer	2
290.631(3)	Pub trst	G	Weights and measures	5
290.650	Person	G	Motor fuels —assaulting/obstructing director or authorized representative	2
290.650b(3)	Pub trst	H	Motor fuels violations	2

P.A.1927, No. 175, c. XVII, § 12n, added by P.A.2002, No. 34, Eff. April 1, 2002.

777.13. Application of chapter to Michigan Compiled Laws chapters 300 to 399

Sec. 13. This chapter applies to felonies enumerated in chapters 300 to 399 of the Michigan Compiled Laws as set forth in sections 13a to 13p of this chapter. [1]

P.A.1927, No. 175, c. XVII, § 13, added by P.A.1998, No. 317, Eff. Dec. 15, 1998. Amended by P.A.1999, No. 61, Eff. Sept. 1, 1999; P.A.2000, No. 279, Eff. Oct. 1, 2000; P.A.2000, No. 304, Eff. Jan. 1, 2001; P.A.2000, No. 315, Eff. Jan. 1, 2001; P.A.2000, No. 412, Eff. March 28, 2001; P.A.2001, No. 13, Eff. July 1, 2001; P.A.2001, No. 156, Eff. Jan. 1, 2002; P.A. 2002, No. 30, Eff. April 1, 2002.

[1] M.C.L.A. §§ 777.13a to 777.13p.

777.13b. Application of chapter to Michigan Compiled Laws chapter 324, sections 324.1608 to 324.2157; enumerated felonies

Sec. 13b. This chapter applies to the following felonies enumerated in chapter 324 of the Michigan Compiled Laws:

M.C.L.	Category	Class	Description	Stat Max
324.1608	Person	G	Resisting and obstructing conservation officer	2
324.2157(1)(c)	Property	E	Damage to state property involving $1,000 to $20,000 or with prior convictions	5
324.2157(1)(d)	Property	D	Damage to state property involving $20,000	

M.C.L.	Category	Class	Description	Stat Max
			or more or with prior convictions	10

P.A.1927, No. 175, c. XVII, § 13b, added by P.A.2002, No. 30, Eff. April 1, 2002.

777.13c. Application of chapter to Michigan Compiled Laws chapter 324, sections 324.3115 to 324.21548; enumerated felonies

Sec. 13c. This chapter applies to the following felonies enumerated in chapter 324 of the Michigan Compiled Laws:

M.C.L.	Category	Class	Description	Stat Max
324.3115(2)	Pub saf	H	Water pollution	2
324.3115(4)	Pub saf	G	Water pollution —substantial endangerment	5
324.5531(4)	Pub saf	H	Knowingly releasing air pollutants	2
324.5531(5)	Pub saf	G	Knowingly releasing air pollutants — causing death or serious bodily injury	6
324.5531(6)	Pub saf	C	Knowingly releasing air pollutants — intentionally causing death or serious bodily injury	15
324.8905(2)	Pub saf	H	Littering—infectious waste/pathological waste/ sharps	2
324.8905(3)	Pub saf	G	Littering—infectious waste/pathological waste/ sharps —subsequent offense	5
324.11151(2)	Pub saf	H	Hazardous waste—subsequent offense	2
324.11151(3)	Pub saf	H	Hazardous waste—disregard for human life	2
324.11151(3)	Pub saf	G	Hazardous waste—extreme indifference for human life	5
324.11549(2)	Pub saf	G	Solid waste—importing from foreign country	2
324.11719(2)	Pub saf	G	Septage—false statement or entry in a license application or other record	2
324.12116(2)	Pub saf	H	Liquid industrial waste—false statement in a license application	2
324.20139(3)	Pub saf	H	Hazardous substance—knowingly releasing or causing release	2
324.21324(1)	Pub saf	G	Underground storage tanks— false or misleading information	5
324.21548(1)	Pub trst	H	Underground storage tanks— false request for payment	5

P.A.1927, No. 175, c. XVII, § 13c, added by P.A.2002, No. 30, Eff. April 1, 2002. Amended by P.A.2004, No. 382, Imd. Eff. Oct. 12, 2004; P.A.2006, No. 59, Imd. Eff. March 13, 2006.

777.13d. Application of chapter to Michigan Compiled Laws chapter 324, sections 324.30316 to 324.33939; enumerated felonies

Sec. 13d. This chapter applies to the following felonies enumerated in chapter 324 of the Michigan Compiled Laws:

M.C.L.	Category	Class	Description	Stat Max
324.30316(3)	Pub saf	H	NREPA violation —subsequent offense	2
324.31525	Person	G	NREPA —imminent danger of death or serious injury —subsequent offense	2
324.33939(1)	Pub trst	H	NREPA violation for commercial purposes	2

P.A.1927, No. 175, c. XVII, § 13d, added by P.A.2002, No. 30, Eff. April 1, 2002.

777.13e. Application of chapter to Michigan Compiled Laws chapter 324, sections 324.40118 to 324.52908; enumerated felonies

Sec. 13e. This chapter applies to the following felonies enumerated in chapter 324 of the Michigan Compiled Laws:

M.C.L.	Category	Class	Description	Stat Max
324.40118(11)	Pub ord	G	Wildlife conservation —buying/selling protected animals —subsequent offense	4
324.41309(3)(b)	Property	G	Possession of prohibited species	2
324.41309(4)(a)	Property	G	Possession of restricted or nonnative species —intent to damage resources	2
324.41309(4)(b)	Property	F	Possession of prohibited or genetically engineered species —intent to damage resources	4
324.41309(8)	Property	G	Introduction of prohibited or genetically engineered species —knowing identity of organism	2
324.41309(9)(a)	Property	G	Introduction of restricted or nonnative species — knowing introduction is unlawful	2
324.41309(9)(b)	Property	F	Introduction of prohibited or genetically engineered species —knowing introduction is unlawful	4
324.41309(10)(a)	Property	F	Introduction of restricted or nonnative species —intent to damage resources	3
324.41309(10)(b)	Property	E	Introduction of prohibited or genetically engineered species —intent to damage resources	5
324.48738(4)	Property	E	Possession, importation, or planting of genetically engineered fish	5
324.51120(2)	Property	H	Removing forest products over $2,500	3
324.51512	Pub saf	D	Willfully setting forest fires	10
324.52908(1)(c)	Property	E	Damage to plant involving $1,000 to $20,000 or with prior convictions	5
324.52908(1)(d)	Property	D	Damage to plant involving $20,000 or	

M.C.L.	Category	Class	Description	Stat Max
			more or with prior convictions	10

P.A.1927, No. 175, c. XVII, § 13e, added by P.A.2002, No. 30, Eff. April 1, 2002. Amended by P.A.2003, No. 269, Eff. March 30, 2004; P.A.2005, No. 81, Eff. Sept. 1, 2005.

777.13f. Application of chapter to Michigan Compiled Laws chapter 324, sections 324.61511 to 324.61521; enumerated felonies

Sec. 13f. This chapter applies to the following felonies enumerated in chapter 324 of the Michigan Compiled Laws:

M.C.L.	Category	Class	Description	Stat Max
324.61511	Pub trst	G	False affidavit under NREPA	5
324.61521(1)	Pub trst	G	Evading rule under NREPA	3

P.A.1927, No. 175, c. XVII, § 13f, added by P.A.2002, No. 30, Eff. April 1, 2002.

777.13g. Application of chapter to Michigan Compiled Laws chapter 324, sections 324.76107 to 324.82160; enumerated felonies

Sec. 13g. This chapter applies to the following felonies enumerated in chapter 324 of the Michigan Compiled Laws:

M.C.L.	Category	Class	Description	Stat Max
324.76107(3)	Pub ord	D	Removing or mutilating human body from Great Lakes bottomland	10
324.76107(4)(c)	Property	E	Recovering abandoned property in Great Lakes having value of $1,000 to $20,000 or with prior convictions	5
324.76107(4)(d)	Property	D	Recovering abandoned property in Great Lakes having value of $20,000 or more or with prior convictions	10
324.80130d(1)	Pub ord	H	False representation to obtain personal information	4
324.80130d(2)	Pub ord	G	False representation to obtain personal information—second offense	7
324.80130d(3)	Pub ord	C	False representation to obtain personal information—third or subsequent offense	15
324.80134a(2)	Person	E	Failure to stop at scene of marine accident causing serious impairment or death	5
324.80134a(3)	Person	C	Failure to stop at scene of marine accident causing death when at fault	15
324.80172	Person	G	Negligent crippling or homicide by vessel	2
324.80173	Person	G	Felonious operation of a vessel	2
324.80176(4)	Person	C	Operating a vessel under the influence causing death	15
324.80176(5)	Person	E	Operating a vessel under the influence causing serious impairment	5
324.80177(1)(c)	Pub saf	E	Operating a vessel under the influence—third or subsequent offense	5
324.80319a(1)	Pub ord	H	False representation to obtain personal information	4
324.80319a(2)	Pub ord	G	False representation to obtain personal information—second offense	7
324.80319a(3)	Pub ord	C	False representation to obtain personal information—third or subsequent offense	15
324.81120(1)	Pub ord	H	False representation to obtain personal information	4
324.81120(2)	Pub ord	G	False representation to obtain personal information—second offense	7
324.81120(3)	Pub ord	C	False representation to obtain personal information—third or subsequent offense	15
324.81134(6)	Pub saf	E	Operating an ORV under the influence—third or subsequent offense	5
324.81134(7)	Person	C	Operating an ORV under the influence causing death	15
324.81134(8)	Person	E	Operating an ORV under the influence causing serious impairment	5
324.82126c(1)	Person	G	Operating a snowmobile carelessly or negligently causing death or serious impairment	2
324.82126c(2)	Person	G	Operating a snowmobile without regard to safety causing serious impairment	2
324.82127(4)	Person	C	Operating a snowmobile under the influence causing death	15
324.82127(5)	Person	E	Operating a snowmobile under the influence causing serious impairment	5
324.82128(1)(c)	Pub saf	E	Operating a snowmobile under the influence—third or subsequent offense	5

M.C.L.	Category	Class	Description	Stat Max
324.82160(1)	Pub ord	H	False representation to obtain personal information	4
324.82160(2)	Pub ord	G	False representation to obtain personal information—second offense	7
324.82160(3)	Pub ord	C	False representation to obtain personal information—third or subsequent offense	15

P.A.1927, No. 175, c. XVII, § 13g, added by P.A.2002, No. 30, Eff. April 1, 2002. Amended by P.A.2003, No. 232, Eff. April 1, 2004.

777.13j. Application of chapter to Michigan Compiled Laws chapters 325 to 332; enumerated felonies

Sec. 13j. This chapter applies to the following felonies enumerated in chapters 325 to 332 of the Michigan Compiled Laws:

M.C.L.	Category	Class	Description	Stat Max
328.232	Property	E	Conversion of funeral contracts	5
330.1944	Pub saf	F	Criminal sexual psychopath leaving state without permission	4

P.A.1927, No. 175, c. XVII, § 13j, added by P.A.2002, No. 30, Eff. April 1, 2002. Amended by P.A.2006, No. 655, Imd. Eff. Jan. 9, 2007.

777.13k. Application of chapter to Michigan Compiled Laws chapter 333, sections 333.2685 to 333.5661; enumerated felonies

Sec. 13k. This chapter applies to the following felonies enumerated in chapter 333 of the Michigan Compiled Laws:

M.C.L.	Category	Class	Description	Stat Max
333.2685	Person	E	Use of a live human embryo, fetus for nontherapeutic research	5
333.2688	Person	E	Research on dead embryo or fetus without mother's consent	5
333.2689	Person	E	Abortion to obtain embryo	5
333.2690	Person	E	Sale or delivery of fetus or embryo	5
333.2813(3)	Pub trst	F	Unauthorized disclosure of social security number —subsequent offense	4
333.2835(9)	Pub trst	G	Disclosing confidential information —abortion	3
333.5210	Person	F	AIDS —sexual penetration with uninformed partner	4
333.5661	Person	F	Fraud resulting in patient death	4

P.A.1927, No. 175, c. XVII, § 13k, added by P.A.2002, No. 30, Eff. April 1, 2002.

777.13m. Application of chapter to Michigan Compiled Laws chapter 333, sections 333.7340 to 333.7410a; enumerated felonies

Sec. 13m. This chapter applies to the following felonies enumerated in chapter 333 of the Michigan Compiled Laws:

M.C.L.	Category	Class	Description	Stat Max
333.7340	CS	F	Sale, distribution, or delivery of product containing ephedrine or pseudoephedrine by mail, internet, or telephone	4
333.7341(8)	CS	G	Delivery or manufacture of imitation controlled substance	2
333.7401(2)(a)(*i*)	CS	A	Delivery or manufacture of 1,000 or more grams of certain schedule 1 or 2 controlled substances	Life
333.7401(2)(a)(*ii*)	CS	A	Delivery or manufacture of 450 or more but less than 1,000 grams of certain schedule 1 or 2 controlled substances	30
333.7401(2)(a)(*iii*)	CS	B	Delivery or manufacture of 50 or more but less than 450 grams of certain schedule 1 or 2 controlled substances	20
333.7401(2)(a)(*iv*)	CS	D	Delivery or manufacture of less than 50 grams of certain schedule 1 or 2 controlled substances	20
333.7401(2)(b)(*i*)	CS	B	Delivery or manufacture of methamphetamine or 3, 4–methylenedioxymethamphetamine	20
333.7401(2)(b)(*ii*)	CS	E	Delivery or manufacture of certain schedule 1, 2, or 3 controlled substances	7
333.7401(2)(c)	CS	F	Delivery or manufacture of schedule 4 controlled substance	4
333.7401(2)(d)(*i*)	CS	C	Delivery or manufacture of 45 or more kilograms of marijuana	15
333.7401(2)(d)(*ii*)	CS	D	Delivery or manufacture of 5 or more but less than 45 kilograms of marijuana	7
333.7401(2)(d)(*iii*)	CS	F	Delivery or manufacture of less than 5 kilograms or 20 plants of marijuana	4
333.7401(2)(e)	CS	G	Delivery or manufacture of schedule 5 controlled substance	2
333.7401(2)(f)	CS	D	Delivery or manufacture of an official or counterfeit prescription form	20
333.7401(2)(g)	CS	D	Delivery or manufacture of prescription or counterfeit	

M.C.L.	Category	Class	Description	Stat Max
			form (other than official)	7
333.7401a	Person	B	Delivering a controlled substance or GBL with intent to commit criminal sexual conduct	20
333.7401b(3)(a)	CS	E	Delivery or manufacture of GBL	7
333.7401b(3)(b)	CS	G	Possession of GBL	2
333.7401c(2)(a)	CS	D	Operating or maintaining controlled substance laboratory	10
333.7401c(2)(b)	CS	B	Operating or maintaining controlled substance laboratory in presence of minor	20
333.7401c(2)(c)	CS	B	Operating or maintaining controlled substance laboratory involving hazardous waste	20
333.7401c(2)(d)	CS	B	Operating or maintaining controlled substance laboratory near certain places	20
333.7401c(2)(e)	CS	A	Operating or maintaining controlled substance laboratory involving firearm or other harmful device	25
333.7401c(2)(f)	CS	B	Operating or maintaining controlled substance laboratory involving methamphetamine	20
333.7402(2)(a)	CS	D	Delivery or manufacture of certain imitation controlled substances	10
333.7402(2)(b)	CS	E	Delivery or manufacture of schedule 1, 2, or 3 imitation controlled substance	5
333.7402(2)(c)	CS	F	Delivery or manufacture of imitation schedule 4 controlled substance	4
333.7402(2)(d)	CS	G	Delivery or manufacture of imitation schedule 5 controlled substance	2
333.7402(2)(e)	CS	C	Delivery or manufacture of controlled substance analogue	15
333.7403(2)(a)(*i*)	CS	A	Possession of 1,000 or more grams of certain schedule 1 or 2 controlled substances	Life
333.7403(2)(a)(*ii*)	CS	A	Possession of 450 or more but less than 1,000 grams of certain schedule 1 or 2 controlled substances	30
333.7403(2)(a)(*iii*)	CS	B	Possession of 50 or more but less than 450 grams of certain schedule 1 or 2 controlled substances	20
333.7403(2)(a)(*iv*)	CS	G	Possession of 25 or more but less than 50 grams of certain schedule 1 or 2 controlled substances	4
333.7403(2)(a)(*v*)	CS	G	Possession of less than 25 grams of certain schedule 1 or 2 controlled substances	4
333.7403(2)(b)(*i*)	CS	D	Possession of methamphetamine or 3, 4–methylenedioxymethamphetamine	10
333.7403(2)(b)(*ii*)	CS	G	Possession of certain schedule 1, 2, 3, or 4 controlled substances or controlled substances analogue	2
333.7405(a)	CS	G	Controlled substance violations by licensee	2
333.7405(b)	CS	G	Manufacturing or distribution violations by licensee	2
333.7405(c)	CS	G	Refusing lawful inspection	2
333.7405(d)	CS	G	Maintaining drug house	2
333.7407(1)(a)	CS	G	Controlled substance violations by licensee	4
333.7407(1)(b)	CS	G	Use of fictitious, revoked, or suspended license number	4
333.7407(1)(c)	CS	G	Obtaining controlled substance by fraud	4
333.7407(1)(d)	CS	G	False reports under controlled substance article	4
333.7407(1)(e)	CS	G	Possession of counterfeiting implements	4
333.7407(1)(f)	CS	F	Disclosing or obtaining prescription information	4
333.7407(1)(g)	CS	F	Possession of counterfeit prescription form	4
333.7407(2)	CS	G	Refusing to furnish records under controlled substance article	4
333.7410a	CS	G	Controlled substance offense or offense involving GBL in or near a park	2

P.A.1927, No. 175, c. XVII, § 13m, added by P.A. 2002, No. 30, Eff. April 1, 2002. Amended by P.A. 2002, No. 666, Eff. March 1, 2003; P.A.2002, No. 711, Eff. April 1, 2003; P.A.2003, No. 311, Eff. April 1, 2004; P.A.2006, No. 259, Eff. Oct. 1, 2006.

777.13n. Application of chapter to Michigan Compiled Laws chapter 333, sections 333.10204 to 333.21792; enumerated felonies

Sec. 13n. This chapter applies to the following felonies enumerated in chapter 333 of the Michigan Compiled Laws:

M.C.L.	Category	Class	Description	Stat Max
333.10204(1)	Pub ord	F	Transferring a human organ for valuable consideration	4
333.10204(4)	Pub saf	F	Removal of a human organ by an unauthorized individual	4
333.10205	Pub saf	F	Removal of a human organ in an unapproved facility	4
333.13738(2)	Pub saf	F	Waste disposal violations —second offense	5

M.C.L.	Category	Class	Description	Stat Max
333.13738(3)	Pub saf	F	Disposing of waste —indifference to human life	2
	Pub saf	B	Disposing of waste —extreme indifference to human life	20
333.16170(3)	Pub trst	F	False representation —health professional recovery program	4
333.16294	Pub saf	F	Health profession —unauthorized practice	4
333.17764(3)	Pub saf	G	Adulterate, misbrand, remove, or substitute a drug or device	2
333.17764(4)	Pub saf	F	Adulterate, misbrand, remove, or substitute a drug or device causing personal injury	4
333.17764(5)	Pub saf	E	Adulterate, misbrand, remove, or substitute a drug or device causing serious impairment of a body function	5
333.17764(6)	Pub saf	C	Adulterate, misbrand, remove, or substitute a drug or device causing death	15
333.17766c(2)	CS	G	Possession of more than 12 grams ephedrine or pseudoephedrine	2
333.20142(5)	Pub trst	F	False statement —application licensure health facility	4
333.21792	Pub trst	G	Nursing homes —referral fees/bribing officials/accepting bribes	4

P.A.1927, No. 175, c. XVII, § 13n, added by P.A.2002, No. 30, Eff. April 1, 2002. Amended by P.A.2003, No. 309, Eff. April 1, 2004; P.A.2004, No. 215, Eff. Oct. 12, 2004.

777.13p. Application of chapter to Michigan Compiled laws chapter 338 to 399; enumerated felonies

Sec. 13p. This chapter applies to the following felonies enumerated in chapters 338 to 399 of the Michigan Compiled Laws:

M.C.L.	Category	Class	Description	Stat Max
338.823	Pub trst	F	Private detective license act violation	4
338.1053	Pub trst	F	Private security business and security alarm act violation	4
338.3434a(2)	Pub trst	F	Unauthorized disclosure of a social security number —subsequent offense	4
338.3471(1)(b)	Pub trst	G	Michigan immigration clerical assistant act violation —subsequent offense	2
339.735	Pub trst	E	Unauthorized practice of public accounting	5
380.1230d(3)(a)	Pub saf	G	Failure by school employee to report charge or conviction	2
380.1816	Pub trst	F	Improper use of bond proceeds	4
388.936	Pub trst	F	Knowingly making false statement —school district loans	4
388.1937	Pub trst	F	Making false statement or concealing material information to obtain qualification of school bond issue or improperly using proceeds of school bonds	4

P.A.1927, No. 175, c. XVII, § 13p, added by P.A.2002, No. 30, Eff. April 1, 2002. Amended by P.A.2002, No. 475, Eff. Oct. 1, 2002; P.A.2004, No. 162, Eff. Oct. 1, 2004; P.A.2004, No. 418, eff. March 30, 2005; P.A. 2005, No. 96, Imd. Eff. July 20, 2005; P.A.2005, No. 125, Imd. Eff. Sept. 29, 2005; P.A.2005, No. 279, Imd. Eff. Dec. 19, 2005.

777.14. Application of chapter to Michigan Compiled Laws chapters 400 to 499

Sec. 14. This chapter applies to felonies enumerated in chapters 400 to 499 of the Michigan Compiled Laws as set forth in sections 14a to 14p. [1]

P.A.1927, No. 175, c. XVII, § 14, added by P.A.1998, No. 317, Eff. Dec. 15, 1998. Amended by P.A.2000, No. 279, Eff. Oct. 1, 2000; P.A.2000, No. 363, Eff. July 1, 2001; P.A.2002, No. 29, Eff. April 1, 2002.

[1] M.C.L.A. §§ 777.14a to 777.14p.

777.14a. Application of chapter to Michigan Compiled Laws chapters 400 to 407; enumerated felonies

Sec. 14a. This chapter applies to the following felonies enumerated in chapters 400 to 407 of the Michigan Compiled Laws:

M.C.L.	Category	Class	Description	Stat Max
400.60(2)	Property	H	Welfare —obtaining over $500 by failure to inform	4
400.603	Pub trst	G	Medicaid fraud —false statement in benefit/concealing information	4
400.604	Pub trst	G	Medicaid fraud —kickback/referral fees	4
400.605	Pub trst	G	Medicaid fraud —false statement regarding institutions	4
400.606	Property	E	Medicaid fraud —conspiracy	10
400.607	Pub trst	G	Medicaid fraud —false claim/medically unnecessary	4
400.609	Property	D	Medicaid fraud —fourth or subsequent offense	10
400.713(13)	Pub saf	H	Adult foster care —unlicensed facility	2
	Pub saf	F	Adult foster care —unlicensed facility —subsequent violation	5
400.722(4)	Pub saf	F	Adult foster care —maintaining operation after refusal of licensure	5

P.A.1927, No. 175, c. XVII, § 14a, added by P.A.2002, No. 29, Eff. April 1, 2002.

777.14b. Application of chapter to Michigan Compiled Laws chapters 408 to 420; enumerated felonies

Sec. 14b. This chapter applies to the following felonies enumerated in chapters 408 to 420 of the Michigan Compiled Laws:

M.C.L.	Category	Class	Description	Stat Max
408.1035(5)	Person	H	MIOSHA violation causing employee death	1
	Person	G	MIOSHA violation causing employee death —subsequent offense	3
408.1035a(5)	Person	H	MIOSHA violation causing employee death	1
	Person	G	MIOSHA violation causing employee death —subsequent offense	3
409.122(2)	Person	G	Employment of children during certain hours —second offense	2
	Person	E	Employment of children during certain hours —third or subsequent offense	10
409.122(3)	Person	D	Employment of children in child sexually abusive activity	20

P.A.1927, No. 175, c. XVII, § 14b, added by P.A.2002, No. 29, Eff. April 1, 2002.

777.14c. Application of chapter to Michigan Compiled Laws chapter 421; enumerated felonies

Sec. 14c. This chapter applies to the following felonies enumerated in chapter 421 of the Michigan Compiled Laws:

M.C.L.	Category	Class	Description	Stat Max
421.54(a)(*ii*)(B)	Property	H	Unemployment comp fraud —failure to comply with act/rule $25,000–$100,000	2
421.54(a)(*ii*)(C)	Property	G	Unemployment comp fraud —failure to comply with act/rule over $100,000	5
421.54(a)(*iv*)(B)	Property	H	Unemployment comp fraud —willful violation of act/rule over $100,000	2
421.54(b)(*ii*)(B)	Property	H	Unemployment comp fraud —false statement or misrepresentation over $25,000	2
421.54(b)(*ii*)(C)	Property	H	Unemployment comp fraud —false statement or misrepresentation without actual loss	2
421.54(d)	Property	H	Unemployment comp fraud —disclose confidential information for financial gain	1
421.54a	Property	G	Unemployment comp fraud —false statement as condition of employment	10
421.54b(b)(*i*)	Property	H	Unemployment comp fraud —conspiracy with loss of $25,000 or less	2
421.54b(b)(*ii*)	Property	G	Unemployment comp fraud —conspiracy with loss over $25,000	5
421.54b(b)(*iii*)	Property	H	Unemployment comp fraud —conspiracy with no actual loss	2
421.54c(b)(*ii*)	Property	H	Unemployment comp fraud —embezzlement of $25,000 to under $100,000	2
421.54c(b)(*iii*)	Property	G	Unemployment comp fraud —embezzlement of $100,000 or more	5
421.54c(b)(*iv*)	Property	H	Unemployment comp fraud —embezzlement with no actual loss	2

P.A.1927, No. 175, c. XVII, § 14c, added by P.A.2002, No. 29, Eff. April 1, 2002.

777.14d. Application of chapter to Michigan Compiled Laws chapters 422 to 432; enumerated felonies

Sec. 14d. This chapter applies to the following felonies enumerated in chapters 422 to 432 of the Michigan Compiled Laws:

M.C.L.	Category	Class	Description	Stat Max
431.257	Pub trst	G	Racing, boxing and exhibition racing	2
431.307(8)	Pub trst	G	Horse racing —testifying falsely to commissioner while under oath	4
431.330(4)	Pub trst	G	Horse racing —administering a drug that could affect racing condition	5
431.332	Pub trst	G	Horse racing —influencing or attempting to influence result of race	5
432.30	Property	G	Lottery —forgery of tickets	5
432.218	Pub ord	D	Casino gaming offenses	10

P.A.1927, No. 175, c. XVII, § 14d, added by P.A.2002, No. 29, Eff. April 1, 2002.

777.14f. Application of chapter to Michigan Compiled Laws chapter 436; enumerated felonies

Sec. 14f. This chapter applies to the following felonies enumerated in chapter 436 of the Michigan Compiled Laws:

M.C.L.	Category	Class	Description	Stat Max
436.1701(2)	Person	D	Selling alcohol to a minor and causing death	10
436.1909(3)	Pub ord	H	Liquor violation	1
436.1919	Pub ord	H	Fraudulent documents, labels, or stamps	1

P.A.1927, No. 175, c. XVII, § 14f, added by P.A.2002, No. 29, Eff. April 1, 2002.

777.14g. Application of chapter to Michigan Compiled Laws chapters 437 to 444; enumerated felonies

Sec. 14g. This chapter applies to the following felonies enumerated in chapters 437 to 444 of the Michigan Compiled Laws:

M.C.L.	Category	Class	Description	Stat Max
438.41	Property	E	Criminal usury	5
440.9320(8)	Property	G	Farming —illegal sale of secured products	3
440.9501	Pub trst	E	Filing a false or fraudulent financing statement with the secretary of state	5
442.219	Pub trst	E	Sales —false statement	5
443.50	Pub trst	E	Issuing warehouse receipt for goods not received	5

M.C.L.	Category	Class	Description	Stat Max
443.52	Pub trst	E	Issuing duplicate warehouse receipt not so marked	5
444.13	Pub trst	H	Warehousemen and warehouse receipts	2
444.107	Pub trst	E	Warehouse certificates —willfully alter or destroy	5

P.A.1927, No. 175, c. XVII, § 14g, added by P.A.2002, No. 29, Eff. April 1, 2002. Amended by P.A.2004, No. 304, Eff. Jan. 1, 2005.

777.14h. Application of chapter to Michigan Compiled Laws chapter 445; enumerated felonies

Sec. 14h. This chapter applies to the following felonies enumerated in chapter 445 of the Michigan Compiled Laws:

M.C.L.	Category	Class	Description	Stat Max
445.65	Pub ord	E	Identity theft	5
445.67	Pub ord	E	Obtain, possess, sell, or transfer personal identifying information of another or falsify a police report with intent to commit identity theft	5
445.408(2)	Pub ord	F	Buying or selling stolen scrap metal	3
445.408(3)	Pub ord	E	Buying or selling stolen scrap metal removed from a utility pole, telecommunications company property, government property, or utility property or jobsite	5
445.487(2)	Pub ord	H	Precious metal and gem dealer failure to record material matter —subsequent offense	2
445.488(2)	Pub ord	H	Precious metal and gem dealer violations —subsequent offense	2
445.489	Pub ord	H	Precious metal and gem dealer violations	2
445.490	Pub ord	H	Precious metal and gem dealer failure to obtain a certificate of registration	2
445.779	Pub ord	H	Antitrust violation	2
445.1505	Pub trst	G	Franchise investment law —fraudulent filing/offers	7
445.1508	Pub trst	G	Franchise investment law —sale without proper disclosure	7
445.1513	Pub trst	G	Franchise investment law —illegal offers/sales	7
445.1520	Pub trst	G	Franchise investment law —keeping records	7
445.1521	Pub trst	G	Franchise investment law —false representation	7
445.1523	Pub trst	G	Franchise investment law —false statements of material fact	7
445.1525	Pub trst	G	Franchise investment law —false advertising	7
445.1528	Pub trst	D	Pyramid/chain promotions —offer or sell	7
445.1671	Pub trst	E	Mortgage brokers, lenders —knowingly giving a false statement	15
445.1679	Pub trst	H	Mortgage brokers act —general violations	3
445.2507(2)	Pub ord	F	Violation of unsolicited commercial e-mail protection act in furtherance of crime	4

P.A.1927, No. 175, c. XVII, § 14h, added by P.A.2002, No. 29, Eff. April 1, 2002. Amended by P.A.2003, No. 134, Eff. Sept. 30, 2003; P.A.2004, No. 457, Eff. Mar. 1, 2005; P.A.2006, No. 594, Eff. March 30, 2007.

777.14j. Application of chapter to Michigan Compiled Laws chapters 450 and 451; enumerated felonies

Sec. 14j. This chapter applies to the following felonies enumerated in chapters 450 and 451 of the Michigan Compiled Laws:

M.C.L.	Category	Class	Description	Stat Max
450.775	Pub ord	H	Corporations —minority and woman owned businesses	2
450.795	Pub ord	H	Corporations —handicapper business opportunity act	2
451.319	Pub trst	G	Securities, real estate, and debt management —violation	2
451.434	Pub trst	H	Debt management act —licensee violations	2
451.501	Pub trst	E	Blue sky laws —fraudulent schemes/statements	10
451.502	Pub trst	E	Blue sky laws —investment advisor/agent fraud	10
451.503	Pub trst	E	Blue sky laws —make/sell false bullion/certificates	10
451.601	Pub trst	E	Blue sky laws —unregistered broker/dealer/agent/advisor	10
451.603(h)	Pub trst	E	Blue sky laws —fail to notify administrator of sanctions	10
451.604(a)(1)(j) to (s) and (v) to (z)	Pub trst	E	Blue sky laws —various violations	10
451.701	Pub trst	E	Blue sky laws —offer/sell unregistered securities	10
451.802	Pub trst	E	Blue sky laws —unlawfully selling securities	10
451.804	Pub trst	E	Blue sky laws —willful false statements	10
451.805(b)	Pub trst	E	Blue sky laws —false representation of administrative approval	10
451.806(b)	Pub trst	E	Blue sky laws —improper disclosure by cor and sec bur employee	10

P.A.1927, No. 175, c. XVII, § 14j, added by P.A.2002, No. 29, Eff. April 1, 2002.

777.14m. Application of chapter to Michigan Compiled Laws chapters 460 to 473; enumerated felonies

Sec. 14m. This chapter applies to the following felonies enumerated in chapters 460 to 473 of the Michigan Compiled Laws:

M.C.L.	Category	Class	Description	Stat Max
462.257(1)	Person	A	Trains —endangering travel	Life
462.353(5)	Pub saf	E	Operating a locomotive under the influence —third or subsequent offense	5

M.C.L.	Category	Class	Description	Stat Max
462.353(6)	Person	C	Operating locomotive under the influence or while impaired causing death	15
462.353(7)	Person	E	Operating locomotive under the influence or while impaired causing serious impairment	5
472.36	Pub saf	A	Street railways —obstruction of track	Life

P.A.1927, No. 175, c. XVII, § 14m, added by P.A. 2002, No. 29, Eff. April 1, 2002. Amended by P.A. 2002, No. 659, Eff. April 1, 2003.

777.14p. Application of chapter to Michigan Compiled Laws chapters 482 to 499; enumerated felonies

Sec. 14p. This chapter applies to the following felonies enumerated in chapters 482 to 499 of the Michigan Compiled Laws:

M.C.L.	Category	Class	Description	Stat Max
482.44	Property	H	Bills of lading —issuance for goods not received	5
482.46	Property	H	Bills of lading —issuance of duplicate negotiable bill with intent to defraud	5
482.48	Property	H	Bills of lading —negotiation when goods not in carriers' possession	5
482.49	Property	H	Bills of lading —inducing carrier to issue when goods have not been received	5
482.50	Property	H	Bills of lading —issuance of non-negotiable bill not so marked	5
487.1042(1)	Pub trst	E	Money transmission services act —intentionally making a false statement, misrepresentation, or certification in a record or document	5
487.1042(2)	Pub trst	E	Criminal fraud in the conduct of money transmission services business	5
487.1042(3)	Pub trst	E	Money transmission services act license violation	5
487.1505(6)	Pub trst	E	BIDCO act —knowingly receiving money or property at an interest rate exceeding 25%	5
492.137(a)	Pub trst	H	Installment sales of motor vehicles	3
493.56a(13)	Pub trst	C	False statement in reports —secondary mortgage	15
493.77(2)	Pub trst	H	Second mortgage loan act licensing violation	3

P.A.1927, No. 175, c. XVII, § 14p, added by P.A.2002, No. 29, Eff. April 1, 2002. Amended by P.A.2006, No. 251, Imd. Eff. July 3, 2006.

777.15. Application of chapter to Michigan Compiled Laws chapters 500 to 749

Sec. 15. This chapter applies to the following felonies enumerated in chapters 500 to 749 of the Michigan Compiled Laws as set forth in sections 15a to 15g of this chapter. [1]

P.A.1927, No. 175, c. XVII, § 15, added by P.A.1998, No. 317, Eff. Dec. 15, 1998. Amended by P.A.2000, No. 279, Eff. Oct. 1, 2000; P.A.2001, No. 10, Imd. Eff. May 29, 2001; P.A.2001, No. 152, Eff. Jan. 1, 2002; P.A.2002, No. 206, Eff. May 1, 2002.

[1] M.C.L.A. §§ 777.15a to 777.15g.

777.15a. Application of chapter to Michigan Compiled Laws chapters 500 to 550; enumerated felonies

Sec. 15a. This chapter applies to the following felonies enumerated in chapters 500 to 550 of the Michigan Compiled Laws:

M.C.L.	Category	Class	Description	Stat Max
500.1325(3)	Pub trst	E	Insurance code — knowingly misrepresenting false financial condition	5
500.1371	Pub trst	H	Holding companies — violation	2
500.1505(2)	Pub trst	C	Insurance code — license and regulatory violations	15
500.4511(1)	Pub trst	F	Insurance code — fraudulent insurance act	4
500.4511(2)	Pub trst	D	Insurance fraud — agreement or conspiracy to commit	10
500.5252(4)	Property	G	Insurance — improper personal interest in transactions	5
500.7034(2)	Pub trst	E	Officer of a MEWA knowingly receive valuables for sale property or loan	10
500.8197(2)	Pub trst	C	Insurance — knowing or willful false statements in application for insurance	15
500.8197(3)	Property	E	Consolidation merger — compensation otherwise than expressed in contract	5

P.A.1927, No. 175, c. XVII, § 15a, added by P.A.2002, No. 206, Eff. May 1, 2002.

777.15b. Application of chapter to Michigan Compiled Laws chapters 551 to 570; enumerated felonies

Sec. 15b. This chapter applies to the following felonies enumerated in chapters 551 to 570 of the Michigan Compiled Laws:

M.C.L.	Category	Class	Description	Stat Max
551.102(2)	Pub trst	F	Unauthorized disclosure of social security number — subsequent offense	4
554.836	Property	E	Real and property — living care disclosure act	7
565.371	Property	G	Fraudulent conveyances — recording with intent to deceive	3
565.827	Pub trst	E	Land sales act — false or fraudulent statement	10
570.152	Property	G	Contractor — fraudulent use of building contract fund	3

M.C.L.	Category	Class	Description	Stat Max
570.1110(c)	Property	E	Contractor — false sworn statement involving $1,000 to $20,000 or with prior convictions	5
570.1110(d)	Property	D	Contractor — false sworn statement involving $20,000 or more or with prior convictions	10
570.1207	Property	G	Construction liens — false information	4

P.A.1927, No. 175, c. XVII, § 15b, added by P.A.2002, No. 206, Eff. May 1, 2002.

777.15d. Application of chapter to Michigan Compiled Laws chapter 600; enumerated felonies

Sec. 15d. This chapter applies to the following felonies enumerated in chapter 600 of the Michigan Compiled Laws:

M.C.L.	Category	Class	Description	Stat Max
600.908(8)	Pub trst	E	Immunity to witness — committing perjury	15
600.2136	Pub trst	E	Library record, book, paper — false certification in court	15
600.2907a	Property	G	Recording documents affecting property without lawful cause	3
600.2916	Pub saf	G	Revised judicature act — lethal gases for fumigation	4
600.8713	Pub trst	G	Revised judicature act — false statement by authorized local officials	15
600.8813	Pub trst	E	Law enforcement officer — knowingly making false statement in a citation	15

P.A.1927, No. 175, c. XVII, § 15d, added by P.A.2002, No. 206, Eff. May 1, 2002.

777.15f. Application of chapter to Michigan Compiled Laws chapters 700 to 720; enumerated felonies

Sec. 15f. This chapter applies to the following felonies enumerated in chapters 700 to 720 of the Michigan Compiled Laws:

M.C.L.	Category	Class	Description	Stat Max
710.54(11)	Pub trst	F	Offer to give other consideration — adoption — subsequent violation	4
710.55(1)	Pub trst	F	Adoption — persons not authorized placing child — subsequent violation	4
710.69	Person	F	Michigan adoption law — subsequent offense	4
711.1(8)	Pub trst	E	Intentional false statement in petition for name change	15
712A.6b(3)	Pub ord	G	Violation of court order — subsequent conviction	2

P.A.1927, No. 175, c. XVII, § 15f, added by P.A.2002, No. 206, Eff. May 1, 2002.

777.15g. Application of chapter to Michigan Compiled Laws chapters 721 to 730; enumerated felonies

Sec. 15g. This chapter applies to the following felonies enumerated in chapters 721 to 730 of the Michigan Compiled Laws:

M.C.L.	Category	Class	Description	Stat Max
722.115e(2)(a)	Pub saf	G	Failure to report arraignment for criminal charges —child care centers, day care centers, and employees	2
722.115f(8)(a)	Pub saf	G	Failure to report arraignment for criminal charges —family day care homes and group day care homes	2
722.633(5)(b)	Person	F	Intentional false report of child abuse constituting a felony	Variable
722.675	Pub ord	E	Distributing obscene matter to children	2
722.857	Person	E	Surrogate parenting contracts involving minors, mentally retarded, etc.	5
722.859(3)	Person	E	Surrogate parenting contracts for compensation	5

P.A.1927, No. 175, c. XVII, § 15g, added by P.A.2002, No. 206, Eff. May 1, 2002. Amended by P.A.2005, No. 106, Imd. Eff. Sept. 14, 2005; P.A.2005, No. 134, Eff. Jan. 1, 2006.

777.16. Application of chapter to Michigan Compiled Laws chapter 750

Sec. 16. This chapter applies to felonies enumerated in chapter 750 of the Michigan Compiled Laws as set forth in sections 16a to 16z of this chapter. [1]

P.A.1927, No. 175, c. XVII, § 16, added by P.A.1998, No. 317, Eff. Dec. 15, 1998.

[1] M.C.L.A. §§ 777.16a to 777.16z.

777.16a. Application of chapter to Michigan Compiled Laws chapter 750, sections 750.11 to 750.32; enumerated felonies

Sec. 16a. This chapter applies to the following felonies enumerated in chapter 750 of the Michigan Compiled Laws:

M.C.L.	Category	Class	Description	Stat Max
750.11	Person	A	Taking a woman and compelling her to marry	Life
750.12	Person	H	Taking a woman with intent to compel her to marry	10
750.13	Person	D	Enticing female under 16 for immoral purposes	10
750.14	Person	C	Abortion resulting in death of female	15
	Person	G	Abortion	4
750.16(1)	Person	G	Adulterate, misbrand, remove, or substitute a drug or medicine	2
750.16(2)	Person	F	Adulterate, misbrand, remove, or substitute a	4

M.C.L.	Category	Class	Description	Stat Max
			drug or medicine causing personal injury	
750.16(3)	Person	E	Adulterate, misbrand, remove, or substitute a drug or medicine resulting in serious impairment of body function	5
750.16(4)	Person	C	Adulterate, misbrand, remove, or substitute a drug or medicine resulting in death	15
750.18(3)	Person	G	Mix, color, stain, or powder a drug or medicine with an ingredient or material so as to injuriously affect its quality or potency	2
750.18(4)	Person	F	Mix, color, stain, or powder a drug or medicine with an ingredient or material so as to injuriously affect its quality or potency resulting in personal injury	4
750.18(5)	Person	E	Mix, color, stain, or powder a drug or medicine with an ingredient or material so as to injuriously affect its quality or potency resulting in serious impairment of body function	5
750.18(6)	Person	C	Mix, color, stain, or powder a drug or medicine with an ingredient or material so as to injuriously affect its quality or potency resulting in death	15
750.30	Pub ord	H	Adultery	4
750.32	Pub ord	H	Cohabitation of divorced parties	4

P.A.1927, No. 175, c. XVII, § 16a, added by P.A.1998, No. 317, Eff. Dec. 15, 1998. Amended by P.A.2000, No. 279, Eff. Oct. 1, 2000; P.A.2004, No. 216, Eff. Oct. 12, 2004.

777.16b. Application of chapter to Michigan Compiled Laws chapter 750, sections 750.49 to 750.68; enumerated felonies

Sec. 16b. This chapter applies to the following felonies enumerated in chapter 750 of the Michigan Compiled Laws:

M.C.L.	Category	Class	Description	Stat Max
750.49(2)(a) to (d)	Pub ord	F	Fighting animals or providing facilities for animal fights	4
750.49(2)(e)	Pub ord	F	Organizing or promoting animal fights	4
750.49(2)(f)	Pub ord	H	Attending animal fight	4
750.49(2)(g)	Pub ord	F	Breeding or selling fighting animals	4
750.49(2)(h)	Pub ord	F	Selling or possessing equipment for animal fights	4
750.49(8)	Person	A	Inciting fighting animal resulting in death	Life
750.49(9)	Person	F	Inciting fighting animal to attack	4
750.49(10)	Person	D	Fighting animal attacking without provocation and death resulting	15
750.50(4)	Pub ord	G	Animal neglect or cruelty —second offense	2
	Pub ord	F	Animal neglect or cruelty —third or subsequent offense	4
750.50b(2)	Property	F	Killing or torturing animals	4
750.50c(5)	Pub ord	E	Killing or causing serious physical harm to law enforcement animal or search and rescue dog	5
750.50c(7)	Pub saf	H	Harassing or causing harm to law enforcement animal or search and rescue dog while committing crime	2
750.68	Property	G	Changing brands with intent to steal	4

P.A.1927, No. 175, c. XVII, § 16b, added by P.A.1998, No. 317, Eff. Dec. 15, 1998. Amended by P.A.2000, No. 279, Eff. Oct. 1, 2000; P.A.2006, No. 518, Imd. Eff. Dec. 29, 2006.

777.16c. Application of chapter to Michigan Compiled Laws chapter 750, sections 750.72 to 750.80; enumerated felonies

Sec. 16c. This chapter applies to the following felonies enumerated in chapter 750 of the Michigan Compiled Laws:

M.C.L.	Category	Class	Description	Stat Max
750.72	Person	B	Arson of a dwelling house	20
750.73	Property	D	Arson of real property	10
750.74	Person	E	Arson of personal property having a value of $1,000 to $20,000 or with prior convictions	5
750.74(1)(d)	Person	D	Arson of personal property of $20,000 or more or with prior convictions	10
750.75	Property	D	Arson of insured property	10
750.77(1)(c)	Person	E	Preparing to burn personal property having a value of $1,000 to $20,000 or with prior convictions	5
750.77(1)(d)	Person	D	Preparing to burn personal property of $20,000 or more or with prior convictions	10
750.78	Pub saf	F	Arson of woods and prairies	4
750.79	Pub saf	F	Violating township rules concerning clearing of land and burning	4
750.80	Property	D	Arson of mines	Life

P.A.1927, No. 175, c. XVII, § 16c, added by P.A.1998, No. 317, Eff. Dec. 15, 1998. Amended by P.A.2000, No. 279, Eff. Oct. 1, 2000.

777.16d. Application of chapter to Michigan Compiled Laws chapter 750, sections 750.81 to 750.91; enumerated felonies

Sec. 16d. This chapter applies to the following felonies enumerated in chapter 750 of the Michigan Compiled Laws:

M.C.L.	Category	Class	Description	Stat Max
750.81(4)	Person	G	Domestic assault with prior convictions	2
750.81a(3)	Person	G	Aggravated domestic assault with prior convictions	2

M.C.L.	Category	Class	Description	Stat Max
750.81d(1)	Person	G	Assaulting, resisting, or obstructing certain persons	2
750.81d(2)	Person	F	Assaulting, resisting, or obstructing certain persons causing injury	4
750.81d(3)	Person	C	Assaulting, resisting, or obstructing certain persons causing serious impairment	15
750.81d(4)	Person	B	Assaulting, resisting, or obstructing certain persons causing death	20
750.82(1)	Person	F	Felonious assault	4
750.82(2)	Person	F	Felonious assault — weapon-free school zone	4
750.83	Person	A	Assault with intent to murder	Life
750.84	Person	D	Assault with intent to do great bodily harm less than murder	10
750.85	Person	A	Torture	Life
750.86	Person	D	Assault with intent to maim	10
750.87	Person	D	Assault with intent to commit a felony	10
750.88	Person	C	Assault with intent to commit unarmed robbery	15
750.89	Person	A	Assault with intent to commit armed robbery	Life
750.90	Person	D	Sexual intercourse under pretext of medical treatment	10
750.90a	Person	A	Assault against a pregnant individual causing miscarriage, stillbirth, or death to embryo or fetus with intent or recklessness	Life
750.90b(a)	Person	C	Assault against a pregnant individual resulting in miscarriage, stillbirth, or death to embryo or fetus	15
750.90b(b)	Person	D	Assault against a pregnant individual resulting in great bodily harm to embryo or fetus	10
750.90c(a)	Person	C	Gross negligence against a pregnant individual resulting in miscarriage, stillbirth, or death to embryo or fetus	15
750.90c(b)	Person	E	Gross negligence against a pregnant individual resulting in great bodily harm to embryo or fetus	5
750.90d(a)	Person	C	Operating a vehicle under the influence or while impaired causing miscarriage, stillbirth, or death to embryo or fetus	15
750.90d(b)	Person	E	Operating a vehicle under the influence or while impaired causing serious or aggravated injury to embryo or fetus	5
750.90e	Person	G	Careless or reckless driving causing miscarriage, stillbirth, or death to embryo or fetus	2
750.90g(3)	Person	A	Performance of procedure on live infant with intent to cause death	Life
750.91	Person	A	Attempted murder	Life

P.A.1927, No. 175, c. XVII, § 16d, added by P.A.1998, No. 317, Eff. Dec. 15, 1998. Amended by P.A.1999, No. 192, Eff. March 10, 2000; P.A.2000, No. 279, Eff. Oct. 1, 2000; P.A.2001, No. 2, Eff. June 1, 2001; P.A.2001, No. 20, Eff. Sept. 1, 2001; P.A.2002, No. 269, Eff. July 15, 2002; P.A.2005, No. 336, Eff. March 1, 2006.

777.16e. Application of chapter to Michigan Compiled Laws chapter 750, sections 750.93 to 750.106; enumerated felonies

Sec. 16e. This chapter applies to the following felonies enumerated in chapter 750 of the Michigan Complied Laws:

M.C.L.	Category	Class	Description	Stat Max
750.93	Property	G	Removing or destroying bonds in state treasury	10
750.94	Property	G	Issuing bank notes without complying with requirements	10
750.95	Property	G	Fraudulent bank notes	10
750.96	Property	G	Fraudulent disposal of bank property	4
750.97	Property	H	Statements derogatory to financial condition of bank	4
750.98	Pub ord	G	Private banking	4
750.99	Pub trst	G	Certifying checks without sufficient funds	4
750.100	Pub trst	E	Banks—conducting business when insolvent	5
750.101	Pub trst	E	Violating financial institutions act	5
750.104	Property	F	Fitting boat with intent to destroy	4
750.105	Property	G	Making false cargo invoice for boat	4
750.106	Property	G	Boats—making or procuring false protest	4

P.A.1927, No. 175, c. XVII, § 16e, added by P.A.1998, No. 317, Eff. Dec. 15, 1998.

777.16f. Application of chapter to Michigan Compiled Laws chapter 750, sections 750.110 to 750.131a; enumerated felonies

Sec. 16f. This chapter applies to the following felonies enumerated in chapter 750 of the Michigan Compiled Laws:

M.C.L.	Category	Class	Description	Stat Max
750.110	Property	D	Breaking and entering with intent to commit felony or larceny	10
750.110a(2)	Person	B	Home invasion—first degree	20
750.110a(3)	Person	C	Home invasion—second degree	15
750.110a(4)	Person	E	Home invasion—third degree	5
750.111	Property	E	Entering without breaking with intent to commit felony or larceny	5
750.112	Person	A	Burglary with explosives	Life
750.116	Property	E	Possession of burglar's tools	10

M.C.L.	Category	Class	Description	Stat Max
750.117	Pub trst	F	Bribing a public officer	4
750.118	Pub trst	D	Public officer accepting bribe	10
750.119(1)(a)	Pub trst	F	Bribing a juror or other person	4
750.119(1)(b)	Pub trst	D	Bribing a juror or other person in case punishable by more than 10 years	10
750.120	Pub trst	F	Juror or other person accepting a bribe	4
750.120a(2)(a)	Pub ord	F	Juror intimidation	4
750.120a(2)(b)	Pub ord	D	Juror intimidation in case punishable by more than 10 years	10
750.120a(2)(c)	Person	C	Juror intimidation by committing crime or threatening to kill or injure	15
750.120a(4)	Person	D	Retaliating against juror	10
750.121	Pub trst	F	Bribing a public officer to influence contract	4
750.122(7)(a)	Pub ord	F	Bribing or intimidating witness	4
750.122(7)(b)	Pub ord	D	Bribing or intimidating witness in case punishable by more than 10 years	10
750.122(7)(c)	Person	C	Intimidating witness by committing crime or threatening to kill or injure	15
750.122(8)	Person	D	Retaliating against witness	10
750.124	Pub trst	G	Bribing an athlete	4
750.128	Pub ord	H	Bucket shop violation	2
750.131(3)(b)(*ii*)	Property	G	NSF checks—$100 to $500—third or subsequent offense	2
750.131(3)(c)	Property	G	NSF checks—$500 or more	2
750.131a(1)	Property	H	No account checks	2
750.131a(2)	Property	H	NSF checks, 3 or more within 10 days	2

P.A.1927, No. 175, c. XVII, § 16f, added by P.A.1998, No. 317, Eff. Dec. 15, 1998. Amended by P.A.1999, No. 45, Eff. Oct. 1, 1999; P.A.2000, No. 279, Eff. Oct. 1, 2000; P.A.2000, No. 498, Eff. March 28, 2001.

777.16g. Application of chapter to Michigan Compiled Laws chapter 750, sections 750.135 to 750.147b; enumerated felonies

Sec. 16g. (1) This chapter applies to the following felonies enumerated in chapter 750 of the Michigan Compiled Laws:

M.C.L.	Category	Class	Description	Stat Max
750.135	Person	D	Exposing children with intent to injure or abandon	10
750.136b(2)	Person	B	Child abuse —first degree	15
750.136b(4)	Person	F	Child abuse —second degree	4
750.136b(5)	Person	G	Child abuse —third degree	2
750.136c	Person	B	Buying or selling an individual	20
750.145a	Person	F	Soliciting child to commit an immoral act	4
750.145b	Person	D	Accosting children for immoral purposes with prior conviction	10
750.145c(2)	Person	B	Child sexually abusive activity or materials —active involvement	20
750.145c(3)	Person	D	Child sexually abusive activity or materials —distributing, promoting, or financing	7
750.145c(4)	Person	F	Child sexually abusive activities or materials —possession	4
750.145d(2)(b)	Variable	G	Using internet or computer to commit crime punishable by a maximum term of imprisonment of at least 1 year but less than 2 years	2
750.145d(2)(c)	Variable	F	Using internet or computer to commit crime punishable by a maximum term of imprisonment of at least 2 years but less than 4 years	4
750.145d(2)(d)	Variable	D	Using internet or computer to commit crime punishable by a maximum term of imprisonment of at least 4 years but less than 10 years	10
750.145d(2)(e)	Variable	C	Using internet or computer to commit crime punishable by a maximum term of imprisonment of at least 10 years but less than 15 years	15
750.145d(2)(f)	Variable	B	Using internet or computer to commit crime punishable by a maximum term of imprisonment of at least 15 years or for life	20
750.145n(1)	Person	C	Vulnerable adult abuse —first degree	15
750.145n(2)	Person	F	Vulnerable adult abuse —second degree	4
750.145n(3)	Person	G	Vulnerable adult abuse —third degree	2
750.145o	Person	E	Death of vulnerable adult caused by unlicensed caretaker	5
750.145p(1)	Person	G	Vulnerable adult —commingling funds, obstructing investigation, or filing false information	2
750.145p(2)	Person	G	Retaliation or discrimination by caregiver against vulnerable adult	2
750.145p(5)	Person	E	Vulnerable adult —caregiver violations —subsequent offense	5
750.147b	Person	G	Ethnic intimidation	2

(2) For a violation of section 145d of the Michigan penal code, 1931 PA 328, MCL 750.145d, determine the offense category, offense variable level, and prior record variable level based on the underlying offense.

P.A.1927, No. 175, c. XVII, § 16g, added by P.A.1998, No. 317, Eff. Dec. 15, 1998. Amended by P.A.1999, No. 39, Eff. Aug. 1, 1999; P.A.2000, No. 183, Eff. Sept. 19, 2000; P.A.2000, No. 279, Eff. Oct. 1, 2000; P.A.2002, No. 47, Eff. June 1, 2002; P.A.2002, No. 630, Eff. March 31, 2003.

777.16h. Application of chapter to Michigan Compiled Laws chapter 750, sections 750.149 to 750.157w; enumerated felonies

Sec. 16h. This chapter applies to the following felonies enumerated in chapter 750 of the Michigan Compiled Laws:

M.C.L.	Category	Class	Description	Stat Max
750.149	Pub saf	F	Concealing an offense punishable by life	4
750.157a(b)	Pub ord	H	Conspiracy —gambling	5
750.157a(d)	Pub ord	G	Conspiracy to commit legal act in illegal manner	5
750.157b(2)	Person	A	Solicitation of murder	Life
750.157b(3)(a)	Pub ord	E	Solicitation of felony punishable by life or 5 or more years	5
750.157b(3)(b)	Pub ord	G	Solicitation of felony punishable by less than 5 years	2
750.157n(1)	Property	H	Financial transaction device —stealing, retaining, or using without consent	4
750.157n(2)	Property	H	Possessing fraudulent or altered financial transaction device	4
750.157p	Property	H	Possessing financial transaction device without permission and with intent to use or sell	4
750.157q	Property	H	Delivery or sale of fraudulent financial transaction device	4
750.157r	Property	H	Financial transaction device —forgery, alteration, or counterfeiting	4
750.157s(1)(b)(*ii*)	Property	H	Using revoked or canceled financial transaction device involving $100 to $500 with prior convictions	2
750.157s(1)(c)	Property	H	Use of revoked or canceled financial transaction device involving $500 or more	2
750.157t	Property	H	Furnishing goods or services to person committing violation with financial transaction device	4
750.157u	Property	H	Overcharging person using financial transaction device	4
750.157v	Property	H	False statement of identity to obtain financial transaction device	4
750.157w(1)(c)	Property	E	Fraudulently withdrawing or transferring $1,000 to $20,000 with financial transaction device	5
750.157w(1)(d)	Property	D	Fraudulently withdrawing or transferring $20,000 or more with financial transaction device	10

P.A.1927, No. 175, c. XVII, § 16h, added by P.A.1998, No. 317, Eff. Dec. 15, 1998. Amended by P.A.2000, No. 279, Eff. Oct. 1, 2000.

777.16i. Application of chapter to Michigan Compiled Laws chapter 750, sections 750.158 to 750.182a; enumerated felonies

Sec. 16i. This chapter applies to the following felonies enumerated in chapter 750 of the Michigan Compiled Laws:

M.C.L.	Category	Class	Description	Stat Max
750.158	Pub ord	E	Sodomy	15
750.159j	Pub saf	B	Racketeering	20
750.160	Pub ord	D	Disinterring or mutilating dead human body	10
750.160a	Pub ord	H	Photographing dead human body	2
750.160c	Pub ord	D	Improper disposal of dead human body after more than 180 days	10
750.161	Pub ord	G	Desertion/abandonment/nonsupport	3
750.164	Pub ord	F	Desertion to escape prosecution	4
750.165	Pub ord	F	Failing to pay support	4
750.168(2)(a)	Pub ord	G	Disorderly conduct at a funeral	2
750.168(2)(b)	Pub ord	F	Disorderly conduct at a funeral—subsequent offense	4
750.171	Person	E	Duelling	10
750.174(4)	Property	E	Embezzlement by agent of $200 to $1,000 from nonprofit corporation or charitable organization, of $1,000 to $20,000, or with prior convictions	5
750.174(5)	Property	D	Embezzlement by agent of $1,000 to $20,000 from nonprofit corporation or charitable organization, of $20,000 or more but less than $50,000, or of $1,000 to $20,000 with prior convictions	10
750.174(6)	Property	C	Embezzlement by agent of $50,000 or more but less than $100,000	15
750.174(7)	Property	B	Embezzlement by agent of $100,000 or more	20
750.174a(4)	Property	E	Embezzlement by person in a relationship of trust with a vulnerable adult of $1,000 to $20,000 or with prior convictions	5
750.174a(5)	Property	D	Embezzlement by person in a relationship of trust with a vulnerable adult of $20,000 or more or $1,000 to $20,000 with prior convictions	10
750.175	Pub trst	D	Embezzlement by public official over $50	10
750.176	Pub trst	E	Embezzlement by administrator/executor/guardian	10
750.177(2)	Property	D	Embezzlement by chattel mortgagor of $20,000 or more or $1,000 to $20,000 with prior convictions	10
750.177(3)	Property	E	Embezzlement by chattel mortgagor of $1,000 to $20,000 or with prior convictions	5
750.178(2)	Property	D	Embezzlement of mortgaged or leased property of $20,000 or more or $1,000 to $20,000 with prior convictions	10
750.178(3)	Property	E	Embezzling mortgaged or leased property with value of $1,000 to $20,000 or with prior convictions	5
750.180	Property	D	Embezzlement by financial institutions	20
750.181(4)	Property	E	Embezzling jointly held property with value of $1,000 to $20,000 or with prior convictions	5
750.181(5)	Property	D	Embezzling jointly held property with value of $20,000 or more or	10

M.C.L.	Category	Class	Description	Stat Max
			$1,000 to $20,000 with prior convictions	
750.182	Property	G	Embezzlement by warehouses	4
750.182a	Pub trst	H	Falsifying school records	2

P.A.1927, No. 175, c. XVII, § 16i, added by P.A.1998, No. 317, Eff. Dec. 15, 1998. Amended by P.A.2000, No. 223, Eff. Sept. 26, 2000; P.A.2000, No. 279, Eff. Oct. 1, 2000; P.A.2002, No. 278, Imd. Eff. May 9, 2002; P.A.2003, No. 268, Eff. April 1, 2004; P.A.2006, No. 149, Eff. Aug. 22, 2006; P.A.2006, No. 151, Eff. Aug. 22, 2006; P.A.2006, No. 574, Eff. March 30, 2007.

777.16j. Application of chapter to Michigan Compiled Laws chapter 750, sections 750.183 to 750.199a; enumerated felonies

Sec. 16j. This chapter applies to the following felonies enumerated in chapter 750 of the Michigan Compiled Laws:

M.C.L.	Category	Class	Description	Stat Max
750.183	Pub saf	E	Aiding escaping prisoner	7
750.186a(1)	Pub saf	F	Escape from a juvenile facility	4
750.189	Pub saf	H	Officer negligently allowing prisoner to escape or refusing to receive prisoner	2
750.190	Pub saf	G	Officer receiving reward to assist or permit escape	2
750.193	Pub saf	E	Escape from prison	5
750.195(1)	Pub saf	H	Escape from a misdemeanor jail sentence	2
750.195(2)	Pub saf	F	Escape from a felony jail sentence	4
750.197(1)	Pub saf	H	Escape while awaiting trial for misdemeanor	2
750.197(2)	Pub saf	F	Escape while awaiting trial for felony	4
750.197c	Pub saf	E	Escape from jail through violence	5
750.199(3)	Pub saf	F	Harboring a person for whom felony warrant has been issued	4
750.199a	Pub ord	F	Absconding on or forfeiting bond	4

P.A.1927, No. 175, c. XVII, § 16j, added by P.A.1998, No. 317, Eff. Dec. 15, 1998. Amended by P.A.2006, No. 243, Imd. Eff. June 30, 2006; P.A.2006, No. 536, Imd. Eff. Dec. 29, 2006.

777.16k. Application of chapter to Michigan Compiled Laws chapter 750, sections 750.200 to 750.212a; enumerated felonies

Sec. 16k. This chapter applies to the following felonies enumerated in chapter 750 of the Michigan Compiled Laws:

M.C.L.	Category	Class	Description	Stat Max
750.200	Pub saf	E	Transporting an explosive by common carrier	5
750.200i(2)(a)	Pub saf	C	Manufacturing or using a harmful device	15
750.200i(2)(b)	Property	B	Harmful device causing property damage	20
750.200i(2)(c)	Person	A	Harmful device causing personal injury	25
750.200i(2)(d)	Person	A	Harmful device causing serious impairment	Life
750.200j(2)(a)	Person	E	Irritant or irritant device	5
750.200j(2)(b)	Property	E	Irritant or irritant device causing property damage	7
750.200j(2)(c)	Person	D	Irritant or irritant device causing personal injury	10
750.200j(2)(d)	Person	A	Irritant or irritant device causing serious impairment	25
750.200j(2)(e)	Person	A	Irritant or irritant device causing death	Life
750.200*l*	Person	E	Falsely exposing person to harmful substance or device	5
750.201	Pub saf	E	Transporting certain types of explosives	5
750.202	Pub saf	F	Shipping an explosive with false markings or invoice	4
750.204(2)(a)	Pub saf	C	Sending an explosive with malicious intent	15
750.204(2)(b)	Property	B	Sending an explosive causing property damage	20
750.204(2)(c)	Person	A	Sending an explosive causing physical injury	25
750.204(2)(d)	Person	A	Sending an explosive causing serious impairment	Life
750.204a	Pub saf	E	Sending or transporting an imitation explosive device with malicious intent	5
750.207(2)(a)	Pub saf	C	Placing an explosive with malicious intent	15
750.207(2)(b)	Property	B	Placing an explosive causing property damage	20
750.207(2)(c)	Person	A	Placing an explosive causing physical injury	25
750.207(2)(d)	Person	A	Placing an explosive causing serious impairment	Life
750.209(1)(a)	Pub saf	C	Placing an offensive or injurious substance with intent to injure	15
750.209(1)(b)	Property	B	Placing an offensive or injurious substance causing property damage	20
750.209(1)(c)	Person	A	Placing an offensive or injurious substance causing physical injury	25
750.209(1)(d)	Person	A	Placing an offensive or injurious substance causing serious impairment	Life
750.209(2)	Pub saf	E	Placing an offensive or injurious substance with intent to alarm or annoy	5
750.209a	Pub saf	D	Possessing an explosive device in public place	10
750.210(2)(a)	Pub saf	C	Possessing or carrying an explosive or combustible substance with malicious intent	15
750.210(2)(b)	Property	B	Possessing or carrying an explosive or combustible substance causing property damage	20
750.210(2)(c)	Person	A	Possessing or carrying an explosive or combustible substance causing physical injury	25
750.210(2)(d)	Person	A	Possessing or carrying an explosive or combustible substance causing serious impairment	Life
750.210a	Pub saf	H	Sale of valerium	5
750.211a(2)(a)	Pub saf	F	Manufacturing or possessing a Molotov cock-	4

M.C.L.	Category	Class	Description	Stat Max
			tail or similar device designed to explode upon impact or by heat or flame or that is highly incendiary	
750.211a(2)(b)	Pub saf	C	Manufacturing or possessing an explosive or incendiary device with malicious intent	15
750.211a(2)(c)	Property	B	Manufacturing or possessing an explosive or incendiary device causing property damage	20
750.211a(2)(d)	Person	A	Manufacturing or possessing an explosive or incendiary device causing physical injury	25
750.211a(2)(e)	Person	A	Manufacturing or possessing an explosive or incendiary device causing serious impairment	Life
750.212a	Person	B	Explosives violation involving a vulnerable target causing death or injury	20

P.A.1927, No. 175, c. XVII, § 16k, added by P.A.1998, No. 317, Eff. Dec. 15, 1998. Amended by P.A.2000, No. 279, Eff. Oct. 1, 2000; P.A.2001, No. 136, Imd. Eff. Oct. 23, 2001; P.A.2004, No. 524, Eff. April 1, 2005.

777.16*l*. Application of chapter to Michigan Compiled Laws chapter 750, sections 750.213 to 750.219f; enumerated felonies

Sec. 16*l*. This chapter applies to the following felonies enumerated in chapter 750 of the Michigan Compiled Laws:

M.C.L.	Category	Class	Description	Stat Max
750.213	Person	B	Threats to extort money	20
750.215(3)	Pub saf	F	Impersonating peace officer	4
750.217b	Pub saf	G	Impersonating public utility employee	2
750.217c(3)	Pub ord	H	Impersonating public officer or employee	2
750.217c(4)	Pub ord	G	Impersonating public officer or employee — third or subsequent conviction	4
750.217d	Pub saf	C	False representation or practice as health professional	15
750.217e	Pub ord	G	Impersonating a DHS employee	2
750.217f	Pub saf	G	Impersonating a firefighter or emergency medical service personnel	2
750.218(4)	Property	E	False pretenses involving $1,000 to $20,000 or with prior convictions	5
750.218(5)	Property	D	False pretenses involving $20,000 or more or $1,000 to $20,000 with prior convictions	10
750.219a(2)(c)	Property	E	Telecommunications fraud with 1 or more prior convictions or involving a value of $1,000 to $20,000	5
750.219a(2)(d)	Property	D	Telecommunications fraud with 2 or more prior convictions or involving a value of $20,000 or more	10
750.219e	Property	F	Receiving, possessing, preparing, or submitting an unauthorized credit application or receiving or possessing proceeds	4
750.219f	Property	F	Receiving with intent to forward, possessing with intent to forward, or forwarding an unauthorized credit application or proceeds	4

P.A.1927, No. 175, c. XVII, § 16*l*, added by P.A.1998, No. 317, Eff. Dec. 15, 1998. Amended by P.A.1999, No. 165, Eff. Feb. 3, 2000; P.A.1999, No. 168, Eff. March 10, 2000; P.A.2000, No. 279, Eff. Oct. 1, 2000; P.A.2001, No. 19, Eff. Sept. 1, 2001; P.A.2003, No. 16, Eff. Sept. 1, 2003; P.A.2005, No. 171, Eff. Jan. 1, 2006.

777.16m. Application of chapter to Michigan Compiled Laws chapter 750, sections 750.223 to 750.237; enumerated felonies

Sec. 16m. This chapter applies to the following felonies enumerated in chapter 750 of the Michigan Compiled Laws:

M.C.L.	Category	Class	Description	Stat Max
750.223(2)	Pub saf	F	Sale of firearm to minor —subsequent offense	4
750.223(3)	Pub ord	D	Sale of firearm to person prohibited from possessing	10
750.224	Pub saf	E	Manufacture or sale of silencer, bomb, blackjack, automatic weapon, gas spray, etc.	5
750.224a	Pub saf	F	Possession or sale of electrical current weapons	4
750.224b	Pub saf	E	Possession of short barreled shotgun or rifle	5
750.224c	Pub saf	F	Armor piercing ammunition	4
750.224d(2)	Person	G	Using self-defense spray device	2
750.224e	Pub saf	F	Manufacture/sale/possession of devices to convert semiautomatic weapons	4
750.224f	Pub saf	E	Possession or sale of firearm by felon	5
750.226	Pub saf	E	Carrying firearm or dangerous weapon with unlawful intent	5
750.227	Pub saf	E	Carrying a concealed weapon	5
750.227a	Pub saf	F	Unlawful possession of pistol	4
750.227c	Pub saf	G	Possessing a loaded firearm in or upon a vehicle	2
750.227f	Pub saf	F	Wearing body armor during commission of certain crimes	4
750.227g(1)	Pub saf	F	Felon purchasing, owning, possessing, or using body armor	4
750.230	Pub saf	G	Altering ID mark on firearm	2
750.232a(3)	Pub saf	G	False statement in a pistol application	4
750.234a	Pub saf	F	Discharging firearm from vehicle	4
750.234b	Pub saf	F	Discharging firearm in or at a building	4
750.234c	Pub saf	F	Discharging firearm at emergency/police vehicle	4

M.C.L.	Category	Class	Description	Stat Max
750.236	Person	C	Setting spring gun — death resulting	15
750.237(3)	Person	E	Using firearm while under the influence or impaired causing serious impairment	5
750.237(4)	Person	C	Using firearm while under the influence or impaired causing death	15

P.A.1927, No. 175, c. XVII, § 16m, added by P.A. 1998, No. 317, Eff. Dec. 15, 1998. Amended by P.A.2000, No. 225, Eff. Oct. 1, 2000; P.A.2000, No. 279, Eff. Oct. 1, 2000; P.A.2001, No. 166, Eff. Feb. 1, 2002; P.A.2005, No. 106, Imd. Eff. Sept. 14, 2005.

777.16n. Application of chapter to Michigan Compiled Laws chapter 750, sections 750.241 to 750.263; enumerated felonies

Sec. 16n. This chapter applies to the following felonies enumerated in chapter 750 of the Michigan Compiled Laws:

M.C.L.	Category	Class	Description	Stat Max
750.241(2)	Pub saf	F	Obstructing public service facility personnel in civil disturbance	4
750.248	Property	E	Forgery	14
750.248a	Property	F	Uttering and publishing financial transaction device	4
750.249	Property	E	Uttering and publishing forged records	14
750.249a	Property	H	Molds or dies to forge financial transaction device	4
750.250	Property	E	Forgery of treasury notes	7
750.251	Property	E	Forgery of bank bills	7
750.252	Property	E	Possessing counterfeit notes	7
750.253	Property	G	Uttering counterfeit notes	5
750.254	Property	E	Possession of counterfeit notes or bills	5
750.255	Property	E	Possession of counterfeiting tools	10
750.260	Property	E	Counterfeiting coins or possession of 5 or more counterfeit coins	Life
750.261	Property	E	Possession of 5 or fewer counterfeit coins	10
750.262	Property	E	Manufacture or possession of tools to counterfeit coins	10
750.263(3)	Property	E	Delivery, use, or display of items with counterfeit mark —subsequent offense or over $1,000 or 100 items	5
750.263(4)	Property	E	Manufacturing items with counterfeit mark	5

P.A.1927, No. 175, c. XVII, § 16n, added by P.A.1998, No. 317, Eff. Dec. 15, 1998. Amended by P.A.2002, No. 272, Eff. July 15, 2002; P.A.2002, No. 321, Eff. July 15, 2002.

777.16o. Application of chapter to Michigan Compiled Laws chapter 750, sections 750.271 to 750.313; enumerated felonies

Sec. 16o. This chapter applies to the following felonies enumerated in chapter 750 of the Michigan Compiled Laws:

M.C.L.	Category	Class	Description	Stat Max
750.271	Property	E	Fraudulently issuing or selling domestic securities	10
750.272	Property	G	Sale of fraudulent stock of foreign corporations	10
750.273	Property	E	Obtaining signature to financial document with intent to defraud	10
750.274	Property	E	Fraud —purchasing/collecting on fraudulent financial document	10
750.276	Property	G	Fraud —promise to vendee of grain at fictitious price	4
750.277	Pub trst	G	Promise to vendee of grain to sell at a fictitious price—sale and transfer	4
750.278	Property	G	Fraud —warehouse receipts	5
750.279	Property	G	Fraud —disposition of exhausted property	4
750.280	Property	E	Gross frauds/cheats at common law	10
750.282	Pub ord	G	Public utility —fraudulent use over $500	4
750.300	Pub ord	G	Animals —killing/injuring to defraud insurance company	2
750.300a(1)(a)	Property	G	Food stamp fraud —$250 or less —second offense	5
	Property	G	Food stamp fraud —$250 or less —third or subsequent offense	10
750.300a(1)(b)	Property	E	Food stamp fraud —more than $250 to $1,000	5
	Property	E	Food stamp fraud —more than $250 to $1,000 —subsequent offense	10
750.300a(1)(c)	Property	E	Food stamp fraud —over $1,000	10
750.303	Pub ord	H	Gaming	2
750.313	Pub ord	H	Gambling —stocks/bonds/commodities	2

P.A.1927, No. 175, c. XVII, § 16*o*, added by P.A.1998, No. 317, Eff. Dec. 15, 1998. Amended by P.A.2000, No. 279, Eff. Oct. 1, 2000; P.A.2000, No. 389, Eff. April 1, 2001; P.A.2004, No. 457, Eff. Mar. 1, 2005.

777.16p. Application of chapter to Michigan Compiled Laws chapter 750, sections 750.317 to 750.329a; enumerated felonies

Sec. 16p. This chapter applies to the following felonies enumerated in chapter 750 of the Michigan Compiled Laws:

M.C.L.	Category	Class	Description	Stat Max
750.317	Person	M2	Second degree murder	Life
750.317a	Person	A	Delivery of controlled substance causing death	Life
750.321	Person	C	Manslaughter	15
750.322	Person	C	Willful killing of unborn quick child	15
750.323	Person	C	Abortion resulting in death	15
750.324	Person	G	Negligent homicide	2
750.327	Person	A	Death by explosives on vehicle or vessel	Life
750.328	Person	A	Death by explosives in or near building	Life

M.C.L.	Category	Class	Description	Stat Max
750.329	Person	C	Homicide–weapon aimed with intent but not malice	15
750.329a	Person	E	Assisting a suicide	5

P.A.1927, No. 175, c. XVII, § 16p, added by P.A.1998, No. 317, Eff. Dec. 15, 1998. Amended by P.A.2000, No. 279, Eff. Oct. 1, 2000; P.A.2005, No. 168, Eff. Jan. 1, 2006.

777.16q. Application of chapter to Michigan Compiled Laws, sections 750.332 to 750.350a; enumerated felonies

Sec. 16q. This chapter applies to the following felonies enumerated in chapter 750 of the Michigan Compiled Laws:

M.C.L.	Category	Class	Description	Stat Max
750.332	Property	H	Entering horse in race under false name	4
750.335a(2)(b)	Person	G	Aggravated indecent exposure	2
750.335a(2)(c)	Person	A	Indecent exposure by sexually delinquent person	Life
750.338	Pub ord	G	Gross indecency between males	5
	Pub ord	A	Gross indecency between males involving sexually delinquent person	Life
750.338a	Pub ord	G	Gross indecency between females	5
	Pub ord	A	Gross indecency between females involving sexually delinquent person	Life
750.338b	Pub ord	G	Gross indecency between males and females	5
	Pub ord	A	Gross indecency between males and females involving sexually delinquent person	Life
750.349	Person	A	Kidnapping	Life
750.349a	Person	A	Prisoner taking a hostage	Life
750.349b	Person	C	Unlawful imprisonment	15
750.350	Person	A	Kidnapping —child enticement	Life
750.350a	Person	H	Kidnapping —custodial interference	1

P.A.1927, No. 175, c. XVII, § 16q, added by P.A.1998, No. 317, Eff. Dec. 15, 1998. Amended by P.A.2002, No. 261, Imd. Eff. May 1, 2002; P.A.2005, No. 302, Eff. Feb. 1, 2006; P.A.2006, No. 164, Eff. Aug. 24, 2006.

777.16r. Application of chapter to Michigan Compiled Laws chapter 750, sections 750.356 to 750.374; enumerated felonies

Sec. 16r. This chapter applies to the following felonies enumerated in chapter 750 of the Michigan Compiled Laws:

M.C.L.	Category	Class	Description	Stat Max
750.356(2)	Property	D	Larceny involving $20,000 or more or with prior convictions	10
750.356(3)	Property	E	Larceny involving $1,000 to $20,000 or with prior convictions	5
750.356a(1)	Property	G	Larceny from a motor vehicle	5
750.356a(2)(c)	Property	E	Breaking and entering a vehicle to steal $1,000 to $20,000 or with prior convictions	5
750.356a(2)(d)	Property	D	Breaking and entering a vehicle to steal $20,000 or more or with prior convictions	10
750.356a(3)	Property	G	Breaking and entering a vehicle to steal causing damage	5
750.356b	Property	G	Breaking and entering a coin telephone	4
750.356c	Property	E	Retail fraud — first degree	5
750.357	Person	D	Larceny from the person	10
750.357a	Property	G	Larceny of livestock	4
750.357b	Property	E	Larceny — stealing firearms of another	5
750.358	Property	G	Larceny from burning building	5
750.360	Property	G	Larceny in a building	4
750.360a(2)(b)	Property	F	Theft detection device offense with prior conviction	4
750.361	Property	H	Trains — stealing/maliciously removing parts	2
750.362	Property	E	Larceny by conversion involving $1,000 to $20,000 or with prior convictions	5
	Property	D	Larceny by conversion involving $20,000 or more or with prior convictions	10
750.362a(2)	Property	D	Larceny of rental property involving $20,000 or more or with prior convictions	10
750.362a(3)	Property	E	Larceny of rental property involving $1,000 to $20,000 or with prior convictions	5
750.363	Property	E	Larceny by false personation involving $1,000 to $20,000 or with prior convictions	5
	Property	D	Larceny by false personation involving $20,000 or more	10
750.365	Person	D	Larceny from car or persons detained or injured by accident	20
750.367	Property	E	Larceny of trees or shrubs involving $1,000 to $20,000 or with prior convictions	5
	Property	D	Larceny of a tree or shrub involving $20,000 or more or with prior convictions	10
750.367b	Property	E	Airplanes — taking possession	5
750.368(5)	Pub ord	G	Preparing, serving, or executing unauthorized process —third or subsequent offense	4
750.372	Pub ord	H	Running or allowing lottery	2
750.373	Pub ord	H	Selling or possessing lottery tickets	2
750.374	Pub ord	H	Lottery violations — subsequent offense	4

P.A.1927, No. 175, c. XVII, § 16r, added by P.A.1998, No. 317, Eff. Dec. 15, 1998. Amended by P.A.2000, No. 279, Eff. Oct. 1, 2000; P.A.2002, No. 102, Eff. July 1, 2002; P.A.2002, No. 279, Imd. Eff. May 9, 2002.

777.16s. Application of chapter to Michigan Compiled Laws chapter 750, sections 750.377a to 750.406; enumerated felonies

Sec. 16s. This chapter applies to the following felonies enumerated in chapter 750 of the Michigan Compiled Laws:

M.C.L.	Category	Class	Description	Stat Max
750.377a(1)(a)	Property	D	Malicious destruction of personal property involving $20,000 or more or with prior convictions	10
750.377a(1)(b)	Property	E	Malicious destruction of personal property involving $1,000 to $20,000 or with prior convictions	5
750.377b	Property	F	Malicious destruction of fire/police property	4
750.377c	Property	E	School bus —intentional damage	5
750.378	Property	F	Malicious destruction of property —dams/canals/mills	4
750.379	Property	F	Malicious destruction of property —bridges/railroads/locks	4
750.380(2)	Property	D	Malicious destruction of building involving $20,000 or more or with prior convictions	10
750.380(3)	Property	E	Malicious destruction of a building involving $1,000 to $20,000 or with prior convictions	5
750.382(1)(c)	Property	E	Malicious destruction of plants or turf involving $1,000 to $20,000 or with prior convictions	5
750.382(1)(d)	Property	D	Malicious destruction of plants or turf involving $20,000 or more or with prior convictions	10
750.383a	Property	F	Malicious destruction of utility equipment	4
750.386	Property	E	Malicious destruction of mine property	20
750.387(5)	Property	E	Malicious destruction of a tomb or memorial involving $1,000 to $20,000 or with prior convictions	5
750.387(6)	Property	D	Malicious destruction of a tomb or memorial involving $20,000 or more or with prior convictions	10
750.392	Property	E	Malicious destruction of property —vessels	10
750.394(2)(c)	Person	F	Throwing or dropping dangerous object at vehicle causing injury	4
750.394(2)(d)	Person	D	Throwing or dropping dangerous object at vehicle causing serious impairment	10
750.394(2)(e)	Person	C	Throwing or dropping dangerous object at vehicle causing death	15
750.395(2)(c)	Property	E	Damaging or destroying research property with a value between $1,000 and $20,000 or with prior convictions	5
750.395(2)(d)	Property	E	Damaging or destroying research property with a value of $20,000 or more or 2 or more prior convictions	5
750.395(2)(e)	Person	E	Damaging or destroying research property resulting in physical injury	5
750.395(2)(f)	Person	D	Damaging or destroying research property resulting in serious impairment of body function	10
750.395(2)(g)	Person	C	Damaging or destroying research property resulting in death	15
750.397	Person	D	Mayhem	10
750.397a	Person	D	Placing harmful objects in food	10
750.405	Pub saf	E	Inciting soldiers to desert	5
750.406	Pub saf	E	Military stores —larceny, embezzlement or destruction	5

P.A.1927, No. 175, c. XVII, § 16s, added by P.A.1998, No. 317, Eff. Dec. 15, 1998. Amended by P.A.2000, No. 279, Eff. Oct. 1, 2000; P.A.2003, No. 183, Eff. Jan. 1, 2004; P.A.2004, No. 519, Eff. April 1, 2005; P.A.2005, No. 106, Imd. Eff. Sept. 14, 2005.

777.16t. Application of chapter to Michigan Compiled Laws chapter 750, sections 750.410a to 750.411t; enumerated felonies

Sec. 16t. This chapter applies to the following felonies enumerated in chapter 750 of the Michigan Compiled Laws:

M.C.L.	Category	Class	Description	Stat Max
750.410a	Person	G	Conspiracy to commit a person to state hospital unjustly	4
750.411a(1)(b)	Pub ord	F	False report of a felony	4
750.411a(3)(a)	Pub ord	F	Threat or false report of an explosive or harmful device, substance, or material	4
750.411a(3)(b)	Pub ord	D	Threat or false report of an explosive or harmful device, substance, or material—subsequent offense	10
750.411b	Pub trst	G	Excess fees to members of legislature	4
750.411h(2)(b)	Person	E	Stalking of a minor	5
750.411i(3)(a)	Person	E	Aggravated stalking	5
750.411i(3)(b)	Person	D	Aggravated stalking of a minor	10
750.411*l*	Pub ord	H	Money laundering—fourth degree	2
750.411m	Pub ord	E	Money laundering—third degree	5
750.411n	Pub ord	D	Money laundering—second degree	10
750.411o	Pub ord	B	Money laundering—first degree	20
750.411p(2)(a)	Property	B	Money laundering of proceeds from controlled substance offense involving $10,000 or more	20

M.C.L.	Category	Class	Description	Stat Max
750.411p(2)(b)	Property	D	Money laundering of proceeds from controlled substance offense or other proceeds involving $10,000 or more	10
750.411p(2)(c)	Property	E	Money laundering —transactions involving represented proceeds	5
750.411s(2)(a)	Person	G	Unlawful posting of message	2
750.411s(2)(b)	Person	E	Unlawful posting of message with aggravating circumstances	5
750.411t(2)(b)	Person	E	Hazing resulting in serious impairment	5
750.411t(2)(c)	Person	C	Hazing resulting in death	15

P.A.1927, No. 175, c. XVII, § 16t, added by P.A.1998, No. 317, Eff. Dec. 15, 1998. Amended by P.A.2000, No. 279, Eff. Oct. 1, 2000; P.A.2000, No. 371, Eff. April 1, 2001; P.A.2004, No. 112, Eff. Aug. 18, 2004.

777.16u. Application of chapter to Michigan Compiled Laws chapter 750, sections 750.413 to 750.421b; enumerated felonies

Sec. 16u. This chapter applies to the following felonies enumerated in chapter 750 of the Michigan Compiled Laws:

M.C.L.	Category	Class	Description	Stat Max
750.413	Property	E	Unlawful driving away of an automobile	5
750.414	Property	H	Unlawful use of an automobile	2
750.415(2)	Property	G	Motor vehicles— conceal/misrepresent identity with intent to mislead	4
750.415(5)	Property	G	Motor vehicles — buy/sell/exchange/give away paraphernalia capable of changing/misrepresenting identity	4
750.415(6)	Property	E	Motor vehicles— buy/receive/obtain a motor vehicle or motor vehicle part with intent to sell or dispose knowing the VIN has been removed or altered	10
750.417	Property	H	Motor vehicle— mortgaged— removal from state	4
750.418	Property	H	Removing a vehicle out of state without vendor's consent	4
750.420	Pub saf	H	Motor vehicle— equipping to release smoke/gas	4
750.421	Pub saf	H	Motor vehicle— designed for attack	5
750.421b	Pub saf	H	Hinder transport of farm/commercial products —subsequent offense	2

P.A.1927, No. 175, c. XVII, § 16u, added by P.A.1998, No. 317, Eff. Dec. 15, 1998. Amended by P.A.2000, No. 218, Eff. Oct. 1, 2000; P.A.2000, No. 279, Eff. Oct. 1, 2000.

777.16v. Application of chapter to Michigan Compiled Laws chapter 750, sections 750.422 to 750.443; enumerated felonies

Sec. 16v. This chapter applies to the following felonies enumerated in chapter 750 of the Michigan Compiled Laws:

M.C.L.	Category	Class	Description	Stat Max
750.422	Pub trst	C	Perjury committed in court —noncapital crime	15
	Pub trst	B	Perjury committed in court —capital crime	Life
750.423	Pub trst	E	Perjury by falsely swearing	15
750.424	Pub trst	C	Subornation of perjury	15
750.425	Pub trst	E	Inciting or procuring perjury but perjury not committed	5
750.430a	Person	D	Human cloning	10
750.436(2)(a)	Pub saf	C	Poisoning food, drink, medicine, or water supply	15
750.436(2)(b)	Property	B	Poisoning food, drink, medicine, or water supply causing property damage	20
750.436(2)(c)	Person	A	Poisoning food, drink, medicine, or water supply causing injury	25
750.436(2)(d)	Person	A	Poisoning food, drink, medicine, or water supply causing serious impairment	Life
750.436(3)(a)	Pub ord	F	False report of poisoning food, drink, medicine, or water supply	4
750.436(3)(b)	Pub ord	D	False report of poisoning food, drink, medicine, or water supply with prior conviction	10
750.439	Pub ord	G	Polygamy	4
750.440	Pub ord	G	Polygamy —knowingly entering a prohibited marriage	4
750.441	Pub ord	G	Teaching or advocating polygamy	4
750.442	Pub ord	G	Participating in prizefights	4
750.443	Pub ord	G	Prizefights —training	4

P.A.1927, No. 175, c. XVII, § 16v, added by P.A.1998, No. 317, Eff. Dec. 15, 1998. Amended by P.A.2000, No. 279, Eff. Oct. 1, 2000; P.A.2002, No. 123, Eff. April 22, 2002.

777.16w. Application of chapter to Michigan Compiled Laws chapter 750, sections 750.451 to 750.465a; enumerated felonies

Sec. 16w. This chapter applies to the following felonies enumerated in chapter 750 of the Michigan Compiled Laws:

M.C.L.	Category	Class	Description	Stat Max
750.451	Pub ord	G	Prostitution —various offenses —third or subsequent offense	2
750.452	Pub ord	E	Keeping a house of prostitution	5
750.455	Pub ord	G	Pandering	20
750.456	Person	B	Placing spouse into prostitution	20
750.457	Pub ord	G	Accepting earnings of a prostitute	20
750.458	Person	B	Prostitution —detaining female for debt	20

M.C.L.	Category	Class	Description	Stat Max
750.459	Person	B	Transporting a female for prostitution	20
750.462b(1)	Person	D	Human trafficking —forced labor through physical harm	10
750.462b(2)	Person	C	Human trafficking —forced labor through physical harm causing injury	15
750.462b(3)	Person	A	Human trafficking —forced labor through physical harm causing death	Life
750.462c(1)	Person	D	Human trafficking —forced labor through physical restraint	10
750.462c(2)	Person	C	Human trafficking —forced labor through physical restraint causing injury	15
750.462c(3)	Person	A	Human trafficking —forced labor through physical restraint causing death	Life
750.462d(1)	Person	D	Human trafficking —forced labor through abuse of legal process	10
750.462d(2)	Person	C	Human trafficking —forced labor through abuse of legal process causing injury	15
750.462d(3)	Person	A	Human trafficking —forced labor through abuse of legal process causing death	Life
750.462e(1)	Person	D	Human trafficking —forced labor through destruction of ID document	10
750.462e(2)	Person	C	Human trafficking —forced labor through destruction of ID document causing injury	15
750.462e(3)	Person	A	Human trafficking —forced labor through destruction of ID document causing death	Life
750.462f(1)	Person	D	Human trafficking —forced labor through blackmail	10
750.462f(2)	Person	C	Human trafficking —forced labor through blackmail causing injury	15
750.462f(3)	Person	A	Human trafficking —forced labor through blackmail causing death	Life
750.462g(1)	Person	B	Human trafficking —obtain minor for child sexual abusive activity	20
750.462h(2)	Person	D	Human trafficking —recruit minor for forced labor	10
750.462h(3)	Person	C	Human trafficking —recruit minor for forced labor causing injury	15
750.462h(4)	Person	A	Human trafficking —recruit minor for forced labor causing death	Life
750.462i	Person	A	Human trafficking —compound felony	Life
750.465a(1)(b)	Property	G	Operating audiovisual recording device in a theatrical facility —second offense	2
750.465a(1)(c)	Property	F	Operating audiovisual recording device in a theatrical facility —third or subsequent offense	4

P.A.1927, No. 175, c. XVII, § 16w, added by P.A.1998, No. 317, Eff. Dec. 15, 1998. Amended by P.A.2000, No. 279, Eff. Oct. 1, 2000; P.A.2004, No. 424, Imd. Eff. Dec. 15, 2004; P.A.2006, No. 156, Eff. Aug. 24, 2006.

777.16x. Application of chapter to Michigan Compiled Laws chapter 750, sections 750.478a to 750.512; enumerated felonies

Sec. 16x. This chapter applies to the following felonies enumerated in chapter 750 of the Michigan Compiled Laws:

M.C.L.	Category	Class	Description	Stat Max
750.478a(2)	Pub ord	H	Unauthorized process to obstruct a public officer or employee	2
750.478a(3)	Pub ord	G	Unauthorized process to obstruct a public officer or employee —subsequent offense	4
750.479(2)	Person	G	Assaulting or obstructing certain officials	2
750.479(3)	Person	G	Assaulting or obstructing certain officials causing injury	4
750.479(4)	Person	D	Assaulting or obstructing certain officials causing serious impairment	10
750.479(5)	Person	B	Assaulting or obstructing certain officials causing death	20
750.479a(2)	Pub saf	G	Fleeing and eluding —fourth degree	2
750.479a(3)	Pub saf	E	Fleeing and eluding —third degree	5
750.479a(4)	Person	D	Fleeing and eluding —second degree	10
750.479a(5)	Person	C	Fleeing and eluding —first degree	15
750.479b(1)	Person	F	Disarming peace officer —nonfirearm	4
750.479b(2)	Person	D	Disarming peace officer —firearm	10
750.480	Pub trst	F	Public officers —refusing to turn over books/money to successor	4
750.483a(2)(b)	Person	D	Withholding evidence, preventing report of crime, or retaliating for reporting crime punishable by more than 10 years	10
750.483a(4)(b)	Person	D	Interfering with police investigation by committing crime or threatening to kill or injure	10
750.483a(6)(a)	Pub ord	F	Tampering with evidence or offering false evidence	4
750.483a(6)(b)	Pub ord	D	Tampering with evidence or offering false evidence in case punishable by more than 10 years	10
750.488	Pub trst	H	Public officers —state official —retaining fees	2
750.490	Pub trst	H	Public money —safekeeping	2
750.491	Pub trst	H	Public records —removal/mutilation/destruction	2
750.492a(1)(a)	Pub trst	G	Medical record —intentional place false information —health care provider	4
750.492a(2)	Pub trst	G	Medical record —health care provider —altering to conceal injury/death	4
750.495a(2)	Person	F	Concealing objects in trees or wood products —causing injury	4
750.495a(3)	Person	C	Concealing objects in trees or wood products —causing death	15

M.C.L.	Category	Class	Description	Stat Max
750.498b(2)(a)	Person	E	Tampering with, taking, or removing marine safety device without authority causing serious impairment	5
750.498b(2)(b)	Person	C	Tampering with, taking, or removing marine safety device without authority causing death	15
750.502d	Pub saf	F	Unlawfully possessing or transporting anhydrous ammonia or tampering with containers	4
750.505	Pub ord	E	Common law offenses	5
750.508(2)(b)	Pub ord	G	Carrying or possessing a scanner in the commission of a crime	2
750.511	Person	A	Blocking or wrecking railroad track	Life
750.512	Property	E	Uncoupling railroad cars	10

P.A.1927, No. 175, c. XVII, § 16x, added by P.A.1998, No. 317, Eff. Dec. 15, 1998. Amended by P.A.2000, No. 279, Eff. Oct. 1, 2000; P.A.2000, No. 473, Eff. March 28, 2001; P.A.2002, No. 271, Eff. July 15, 2002; P.A.2002, No. 320, Eff. July 15, 2002; P.A. 2003, No. 313, Eff. April 1, 2004; P.A.2006, No. 40, Imd. Eff. March 2, 2006; P.A.2006, No. 234, Eff. July 1, 2006.

777.16y. Application of chapter to Michigan Compiled Laws chapter 750, sections 750.520b to 750.532; enumerated felonies

Sec. 16y. This chapter applies to the following felonies enumerated in chapter 750 of the Michigan Compiled Laws:

M.C.L.	Category	Class	Description	Stat Max
750.520b(2)	Person	A	First degree criminal sexual conduct	Life
750.520c	Person	C	Second degree criminal sexual conduct	15
750.520d	Person	B	Third degree criminal sexual conduct	15
750.520e	Person	G	Fourth degree criminal sexual conduct	2
750.520g(1)	Person	D	Assault with intent to commit sexual penetration	10
750.520g(2)	Person	E	Assault with intent to commit sexual contact	5
750.520n	Pub saf	G	Electronic monitoring device violation	2
750.528	Pub saf	F	Destroying dwelling house or other property during riot or unlawful assembly	4
750.528a	Pub saf	F	Civil disorders —firearms/explosives	4
750.529	Person	A	Armed robbery	Life
750.529a	Person	A	Carjacking	Life
750.530	Person	C	Unarmed robbery	15
750.531	Person	C	Bank robbery/safebreaking	Life
750.532	Person	H	Seduction	5

P.A.1927, No. 175, c. XVII, § 16y, added by P.A.1998, No. 317, Eff. Dec. 15, 1998. Amended by P.A.2000, No. 279, Eff. Oct. 1, 2000; P.A.2005, No. 304, Eff. April 15, 2006; P.A.2006, No. 166, Eff. Aug. 28, 2006; P.A.2006, No. 655, Imd. Eff. Jan. 9, 2007.

777.16z. Application of chapter to Michigan Compiled Laws chapter 750, sections 750.520b to 750.552c; enumerated felonies

Sec. 16z. This chapter applies to the following felonies enumerated in chapter 750 of the Michigan Compiled Laws:

M.C.L.	Category	Class	Description	Stat Max
750.520b(2)	Property	D	Receiving or concealing stolen property having a value of $20,000 or more or with prior convictions	10
750.535(3)	Property	E	Receiving or concealing stolen property having a value of $1,000 to $20,000 or with prior convictions	5
750.535(7)	Property	E	Receiving or concealing stolen motor vehicle	5
750.535a(2)	Pub ord	D	Operating a chop shop	10
750.535a(3)	Pub ord	D	Operating a chop shop, subsequent violation	10
750.535b	Pub saf	E	Stolen firearms or ammunition	10
750.539c	Pub ord	H	Eavesdropping	2
750.539d(3)(a)(*i*)	Pub ord	H	Installing, placing, or using eavesdropping device	2
750.539d(3)(a)(*ii*)	Pub ord	E	Installing, placing, or using eavesdropping device —subsequent offense	5
750.539d(3)(b)	Pub ord	E	Distributing, disseminating, or transmitting recording or image obtained by eavesdropping	5
750.539e	Pub ord	H	Divulging or using information obtained by eavesdropping	2
750.539f	Pub ord	H	Manufacture or possession of eavesdropping device	2
750.539j(2)(a)(*i*)	Pub ord	H	Lewd surveillance or capturing lewd image	2
750.539j(2)(a)(*ii*)	Pub ord	E	Lewd surveillance or capturing lewd image —subsequent offense	5
750.539j(2)(b)	Pub ord	E	Distributing, disseminating, or transmitting visual image obtained by surveillance	5
750.540(5)(a)	Pub ord	H	Damaging, destroying, using, or obstructing use of electronic medium of communication	2
750.540(5)(b)	Person	F	Damaging, destroying, using, or obstructing use of electronic medium of communication resulting in injury or death	4
750.540c(4)	Property	F	Telecommunication violation	4
750.540f(2)	Property	E	Knowingly publishing a communications access device with prior convictions	5
750.540g(1)(c)	Property	E	Diverting telecommunication services having a value of $1,000 to $20,000 or with prior convictions	5
750.540g(1)(d)	Property	D	Diverting telecommunications services having a value of $20,000 or more or with prior convictions	10
750.543f	Person	A	Terrorism without causing death	Life

M.C.L.	Category	Class	Description	Stat Max
750.543h(3)(a)	Pub ord	B	Hindering prosecution of terrorism —certain terrorist acts	20
750.543h(3)(b)	Pub ord	A	Hindering prosecution of terrorism —act of terrorism	Life
750.543k	Pub saf	B	Soliciting or providing material support for terrorism or terrorist acts	20
750.543m	Pub ord	B	Threat or false report of terrorism	20
750.543p	Pub saf	B	Use of internet or telecommunications to commit certain terrorist acts	20
750.543r	Pub saf	B	Possession of vulnerable target information with intent to commit certain terrorist acts	20
750.545	Pub ord	E	Misprision of treason	5
750.552b	Property	F	Trespassing on correctional facility property	4
750.552c	Pub saf	F	Trespass upon key facility	4

P.A.1927, No. 175, c. XVII, § 16z, added by P.A.1998, No. 317, Eff. Dec. 15, 1998. Amended by P.A.1999, No. 186, Eff. April 1, 2000; P.A.2000, No. 279, Eff. Oct. 1, 2000; P.A.2002, No. 122, Eff. April 22, 2002; P.A.2002, No. 271, Eff. July 15, 2002; P.A.2004, No. 2, Imd. Eff. Feb. 12, 2004; P.A.2004, No. 157, Imd. Eff. June 16, 2004; P.A.2006, No. 62, Eff. June 1, 2006; P.A.2006, No. 655, Imd. Eff. Jan. 9, 2007.

777.17. Application of chapter to Michigan Compiled Laws chapters 751 to 830

Sec. 17. This chapter applies to the following felonies enumerated in chapters 751 to 830 of the Michigan Compiled Laws as set forth in sections 17a to 17g of this chapter. [1]

P.A.1927, No. 175, c. XVII, § 17, added by P.A.1998, No. 317, Eff. Dec. 15, 1998. Amended by P.A.1999, No. 67, Eff. Aug. 1, 1999; P.A.2000, No. 178, Eff. Sept. 19, 2000; P.A.2000, No. 279, Eff. Oct. 1, 2000; P.A.2000, No. 300, Eff. Jan. 1, 2001; P.A.2001, No. 136, Eff. Feb. 1, 2002; P.A.2002, No. 28, Eff. April 1, 2002.

[1] M.C.L.A. §§ 777.17a to 777.17g.

777.17b. Application of chapter to Michigan Compiled Laws chapter 752, sections 752.272a to 752.543; enumerated felonies

Sec. 17b. This chapter applies to the following felonies enumerated in chapter 752 of the Michigan Compiled Laws:

M.C.L.	Category	Class	Description	Stat Max
752.272a(2)(c)	Pub saf	F	Sale or distribution of nitrous oxide device —2 or more prior convictions	4
752.365(3)	Pub ord	G	Obscenity —subsequent offense	2
752.541	Pub saf	D	Riot	10
752.542	Pub saf	D	Incitement to riot	10
752.542a	Pub saf	D	Riot in state correctional facilities	10
752.543	Pub saf	G	Unlawful assembly	5

P.A.1927, No. 175, c. XVII, § 17b, added by P.A.2002, No. 28, Eff. April 1, 2002.

777.17c. Application of chapter to Michigan Compiled Laws chapter 752, section 752.797; enumerated felonies

Sec. 17c. (1) This chapter applies to the following felonies enumerated in chapter 752 of the Michigan Compiled Laws:

M.C.L.	Category	Class	Description	Stat Max
752.797(1)(c)	Property	E	Computer fraud —2 prior convictions or value of $1,000 to $20,000	5
752.797(1)(d)	Property	D	Computer fraud —3 or more prior convictions or value of $20,000 or more	10
752.797(2)(a)	Property	E	Unlawfully accessing computer, computer system, or computer program	5
752.797(2)(b)	Property	D	Unlawfully accessing computer, computer system, or computer program, with prior conviction	10
752.797(3)(b)	Variable	G	Using computer to commit crime punishable by a maximum term of imprisonment of more than 1 year but less than 2 years	2
752.797(3)(c)	Variable	F	Using computer to commit crime punishable by a maximum term of imprisonment of at least 2 years but less than 4 years	4
752.797(3)(d)	Variable	D	Using computer to commit crime punishable by a maximum term of imprisonment of at least 4 years but less than 10 years	7
752.797(3)(e)	Variable	D	Using computer to commit crime punishable by a maximum term of imprisonment of at least 10 years but less than 20 years	10
752.797(3)(f)	Variable	B	Using computer to commit crime punishable by a maximum term of imprisonment of at least 20 years or for life	20

(2) For a violation of section 797(3) of 1979 PA 53, MCL 752.797, determine the offense category, offense variable level, and prior record variable level based on the underlying offense.

P.A.1927, No. 175, c. XVII, § 17c, added by P.A.2002, No. 28, Eff. April 1, 2002.

777.17d. Application of chapter to Michigan Compiled Laws chapter 752, sections 752.802 to 752.1054; enumerated felonies

Sec. 17d. This chapter applies to the following felonies enumerated in chapter 752 of the Michigan Compiled Laws:

M.C.L.	Category	Class	Description	Stat Max
752.802	Property	H	Vending machines — manufacture/sale of slugs	5
752.811	Property	H	Breaking and entering a coin operated device	3
752.861	Person	G	Careless discharge of firearm causing injury or death	2
752.881	Person	G	Reckless use of bow and arrow resulting in injury or death	2
752.1003	Property	F	Health care fraud — false claim/state, unnecessary, conceal information	4
752.1004	Property	F	Health care fraud — kickbacks/referral fees	4
752.1005	Property	H	Health care fraud — conspiracy	10
752.1006	Property	D	Health care fraud —subsequent offense	20
752.1054(2)	Property	G	Copying audio/video recordings for gain	5

P.A.1927, No. 175, c. XVII, § 17d, added by P.A.2002, No. 28, Eff. April 1, 2002.

777.17f. Application of chapter to Michigan Compiled Laws chapters 760 to 799; enumerated felonies

Sec. 17f. This chapter applies to the following felonies enumerated in chapters 760 to 799 of the Michigan Compiled Laws:

M.C.L.	Category	Class	Description	Stat Max
764.1e	Pub trst	C	Peace officer —false statement in a complaint	15
767.4a	Pub trst	F	Disclosing or possessing grand jury information	4
767A.9(1)(a)	Pub trst	C	Perjury committed in prosecutor's investigative hearing —noncapital crime	15
767A.9(1)(b)	Pub trst	B	Perjury committed in prosecutor's investigative hearing —capital crime	Life
791.236(17)	Pub ord	F	Failure to provide correct notice of proposed domicile by sex offender	4

P.A.1927, No. 175, c. XVII, § 17f, added by P.A.2002, No. 28, Eff. April 1, 2002. Amended by P.A.2006, No. 404, Eff. Dec. 1, 2006.

777.17g. Application of chapter to Michigan Compiled Laws chapters 800 to 830; enumerated felonies

Sec. 17g. This chapter applies to the following felonies enumerated in chapters 800 to 830 of the Michigan Compiled Laws:

M.C.L.	Category	Class	Description	Stat Max
800.281(1)	Pub saf	H	Furnishing prisoner with contraband	5
800.281(2)	Pub saf	H	Furnishing prisoner with contraband outside	5
800.281(3)	Pub saf	H	Bringing contraband into prisons	5
800.281(4)	Pub saf	E	Prisoner possessing contraband	5
800.283(1)	Pub saf	E	Furnishing weapon to prisoner in prison	5
800.283(2)	Pub saf	E	Prisons —knowledge of a weapon in a correctional facility	5
800.283(3)	Pub saf	E	Bringing weapon into prison	5
800.283(4)	Pub saf	E	Prisoner possessing weapon	5
800.283a	Pub saf	E	Furnishing cell phone to prisoner	5
801.262(1)(a)	Pub saf	E	Bringing weapon into jail	5
801.262(1)(b)	Pub saf	E	Furnishing weapon to prisoner in jail	5
801.262(2)	Pub saf	E	Prisoner in jail possessing weapon	5
801.263(1)	Pub saf	H	Furnishing contraband to prisoner in jail	5
801.263(2)	Pub saf	H	Prisoner in jail possessing contraband	5

P.A.1927, No. 175, c. XVII, § 17g, added by P.A.2002, No. 28, Eff. April 1, 2002. Amended by P.A.2006, No. 541, Imd. Eff. Dec. 29, 2006.

777.18. Application of chapter to Michigan Compiled Laws chapters 333 and 750; enumerated felonies

Sec. 18. This chapter applies to the following felonies:

M.C.L.	Category	Description	Stat Max
333.7410	CS	Controlled substance offense or offense involving GBL on or near school property or library	Variable
333.7413(2) or (3)	Pub trst	Subsequent controlled substance violations	Variable
333.7416(1)(a)	CS	Recruiting or inducing a minor to commit a controlled substance felony	Variable
750.157a(a)	Pub saf	Conspiracy	Variable
750.157c	Person	Inducing minor to commit a felony	Variable
750.188	Pub ord	Voluntarily suffering prisoner to escape	Variable
750.237a	Pub saf	Felony committed in a weapon-free school zone	Variable
750.367a	Property	Larceny of rationed goods	Variable

P.A.1927, No. 175, c. XVII, § 18, added by P.A.1998, No. 317, Eff. Dec. 15, 1998. Amended by P.A.2000, No. 279, Eff. Oct. 1, 2000; P.A.2000, No. 304, Eff. Jan. 1, 2001; P.A.2006, No. 553, Eff. March 30, 2007.

777.19. Application of chapter to attempted offenses; attempt to commit class H offense; offense categories for attempted offenses

Sec. 19. (1) This chapter applies to an attempt to commit an offense enumerated in this part if the attempted violation is a felony. This chapter does not apply to an attempt to commit a class H offense enumerated in this part.

(2) For an attempt to commit an offense enumerated in this part, the offense category is the same as the attempted offense.

(3) For an attempt to commit an offense enumerated in this part, the offense class is as follows:

(a) Class E if the attempted offense is in class A, B, C, or D.

(b) Class H if the attempted offense is in class E, F, or G.

P.A.1927, No. 175, c. XVII, § 19, added by P.A.1998, No. 317, Eff. Dec. 15, 1998. Amended by P.A.2000, No. 279, Eff. Oct. 1, 2000.

PART 3. SCORING INSTRUCTIONS FOR SENTENCING GUIDELINES

777.21. Determination of recommended minimum sentence range for offense

Sec. 21. (1) Except as otherwise provided in this section, for an offense enumerated in part 2 [1] of this chapter, determine the recommended minimum sentence range as follows:

(a) Find the offense category for the offense from part 2 of this chapter. From section 22 [2] of this chapter, determine the offense variables to be scored for that offense category and score only those offense variables for the offender as provided in part 4 [3] of this chapter. Total those points to determine the offender's offense variable level.

(b) Score all prior record variables for the offender as provided in part 5 [4] of this chapter. Total those points to determine the offender's prior record variable level.

(c) Find the offense class for the offense from part 2 of this chapter. Using the sentencing grid for that offense class in part 6 [5] of this chapter, determine the recommended minimum sentence range from the intersection of the offender's offense variable level and prior record variable level. The recommended minimum sentence within a sentencing grid is shown as a range of months or life.

(2) If the defendant was convicted of multiple offenses, subject to section 14 [6] of chapter XI, score each offense as provided in this part.

(3) If the offender is being sentenced under section 10, 11, or 12 [7] of chapter IX, determine the offense category, offense class, offense variable level, and prior record variable level based on the underlying offense. To determine the recommended minimum sentence range, increase the upper limit of the recommended minimum sentence range determined under part 6 for the underlying offense as follows:

(a) If the offender is being sentenced for a second felony, 25%.

(b) If the offender is being sentenced for a third felony, 50%.

(c) If the offender is being sentenced for a fourth or subsequent felony, 100%.

(4) If the offender is being sentenced for a violation described in section 18 [8] of this chapter, both of the following apply:

(a) Determine the offense variable level by scoring the offense variables for the underlying offense and any additional offense variables for the offense category indicated in section 18 of this chapter.

(b) Determine the offense class based on the underlying offense. If there are multiple underlying felony offenses, the offense class is the same as that of the underlying felony offense with the highest crime class. If there are multiple underlying offenses but only 1 is a felony, the offense class is the same as that of the underlying felony offense. If no underlying offense is a felony, the offense class is G.

(5) If the offender is being sentenced for an attempted felony described in section 19 [9] of this chapter, determine the offense variable level and prior record variable level based on the underlying attempted offense.

P.A.1927, No. 175, c. XVII, § 21, added by P.A.1998, No. 317, Eff. Dec. 15, 1998. Amended by P.A.2000, No. 279, Eff. Oct. 1, 2000; P.A.2006, No. 655, Imd. Eff. Jan. 9, 2007.

[1] M.C.L.A. § 777.11 et seq.

[2] M.C.L.A. § 777.22.

[3] M.C.L.A. § 777.31 et seq.

[4] M.C.L.A. § 777.50 et seq.

[5] M.C.L.A. § 777.61 et seq.

[6] M.C.L.A. § 771.14.

[7] M.C.L.A. §§ 769.10, 769.11, or 769.12.

[8] M.C.L.A. § 777.18.

[9] M.C.L.A. § 777.19.

777.22. Scoring of offense variables

Sec. 22. (1) For all crimes against a person, score offense variables 1, 2, 3, 4, 7, 8, 9, 10, 11, 12, 13, 14, 19, and 20. Score offense variables 5 and 6 for homicide, attempted homicide, conspiracy or solicitation to commit a homicide, or assault with intent to commit murder. Score offense variable 16 under this subsection for a violation or attempted violation of section 110a of the Michigan penal code, 1931 PA 328, MCL 750.110a. Score offense variables 17 and 18 if the offense or attempted offense involves the operation of a vehicle, vessel, ORV, snowmobile, aircraft, or locomotive.

(2) For all crimes against property, score offense variables 1, 2, 3, 4, 9, 10, 12, 13, 14, 16, 19, and 20.

(3) For all crimes involving a controlled substance, score offense variables 1, 2, 3, 12, 13, 14, 15, 19, and 20.

(4) For all crimes against public order and all crimes against public trust, score offense variables 1, 3, 4, 9, 10, 12, 13, 14, 16, 19, and 20.

(5) For all crimes against public safety, score offense variables 1, 3, 4, 9, 10, 12, 13, 14, 16, 19, and 20. Score offense variable 18 if the offense or attempted offense involves the operation of a vehicle, vessel, ORV, snowmobile, aircraft, or locomotive.

P.A.1927, No. 175, c. XVII, § 22, added by P.A.1998, No. 317, Eff. Dec. 15, 1998. Amended by P.A.2000, No. 279, Eff. Oct. 1, 2000; P.A.2002, No. 143, Eff. April 22, 2002; P.A.2003, No. 134, Eff. Sept. 30, 2003.

PART 4. OFFENSE VARIABLES

777.31. Scoring offense variable 1, aggravated use of weapon

Sec. 31. (1) Offense variable 1 is aggravated use of a weapon. Score offense variable 1 by determining which of the following apply and by assigning the number of points attributable to the one that has the highest number of points:

(a) A firearm was discharged at or toward a human being or a victim was cut or stabbed with a knife or other cutting or stabbing weapon	25 points
(b) The victim was subjected or exposed to a harmful biological substance, harmful biological device, harmful chemical substance, harmful chemical device, harmful radioactive material, harmful radioactive device, incendiary device, or explosive device	20 points
(c) A firearm was pointed at or toward a victim or the victim had a reasonable apprehension of an immediate battery when threatened with a knife or other cutting or stabbing weapon	15 points
(d) The victim was touched by any other type of weapon	10 points
(e) A weapon was displayed or implied	5 points
(f) No aggravated use of a weapon occurred	0 points

(2) All of the following apply to scoring offense variable 1:

(a) Count each person who was placed in danger of injury or loss of life as a victim.

(b) In multiple offender cases, if 1 offender is assessed points for the presence or use of a weapon, all offenders shall be assessed the same number of points.

(c) Score 5 points if an offender used an object to suggest the presence of a weapon.

(d) Score 5 points if an offender used a chemical irritant, chemical irritant device, smoke device, or imitation harmful substance or device.

(e) Do not score 5 points if the conviction offense is a violation of section 82 or 529 of the Michigan penal code, 1931 PA 328, MCL 750.82 and 750.529.

(3) As used in this section:

(a) "Chemical irritant", "chemical irritant device", "harmful biological substance", " harmful biological device", "harmful chemical substance", "harmful chemical device", " harmful radioactive material", "harmful radioactive device", and "imitation harmful substance or device" mean those terms as defined in section 200h of the Michigan penal code, 1931 PA 328, MCL 750.200h.

(b) "Incendiary device" includes gasoline or any other flammable substance, a blowtorch, fire bomb, Molotov cocktail, or other similar device.

P.A.1927, No. 175, c. XVII, § 31, added by P.A.1998, No. 317, Eff. Dec. 15, 1998. Amended by P.A.1999, No. 227, Imd. Eff. Dec. 28, 1999; P.A.2001, No. 136, Imd. Eff. Oct. 23, 2001; P.A.2002, No. 137, Eff. April 22, 2002.

777.32. Scoring offense variable 2, lethal potential of weapon possessed or used

Sec. 32. (1) Offense variable 2 is lethal potential of the weapon possessed or used. Score offense variable 2 by determining which of the following apply and by assigning the number of points attributable to the one that has the highest number of points:

(a) The offender possessed or used a harmful biological substance, harmful biological device, harmful chemical substance, harmful chemical device, harmful radioactive material, or harmful radioactive device .... 15 points
(b) The offender possessed or used an incendiary device, an explosive device, or a fully automatic weapon .... 15 points
(c) The offender possessed or used a short-barreled rifle or a short-barreled shotgun .... 10 points
(d) The offender possessed or used a pistol, rifle, shotgun, or knife or other cutting or stabbing weapon.... 5 points
(e) The offender possessed or used any other potentially lethal weapon .... 1 point
(f) The offender possessed or used no weapon .... 0 points

(2) In multiple offender cases, if 1 offender is assessed points for possessing a weapon, all offenders shall be assessed the same number of points.

(3) As used in this section:

(a) "Harmful biological substance", "harmful biological device", "harmful chemical substance", "harmful chemical device", "harmful radioactive material", and "harmful radioactive device" mean those terms as defined in section 200h of the Michigan penal code, 1931 PA 328, MCL 750.200h.

(b) "Fully automatic weapon" means a firearm employing gas pressure or force of recoil or other means to eject an empty cartridge from the firearm after a shot, and to load and fire the next cartridge from the magazine, without renewed pressure on the trigger for each successive shot.

(c) "Pistol", "rifle", or " shotgun" includes a revolver, semi-automatic pistol, rifle, shotgun, combination rifle and shotgun, or other firearm manufactured in or after 1898 that fires fixed ammunition, but does not include a fully automatic weapon or short-barreled shotgun or short-barreled rifle.

(d) "Incendiary device" includes gasoline or any other flammable substance, a blowtorch, fire bomb, Molotov cocktail, or other similar device.

P.A.1927, No. 175, c. XVII, § 32, added by P.A.1998, No. 317, Eff. Dec. 15, 1998. Amended by P.A.2001, No. 136, Imd. Eff. Oct. 23, 2001.

777.33. Scoring offense variable 3, physical injury to victim

Sec. 33. (1) Offense variable 3 is physical injury to a victim. Score offense variable 3 by determining which of the following apply and by assigning the number of points attributable to the one that has the highest number of points:

(a) A victim was killed............... 100 points
(b) A victim was killed................ 50 points
(c) Life threatening or permanent incapacitating injury occurred to a victim .... 25 points
(d) Bodily injury requiring medical treatment occurred to a victim .... 10 points
(e) Bodily injury not requiring medical treatment occurred to a victim .... 5 points
(f) No physical injury occurred to a victim .... 0 points

(2) All of the following apply to scoring offense variable 3:

(a) In multiple offender cases, if 1 offender is assessed points for death or physical injury, all offenders shall be assessed the same number of points.

(b) Score 100 points if death results from the commission of a crime and homicide is not the sentencing offense.

(c) Score 50 points if death results from the commission of a crime and the offense or attempted offense involves the operation of a vehicle, vessel, ORV, snowmobile, aircraft, or locomotive and any of the following apply:

(*i*) The offender was under the influence of or visibly impaired by the use of alcoholic liquor, a controlled substance, or a combination of alcoholic liquor and a controlled substance.

(*ii*) The offender had an alcohol content of 0.08 grams or more per 100 milliliters of blood, per 210 liters of breath, or per 67 milliliters of urine or, beginning October 1, 2013, the offender had an alcohol content of 0.10 grams or more per 100 milliliters of blood, per 210 liters of breath, or per 67 milliliters of urine.

(*iii*) The offender's body contained any amount of a controlled substance listed in schedule 1 under section 7212 of the public health code, 1978 PA 368, MCL 333.7212, or a rule promulgated under that section, or a controlled substance described in section 7214(a)(*iv*) of the public health code, 1978 PA 368, MCL 333.7214.

(d) Do not score 5 points if bodily injury is an element of the sentencing offense.

(3) As used in this section, "requiring medical treatment" refers to the necessity for treatment and not the victim's success in obtaining treatment.

P.A.1927, No. 175, c. XVII, § 33, added by P.A.1998, No. 317, Eff. Dec. 15, 1998. Amended by P.A.2000, No. 279, Eff. Oct. 1, 2000; P.A.2003, No. 134, Eff. Sept. 30, 2003.

777.34. Scoring offense variable 4, psychological injury to victim

Sec. 34. (1) Offense variable 4 is psychological injury to a victim. Score offense variable 4 by determining which of the following apply and by assigning the number of points attributable to the one that has the highest number of points:

(a) Serious psychological injury requiring professional treatment occurred to a victim .... 10 points

(b) No serious psychological injury requiring professional treatment occurred to a victim .... 0 points

(2) Score 10 points if the serious psychological injury may require professional treatment. In making this determination, the fact that treatment has not been sought is not conclusive.

P.A.1927, No. 175, c. XVII, § 34, added by P.A.1998, No. 317, Eff. Dec. 15, 1998.

777.35. Scoring offense variable 5, psychological injury to member of victim's family

Sec. 35. (1) Offense variable 5 is psychological injury to a member of a victim's family. Score offense variable 5 by determining which of the following apply and by assigning the number of points attributable to the one that has the highest number of points:

(a) Serious psychological injury requiring professional treatment occurred to a victim's family .... 15 points

(b) No serious psychological injury requiring professional treatment occurred to a victim's family .... 0 points

(2) Score 15 points if the serious psychological injury to the victim's family may require professional treatment. In making this determination, the fact that treatment has not been sought is not conclusive.

P.A.1927, No. 175, c. XVII, § 35, added by P.A.1998, No. 317, Eff. Dec. 15, 1998. Amended by P.A.2000, No. 279, Eff. Oct. 1, 2000.

777.36. Scoring offense variable 6, offender's intent to kill or injure another individual

Sec. 36. (1) Offense variable 6 is the offender's intent to kill or injure another individual. Score offense variable 6 by determining which of the following apply and by assigning the number of points attributable to the one that has the highest number of points:

(a) The offender had premeditated intent to kill or the killing was committed while committing or attempting to commit arson, criminal sexual conduct in the first or third degree, child abuse in the first degree, a major controlled substance offense, robbery, breaking and entering of a dwelling, home invasion in the first or second degree, larceny of any kind, extortion, or kidnapping or the killing was the murder of a peace officer or a corrections officer .... 50 points

(b) The offender had unpremeditated intent to kill, the intent to do great bodily harm, or created a very high risk of death or great bodily harm knowing that death or great bodily harm was the probable result.... 25 points

(c) The offender had intent to injure or the killing was committed in an extreme emotional state caused by an adequate provocation and before a reasonable amount of time elapsed for the offender to calm or there was gross negligence amounting to an unreasonable disregard for life .... 10 points

(d) The offender had no intent to kill or injure........................... 0 points

(2) All of the following apply to scoring offense variable 6.

(a) The sentencing judge shall score this variable consistent with a jury verdict unless the judge has information that was not presented to the jury.

(b) Score 10 points if a killing is intentional within the definition of second degree murder or voluntary manslaughter, but the death occurred in a combative situation or in response to victimization of the offender by the decedent.

P.A.1927, No. 175, c. XVII, § 36, added by P.A.1998, No. 317, Eff. Dec. 15, 1998.

777.37. Scoring offense variable 7, aggravated physical abuse

Sec. 37. (1) Offense variable 7 is aggravated physical abuse. Score offense variable 7 by determining which of the following apply and by assigning the number of points attributable to the one that has the highest number of points:

(a) A victim was treated with sadism, torture, or excessive brutality or conduct designed to substantially increase the fear and anxiety a victim suffered during the offense .... 50 points

(b) No victim was treated with sadism, torture, or excessive brutality or conduct designed to substantially increase the fear and anxiety a victim suffered during the offense .... 0 points

(2) Count each person who was placed in danger of injury or loss of life as a victim.

(3) As used in this section, "sadism" means conduct that subjects a victim to extreme or prolonged pain or humiliation and is inflicted to produce suffering or for the offender's gratification.

P.A.1927, No. 175, c. XVII, § 37, added by P.A.1998, No. 317, Eff. Dec. 15, 1998. Amended by P.A.2002, No. 137, Eff. April 22, 2002.

777.38. Scoring offense variable 8, victim asportation or captivity

Sec. 38. (1) Offense variable 8 is victim asportation or captivity. Score offense variable 8 by determining which of the following apply and by assigning the number of points attributable to the one that has the highest number of points:

(a) A victim was asported to another place of greater danger or to a situation of greater danger or was held captive beyond the time necessary to commit the offense.............. 15 points

(b) No victim was asported or held captive.................................. 0 points

(2) All of the following apply to scoring offense variable 8:

(a) Count each person who was placed in danger of injury or loss of life as a victim.

(b) Score 0 points if the sentencing offense is kidnapping.

P.A.1927, No. 175, c. XVII, § 38, added by P.A.1998, No. 317, Eff. Dec. 15, 1998.

777.39. Scoring of offense variable 9, number of victims

Sec. 39. (1) Offense variable 9 is number of victims. Score offense variable 9 by determining which of the following apply and by assigning the number of points attributable to the one that has the highest number of points:

(a) Multiple deaths occurred .... 100 points

(b) There were 10 or more victims who were placed in danger of physical injury or death, or 20 or more victims who were placed in danger of property loss .... 25 points

(c) There were 2 to 9 victims who were placed in danger of physical injury or death, or 4 to 19 victims who were placed in danger of property loss .... 10 points

(d) There were fewer than 2 victims who were placed in danger of physical injury or death, or fewer than 4 victims who were placed in danger of property loss .... 0 points

(2) All of the following apply to scoring offense variable 9:

(a) Count each person who was placed in danger of physical injury or loss of life or property as a victim.

(b) Score 100 points only in homicide cases.

P.A.1927, No. 175, c. XVII, § 39, added by P.A.1998, No. 317, Eff. Dec. 15, 1998. Amended by P.A.2006, No. 548, Eff. March 30, 2007.

777.40. Scoring offense variable 10, exploitation of vulnerable victim

Sec. 40. (1) Offense variable 10 is exploitation of a vulnerable victim. Score offense variable 10 by determining which of the following apply and by assigning the number of points attributable to the one that has the highest number of points:

(a) Predatory conduct was involved .... 15 points

(b) The offender exploited a victim's physical disability, mental disability, youth or agedness, or a domestic relationship, or the offender abused his or her authority status.... 10 points

(c) The offender exploited a victim by his or her difference in size or strength, or both, or exploited a victim who was intoxicated, under the influence of drugs, asleep, or unconscious .... 5 points

(d) The offender did not exploit a victim's vulnerability.................. 0 points

(2) The mere existence of 1 or more factors described in subsection (1) does not automatically equate with victim vulnerability.

(3) As used in this section:

(a) "Predatory conduct" means preoffense conduct directed at a victim for the primary purpose of victimization.

(b) "Exploit" means to manipulate a victim for selfish or unethical purposes.

(c) "Vulnerability" means the readily apparent susceptibility of a victim to injury, physical restraint, persuasion, or temptation.

(d) "Abuse of authority status" means a victim was exploited out of fear or deference to an authority figure, including, but not limited to, a parent, physician, or teacher.

P.A.1927, No. 175, c. XVII, § 40, added by P.A.1998, No. 317, Eff. Dec. 15, 1998.

777.41. Scoring offense variable 11, criminal sexual penetration

Sec. 41. (1) Offense variable 11 is criminal sexual penetration. Score offense variable 11 by determining which of the following apply and by assigning the number of points attributable to the one that has the highest number of points:

(a) Two or more criminal sexual penetrations occurred .... 50 points

(b) One criminal sexual penetration occurred .... 25 points

(c) No criminal sexual penetration occurred .... 0 points

(2) All of the following apply to scoring offense variable 11:

(a) Score all sexual penetrations of the victim by the offender arising out of the sentencing offense.

(b) Multiple sexual penetrations of the victim by the offender extending beyond the sentencing offense may be scored in offense variables 12 or 13.

(c) Do not score points for the 1 penetration that forms the basis of a first- or third-degree criminal sexual conduct offense.

P.A.1927, No. 175, c. XVII, § 41, added by P.A.1998, No. 317, Eff. Dec. 15, 1998.

777.42. Scoring offense variable 12, contemporaneous felonious criminal acts

Sec. 42. (1) Offense variable 12 is contemporaneous felonious criminal acts. Score offense variable 12 by determining which of the following apply and by assigning the number of points attributable to the one that has the highest number of points:

(a) Three or more contemporaneous felonious criminal acts involving crimes against a person were committed .... 25 points

(b) Two contemporaneous felonious criminal acts involving crimes against a person were committed .... 10 points

(c) Three or more contemporaneous felonious criminal acts involving other crimes were committed .... 10 points

(d) One contemporaneous felonious criminal act involving a crime against a person was committed .... 5 points

(e) Two contemporaneous felonious criminal acts involving other crimes were committed .... 5 points

(f) One contemporaneous felonious criminal act involving any other crime was committed .... 1 point

(g) No contemporaneous felonious criminal acts were committed .... 0 points

(2) All of the following apply to scoring offense variable 12:

(a) A felonious criminal act is contemporaneous if both of the following circumstances exist:

(*i*) The act occurred within 24 hours of the sentencing offense.

(*ii*) The act has not and will not result in a separate conviction.

(b) A violation of section 227b of the Michigan penal code, 1931 PA 328, MCL 750.227b, should not be considered for scoring this variable.

(c) Do not score conduct scored in offense variable 11.

P.A.1927, No. 175, c. XVII, § 42, added by P.A.1998, No. 317, Eff. Dec. 15, 1998.

777.43. Scoring offense variable 13, continuing pattern of criminal behavior

Sec. 43. (1) Offense variable 13 is continuing pattern of criminal behavior. Score offense variable 13 by determining which of the following apply and by assigning the number of points attributable to the one that has the highest number of points:

(a) The offense was part of a pattern of felonious criminal activity involving 3 or more sexual penetrations against a person or persons less than 13 years of age 50 points

(b) The offense was part of a pattern of felonious criminal activity involving 3 or more crimes against a person .... 25 points

(c) The offense was part of a pattern of felonious criminal activity involving a combination of 3 or more crimes against a person or property or a violation of section 7401(2)(a)(*i*) to (*iii*) or section 7403(2)(a)(*i*) to (*iii*)[1] .... 10 points

(d) The offense was part of a pattern of felonious criminal activity directly related to membership in an organized criminal group ..... 10 points

(e) The offense was part of a pattern of felonious criminal activity involving a combination of 3 or more violations of section 7401(2)(a)(*i*) to (*iii*) or section 7403(2)(a)(*i*) to (*iii*)............. 10 points

(f) The offense was part of a pattern of felonious criminal activity involving 3 or more crimes against property........................ 5 points

(g) No pattern of felonious criminal activity existed................. 0 points

(2) All of the following apply to scoring offense variable 13:

(a) For determining the appropriate points under this variable, all crimes within a 5–year period, including the sentencing offense, shall be counted regardless of whether the offense resulted in a conviction.

(b) The presence or absence of multiple offenders, the age of the offenders, or the degree of sophistication of the organized criminal group is not as important as the fact of the group's existence, which may be reasonably inferred from the facts surrounding the sentencing offense.

(c) Except for offenses related to membership in an organized criminal group, do not score conduct scored in offense variable 11 or 12.

(d) Score 50 points only if the sentencing offense is first degree criminal sexual conduct.

(e) Do not count more than 1 controlled substance offense arising out of the criminal episode for which the person is being sentenced.

(f) Do not count more than 1 crime involving the same controlled substance. For example, do not count conspiracy and a substantive offense involving the same amount of controlled substances or possession and delivery of the same amount of controlled substances.

P.A.1927, No. 175, c. XVII, § 43, added by P.A.1998, No. 317, Eff. Dec. 15, 1998. Amended by P.A.1999, No. 227, Imd. Eff. Dec. 28, 1999; P.A.2000, No. 279, Eff. Oct. 1, 2000; P.A.2002, No. 666, Eff. March 1, 2003.

[1] M.C.L.A. §§ 333.7401 or 333.7403.

777.44. Scoring offense variable 14, offender's role

Sec. 44. (1) Offense variable 14 is the offender's role. Score offense variable 14 by determining which of the following apply and by assigning the number of points attributable to the one that has the highest number of points:

(a) The offender was a leader in a multiple offender situation .... 10 points

(b) The offender was not a leader in a multiple offender situation .... 0 points

(2) All of the following apply to scoring offense variable 14:

(a) The entire criminal transaction should be considered when scoring this variable.

(b) If 3 or more offenders were involved, more than 1 offender may be determined to have been a leader.

P.A.1927, No. 175, c. XVII, § 44, added by P.A.1998, No. 317, Eff. Dec. 15, 1998.

777.45. Scoring offense variable 15, aggravated controlled substance offenses

Sec. 45. (1) Offense variable 15 is aggravated controlled substance offenses. Score offense variable 15 by determining which of the following apply and by assigning the number of points attributable to the one that has the highest number of points:

(a) The offense involved the manufacture, creation, delivery, possession, or possession with intent to manufacture, create, or deliver of 1, 000 or more grams of any mixture containing a controlled substance classified in schedule 1 or 2 that is a narcotic drug or a drug described in section 7214(a)(*iv*)[1] .... 100 points

(b) The offense involved the manufacture, creation, delivery, possession, or possession with intent to manufacture, create, or deliver of 450 grams or more but less than 1,000 grams of any mixture containing a controlled substance classified in schedule 1 or 2 that is a narcotic drug or a drug described in section 7214(a)(*iv*)..................... 75 points

(c) The offense involved the manufacture, creation, delivery, possession, or possession with intent to manufacture, create, or deliver of 50 or more grams but less than 450 grams of any mixture containing a controlled substance classified in schedule 1 or 2 that is a narcotic drug or a drug described in section 7214(a)(*iv*) .... 50 points

(d) The offense involved the sale or delivery of a controlled substance other than marihuana or a mixture containing a controlled substance other than marihuana by the offender who was 18 years of age or older to a minor who was 3 or more years younger than the offender .... 25 points

(e) The offense involved the sale, delivery, or possession with intent to sell or deliver 45 kilograms or more of marihuana or 200 or more of marihuana plants .... 10 points

(f) The offense is a violation of section 7401(2)(a)(*i*) to (*iii*)[2] pertaining to a controlled substance classified in schedule 1 or 2 that is a narcotic drug or a drug described in section 7214(a)(*iv*) and was committed in a minor's abode, settled home, or domicile, regardless of whether the minor was present .... 10 points

(g) The offense involved the delivery or possession with intent to deliver marihuana or any other controlled substance or a counterfeit controlled substance or possession of controlled substances or counterfeit controlled substances having a value or under such circumstances as to indicate trafficking .... 5 points

(h) The offense was not an offense described in subdivisions (a) through (g) .... 0 points

(2) As used in this section:

(a) "Deliver" means the actual or constructive transfer of a controlled substance from 1 individual to another regardless of remuneration.

(b) "Minor" means an individual 17 years of age or less.

(c) "Trafficking" means the sale or delivery of controlled substances or counterfeit controlled substances on a continuing basis to 1 or more other individuals for further distribution.

P.A.1927, No. 175, c. XVII, § 45, added by P.A.1998, No. 317, Eff. Dec. 15, 1998. Amended by P.A.2002, No. 666, Eff. March 1, 2003.

[1] M.C.L.A. § 333.7214.

[2] M.C.L.A. § 333.7401.

777.46. Scoring offense variable 16, property obtained, damaged, lost, or destroyed

Sec. 46. (1) Offense variable 16 is property obtained, damaged, lost, or destroyed. Score offense variable 16 by determining which of the following apply and by assigning the number of points attributable to the one that has the highest number of points:

(a) Wanton or malicious damage occurred beyond that necessary to commit the crime for which the offender is not charged and will not be charged .... 10 points

(b) The property had a value of more than $20,000.00 or had significant historical, social, or sentimental value .... 10 points

(c) The property had a value of $1,000.00 or more but not more than $20,000.00 .... 5 points

(d) The property had a value of $200.00 or more but not more than $1,000.00 .... 1 point

(e) No property was obtained, damaged, lost, or destroyed or the property had a value of less than $200.00. .... 0 points

(2) All of the following apply to scoring offense variable 16:

(a) In multiple offender or victim cases, the appropriate points may be determined by adding together the aggregate value of the property involved, including property involved in uncharged offenses or charges dismissed under a plea agreement.

(b) In cases in which the property was obtained unlawfully, lost to the lawful owner, or destroyed, use the value of the property in scoring this variable. If the property was damaged, use the monetary amount appropriate to restore the property to pre-offense condition in scoring this variable.

(c) The amount of money or property involved in admitted but uncharged offenses or in charges that have been dismissed under a plea agreement may be considered.

P.A.1927, No. 175, c. XVII, § 46, added by P.A.1998, No. 317, Eff. Dec. 15, 1998. Amended by P.A.1999, No. 227, Imd. Eff. Dec. 28, 1999.

777.47. Scoring offense variable 17, degree of negligence exhibited

Sec. 47. (1) Offense variable 17 is degree of negligence exhibited. Score offense variable 17 by determining which of the following apply and by assigning the number of points attributable to the one that has the highest number of points:

(a) The offender showed a wanton or reckless disregard for the life or property of another person .... 10 points

(b) The offender failed to show the degree of care that a person of ordinary prudence in a similar situation would have shown .... 5 points

(c) The offender was not negligent..... 0 points

(2) Do not score 10 points if points are given in offense variable 6.

P.A.1927, No. 175, c. XVII, § 47, added by P.A.1998, No. 317, Eff. Dec. 15, 1998.

777.48. Scoring offense variable 18, operator ability affected by alcohol or drugs

Sec. 48. (1) Offense variable 18 is operator ability affected by alcohol or drugs. Score offense variable 18 by determining which of the following apply and by assigning the number of points attributable to the one that has the highest number of points:

(a) The offender operated a vehicle, vessel, ORV, snowmobile, aircraft, or locomotive when his or her bodily alcohol content was 0.20 grams or more per 100 milliliters of blood, per 210 liters of breath, or per 67 milliliters of urine .... 20 points

(b) The offender operated a vehicle, vessel, ORV, snowmobile, aircraft, or locomotive when his or her bodily alcohol content was 0.15 grams or more but less than 0.20 grams per 100 milliliters of blood, per 210 liters of breath, or per 67 milliliters of urine .... 15 points

(c) The offender operated a vehicle, vessel, ORV, snowmobile, aircraft, or locomotive while the offender was under the influence of alcoholic or intoxicating liquor, a controlled substance, or a combination of alcoholic or intoxicating liquor and a controlled substance; or while the offender's body contained any amount of a controlled substance listed in schedule 1 under section 7212 of the public health code, 1978 PA 368, MCL 333.7212, or a rule promulgated under that section, or a controlled substance described in section 7214(a)(*iv*) of the public health code, 1978 PA 368, MCL 333.7214; or while the offender had an alcohol content of 0.08 grams or more but less than 0.15 grams per 100 milliliters of blood, per 210 liters of breath, or per 67 milliliters of urine or, beginning October 1, 2013, the offender had an alcohol content of 0.10 grams or more but less than 0.15 grams per 100 milliliters of blood, per 210 liters of breath, or per 67 milliliters of urine .... 10 points

(d) The offender operated a vehicle, vessel, ORV, snowmobile, aircraft, or locomotive while he or she was visibly impaired by the use of alcoholic or intoxicating liquor or a controlled substance or a combination of alcoholic or intoxicating liquor and a controlled substance, or was less than 21 years of age and had any bodily alcohol content .... 5 points

(e) The offender's ability to operate a vehicle, vessel, ORV, snowmobile, aircraft, or locomotive was not affected by an alcoholic or intoxicating liquor or a controlled substance or a combination of alcoholic or intoxicating liquor and a controlled substance..... 0 points

(2) As used in this section, "any bodily alcohol content" means either of the following:

(a) An alcohol content of 0.02 grams or more but less than 0.08 grams per 100 milliliters of blood, per 210 liters of breath, or per 67 milliliters of urine or, beginning October 1, 2013, 0.02 grams or more but less than 0.10 grams per 100 milliliters of blood, per 210 liters of breath, or per 67 milliliters of urine.

(b) Any presence of alcohol within an individual's body resulting from the consumption of alcoholic or intoxicating liquor other than the consumption of alcoholic or intoxicating liquor as part of a generally recognized religious service or ceremony.

P.A.1927, No. 175, c. XVII, § 48, added by P.A.1998, No. 317, Eff. Dec. 15, 1998. Amended by P.A.1999, No. 227, Imd. Eff. Dec. 28, 1999; P.A.2000, No. 279, Eff. Oct. 1, 2000; P.A.2003, No. 134, Eff. Sept. 30, 2003.

777.49. Scoring offense variable 19, threat to security of penal institution or court or interference with administration of justice or rendering of emergency services

Sec. 49. Offense variable 19 is threat to the security of a penal institution or court or interference with the administration of justice or the rendering of emergency services. Score offense variable 19 by determining which of the following apply and by assigning the number of points attributable to the one that has the highest number of points:

(a) The offender by his or her conduct threatened the security of a penal institution or court .... 25 points

(b) The offender used force or the threat of force against another person or the property of another person to interfere with, attempt to interfere with, or that results in the interference with the administration of justice or the rendering of emergency services 15 points

(c) The offender otherwise interfered with or attempted to interfere with the administration of justice ..... 10 points

(d) The offender did not threaten the security of a penal institution or court or interfere with or attempt to interfere with the administration of justice or the rendering of emergency services by force or threat of force .... 0 points

P.A.1927, No. 175, c. XVII, § 49, added by P.A.1998, No. 317, Eff. Dec. 15, 1998. Amended by P.A.2001, No. 136, Imd. Eff. Oct. 23, 2001; P.A.2002, No. 137, Eff. April 22, 2002.

777.49a. Scoring offense variable 20, terrorism

Sec. 49a. (1) Offense variable 20 is terrorism. Score offense variable 20 by determining which of the following applies and by assigning the number of points attributable to the one that has the highest number of points:

(a) The offender committed an act of terrorism by using or threatening to use a harmful biological substance, harmful biological device, harmful chemical substance, harmful chemical device, harmful radioactive material, harmful radioactive device, incendiary device, or explosive device .... 100 points

(b) The offender committed an act of terrorism without using or threatening to use a harmful biological substance, harmful biological device, harmful chemical substance, harmful chemical device, harmful radioactive material, harmful radioactive device, incendiary device, or explosive device .... 50 points

(c) The offender supported an act of terrorism, a terrorist, or a terrorist organization .... 25 points

(d) The offender did not commit an act of terrorism or support an act of terrorism, a terrorist, or a terrorist organization .... 0 points

(2) As used in this section:

(a) "Act of terrorism" and "terrorist" mean those terms as defined in section 543b of the Michigan penal code, 1931 PA 328, MCL 750.543b.

(b) "Harmful biological substance", "harmful biological device", "harmful chemical substance", "harmful chemical device", "harmful radioactive material", and "harmful radioactive device" mean those terms as defined in section 200h of the Michigan penal code, 1931 PA 328, MCL 750.200h.

(c) "Incendiary device" includes gasoline or any other flammable substance, a blowtorch, fire bomb, Molotov cocktail, or other similar device.

(d) "Terrorist organization" means that term as defined in section 543c of the Michigan penal code, 1931 PA 328, MCL 750.543c.

P.A.1927, No. 175, c. XVII, § 49a, added by P.A.2002, No. 137, Eff. April 22, 2002.

PART 5. PRIOR RECORD VARIABLES

777.50. Scoring prior record variables 1 to 5

Sec. 50. (1) In scoring prior record variables 1 to 5, do not use any conviction or juvenile adjudication that precedes a period of 10 or more years between the discharge date from a conviction or juvenile adjudication and the defendant's commission of the next offense resulting in a conviction or juvenile adjudication.

(2) Apply subsection (1) by determining the time between the discharge date for the prior conviction or juvenile adjudication most recently preceding the commission date of the sentencing offense. If it is 10 or more years, do not use that prior conviction or juvenile adjudication and any earlier conviction or juvenile adjudication in scoring prior record variables. If it is less than 10 years, use that prior conviction or juvenile adjudication in scoring prior record variables and determine the time between the commission date of that prior conviction and the discharge date of the next earlier prior conviction or juvenile adjudication. If that period is 10 or more years, do not use that prior conviction or juvenile adjudication and any earlier conviction or

juvenile adjudication in scoring prior record variables. If it is less than 10 years, use that prior conviction or juvenile adjudication in scoring prior record variables and repeat this determination for each remaining prior conviction or juvenile adjudication until a period of 10 or more years is found or no prior convictions or juvenile adjudications remain.

(3) If a discharge date is not available, add either the time defendant was sentenced to probation or the length of the minimum incarceration term to the date of the conviction and use that date as the discharge date.

(4) As used in this part:

(a) "Conviction" includes any of the following:

(*i*) Assignment to youthful trainee status under sections 11 to 15 of chapter II. [1]

(*ii*) A conviction set aside under 1965 PA 213, MCL 780.621 to 780.624

(b) "Discharge date" means the date an individual is discharged from the jurisdiction of the court or the department of corrections after being convicted of or adjudicated responsible for a crime or an act that would be a crime if committed by an adult.

(c) "Juvenile adjudication" includes an adjudication set aside under section 18e of chapter XIIA of 1939 PA 288, MCL 712A.18e, or expunged.

P.A.1927, No. 175, c. XVII, § 50, added by P.A.1998, No. 317, Eff. Dec. 15, 1998.

[1] M.C.L.A. §§ 762.11 to 762.15.

777.51. Scoring prior record variable 1, prior high severity felony convictions

Sec. 51. (1) Prior record variable 1 is prior high severity felony convictions. Score prior record variable 1 by determining which of the following apply and by assigning the number of points attributable to the one that has the highest number of points:

(a) The offender has 3 or more prior high severity felony convictions ... 75 points
(b) The offender has 2 prior high severity felony convictions .... 50 points
(c) The offender has 1 prior high severity felony conviction .... 25 points
(d) The offender has no prior high severity felony convictions .... 0 points

(2) As used in this section, "prior high severity felony conviction" means a conviction for any of the following, if the conviction was entered before the sentencing offense was committed:

(a) A crime listed in offense class M2, A, B, C, or D.

(b) A felony under a law of the United States or another state corresponding to a crime listed in offense class M2, A, B, C, or D.

(c) A felony that is not listed in offense class M2, A, B, C, D, E, F, G, or H and that is punishable by a maximum term of imprisonment of 10 years or more.

(d) A felony under a law of the United States or another state that does not correspond to a crime listed in offense class M2, A, B, C, D, E, F, G, or H and that is punishable by a maximum term of imprisonment of 10 years or more.

P.A.1927, No. 175, c. XVII, § 51, added by P.A.1998, No. 317, Eff. Dec. 15, 1998. Amended by P.A.2006, No. 655, Imd. Eff. Jan. 9, 2007.

777.52. Scoring prior record variable 2, prior low severity felony convictions

Sec. 52. (1) Prior record variable 2 is prior low severity felony convictions. Score prior record variable 2 by determining which of the following apply and by assigning the number of points attributable to the one that has the highest number of points:

(a) The offender has 4 or more prior low severity felony convictions .... 30 points
(b) The offender has 3 prior low severity felony convictions .... 20 points
(c) The offender has 2 prior low severity felony convictions .... 10 points
(d) The offender has 1 prior low severity felony conviction .... 5 points
(e) The offender has no prior low severity felony convictions .... 0 points

(2) As used in this section, "prior low severity felony conviction" means a conviction for any of the following, if the conviction was entered before the sentencing offense was committed:

(a) A crime listed in offense class E, F, G, or H.

(b) A felony under a law of the United States or another state that corresponds to a crime listed in offense class E, F, G, or H.

(c) A felony that is not listed in offense class M2, A, B, C, D, E, F, G, or H and that is punishable by a maximum term of imprisonment of less than 10 years.

(d) A felony under a law of the United States or another state that does not correspond to a crime listed in offense class M2, A, B, C, D, E, F, G, or H and that is punishable by a maximum term of imprisonment of less than 10 years.

P.A.1927, No. 175, c. XVII, § 52, added by P.A.1998, No. 317, Eff. Dec. 15, 1998. Amended by P.A.2006, No. 655, Imd. Eff. Jan. 9, 2007.

777.53. Scoring prior record variable 3, prior high severity juvenile adjudications

Sec. 53. (1) Prior record variable 3 is prior high severity juvenile adjudications. Score prior record variable 3 by determining which of the following apply and by assigning the number of points attributable to the one that has the highest number of points:

(a) The offender has 3 or more prior high severity juvenile adjudications 50 points
(b) The offender has 2 prior high severity juvenile adjudications....... 25 points
(c) The offender has 1 prior high severity juvenile adjudication .... 10 points
(d) The offender has no prior high severity juvenile adjudications....... 0 points

(2) As used in this section, "prior high severity juvenile adjudication" means a juvenile adjudication for conduct that would be any of the following if committed by an adult, if the order of disposition was entered before the sentencing offense was committed:

(a) A crime listed in offense class M2, A, B, C, or D.

(b) A felony under a law of the United States or another state corresponding to a crime listed in offense class M2, A, B, C, or D.

(c) A felony that is not listed in offense class M2, A, B, C, D, E, F, G, or H and that is punishable by a maximum term of imprisonment of 10 years or more.

(d) A felony under a law of the United States or another state that does not correspond to a crime listed in offense class M2, A, B, C, D, E, F, G, or H and that is punishable by a maximum term of imprisonment of 10 years or more.

P.A.1927, No. 175, c. XVII, § 53, added by P.A.1998, No. 317, Eff. Dec. 15, 1998. Amended by P.A.2006, No. 655, Imd. Eff. Jan. 9, 2007.

777.54. Scoring prior record variable 4, prior low severity juvenile adjudications

Sec. 54. (1) Prior record variable 4 is prior low severity juvenile adjudications. Score prior record variable 4 by determining which of the following apply and by assigning the number of points attributable to the one that has the highest number of points:

(a) The offender has 6 or more prior low severity juvenile adjudications 20 points
(b) The offender has 5 prior low severity juvenile adjudications .... 15 points
(c) The offender has 3 or 4 prior low severity juvenile adjudications..... 10 points
(d) The offender has 2 prior low severity juvenile adjudications .... 5 points
(e) The offender has 1 prior low severity juvenile adjudication .... 2 points
(f) The offender has no prior low severity juvenile adjudications....... 0 points

(2) As used in this section, "prior low severity juvenile adjudication" means a juvenile adjudication for conduct that would be any of the following if committed by an adult, if the order of disposition was entered before the sentencing offense was committed:

(a) A crime listed in offense class E, F, G, or H.

(b) A felony under a law of the United States or another state corresponding to a crime listed in offense class E, F, G, or H.

(c) A felony that is not listed in offense class M2, A, B, C, D, E, F, G, or H and that is punishable by a maximum term of imprisonment of less than 10 years.

(d) A felony under a law of the United States or another state that does not correspond to a crime listed in offense class M2, A, B, C, D, E, F, G, or H and that is punishable by a maximum term of imprisonment of less than 10 years.

P.A.1927, No. 175, c. XVII, § 54, added by P.A.1998, No. 317, Eff. Dec. 15, 1998. Amended by P.A.2000, No. 279, Eff. Oct. 1, 2000; P.A.2006, No. 655, Imd. Eff. Jan. 9, 2007.

777.55. Scoring prior record variable 5, prior misdemeanor convictions or prior misdemeanor juvenile adjudications

Sec. 55. (1) Prior record variable 5 is prior misdemeanor convictions or prior misdemeanor juvenile adjudications. Score prior record variable 5 by determining which of the following apply and by assigning the number of points attributable to the one that has the highest number of points:

(a) The offender has 7 or more prior misdemeanor convictions or prior misdemeanor juvenile adjudications .... 20 points
(b) The offender has 5 or 6 prior misdemeanor convictions or prior misdemeanor juvenile adjudications .... 15 points
(c) The offender has 3 or 4 prior misdemeanor convictions or prior misdemeanor juvenile adjudications .... 10 points
(d) The offender has 2 prior misdemeanor convictions or prior misdemeanor juvenile adjudications .... 5 points
(e) The offender has 1 prior misdemeanor conviction or prior misdemeanor juvenile adjudication. .... 2 points
(f) The offender has no prior misdemeanor convictions or prior misdemeanor juvenile adjudications .... 0 points

(2) All of the following apply to scoring record variable 5:

(a) Except as provided in subdivision (b), count a prior misdemeanor conviction or prior misdemeanor juvenile adjudication only if it is an offense against a person or property, a controlled substance offense, or a weapon offense. Do not count a prior conviction used to enhance the sentencing offense to a felony.

(b) Count all prior misdemeanor convictions and prior misdemeanor juvenile adjudications for operating or attempting to operate a vehicle, vessel, ORV, snowmobile, aircraft, or locomotive while under the influence of or impaired by alcohol, a controlled substance, or a combination of alcohol and a controlled substance. Do not count a prior conviction used to enhance the sentencing offense to a felony.

(3) As used in this section:

(a) "Prior misdemeanor conviction" means a conviction for a misdemeanor under a law of this state, a political subdivision of this state, another state, a political subdivision of another state, or the United States if the conviction was entered before the sentencing offense was committed.

(b) "Prior misdemeanor juvenile adjudication" means a juvenile adjudication for conduct that if committed by an adult would be a misdemeanor under a law of this state, a political subdivision of this state, another state, a political subdivision of another state, or the United States if the order of disposition was entered before the sentencing offense was committed.

P.A.1927, No. 175, c. XVII, § 55, added by P.A.1998, No. 317, Eff. Dec. 15, 1998. Amended by P.A.2000, No. 279, Eff. Oct. 1, 2000.

777.56. Scoring prior record variable 6, relationship to criminal justice system

Sec. 56. (1) Prior record variable 6 is relationship to the criminal justice system. Score prior record variable 6 by determining which of the following apply and by assigning the number of points attributable to the one that has the highest number of points:

(a) The offender is a prisoner of the department of corrections or serving a sentence in jail .... 20 points
(b) The offender is incarcerated in jail awaiting adjudication or sentencing on a conviction or probation violation .... 15 points
(c) The offender is on parole, probation, or delayed sentence status or on bond awaiting adjudication or sentencing for a felony .... 10 points
(d) The offender is on probation or delayed sentence status or on bond awaiting adjudication or sentencing for a misdemeanor .... 5 points
(e) The offender has no relationship to the criminal justice system..... 0 points

(2) Score the appropriate points under this section if the offender is involved with the criminal justice system in another state or United States.

(3) As used in this section:

(a) "Delayed sentence status" includes, but is not limited to, an individual assigned or deferred under any of the following:

(*i*) Section 7411 of the public health code, 1978 PA 368, MCL 333.7411.

(*ii*) Section 1076(4) of the revised judicature act of 1961, 1961 PA 236, MCL 600.1076.

(*iii*) Section 350a of the Michigan penal code, 1931 PA 328, MCL 750.350a.

(*iv*) Section 430 of the Michigan penal code, 1931 PA 328, MCL 750.430.

(*v*) Sections 11 to 15 of chapter II. [1]

(*vi*) Section 4a of chapter IX. [2]

(b) "Prisoner of the department of corrections or serving a sentence in jail" includes an individual who is an escapee.

P.A.1927, No. 175, c. XVII, § 56, added by P.A.1998, No. 317, Eff. Dec. 15, 1998. Amended by P.A.2004, No. 220, Eff. Jan. 1, 2005.

[1] M.C.L.A. §§ 762.11 to 762.15.

[2] M.C.L.A. § 769.4a.

777.57. Scoring prior record variable 7, subsequent or concurrent felony convictions

Sec. 57. (1) Prior record variable 7 is subsequent or concurrent felony convictions. Score prior record variable 7 by determining which of the following apply and by assigning the number of points attributable to the one that has the highest number of points:

(a) The offender has 2 or more subsequent or concurrent convictions .... 20 points

(b) The offender has 1 subsequent or concurrent conviction .... 10 points

(c) The offender has no subsequent or concurrent convictions .... 0 points

(2) All of the following apply to scoring record variable 7:

(a) Score the appropriate point value if the offender was convicted of multiple felony counts or was convicted of a felony after the sentencing offense was committed.

(b) Do not score a felony firearm conviction in this variable.

(c) Do not score a concurrent felony conviction if a mandatory consecutive sentence or a consecutive sentence imposed under section 7401(3) of the public health code, 1978 PA 368, MCL 333.7401, will result from that conviction.

P.A.1927, No. 175, c. XVII, § 57, added by P.A.1998, No. 317, Eff. Dec. 15, 1998. Amended by P.A.1999, No. 227, Imd. Eff. Dec. 28, 1999; P.A.2002, No. 666, Eff. March 1, 2003.

PART 6. SENTENCING GRIDS

777.61. Minimum sentence ranges for class M2

Sec. 61. The following are the minimum sentence ranges for class M2:

	PRIOR RECORD VARIABLE LEVEL					
Offense Variable Level	A 0 points	B 1–9 points	C 10–24 points	D 25–49 points	E 50–74 points	F 75+ points
I 0–49 points	90–150	144–240	162–270	180–300 or life	225–375 or life	270–450 or life
II 50–99 points	144–240	162–270	180–300 or life	225–375 or life	270–450 or life	315–525 or life
III 100+ points	162–270 or life	180–300 or life	225–375 or life	270–450 or life	315–525 or life	365–600 or life

P.A.1927, No. 175, c. XVII, § 61, added by P.A.1998, No. 317, Eff. Dec. 15, 1998.

777.62. Minimum sentence ranges for class A

Sec. 62. The following are the minimum sentence ranges for class A:

	PRIOR RECORD VARIABLE LEVEL					
Offense Variable Level	A 0 points	B 1–9 points	C 10–24 points	D 25–49 points	E 50–74 points	F 75+ points
I 0–19 points	21–35	27–45	42–70	51–85	81–135	108–180
II 20–39 points	27–45	42–70	51–85	81–135	108–180	126–210
III 40–59 points	42–70	51–85	81–135	108–180	126–210	135–225
IV 60–79 points	51–85	81–135	108–180	126–210	135–225	171–285
V 80–99 points	81–135	108–180	126–210	135–225	171–285	225–375 or life
VI 100+ points	108–180	126–210	135–225	171–285	225–375 or life	270–450 or life

P.A.1927, No. 175, c. XVII, § 62, added by P.A.1998, No. 317, Eff. Dec. 15, 1998.

777.63. Minimum sentence ranges for class B

Sec. 63. The following are the minimum sentence ranges for class B:

	PRIOR RECORD VARIABLE LEVEL					
Offense Variable Level	A 0 points	B 1–9 points	C 10–24 points	D 25–49 points	E 50–74 points	F 75+ points
I 0–9 points	0–18	12–20	24–40	36–60	51–85	72–120
II 10–24 points	12–20	15–25	30–50	51–85	72–120	78–130
III 25–34 points	15–25	21–35	36–60	57–95	78–130	84–140
IV 35–49 points	21–35	24–40	45–75	72–120	84–140	87–145
V 50–74 points	24–40	36–60	51–85	78–130	87–145	99–160
VI 75+ points	36–60	45–75	57–95	84–140	99–160	117–160

P.A.1927, No. 175, c. XVII, § 63, added by P.A.1998, No. 317, Eff. Dec. 15, 1998.

777.64. Minimum sentence ranges for class C

Sec. 64. The following are the minimum sentence ranges for class C:

	PRIOR RECORD VARIABLE LEVEL					
Offense Variable Level	A 0 points	B 1–9 points	C 10–24 points	D 25–49 points	E 50–74 points	F 75+ points
I 0–9 points	0–11	0–17	10–19	12–24	19–38	29–57
II 10–24 points	0–17	5–17	12–24	19–38	29–57	36–71
III 25–34 points	10–19	12–24	19–38	29–57	36–71	43–86
IV 35–49 points	12–24	19–38	29–57	36–71	43–86	50–100
V 50–74 points	19–38	29–57	36–71	43–86	50–100	58–114
VI 75+	29–57	36–71	43–86	50–100	58–114	62–114

P.A.1927, No. 175, c. XVII, § 64, added by P.A.1998, No. 317, Eff. Dec. 15, 1998.

777.65. Minimum sentence ranges for class D

Sec. 65. The following are the minimum sentence ranges for class D:

	PRIOR RECORD VARIABLE LEVEL					
Offense Variable Level	A 0 points	B 1–9 points	C 10–24 points	D 25–49 points	E 50–74 points	F 75+ points
I 0–9 points	0–6	0–9	0–11	0–17	5–23	10–23
II 10–24 points points	0–9	0–11	0–17	5–23	10–23	19–38
III 25–34 points	0–11	0–17	5–23	10–23	19–38	29–57
IV 35–49 points	0–17	5–23	10–23	19–38	29–57	34–67
V 50–74 points	5–23	10–23	19–38	29–57	34–67	38–76
VI 75+ points	10–23	19–38	29–57	34–67	38–76	43–76

P.A.1927, No. 175, c. XVII, § 65, added by P.A.1998, No. 317, Eff. Dec. 15, 1998.

777.66. Minimum sentence ranges for class E

Sec. 66. The following are the minimum sentence ranges for class E:

	PRIOR RECORD VARIABLE LEVEL					
Offense Variable Level	A 0 points	B 1–9 points	C 10–24 points	D 25–49 points	E 50–74 points	F 75+ points
I 0–9 points	0–3	0–6	0–9	5–23	7–23	9–23
II 10–24 points	0–6	0–9	0–11	7–23	10–23	12–24
III 25–34 points	0–9	0–11	0–17	10–23	12–24	14–29
IV 35–49 points	0–11	0–17	5–23	12–24	14–29	19–38
V 50–74 points	0–14	5–23	7–23	14–29	19–38	22–38
VI 75+ points	0–17	7–23	12–24	19–38	22–38	24–38

P.A.1927, No. 175, c. XVII, § 66, added by P.A.1998, No. 317, Eff. Dec. 15, 1998.

777.67. Minimum sentence ranges for class F

Sec. 67. The following are the minimum sentence ranges for class F:

	PRIOR RECORD VARIABLE LEVEL					
Offense Variable Level	A 0 points	B 1–9 points	C 10–24 points	D 25–49 points	E 50–74 points	F 75+ points
I 0–9 points	0–3	0–6	0–9	2–17	5–23	10–23
II 10–34 points	0–6	0–9	0–17	5–23	10–23	12–24
III 35–74 points	0–9	0–17	2–17	10–23	12–24	14–29
IV 75+ points	0–17	2–17	5–23	12–24	14–29	17–30

P.A.1927, No. 175, c. XVII, § 67, added by P.A.1998, No. 317, Eff. Dec. 15, 1998.

777.68. Minimum sentence ranges for class G

Sec. 68. The following are the minimum sentence ranges for class G:

	PRIOR RECORD VARIABLE LEVEL					
Offense Variable Level	A 0 points	B 1–9 points	C 10–24 points	D 25–49 points	E 50–74 points	F 75+ points
I 0–9 points	0–3	0–6	0–9	0–11	0–17	2–17
II 10–15 points	0–6	0–9	0–11	0–17	2–17	5–23
III 16+ points	0–9	0–11	0–17	2–17	5–23	7–23

P.A.1927, No. 175, c. XVII, § 68, added by P.A.1998, No. 317, Eff. Dec. 15, 1998.

777.69. Minimum sentence ranges for class H

Sec. 69. The following are the minimum sentence ranges for class H:

	PRIOR RECORD VARIABLE LEVEL					
Offense Variable Level	A 0 points	B 1–9 points	C 10–24 points	D 25–49 points	E 50–74 points	F 75+ points
I 0–9 points	0–1	0–3	0–6	0–9	0–11	0–17
II 10–15 points	0–3	0–6	0–9	0–11	0–17	2–17
III 16+ points	0–6	0–9	0–11	0–17	2–17	5–17

P.A.1927, No. 175, c. XVII, § 69, added by P.A.1998, No. 317, Eff. Dec. 15, 1998.

MICHIGAN COURT RULES OF 1985

Table of Rules

CHAPTER 3. SPECIAL PROCEEDINGS AND ACTIONS

CHAPTER 3. SPECIAL PROCEEDINGS AND ACTIONS

[Chapter in part]

SUBCHAPTER 3.900 PROCEEDINGS INVOLVING JUVENILES

RULE 3.955 SENTENCING OR DISPOSITION IN DESIGNATED CASES

(A) Determining Whether to Sentence or Impose Disposition. If a juvenile is convicted under MCL 712A.2d, sentencing or disposition shall be made as provided in MCL 712A.18(1)(n) and the Crime Victim's Rights Act, MCL 780.751 *et seq.*, if applicable. In deciding whether to enter an order of disposition, or impose or delay imposition of sentence, the court shall consider all the following factors, giving greater weight to the seriousness of the offense and the juvenile's prior record:

(1) the seriousness of the alleged offense in terms of community protection, including but not limited to, the existence of any aggravating factors recognized by the sentencing guidelines, the use of a firearm or other dangerous weapon, and the effect on any victim;

(2) the culpability of the juvenile in committing the alleged offense, including, but not limited to, the level of the juvenile's participation in planning and carrying out the offense and the existence of any aggravating or mitigating factors recognized by the sentencing guidelines;

(3) the juvenile's prior record of delinquency including, but not limited to, any record of detention, any police record, any school record, or any other evidence indicating prior delinquent behavior;

(4) the juvenile's programming history, including, but not limited to, the juvenile's past willingness to participate meaningfully in available programming;

(5) the adequacy of the punishment or programming available in the juvenile justice system; and

(6) the dispositional options available for the juvenile.

The court also shall give the juvenile, the juvenile's lawyer, the prosecutor, and the victim an opportunity to advise the court of any circumstances they believe the court should consider in deciding whether to enter an order of disposition or to impose or delay imposition of sentence.

(B) Burden of Proof. The court shall enter an order of disposition unless the court determines that the best interests of the public would be served by sentencing the juvenile as an adult. The prosecuting attorney has the burden of proving by a preponderance of the evidence that, on the basis of the criteria in subrule (A), it would be in the best interests of the public to sentence the juvenile as an adult.

(C) Sentencing. If the court determines that the juvenile should be sentenced as an adult, either initially or following a delayed imposition of sentence, the sentencing hearing shall be held in accordance with the procedures set forth in MCR 6.425.

(D) Delayed Imposition of Sentence. If the court determines that the juvenile should be sentenced as an adult, the court may, in its discretion, enter an order of disposition delaying imposition of sentence and placing the juvenile on probation on such terms and conditions as it considers appropriate, including ordering any disposition under MCL 712A.18. A delayed sentence may be imposed in accordance with MCR 3.956.

(E) Disposition Hearing. If the court does not determine that the juvenile should be sentenced as an adult, the court shall hold a dispositional hearing and comply with the procedures set forth in MCR 3.943.

[Adopted February 4, 2003, effective May 1, 2003, 467 Mich; amended July 17, 2003, 467 Mich; October 1, 2003, 467 Mich.]

CHAPTER 6. CRIMINAL PROCEDURE

[Chapter in part]

SUBCHAPTER 6.400 TRIALS

RULE 6.425 SENTENCING; APPOINTMENT OF APPELLATE COUNSEL

(A) Presentence Report; Contents. Prior to sentencing, the probation officer must investigate the defendant's background and character, verify material information, and report in writing the results of the investigation to the court. The report must be succinct and, depending on the circumstances, include:

(1) a description of the defendant's prior criminal convictions and juvenile adjudications,

(2) a complete description of the offense and the circumstances surrounding it,

(3) a brief description of the defendant's vocational background and work history, including military record and present employment status,

(4) a brief social history of the defendant, including marital status, financial status, length of residence in the community, educational background, and other pertinent data,

(5) the defendant's medical history, substance abuse history, if any, and, if indicated, a current psychological or psychiatric report,

(6) information concerning the financial, social, psychological, or physical harm suffered by any victim of the offense, including the restitution needs of the victim,

(7) if provided and requested by the victim, a written victim's impact statement as provided by law,

(8) any statement the defendant wishes to make,

(9) a statement prepared by the prosecutor on the applicability of any consecutive sentencing provision,

(10) an evaluation of and prognosis for the defendant's adjustment in the community based on factual information in the report,

(11) a specific recommendation for disposition, and

(12) any other information that may aid the court in sentencing.

Regardless of the sentence imposed, the court must have a copy of the presentence report and of any psychiatric report sent to the Department of Corrections. If the defendant is sentenced to prison, the copies must be sent with the commitment papers.

(B) Presentence Report; Disclosure Before Sentencing. The court must provide copies of the presentence report to the prosecutor and the defendant's lawyer, or the defendant if not represented by a lawyer, at a reasonable time before the day of sentencing. The court may exempt from disclosure information or diagnostic opinion that might seriously disrupt a program of rehabilitation and sources of information that have been obtained on a promise of confidentiality. When part of the report is not disclosed, the court must inform the parties that information has not been disclosed and state on the record the reasons for nondisclosure. To the extent it can do so without defeating the purpose of nondisclosure, the court also must provide the parties with a written or oral summary of the nondisclosed information and give them an opportunity to comment on it. The court must have the information exempted from disclosure specifically noted in the report. The court's decision to exempt part of the report from disclosure is subject to appellate review.

(C) Presentence Report; Disclosure After Sentencing. After sentencing, the court, on written request, must provide the prosecutor, the defendant's lawyer, or the defendant not represented by a lawyer, with a copy of the presentence report and any attachments to it. The court must exempt from disclosure any information the sentencing court exempted from disclosure pursuant to subrule (B).

(D) Sentencing Guidelines. The court must use the sentencing guidelines, as provided by law. Proposed scoring of the guidelines shall accompany the presentence report.

(E) Sentencing Procedure.

(1) The court must sentence the defendant within a reasonably prompt time after the plea or verdict unless the court delays sentencing as provided by law. At sentencing, the court must, on the record:

(a) determine that the defendant, the defendant's lawyer, and the prosecutor have had an opportunity to read and discuss the presentence report,

(b) give each party an opportunity to explain, or challenge the accuracy or relevancy of, any information in the presentence report, and resolve any challenges in accordance with the procedure set forth in subrule (E)(2),

(c) give the defendant, the defendant's lawyer, the prosecutor, and the victim an opportunity to advise the court of any circumstances they believe the court should consider in imposing sentence,

(d) state the sentence being imposed, including the minimum and maximum sentence if applicable, together with any credit for time served to which the defendant is entitled,

(e) if the sentence imposed is not within the guidelines range, articulate the substantial and compelling reasons justifying that specific departure, and

(f) order that the defendant make full restitution as required by law to any victim of the defendant's course of conduct that gives rise to the conviction, or to that victim's estate.

(2) *Resolution of Challenges.* If any information in the presentence report is challenged, the court must allow the parties to be heard regarding the challenge, and make a finding with respect to the challenge or determine that a finding is unnecessary because it will not take the challenged information into account in sentencing. If the court finds merit in the challenge or determines that it will not take the challenged information into account in sentencing, it must direct the probation officer to

(a) correct or delete the challenged information in the report, whichever is appropriate, and

(b) provide defendant's lawyer with an opportunity to review the corrected report before it is sent to the Department of Corrections.

(F) Advice Concerning the Right to Appeal; Appointment of Counsel.

(1) In a case involving a conviction following a trial, immediately after imposing sentence, the court must advise the defendant, on the record, that

(a) the defendant is entitled to appellate review of the conviction and sentence,

(b) if the defendant is financially unable to retain a lawyer, the court will appoint a lawyer to represent the defendant on appeal, and

(c) the request for a lawyer must be made within 42 days after sentencing.

(2) In a case involving a conviction following a plea of guilty or nolo contendere, immediately after imposing sentence, the court must advise the defendant, on the record, that

(a) the defendant is entitled to file an application for leave to appeal;

(b) if the defendant is financially unable to retain a lawyer, the court will appoint a lawyer to represent the defendant on appeal, and

(c) the request for a lawyer must be made within 42 days after sentencing.

(3) The court also must give the defendant a request for counsel form containing an instruction informing the defendant that the form must be completed and returned to the court within 42 days after sentencing if the defendant wants the court to appoint a lawyer.

(4) When imposing sentence in a case in which sentencing guidelines enacted in 1998 PA 317, MCL 777.1 *et seq.*, are applicable, if the court imposes a minimum sentence that is longer or more severe than the range provided by the sentencing guidelines, the court must advise the defendant on the record and in writing that the defendant may seek appellate review of the sentence, by right if the conviction followed trial or by application if the conviction entered by plea, on the ground that it is longer or more severe than the range provided by the sentencing guidelines.

(G) Appointment of Lawyer; Trial Court Responsibilities in Connection with Appeal.

(1) *Appointment of Lawyer.*

(a) Unless there is a postjudgment motion pending, the court must rule on a defendant's request for a lawyer within 14 days after receiving it. If there is a postjudgment motion pending, the court must rule on the request after the court's disposition of the pending motion and within 14 days after that disposition.

(b) In a case involving a conviction following a trial, if the defendant is indigent, the court must enter an order appointing a lawyer if the request is filed within 42 days after sentencing or within the time for filing an appeal of right. The court should liberally grant an untimely request as long as the defendant may file an application for leave to appeal.

(c) In a case involving a conviction following a plea of guilty or nolo contendere, if the defendant is indigent, the court must enter an order appointing a lawyer if the request is filed within 42 days after sentencing.

(d) Scope of Appellate Lawyer's Responsibilities. The responsibilities of the appellate lawyer appointed to represent the defendant include representing the defendant

(i) in available postconviction proceedings in the trial court the lawyer deems appropriate,

(ii) in postconviction proceedings in the Court of Appeals,

(iii) in available proceedings in the trial court the lawyer deems appropriate under MCR 7.208(B) or 7.211(C)(1), and

(iv) as appellee in relation to any postconviction appeal taken by the prosecutor.

(2) *Order to Prepare Transcript.* The appointment order also must

(a) direct the court reporter to prepare and file, within the time limits specified in MCR 7.210,

(i) the trial or plea proceeding transcript,

(ii) the sentencing transcript, and

(iii) such transcripts of other proceedings, not previously transcribed, that the court directs or the parties request, and

(b) provide for the payment of the reporter's fees.

The court must promptly serve a copy of the order on the prosecutor, the defendant, the appointed lawyer, the court reporter, and the Michigan Appellate Assigned Counsel System. If the appointed lawyer timely requests additional transcripts, the trial court shall order such transcripts within 14 days after receiving the request.

(3) *Order as Claim of Appeal; Trial Cases.* In a case involving a conviction following a trial, if the defendant's request for a lawyer, timely or not, was made within the time for filing a claim of appeal, the order described in subrules (G)(1) and (2) must be entered on a form approved by the State Court Administrative Office, entitled "Claim of Appeal and Appointment of Counsel," and the court must immediately send to the Court of Appeals a copy of the order and a copy of the judgment being appealed. The court also must file in the Court of Appeals proof of having made service of the order as required in subrule (G)(2). Entry of the order by the trial court pursuant to this subrule constitutes a timely filed claim of appeal for the purposes of MCR 7.204.

[Statements by the Court and Justices Levin and Cavanagh regarding the October 13, 1995 extension appear in 450 Mich.]

[Statement by Boyle, J., appears in 455 Mich.]

[Statement by Boyle, J., appears in 457 Mich.]

[Statement by Cavanagh and Corrigan, JJ., appear in 461 Mich.]

[Adopted effective October 1, 1989; amended effective July 1, 1994, 445 Mich; amended December 30, 1994, applicable to all crimes committed on or after December 27, 1994 as provided by 1994 PA 374 and 1994 PA 375, effective until further order of the Court after consideration of comments and legislative action, if any, or until April 1, 1995, 447 Mich; by Order of March 31, 1995, December 30, 1994 amendment ordered to remain in effect until June 30, 1995; by Order of June 19, 1995, December 30, 1994 amendment ordered to remain in effect until October 15, 1995, 449 Mich; by Order of October 13, 1995, December 30, 1994 amendment ordered to remain in effect until August 15, 1996, 450 Mich; by Order of July 16, 1996, December 30, 1994 amendment ordered to remain in effect until September 1, 1997, 452 Mich; by Order of July 25, 1997, December 30, 1994 amendment ordered to remain in effect until further order of the Court; amended May 6, 1998, 457 Mich; December 15, 1998, effective January 1, 1999, 459 Mich; March 28, 2000, effective April 1, 2000, 461 Mich; February 1, 2005, effective May 1, 2005, 472 Mich; July 13, 2005, 473 Mich; December 14, 2005, effective January 1, 2006, 474 Mich.]

SUBCHAPTER 6.600 CRIMINAL PROCEDURE IN DISTRICT COURT

RULE 6.610 CRIMINAL PROCEDURE GENERALLY

(A) Precedence. Criminal cases have precedence over civil actions.

(B) Pretrial. The court, on its own initiative or on motion of either party, may direct the prosecutor and the defendant, and, if represented, the defendant's attorney to appear for a pretrial conference. The court may require collateral matters and pretrial motions to be filed and argued no later than this conference.

(C) Record. Unless a writing is permitted, a verbatim record of the proceedings before a court under subrules (D)–(F) must be made.

(D) Arraignment; District Court Offenses.

(1) Whenever a defendant is arraigned on an offense over which the district court has jurisdiction, the defendant must be informed of

(a) the name of the offense;

(b) the maximum sentence permitted by law; and

(c) the defendant's right

(i) to the assistance of an attorney and to a trial;

(ii) (if subrule [D][2] applies) to an appointed attorney; and

(iii) to a trial by jury, when required by law.

The information may be given in a writing that is made a part of the file or by the court on the record.

(2) An indigent defendant has a right to an appointed attorney whenever the offense charged requires on conviction a minimum term in jail or the court determines it might sentence to a term of incarceration, even if suspended.

If an indigent defendant is without an attorney and has not waived the right to an appointed attorney, the court may not sentence the defendant to jail or to a suspended jail sentence.

(3) The right to the assistance of an attorney, to an appointed attorney, or to a trial by jury is not waived unless the defendant

(a) has been informed of the right; and

(b) has waived it in a writing that is made a part of the file or orally on the record.

(4) The court may allow a defendant to enter a plea of not guilty or to stand mute without formal arraignment by filing a written statement

signed by the defendant and any defense attorney of record, reciting the general nature of the charge, the maximum possible sentence, the rights of the defendant at arraignment, and the plea to be entered. The court may require that an appropriate bond be executed and filed and appropriate and reasonable sureties posted or continued as a condition precedent to allowing the defendant to be arraigned without personally appearing before the court.

(E) Pleas of Guilty and Nolo Contendere. Before accepting a plea of guilty or nolo contendere, the court shall in all cases comply with this rule.

(1) The court shall determine that the plea is understanding, voluntary, and accurate. In determining the accuracy of the plea,

(a) if the defendant pleads guilty, the court, by questioning the defendant, shall establish support for a finding that defendant is guilty of the offense charged or the offense to which the defendant is pleading, or

(b) if the defendant pleads nolo contendere, the court shall not question the defendant about the defendant's participation in the crime, but shall make the determination on the basis of other available information.

(2) The court shall inform the defendant of the right to the assistance of an attorney. If the offense charged requires on conviction a minimum term in jail, the court shall inform the defendant that if the defendant is indigent the defendant has the right to an appointed attorney. The court shall also give such advice if it determines that it might sentence to a term of incarceration, even if suspended.

(3) The court shall advise the defendant of the following:

(a) the mandatory minimum jail sentence, if any, and the maximum possible penalty for the offense,

(b) that if the plea is accepted the defendant will not have a trial of any kind and that the defendant gives up the following rights that the defendant would have at trial:

(i) the right to have witnesses called for the defendant's defense at trial,

(ii) the right to cross-examine all witnesses called against the defendant,

(iii) the right to testify or to remain silent without an inference being drawn from said silence,

(iv) the presumption of innocence and the requirement that the defendant's guilt be proven beyond a reasonable doubt.

(4) A defendant or defendants may be informed of the trial rights listed in subrule (3)(b) as follows:

(a) on the record,

(b) in a writing made part of the file, or

(c) in a writing referred to on the record.

If the court uses a writing pursuant to subrule (E)(4)(b) or (c), the court shall address the defendant and obtain from the defendant orally on the record a statement that the rights were read and understood and a waiver of those rights. The waiver may be obtained without repeating the individual rights.

(5) The court shall make the plea agreement a part of the record and determine that the parties agree on all the terms of that agreement. The court shall accept, reject, or indicate on what basis it accepts the plea.

(6) The court must ask the defendant:

(a) (if there is no plea agreement) whether anyone has promised the defendant anything, or (if there is a plea agreement) whether anyone has promised anything beyond what is in the plea agreement;

(b) whether anyone has threatened the defendant; and

(c) whether it is the defendant's own choice to plead guilty.

(7) A plea of guilty or nolo contendere in writing is permissible without a personal appearance of the defendant and without support for a finding that defendant is guilty of the offense charged or the offense to which the defendant is pleading if

(a) the court decides that the combination of the circumstances and the range of possible sentences makes the situation proper for a plea of guilty or nolo contendere;

(b) the defendant acknowledges guilt or nolo contendere, in a writing to be placed in the district court file, and waives in writing the rights enumerated in subrule (3)(b); and

(c) the court is satisfied that the waiver is voluntary.

(8) The following provisions apply where a defendant seeks to challenge the plea.

(a) A defendant may not challenge a plea on appeal unless the defendant moved in the trial court to withdraw the plea for noncompliance with these rules. Such a motion may be made either before or after sentence has been imposed. After imposition of sentence, the defendant may file a motion to withdraw the plea within the time for filing an application for leave to appeal under MCR 7.103(B)(6).

(b) If the trial court determines that a deviation affecting substantial rights occurred, it shall correct the deviation and give the defendant the option of permitting the plea to stand or of withdrawing the plea. If the trial court determines either a deviation did not occur, or that the deviation did not affect substantial rights, it may permit the defendant to withdraw the plea only if it does not cause substantial prejudice to the people because of reliance on the plea.

(c) If a deviation is corrected, any appeal will be on the whole record including the subsequent advice and inquiries.

(9) The State Court Administrator shall develop and approve forms to be used under subrules (E)(4)(b) and (c) and (E)(7)(b) .

(F) Sentencing.

(1) At the sentencing, the court shall:

(a) require the presence of the defendant's attorney, unless the defendant does not have one or has waived the attorney's presence;

(b) give the defendant's attorney or, if the defendant is not represented by an attorney, the defendant an opportunity to review the presentence report, if any, and to advise the court of circumstances the defendant believes should be considered in imposing sentence; and

(c) inform the defendant of credit to be given for time served, if any.

(2) Unless a defendant who is entitled to appointed counsel is represented by an attorney or has waived the right to an attorney, a subsequent charge or sentence may not be enhanced because of this conviction and the defendant may not be incarcerated for violating probation or any other condition imposed in connection with this conviction.

(3) Immediately after imposing a sentence of incarceration, even if suspended, the court must advise the defendant, on the record or in writing, that:

(a) if the defendant wishes to file an appeal and is financially unable to retain a lawyer, the court will appoint a lawyer to represent the defendant on appeal, and

(b) the request for a lawyer must be made within 14 days after sentencing.

(G) Motion for New Trial. A motion for a new trial must be filed within 21 days after the entry of judgment. However, if an appeal has not been taken, a delayed motion may be filed within the time for filing an application for leave to appeal.

(H) Arraignment; Offenses Not Cognizable by the District Court. In a prosecution in which a defendant is charged with a felony or a misdemeanor not cognizable by the district court, the court shall

(1) inform the defendant of the nature of the charge;

(2) inform the defendant of

(a) the right to a preliminary examination;

(b) the right to an attorney, if the defendant is not represented by an attorney at the arraignment;

(c) the right to have an attorney appointed at public expense if the defendant is indigent; and

(d) the right to consideration of pretrial release.

If a defendant not represented by an attorney waives the preliminary examination, the court shall ascertain that the waiver is freely, understandingly, and voluntarily given before accepting it.

[Statement by Cavanagh and Kelly, JJ., appears in 462 Mich.]

[Adopted effective October 1, 1989; amended July 20, 1999, effective October 1, 1999, 460 Mich; June 13, 2000, effective September 1, 2000, 462 Mich; December 21, 2000, effective April 1, 2001, 463 Mich; July 13, 2005, effective January 1, 2006, 473 Mich; January 23, 2007, effective May 1, 2007, 477 Mich.]

SUBCHAPTER 6.900 RULES APPLICABLE TO JUVENILES CHARGED WITH SPECIFIED OFFENSES SUBJECT TO THE JURISDICTION OF THE CIRCUIT OR DISTRICT COURT

RULE 6.931 JUVENILE SENTENCING HEARING

(A) General. If the juvenile has been convicted of an offense listed in MCL 769.1(1)(a)–(*l*), the court must sentence the juvenile in the same manner as an adult. Unless a juvenile is required to be sentenced in the same manner as an adult, a judge of a court having jurisdiction over a juvenile shall conduct a juvenile sentencing hearing unless the hearing is waived as provided in subrule (B). At the conclusion of the juvenile sentencing hearing, the court shall determine whether to impose a sentence against the juvenile as though an adult offender or whether to place the juvenile on juvenile probation and commit the juvenile to state wardship pursuant to MCL 769.1b.

(B) No Juvenile Sentencing Hearing; Consent. The court need not conduct a juvenile sentencing hearing if the prosecuting attorney, the juvenile, and the attorney for the juvenile, consent that it is not in the best interest of the public to sentence the juvenile as though an adult offender. If the juvenile sentence hearing is waived, the court shall not impose a sentence as provided by law for an adult offender. The court must place the juvenile on juvenile probation and commit the juvenile to state wardship.

(C) Notice of Juvenile Sentencing Hearing Following Verdict. If a juvenile sentencing hearing is required, the prosecuting attorney, the juvenile, and the attorney for the juvenile must be advised on the record immediately following conviction of the juvenile by a guilty plea or verdict of guilty that a hearing will be conducted at sentencing, unless waived, to determine whether to sentence the juvenile as an adult or to place the juvenile on juvenile probation and commit the juvenile to state wardship as though a delinquent. The court may announce the scheduled date of the hearing. On request, the court shall notify the victim of the juvenile sentencing hearing.

(D) Review of Reports. The court must give the prosecuting attorney, the juvenile, and the attorney for the juvenile, an opportunity to review the presentence report and the social report before the juvenile sentencing hearing. The court may exempt information from the reports as provided in MCL 771.14 and 771.14a.

(E) Juvenile Sentencing Hearing Procedure.

(1) *Evidence.* At the juvenile sentencing hearing all relevant and material evidence may be received by the court and relied upon to the extent of its probative value, even though such evidence may not be admissible at trial. The rules of evidence do not apply. The court shall receive and consider the presentence report prepared by the probation officer and the social report prepared by the Family Independence Agency.

(2) *Standard of Proof.* The court must sentence the juvenile in the same manner as an adult unless the court determines by a preponderance of the evidence, except as provided in subrule (3)(c), that the best interests of the public would be served by placing the juvenile on probation and committing the juvenile to state wardship.

(3) *Alternative Sentences For Juveniles Convicted of Certain Controlled Substance Offenses.* If a juvenile is convicted of a violation or conspiracy to commit a violation of MCL 333.7403(2)(a)(i), the court shall determine whether the best interests of the public would be served by:

(a) imposing the sentence provided by law for an adult offender;

(b) placing the individual on probation and committing the individual to a state institution or agency as provided in MCL 769.1(3); or

(c) imposing a sentence of imprisonment for any term of years, but not less than 25 years, if the court determines by clear and convincing evidence that such a sentence would serve the best interests of the public.

In making its determination, the court shall use the criteria set forth in subrule (4).

(4) *Criteria.* The court shall consider the following criteria in determining whether to sentence the juvenile as though an adult offender or whether to place the juvenile on juvenile probation and commit the juvenile to state wardship, giving more weight to the seriousness of the

alleged offense and the juvenile's prior record of delinquency:

(a) the seriousness of the alleged offense in terms of community protection, including, but not limited to, the existence of any aggravating factors recognized by the sentencing guidelines, the use of a firearm or other dangerous weapon, and the impact on any victim;

(b) the culpability of the juvenile in committing the alleged offense, including, but not limited to, the level of the juvenile's participation in planning and carrying out the offense and the existence of any aggravating or mitigating factors recognized by the sentencing guidelines;

(c) the juvenile's prior record of delinquency, including, but not limited to, any record of detention, any police record, any school record, or any other evidence indicating prior delinquent behavior;

(d) the juvenile's programming history, including, but not limited to, the juvenile's past willingness to participate meaningfully in available programming;

(e) the adequacy of the punishment or programming available in the juvenile justice system; and

(f) the dispositional options available for the juvenile.

(5) *Findings*. The court must make findings of fact and conclusions of law forming the basis for the juvenile probation and commitment decision or the decision to sentence the juvenile as though an adult offender. The findings and conclusions may be incorporated in a written opinion or stated on the record.

(F) Postjudgment Procedure; Juvenile Probation and Commitment to State Wardship. If the court retains jurisdiction over the juvenile, places the juvenile on juvenile probation, and commits the juvenile to state wardship, the court shall comply with subrules (1) through (11):

(1) The court shall enter a judgment that includes a provision for reimbursement by the juvenile or those responsible for the juvenile's support, or both, for the cost of care and services pursuant to MCL 769.1(7). An order assessing such cost against a person responsible for the support of the juvenile shall not be binding on the person, unless an opportunity for a hearing has been given and until a copy of the order is served on the person, personally or by first class mail to the person's last known address.

(2) The court shall advise the juvenile at sentencing that if the juvenile, while on juvenile probation, is convicted of a felony or a misdemeanor punishable by more than one year's imprisonment, the court must revoke juvenile probation and sentence the juvenile to a term of years in prison not to exceed the penalty that might have been imposed for the offense for which the juvenile was originally convicted.

(3) The court shall assure that the juvenile receives a copy of the social report.

(4) The court shall send a copy of the order and a copy of the written opinion or transcript of the findings and conclusions of law to the Family Independence Agency.

(5) The court shall not place the juvenile on deferred sentencing, as provided in MCL 771.1(2).

(6) The court shall not place the juvenile on life probation for conviction of a controlled substance violation, as set forth in MCL 771.1(4).

(7) The five-year limit on the term of probation for an adult felony offender shall not apply.

(8) The court shall not require as a condition of juvenile probation that the juvenile report to a department of corrections probation officer.

(9) The court shall not, as a condition of juvenile probation, impose jail time against the juvenile except as provided in MCR 6.933(B)(2).

(10) The court shall not commit the juvenile to the Department of Corrections for failing to comply with a restitution order.

(11) The court shall not place the juvenile in a Department of Corrections camp for one year, as otherwise provided in MCL 771.3a(1).

[Adopted effective October 1, 1989; amended September 29, 1993, effective December 1, 1993, 444 Mich; February 4, 2003, effective May 1, 2003, 467 Mich.]

†